SELECTED ARTICLES ON

CENSORSHIP OF SPEECH AND THE PRESS

SELECTED ARTICLES ON

CENSORSHIP OF SPEECH AND THE PRESS

COMPILED BY

LAMAR T. BEMAN, A. M., LL.B.

GREENWOOD PRESS, PUBLISHERS
WESTPORT, CONNECTICUT

Originally published in 1930
by The H. W. Wilson Company, New York

Reprinted from an original copy in the collections
of the University of Illinois Library

First Greenwood Reprinting 1971

Library of Congress Catalogue Card Number 76-98813

SBN 8371-3073-5

Printed in the United States of America

CONTENTS

GENERAL DISCUSSION

AFFIRMATIVE DISCUSSION

NEGATIVE DISCUSSION

PART III. CENSORSHIP OF NEWSPAPERS AND MAGAZINES

BRIEF

Bibliography

General Discussion

Affirmative Discussion

Negative Discussion

Part IV. Censorship of Books

Brief

Bibliography

GENERAL DISCUSSION

AFFIRMATIVE DISCUSSION

NEGATIVE DISCUSSION

PREFACE

Censorship has been used, and as often abused, thru all the ages. From almost the beginning of recorded history those in authority, anxious to preserve the status quo, have used censorship as a means of restraining the utterances and suppressing the ideas of revolutionists, reformers, and advanced thinkers. Few students of history doubt that the net results of the sum total of the world's experience with censorship have been to produce far more harm than good, yet few people today are willing to abandon entirely all forms of censorship, tho its more drastic forms have long since been abandoned in most of the more advanced nations.

Freedom of speech and freedom of the press, altho comparatively new principles in the history of the world, have meant very different things at different times and in different countries. While they have been included in our Federal and State Constitutions, they have been interpreted by our courts to mean different things at different times. This, of course, has been true of many other provisions of our constitutions, for, as Justice Holmes has said, "The provisions of the Constitution are not mathematical formulas having their essence in their form; they are organic living institutions transplanted from English soil."

Freedom of speech and freedom of the press have never been construed to be absolute rights, but on the contrary, they have always been interpreted to permit of many restrictions and limitations. In the United States today censorship, or some restriction and limitation on the freedom of speech and the freedom of the press, is now a live public question. In this year of 1930 a Congressional committee is investigating the activities of the Communist organizations, the *Chicago Tribune* is leading the attack on the Minnesota Nuisance Law, seeking both to secure its repeal in Minnesota and to prevent its adoption in other states, an ex-convict is held for trial in New York city, charged with presenting an obscene and indecent stage play, a number of religious weeklies are attacking the moving pictures, charging that they are undermining the morals of the nation, and in several parts of the country complaints have been made and in a few places official action has been taken against some of the books and magazines of popular fiction that are said to be obscene and indecent.

How best to accept and preserve freedom of speech and the freedom of the press, which all consider as sacred and fundamental rights, and at the same time protect society from their abuse, are among the great problems that confront this country today. This volume deals with different phases of this problem.

LAMAR T. BEMAN

Cleveland, Ohio
July 28, 1930

PART I

CENSORSHIP IN GENERAL

BIBLIOGRAPHY

Bibliographies

American Civil Liberties Union. List of pamphlets, books, leaflets, on civil liberty. 100 Fifth Ave. N.Y.

Ernst, Morris L. and Seagle, William. To the pure: a study of obscenity and the censor. Viking Press. N.Y, '28.

Bibliography p. 311-21.

Library of Congress. List of references on freedom of the press and speech and censorship in time of war (with special reference to the European war). Ap. 20, '17.

†Schroeder, Theodore. Free speech bibliography: covering every method of transmitting ideas. Wilson. N.Y. '22.

†Young, Kimball and Lawrence, Raymond D. Bibliography on censorship and propaganda. Univ. of Oregon Press. '28.

Books and Pamphlets

American Bar Association. Report. 1925:183-99. Liberty and law. Charles E. Hughes.

Bury, John B. History of freedom of thought. Holt. N.Y. '13.

†Chafee, Zechariah, jr. Freedom of speech. Harcourt, Brace and Howe. N.Y. '20.

Curtis, George W. Orations and addresses. Harper. N.Y. '93.

The American doctrine of liberty.

†Draper, John W. History of the conflict between religion and science. Appleton. N.Y. '76.

Encyclopaedia Britannica. 14th ed. '29. vol. 5. p. 114-17. Censorship.

Ernst, Morris L. and Seagle, William. To the pure: a study of obscenity and the censor. Viking Press. N.Y. '28.

Graves, W. Brooke. Readings in public opinion. Appleton. N.Y. '28.

Hays, Arthur G. Let freedom ring. Boni and Liveright. N.Y. '28.

Kallen, Horace M. Freedom in the modern world. Coward-McCann. N.Y. '28.

Lippmann, Walter. Liberty and the news. Harcourt, Brace and Howe. N.Y. '20.

Mill, John Stuart. Liberty. H. M. Caldwell. N.Y. n.d.

†Shipley, Maynard. War on modern science. Knopf. N.Y. '27.

Whipple, Leon. Story of civil liberty in the United States. Vanguard Press. N.Y. '27.

†White, Andrew D. History of the warfare of science with theology in Christendom. 2 vols. Appleton. N.Y. '23.

Periodicals

American Bar Association Journal. 11:563-9. S. '25. Liberty and law. Charles E. Hughes.

American Law Review. 57:385-95. My. '23. Liberty or license? George W. Williams.

American Sociological Society. Publications. 18:127-46. '24. Repression of civil liberties in the United States. Harry F. Ward.

Atlantic Monthly. 124:616-27. N. '20. What modern liberty means. Walter Lippmann.

Case and Comment. 22:457-60. N. '15. Constitutional freedom of speech and of the press. W. W. Ackerly.

Case and Comment. 23:23-7. Je. '16. Our foolish obscenity laws. James F. Morton, jr.

Central Law Journal. 70:184-9, 201-11, 223-8. Mr. 11, 18, 25, '10. Historical interpretation of "Freedom of speech and of the press." Theodore Schroeder.

Columbia Law Review. 28:950-7. N. '28. Enforcement of laws against obscenity in New York.

Commercial and Financial Chronicle. 121:1306-7. S. 12, '25. Perils in attempts to restrict liberty of opinion and action through legislation. Charles E. Hughes.

Current Opinion. 56:298-9. Ap. '14. Is censorship useless as a weapon against literary obscenity?

Current Opinion. 73:451-2. O. '22. Censoring the censors.

Forum. 53:87-99. Ja. '15. Our prudish censorship. Theodore Schroeder.

Forum. 73:742-6. My. '25. Common censorship. W. Pezet.

Independent. 77:432-3. Mr. '30. '14. No censorship.

*Independent. 110:192-3. Mr. 17, '23. Absurdity of censorship. Horace B. Liveright.

*Independent. 110:334-5. My. 26, '23. Growth of the censorship idea. George Haven Putnam.

Indiana Law Journal. 4:445-55. Ap. '29. Freedom of speech and of the press. Hugh E. Willis.

Law Notes. 28:65. Jl. '24. Censorship laws.

Law Notes. 29:104-6. S. '25. Clean books. W. A. Shumaker.

Law Notes. 30:204. F. '27. Dangers of censorship.

Law Notes. 31:63. Jl. '27. Opponents of censorship.

Law Notes. 32:1. Ap. '28. Place of law in civilization.

Law Notes. 32:49-53, 67-70. Je.-Jl. '28. Censorship in the United States. James N. Rosenberg.

Law Notes. 32:99. Ag. '28. Censorship and consequences. Howard B. Morris.

Libertarian. 6:108-11. F. '26. The meaning of free speech. Theodore Schroeder.

Literary Digest. 44:483-4. Mr. 9, '12. England's censorship mania.

Literary Digest. 44:533-4. Mr. 16, '12. Police as literary censors.

Literary Digest. 60:30. Mr. 15, '19. End of the censor's reign of terror.

*Literary Digest. 77:27-9. Je. 23, '23. Censorship or not.

Literary Digest. 92:31-2. F. 19, '27. Revolt against the revolting.

Michigan Law Review. 17:621-65. Je. '19. Freedom of speech and of the press in war time. Thomas F. Carroll.

Missionary Review. 47:10-12. Ja. '24. Save America from ruin. Editorial.

Nation. 128:389-90. Ap. 3, '29. Censorship wave.

*Nation. 130:147-9, 175-8, 241-3, 291-3. F. 5, 12, 26, Mr. 12, '30. Christian Science censor. Henry R. Mussey.

New York Law Review. 5:85-8. Mr. '27. Indecencies in print and on the stage.

†Outlook. 106:795-6. Ap. 11, '14. Passing of the indecent.

Outlook. 149:6-7. My. 2, '28. Natural censorship. Harvey O'Higgins.

Public. 21:1283-4. O. 12, '18. Free speech issue.

Public. 21:1398-9. N. 16, '18. End of censorship.

Publishers' Weekly. 111:1566-9. Ap. 16, '27. A season of censorship discussion.

Publishers' Weekly. 111:2118-20. My. 28, '27. Boston discusses its censorship problem.

Review of Reviews. 75:353-6. Ap. '27. Authorities discuss censorship.

Survey. 33:406-12. Ja. 9, '15. Old freedoms discussed by twentieth century sociologists.

World's Work. 47:171-81. D. '23. American liberty, more or less. William McAndrew.

Yale Law Journal. 30:48-55. N. '20. Freedom of speech and press under the first amendment. E. S. Corwin.

Yale Review. 15:433-47. Ap. '26. Law, liberty, and progress. Henry W. Farnam.

DISCUSSION

HISTORY OF CENSORSHIP[1]

The practice of supervising, restricting, or prohibiting the expression of intellectual conceptions or the dissemination of ideas is as old as the organization of society itself. Some one holding authority or claiming authority was always ready to object to the free circulation of ideas as threatening danger to existing institutions, religious or political. The two earliest authorities recognized, by men, that of the ruler, whether of the family, the clan, or the State, and that of the priest, the representative of the accepted religion, were equally interested in retaining control over the direction and the expression of thought. In the earlier communities, political and religious authority were frequently combined in the same individual. It is probable that in these states the contention for an authoritative control of opinion rested chiefly upon the risk that heretical utterances might interfere with the public peace.

The earliest method of publication was in the form of the lecture or recital. A censorship or control of the utterances of the lecturer could be exercised by the very simple method of prohibiting the lecture, and, in case of contumacy, of imprisoning or killing the lecturer. The decision of the authorities at Athens in 400 B. C. that Socrates must be put to death is often referred to as possibly the earliest recorded example of censorship by the State. It is certain that no organized official censorship ever came into existence in Greece. The philosophers and the poets appear to have lectured and written without hindrance and without supervision.

[1] By George Haven Putnam. Monroe's Cyclopedia of Education. vol. 4. p. 32-41.

There are instances of literary censorship on the part of the imperial authorities of Rome before the institution of the Christian Church. Thus Tacitus remarks that Augustus was the first ruler who undertook to punish a word written or spoken, that is to say, a word unaccompanied by action. The law of the Roman Republic had recognized as deserving of punishment only criminal deeds, but the Emperor brought the authority of the law to bear upon writings described as libellous or scandalous (libelli famosi). He ordered, for instance, that the writings of Labienus should be publicly burned. His successor, Tiberius, issued a still stronger regulation for the supervision of undisciplined or insubordinate writings. Cremutius Cordus was driven from his occupation and left to die through poverty for the offense of speaking of Gaius Cassius as the "last Roman." His writings were ordered to be burned by the aedile.

Tacitus speaks with scorn of those who, in the possession of a little momentary power, undertake to crush out opinions not in accord with their owner to prevent such opinions from being handed down to posterity. The writings of Verjinto were prohibited by Nero. Concerning this prohibition, Tacitus writes: "So long as the possession of these writings was attended by danger, they were eagerly sought and read; when there was no longer any difficulty in securing them, they fell into oblivion." This statement of literary conditions under the early Empire shows a curious resemblance to the results which obtained throughout Europe fourteen centuries later. The books which were formally condemned and the titles of which were placed on the Index obtained an advertisement which secured for them a decided advantage over works of the same general character that had not been fortunate enough to be picked out for reprobation. An edict ascribed to Domitian ordered that the historian Hermogenes and any book dealers who assisted in the distribution of certain writings of his which had libeled the Emperor should be crucified. Severus and certain other bishops Justinian deposed from office, because they had been lax in their supervision of literature and had permitted the wide circulation throughout the realm of prohibited books and of pernicious writings.

With the development of the Church of Rome to the ecclesiastical headship of the civilized world, the claim for the supervision of literature and for the control of the productions of authors was asserted by the Church as the legitimate successor of the imperial authority. The earliest and most sweeping censorship of the Christian Church is probably that contained in the Apostolic Constitutions, which purport to have been written by St. Clement of Rome at the dictation of the Apostles. These constitutions prefigure the Index by forbidding the Christians to read any books of the Gentiles: "The Scriptures should suffice for the believer" (Const. Apost. Lib. 1, CVIII). This general prohibition of St. Clement (which bore date about 95 A. D.) is followed by a series of prohibitions issued by the authorities of the early Church, mainly under the decision of the councils. For instance, in 150, a synod of bishops of Asia Minor, meeting at Ephesus, prohibited the Acta Pauli, an historical romance written a little earlier in the century, and having for its purpose the clarification of the life and labors of St. Paul.

In 325 edicts were issued by the Emperor Constantine and prohibitions by the Council of Nicaea, against the writings of Arius and of Porphyry. The Emperor ordered the penalty of death for any who might conceal copies. In 399 the Emperor Arcadius issued an edict, based upon the recommendation of a council of the Church, ordering the destruction, under penalty of death, of all books of magic art. The various denunciations of books of magic art were, under the influence of the ecclesiastics who might happen to be in control of the proceedings of the councils, utilized for the repression of the writings of their theological opponents. In 399 the Council of Alexandria, presided over by Bishop Theophilus, issued a decree forbidding the owning or the reading of the books of Origen. The Egyptian monks protested, and the bishops were obliged to call in the prefects to enforce the authority of its edicts. In 436 the Emperor Theodosius issued an edict forbidding the possession and reading of the books of the Manicheans and ordering the burning of the same. In 446 Pope Leo I issued an edict ordering the destruction of a long series of writings described as not in accord with the teachings of the synods of Nicaea and, therefore, antagonistic to the Christian religion. The prohibition prescribes that: "Whoever owns or reads these books is to suffer extreme punishment." In 499 Pope Gelasius issued what is later referred to as the first papal Index. It presents a catalogue of books prohibited, but the prohibitions have to do not with private or general, but with public or official reading. In 496 Gelasius issued a decree, confirmed later by the Emperor Gratian, which specified the patristic writings accepted and approved by the Church, and which then proceeded to the condemnation of a long series of apocryphal and heretical writings and writers. The classification of the writings to be condemned is curiously general in terms (Haec et omnia his similia, etc.).

The great impetus given to the distribution of books by the invention of the printing press (1450) had as one result a fresh effort at supervision and control of literary production on the part of the Church. The first measures that were put into shape for the enforcement of such control provided for what has been called preventive censorship; that is, for a requirement, before the printed book could be put into circulation, of an examination and approval by ecclesiastical authorities. It was, however, not until half a century after Gutenberg had printed his first book that official cognizance was taken of the new art in a Papal Bull. And it was nearly half a century later before the Church undertook, through a system of expurgatory and prohibitory indexes, to maintain a systematic censorship upon literature. The invention of printing had as an immediate result an enormous increase in the influence upon the shaping of popular opinion of the written word, which now became the printed word, that is, of thought in the form of literature.

The interference during the earlier centuries of printing on the part of political rulers was fitful and intermittent, and appears at no time to have arrived at the dignity of a continued policy or system. In a number of states, as in Spain, France, and the Holy Roman Empire, while the rulers continued to claim for themselves the exclusive control of the printing press, they were willing to confide to the ecclesiastics the selections of the books to be condemned and prohibited. The Catholic work of censorship, at least in the countries which remained Catholic, fell, therefore, more and more into the hands of the Church, and was as a result carried on with reference to the clerical standard of orthodoxy and morality and to the clerical theories of what was required for the welfare of the community.

The proportion of works of a purely political character that came under condemnation was small as compared with the long list of books condemned on doctrinal grounds. During the two centuries in which censorship exerted the largest influence upon intellectual development, say from 1550 to 1750, the minds of men were directed more largely to doctrinal questions than to political matters. It was not the State, but the Church, whose authority and existence were assailed, and the contest was fought out not over political platforms, but over creeds.

When, with the beginning of the Reformation, it became apparent how great a range of influence was possessed by the printed sheet, the problem that confronted the authorities of the Church was certainly serious in more ways than one. For the space of fifteen centuries the education of the people had remained almost exclusively under the direction of the Church. The faithful had accepted their entire intellectual sustenance at the hands of the priests. In 1516 the leaders of the Reformation, in beginning their long contest against the Church of Rome, promptly availed themselves of the power of the printing press. While the words spoken in the pulpit or in the market place could reach at best but a few hundred hearers, the tracts poured forth from the Wittenberg presses, the "flying leaves" (*Flugschriften*), carried to many thousands the teachings of Luther and Melanchthon, and it was through these "winged words" (*Epea Pteroenta*) that the revolt developed into a revolution.

THE GROWTH OF THE CENSORSHIP IDEA[1]

Censorship of art, literature, morals, and dogma is an active issue of today. This is, however, not a novelty in human experience. It is probable that censorship came into activity with the first development of human expression. We can imagine the cave-dweller inspecting with critical eye the drawing that his neighbor had placed on the wall of his home, and pointing out that the mastodon was out of drawing and that the coloring was too lurid. He might go further and contend that it was not good for the community to have a vain-glorious record, which was also bad art, placed where it could influence the imaginations of the children.

There has always been an urgent desire on the part of some members of the community to restrict the expression and to supervise and control the utterances of their fellows. When some subjective individual, or group of individuals, was able to secure to back up their views on a pending issue the authority of the Government, we have the beginning of censorship, political, religious, or social. An excellent example of the exercise of such censorship was given in the trial of Socrates, 400 B. C. The Athenian philosopher was condemned for the utterance of doctrines that, as the censors

[1] By George Haven Putnam. *Independent.* 110:334-5. May 26, 1923.

of the day claimed, were likely to prove "pernicious for the morals of the citizens and dangerous for the welfare of the State."

The difficulty in the case of censorship by the Government is the fact that the standards of policies change of necessity as one set of administrators is replaced by another. In 1555, for instance, Queen Mary of England prohibited, under serious penalty, the printing and circulation of books by Protestant writers; while in 1559 Queen Elizabeth, with equal partiality, instituted a similar prohibition against the books coming from Catholics. The rulers were, however, troubled not so much on the ground of the religious heresy of such literature as because the books constituted, as claimed, a protest against the existing order and the Crown itself, and tended, therefore, to "subvert the peace of the realm." Such a charge could fairly be made against at least one of the books complained of by Elizabeth, that which contains the edict of excommunication against her by Pope Pius V, with the recommendation that the Queen should be assassinated as a heretic.

The first measures for the protection of property and literature were, as a matter of routine policy, connected with the censorship of the books protected. Shortly after the invention of printing in 1450 the printer-publishers began the practice of securing from the rulers of their respective states "privileges" which gave to the publishers, in form at least, a control or monopoly of the work for a term of years, usually fifteen. It was a necessary condition of the granting of the privilege that the work so protected should, in its purpose and execution, have secured the approval of the State, and this necessitated the institution of official examiners and brought about the development of censorship by the State.

The first prohibition of literature carrying the authority of the Church was issued in 494 by Pope Gelasius 1. From that date the Church may be said to have taken upon itself the guarding of the souls of the faithful against the pernicious influence of heretical literature. This policy was carried out later by the printing of a series of indexes, or lists of books the reading of which was prohibited. The authors and publishers who were responsible for the production and distribution of such books were brought under condemnation and sometimes under excommunication.

The series of indexes compiled under the authority of the Church, and in part under the direct supervision of the Popes, comprised in all fifty-three. The first of the authoritative Church indexes was issued in London in 1526, with an index prepared by the Archbishop of Canterbury. The series closed with the really scholarly index published in Rome in 1900 by Leo XIII.

The Church censorship of heretical literature is now expressed in general principles, on the basis of which principles the bishops and confessors are instructed to guide the reading of the faithful.

There is something almost pathetic in the long series of attempts made by popes, councils, bishops, and confessors to protect the souls of the faithful against the baneful influence of the ever-increasing tide of literature that poured forth from the various publishing centres, and so much of which was calculated to lead men astray from the true doctrines and to bring them into risk of everlasting perdition. The action of the Church in attempting to repress and exterminate such literature was logical and reasonable. It was the only course that was possible for an organization to which, as its rulers believed, the Almighty had confided the care and the spiritual welfare of mankind.

The rulers who have been placed in office under a Government representative of the people, such for instance as the Government of the United States or that of Great Britain, find themselves confronted with special perplexities in regard to this matter of the control of literature. Such terms as the "liberties of the citizen," the right to "freedom of speech," the claim of each man to hold his own theories as to government or the organization of society, or the methods of managing the relations of employers to employes, express the general understanding of the rights of a free man in a free state. On the other hand, patriotic citizens, whether or not they have official responsibilities, may well be troubled with the knowledge that printed matter of doubtful or more than doubtful character is being circulated among comparatively ignorant readers and that a portion of such matter is likely to demoralize these readers. The safety of the Republic rests upon the intelligence and moral character of the individual citizen and there is fair ground for the claim that all measures should be taken which seem likely to secure for such citizens trained minds capable of understanding the issues of the day, sound judgment that would guard them from arriving at hasty or revolutionary decisions, and that would keep them protected against any insidious influence which might lead them astray from its principles.

It is a proper expectation on the part of law-abiding citizens that the peace and welfare of the Republic and of the citizens within the Republic should not be exposed to the "winds of doctrine" of wild anarchistic theories.

It is a fair contention that, as the Government has the responsibility for the protection of life and of property, a duty rests upon the officials to prevent the making of organized propaganda which may incite people to assail the property rights of their neighbors. A person whose utterances, whether oral, written, or printed, have served as an incitement to crime is, under the existing law, held as *particeps criminis*. In a case in which crime has not actually been accomplished but in which the accused has, through his utterances, done what he could to bring about misdeeds, such as manslaughter, arson, assault, sabotage, etc., such person as an instigator to crime is held guilty of criminal action. If a man should push off a piece of coping from a roof into the street, he would be guilty of attempted manslaughter even though no passerby had been struck by the stone. A person who provides the funds for the printing of incendiary utterances or who, having knowledge of their purpose and character, gives cooperation in bringing such propaganda into circulation, is held to be *particeps criminis,* just as he who "utters" (that is to say circulates) forged money, is party to the fraud on the public.

The State has the right and the duty to maintain its own existence and the officials are under obligation to their fellow citizens to neglect no measures that may be necessary to uphold the law, to maintain peace, order and justice, and to protect life and property.

It is equally important under a representative government to prevent the support of law and order from being used for political purposes, that is to say for party purposes. The rights of minorities must be respected; even cranks and fools have the right to claim a hearing; and there should be no restriction of the expression of opinions, even of the expression of foolish opinions, simply on the ground of their unpopularity or because they do not fit in with the views of the party in power. We may recall that under a Dominican Pope the Congregation of the Index was constituted with a Dominican majority, and as a result the works by Franciscans were condemned as heresies. If the succeeding Pope was a Franciscan the writings of the Dominicans suffered in like manner.

In our American communities it is, of course, essential that censorship should be neither Democratic nor Republican. We cannot permit the protectionists to suppress literature upholding freedom of trade, nor would it be in order to interfere with the circulation of books defending the mediaeval rubbish of the protectionists.

Everyone but an extreme pacifist (and I use the term to describe one who would prefer to accept tyrannical domination rather than to lift a hand in defense of the liberties of his country) will admit that when a nation is at war there is requirement for a more strenuous standard of censorship than can properly be permitted in time of peace. The life of a nation often depends upon the readiness of the citizens to take up arms in its defense. Anyone, therefore, who refuses himself to render the service to which the State is entitled, who discourages others from volunteering, and who incites his fellow citizens to refuse to obey the summons of a conscription act, is acting as an enemy to his country as directly as if he were using a gun in the ranks of the invaders.

No ideal of "free speech" should be permitted to stand in the way of prompt repression of utterances, whether spoken or printed, which incite men to refuse to do their share in the defense of the Republic. When the Republic is fighting to preserve not only its own independence but the liberties of all non-aggressive nations, the repression of disloyal teaching becomes a duty not only of the State but of civilization itself, like the suppression of smallpox or the plague.

It may at once be admitted, however, that no plan has as yet been arrived at under which could be secured a censorship that should be absolutely free from partisanship and from the risk of personal animus, and that could, therefore, be trusted to exercise its authority without the risk of bringing about injustice, injustice more serious than the evil it was undertaking to remedy.

We have in New York City a great benevolent society supported by the subscriptions of patriotic citizens, whose purpose has been to protect the community against immoral and pernicious literature. This society has undoubtedly rendered a real service. It would be a rash man who would decide that there was good ground for bringing its operations to a close or for taking away the authority that has been given to it; and yet we must realize that the managers, with their own natural limitations and their share of personal prejudices, have more than once committed serious injustice against an individual or against society itself and have brought their own work and the whole principle of censorship into disrepute. It has happened more than once that a book more or less unsatisfactory in character has, through the operations of this society, achieved a publicity and an influence that could not otherwise have been secured.

I think we may safely take the ground that such a voluntary society, that is a society which was constituted on individual action and whose authority did not have its source with the voters of the country, ought not to be given the final decision in such a matter as that of the censorship of literature. There should always be the privilege of appeal.

The authority placed in the hands of the Postmaster General to prohibit the circulation through the mails of books which in his judgment are undesirable is, it seems to me, unwise and has more than once worked injustice. The Postmaster General should have no authority to issue a prohibition until the book in question had been condemned by a commission representing the authority of a Court. I am inclined on the whole to the conclusion that more mischief has been brought about through unwisely enforced censorship than through leaving in existence certain books the influence of which might possibly prove pernicious. The great majority of such books will fall out of demand and their purpose and character should not be emphasized by unwise attempts at repression.

THE GREAT AMERICAN TRADITION[8]

"I have sworn upon the altar of the living God eternal hostility against every form of tyranny over the mind of man." This powerful blast against all oppression of the human spirit was written by Thomas Jefferson, author of the Declaration of Independence, draftsman of the Virginia statute for religious liberty, and founder of the University of Virginia. And yet, vigorous as it was, this proclamation of freedom by Jefferson was but an echo

[8] By Charles A. Beard. *Nation*. 123:8-9. July 7, 1926.

from an age-long battle waged by those who dare to think against those who, with hemlock, faggot, gallows, irons, and prisons, vainly seek to strangle the irresistible power of inquiry and change.

If a beginning of this great battle must be sought, let it be in the noble words of the *Apology* offered by Socrates twenty-four centuries ago. There he said that if his accusers would spare him on condition that he would cease to search for truth his answer would be:

> Athenians, I love and cherish you, but I shall obey God rather than you, and as long as I draw breath and have the strength, I shall never cease to follow the love of wisdom and to exhort and persuade any one of you whom I happen to meet.

With a smile upon his face and the light of eternity in his eyes, he drained his cup of poison to the dregs. Who remembers the legislators, the judges, and the accusers who brought him to that doom of immortality?

If an immediate forerunner of Jefferson, one in the stream of our own civilization, must be chosen, let it be the blind poet of the Puritans, John Milton. In 1644, a quarter of a century after the landing of the Pilgrims at Plymouth, he issued an indictment of official censorship bearing the title *Areopagitica: a Speech of Mr. John Milton for the Liberty of Unlicensed Printing, to the Parliament of England*—a brief essay that stands out like a gleaming beacon above the dark oppressions of that age. Once a book which good and wise people feared as they did plague and death, it is now read in our schools by tender youth as a work of noble idealism enshrined in the finest imagery of the English tongue. For the timid, shrinking, frightened cowardice of the persecutor who would impose his little designs on the thought of mankind and keep his country asleep in inherited tradition, Milton offered the daring idea of free inquiry and free argument—an idea that would arouse the nation to greater and greater achievement.

> Methinks I see in my mind [he said] a noble puissant nation rousing herself like a strong man after sleep and shaking her invincible locks. Methinks I see her as an eagle mewing her mighty youth and kindling her undazzled eyes at the full mid-day beam; purging and unscaling her long abused sight at the

fountain of heavenly radiance; while the whole noise of timorous and flocking birds, with those also that love the twilight, flutter about, amazed at what she means, and in their envious gabble would prognosticate a year of sects and schisms. . . . Give me liberty to know, to utter, and to argue freely according to conscience, above all liberties.

Nearly a hundred and fifty years after Milton made this eloquent plea the American people wrote in their national Constitution a provision which expressed in a solemn avowal the principle which he had asked from the English Parliament: "Congress shall make no law respecting the establishment of religion or prohibiting the free exercise thereof; or abridging the freedom of speech, or of the press." Jefferson had urged this amendment and rejoiced in its enactment. It was in keeping with his spirit and indeed an inherent part of the American political system.

That system embraced no king ruling by divine right, no house of lords ruling by prescriptive tenure, no established church claiming God's sanction on its monopoly. On the contrary, it was founded on the faith that governments derive their powers from the consent of the governed; that officials are not divinely appointed masters, but elected servants; that periodically the voters should, on reviewing the conduct of their servants, approve or condemn according to their judgment. To give to any set of officials—legislative, executive, or judicial—the power of censoring, controlling, or suppressing the opinions of the people would be to place the servants above the masters, defeat the first principles of the government, and restore a regime of special privilege. An election without discussion would be an impossibility. Discussion without freedom to inquire and to argue would be a farce. Inexorably out of the logic of the American system flowed the principle of freedom of press and speech.

It would of course be doing violence to history to imply that this creed was universally accepted among the founders of this republic. Every school-child knows the history of the Sedition Act of 1798. Frightened by the criticisms of the Jeffersonians bent on ousting them from power, the Federalists hurried through Congress a law drawn in broad and loose language which in effect penalized everyone who passed severe strictures upon the Government of the United States. In fact, this measure gave to Federalist judges, prosecutors, and executive officials the authority to arrest, fine, and imprison any of their political foes who were especially objectionable to them and in practice it was so applied. And all know the verdict of history on this act of partisan fury and tyranny. The party that passed it was buried in oblivion, and for more than a century, in peace and war, no such sweeping violation of political liberty was placed upon the statute books of the United States. Even the Southern Confederacy, recoiling before the irresistible might of Northern armies and assailed by criticism within, did not adopt any measure of law comparable to the Federalist Sedition Act of 1798.

Under these historical circumstances, and in keeping with Jefferson's faith in the long judgment of the people, there grew up in America a great tradition of political liberty. Though difficult to define in law, theory, or practice, though often violated in spirit by mobs and private organizations, that tradition contained certain elements which stand out in undoubted patterns of thought. It did not declare that no alterations might be proposed in our form of government. It did not lay down the rule that in time of war the majority which controls the Government of the United States may exercise the powers and prerogatives of a Caesar. No, the tradition of American political liberty was formulated by fearless and robust men who had the honesty to apply to others the principles they claimed for themselves.

Let us seek what it meant in the language of its first great expounder, Thomas Jefferson. He did not urge the jail and the gallows for those who proposed to dissolve the Union and change our form of government.

In his first inaugural he calmly said: "If there be any among us who would wish to dissolve this Union or change its republican form, let them stand undisturbed as monuments of the safety with which error of opinion may be tolerated where reason is left free to combat it." Jefferson knew that there were limits to the political freedom which he proclaimed. He could read the definition of treason in the Constitution.. It was explicit. It ran:

> Treason against the United States shall consist only in levying war against them or in adhering to their enemies, giving them aid and comfort. No person shall be convicted of treason unless on the testimony of two witnesses to the same overt act, or on confession in open court.

In those lines stood the two words which Jefferson regarded as vital to any limitation on freedom of discussion, namely, *overt act.* In expounding religious liberty he made this firm declaration:

> To suffer the civil magistrate to intrude his powers into the field of opinion and to restrain the profession or propogation of principles on the supposition of their ill tendency is a dangerous fallacy which at once destroys all religious liberty, because he, being of course judge of that tendency, will make his opinions the rule of judgment, and approve or condemn sentiments of others only as they square or differ with his own.

The same principle Jefferson applied again nearly twenty-five years later, showing that it was with him a rooted conviction. In a letter addressed to Elijah Boardman of New Milford, Connecticut, on July 3, 1801 (now in the possession of Dr. George H. Wright, of that town), Jefferson objected to the idea that an opinion could be *an overt act,* and added:

> We have nothing to fear from the demoralizing reasonings of some, if others are left free to demonstrate their errors and especially when the law stands ready to punish the first criminal act produced by the false reasonings; these are safer corrections than the conscience of a judge.

All down through the nineteenth century great leaders of American opinion continued to uphold the principles which Jefferson had expounded. A cloud of witnesses could be summoned to support this statement.

Abraham Lincoln said in his first inaugural address:

> This country, with its institutions, belongs to the people who inhabit it. Whenever they grow weary of the existing Government, they can exercise their constitutional right of amending it or their revolutionary right to dismember or overthrow it.

It is not only liberty that has been celebrated but liberty in season and out. William Ellery Channing said more than a century ago:

> The cry has been that war is declared and that all opposition should therefore be hushed. If the doctrine be admitted, rulers have only to declare war and they are screened at once from scrutiny. . . . We should teach our present and all future rulers that there is no measure for which they must render so solemn an account to their constituents as for a declaration of war; that no measure will be so freely, so fully discussed. . . . In war, then, as in peace assert freedom of speech and of the press.

Years afterward, in the midst of the Mexican war, Theodore Parker exclaimed: "If the people cannot discuss the war they have got to fight and pay for, who under heaven can?" In the very midst of the life and death struggle over which the immortal Lincoln presided, the Democratic Party in its platform declared the war a failure, called for a cessation of hostilities, and protested against the violation of civil rights by the federal Government. Lincoln believed that the Democratic Party was wrong and the judgment of history runs with his opinion, but neither he nor his countrymen thought opposition to war and the advocacy of peace in war time a crime to be suppressed by violent and inquisitorial processes. Interference with the armed forces and the prosecution of the war were of course forbidden and in practice there was no little violation of civil liberty; but the expression of hostile opinions in political discussions (even a demand for immediate peace) was not a crime.

Senator Borah urged long afterward:

> If this blessed old republic cannot rest upon the free and voluntary support and affection of the American people in time

of war as well as in time of peace, if we cannot, as a people, be free to discuss the political problems which involve limb and life, even in time of war, our government rests upon a very brittle foundation.

From the close of the eighteenth to the opening of the twentieth century the great tradition of political liberty was regarded as a sacred element in our political philosophy and practice. In time of war it was often strained by dominant parties; in time of peace it was sometimes violated by mobs; but it was consistently upheld as a guiding principle. Its essential terms were clear. The people were free to criticize and discuss their government and its acts, subject to the law of libel and slander; they were liable to pains and penalties only when their language definitely threatened an immediate overt act.

Broadly speaking, this was where we stood when the storm of the World War broke upon us in 1917. In that year Congress passed the Espionage Act for the entirely proper purposes of preventing interference with the enrolment and operation of the armed forces of the United States. The terms were explicit and the acts against which it was directed were made reasonably definite. This legislation was soon followed by the Sedition Act, and by State statutes often in terms still more general and inclusive. The provisions of these acts and the history of their enforcement established precedents so unusual that the Hon. Charles E. Hughes was led to declare:

> We may well wonder, in view of the precedents now established, whether constitutional government as heretofore maintained in this republic could survive another great war even if victoriously waged.

Surely that is a grave warning that bids us pause and survey our conduct and prepare for the future. And it is best that we should do this in time of peace when the perils of battle do not thunder at our gates and the calm voice of reason can be heard.

CENSORSHIP AND ART

Guaranties for the sociality of art are found in the control society exercises over it.

This control is by *hindrance* and by *furtherance.*

We see *hindrance* in official censors, in the licensing of playhouses, in the suppression of plays, in the exclusion of certain books from the mails, in the shutting out of peace books from garrison libraries. Besides the authorities we have librarians, hanging committees, art juries, monument boards, reputable publishers, and responsible periodicals conspiring to check the raid of the immoral artists upon the public. Behind these hovers a cloud of critics, and every work of art must run the gauntlet of them ere it can gain easy access to the multitude. Flanking these are the Church with its Index, the pulpit with its thunders against the stage, W. C. T. U.'s, Y. M. C. A.'s, mothers' associations and reading clubs down to the local oracle and the village Dogberry. What with censor, police, critic, priest, schoolmaster, and matron, the hindrances society can oppose to a demoralizing work of art are very considerable.

Still more effective is the *furtherance* given to that which is deemed most salutary and wholesome. A great quantity of art-work is selected and paid for by society. The literature conned in the schools, the libraries of barracks and ships, the eloquence of senates, the oratory and poetry of public occasions, the frescoes of public buildings, the collections in public galleries and museums, the repertory of subsidized theatres, the art in churches and cathedrals—on these the social purgation shows as plainly as the patronage of the Bourbons shows on the battle pieces at Versailles. Add now to this the effect of general praise and commendation, the favor shown one class of literature by the church, the fillip given another by the "family" magazine, and it will be

[4] By Edward A. Ross. *Social Control.* p. 272-7.

evident that the policy of society toward art is anything but *laissez faire.*

Even if we abandon all official censorship, so long as society spontaneously ranges itself into leaders and led, into makers and takers of opinion, it will be possible greatly to let or hinder the access of the artist to the public. Let those of influence but appreciate the moral bearing of art, and the impulse of every one to look out for his neighbor's morals will do the rest.

Artists, resenting the yoke of morality, have coined the absurd phrase "art for art's sake," and with it have bewildered not a few. To meet this cry with empty assertions of the "moral purpose of art," the "moral obligations laid upon the artist," is only to heap up chaff. But put "social" for "moral," and the situation becomes clear.

The "realists," "naturalists," and "veritists" assert that art is an individual affair, that a man has the right to speak, print, or publish anything he pleases or that he can get another to like. Art as Master of Revels and Dispenser of Delights cannot, they say, attain its utmost if it be fettered by conventionalities. To naysay the free access of artist to patron is to kill inspiration and cut off humanity from choice springs of enjoyment.

For society to concede any such claim would be sheer folly. What madness, when we are all the time besetting the individual with our theologies and religions and ideals, and can scarcely keep him in order at that, to let the irresponsible artist get at him and undo our work! Why give art *carte blanche* when there is abroad scarcely a speculation regarding the other world which has not been shaped by considerations of this world's discipline? Until sober Reason has won *Lehrfreiheit,* it is over-early to emancipate the Artistic Imagination.

By whom art shall be supervised is quite another question. All attempts to lodge the supervision of it in any man or board have done more harm than good. By brutal suppression they consecrate the established order and turn artists into sycophants or revolutionists. Art should be the hand-maiden, but it should never be made the mere bond-slave and scullion of current morality.

It may be that the fate of the artist's work should be decided by the ten thousand influential, subject to an appeal to the million uninfluential; the latter to ban without ruth or scruple whatever gives moral offence. In this way it may be possible to make art amenable to society without making it amenable to law.

RESISTANCE TO PROGRESS: MOB CENSORSHIP[5]

Progress meets always with resistance and obstacles of all kinds. The bulk of the human race has ever fought its own advancement. Its great men have always been accepted under protest; forward movements have always been resisted not only by the reactionaries but by the entire multitude; the path of progress is strewn with the bones of martyrs to great causes who were overwhelmed by public disapproval. Whenever man has been confronted with a new idea which was counter to the dominant interest or thought he has sought to stamp it out. His cries against those new ideas have been "heresy," "sedition," and "disloyalty," and his actions against those who presented them have been ostracism, banishment, and death. Socrates, when thought was rigid and decadent, was accused and condemned for "corrupting the youth" and given the hemlock. Jesus, when religion was largely form and hypocrisy, and ethics a hollow philosophy, was arraigned before Pilate with the charge, "We found this fellow perverting the nation." Galileo, sentenced to death for "disregard of authority," was forced to swear that the earth did not move. Nor are our own people an exception.

We of this great republic complacently affirm the

[5] **By Joyce O. Hertzler.** ***Social Progress.*** **p. 110-12.**

glory of our national achievements, and are not without temptation to acclaim them as proof of superior craft and judgment. But herein do we forget that we are on record as having cast our vote against every move that has contributed to the present century's development. Not one of its essential factors came into play without an earnest effort on the part of the public to thwart it. We, the people, have stood squarely against each and every innovation that has moved the world beyond the days of Washington.

We raised our voices in contemptuous protest against the first projected highways. Had the locomotive awaited its signal from the people, it would not yet have started. When the electric telegraph was shown to us we brushed it aside as a toy, and laughed its inventor to scorn when he offered to sell us his rights for a few thousand dollars. We put into jail as an imposter the first man who brought anthracite coal to market. We broke to pieces Howe's sewing machine as an invention calculated to ruin the working classes; and we did the same thing to the harvester and binder. We scorned the typewriter as a plaything. We gathered together in mass meetings of indignation at the first proposal to install electric trolley lines; and when Dr. Bell told us he had invented an instrument by means of which we might talk to one another across the town, we responded with accustomed ridicule, and only the reckless among us contributed to its being.

When seventy years ago, William Lloyd Garrison preached the abolition of slavery, we tied a halter about him, and dragged him through the streets of Boston. We rained anathemas upon the memory of Jenner when his disciples undertook to vaccinate us. We hooted Dr. Simpson as an atheist for introducing anesthetics in his surgical practice. We repelled the efforts of our first health officers to establish rules of public hygiene. We stormed in righteous wrath against Robert Ingersoll for suggesting that Moses made mistakes; and when Darwin presented his *Origin of Species,* our outcry was a perfect whirlwind of denunciation, a tempest that blighted men's reputations and cast out professors from universities and clergymen from pulpits.

There is that in our blood as a social organism which craves fixation. Man's first business after the Deluge was to anchor the earth to heaven, and from that time to this have we labored to the same purpose, striving ever to hold the world immobile.

Every discovery and every new thing that has been instrumental in changing the thought and activities of man, came into being in the face of the world's opposition. Each in turn was rejected as unholy or a toy without worth. The advent of each of them found man content with the means at hand. No conscious need of his called other implements to his aid. Necessity was not the mother of any of them. It had no place, no use, for them, until each for itself had created a new field of need and industry. The necessity was not of the world's providing. It sprang from the things themselves.

This resistance to change is an obstacle which only generations of social education and change of social attitude will remove. Men in masses have feared the iconoclast and the new departure. They must be taught that both of these are fundamental if desirable change is to occur; in fact, that almost all the desirable change of the past has come only by means of these.

BRIEF EXCERPTS

There is not and cannot be a standard for the censors to apply.—*Law Notes.* 28:65. *July* 1924.

Any form of censorship is an outrage upon liberty. —*F. Whelen. Graphic.* 80:292. *September* 4, 1909.

To civilized men intolerance is an unpardonable sin.—*New Republic.* 21:254. *January* 28, 1920.

Censorship has run wild in the last six months.—*Saturday Review of Literature.* 6:227. *October* 12, 1929.

Liberty to each to do as he wills in all things produces at once a state of absolute anarchy.—*Law Notes.* 32:1. *April* 1928.

When a man says that he believes in no censorship at all, he probably is not telling the truth. *Heywood Broun. Nation.* 130:36. *January* 8, 1930.

A censorship under any circumstances is not in consonance with American liberty.—*Editorial. Louisville Courier-Journal. March* 19, 1930.

The censor, whatever he may think of himself, is always a ridiculous figure to the impartial observer.—*Robert Herrick. Bookman.* 70:258. *November* 1929.

The power of public opinion in this country and the danger of its debasement cannot be exaggerated.—*George William Curtis. American Doctrine of Liberty.*

Censorship along lines of political appointment is unthinkable. *Owen Johnson. Literary Digest.* 77:29. *June* 23, 1923.

All experience teaches that it is better to err on the side of freedom than on the side of repression.—*John A. Ryan. Publications of the American Sociological Society.* 18:126. 1924.

There was never yet any human mind sufficiently great to compel the rest of the world to think and speak as it directed.—*Editorial. New York Sun. May* 16, 1924.

All censorship is bad, but of two evils a stupid censor is probably more endurable, less likely to do much harm, than a clever one.—*E. H. L. Watson. Dial.* 50:298. *April* 16, 1911.

I do not believe in censorship in the theater, literature, or in any of the arts. No censorship has ever worked.—*Sherwood Anderson. Literary Digest.* 77:60. *June* 23, 1923.

What the censor actually does, in nine cases out of ten, is to suppress the good and advertise the bad.—*Channing Pollock. Current Opinion.* 62:408. *June* 1917.

The people as a whole, unprotected by the despotic judgments of single persons, have enough strength and wisdom to know what is and what is not harmful to themselves.—*John Galsworthy. Inn of Tranquillity.* p. 243.

History proves the danger of entrusting to any officials, however well meaning, the power to prohibit what they disapprove. A compulsory and official censorship is rarely beneficial, always vexatious, and often oppressive.—*Independent.* 77:433. *March* 30, 1914.

I am against censorship of all kinds and degrees. If parents ought to censor their children's reading, let them do it. But I am not willing that they should call in the state to censor mine.—*Heywood Broun. Literary Digest.* 77:29. *June* 23, 1923.

The question of literary and dramatic censorship is not at the moment merely an annoying perplexity in the life of a single city, but is an issue which concerns the whole country.—*William Allen Neilson. Atlantic Monthly.* 145:13. *January* 1930.

Our experience with censorship has not been fortunate, whether in literature, the theatre, or the moving picture. It is easy to demonstrate, however, that we are not yet ready to permit all people to do as they please.—*Bishop Stires. Churchman.* 141:9. *March* 1, 1930.

There is a great deal to be said in favor of relegating all state censorship to the limbo of out-grown and needless governmental interference with the American idea of freedom.—*Editorial. Cleveland Plain Dealer. February* 19, 1929.

The strongest censorship is really the worst. There is nothing which can take the place of liberty even when it goes wrong. If censorship had been applied throughout history we should have hardly a great book or a work of great art today.—*Clarence Darrow. City Club Bulletin. Chicago.* 11:191. *June* 3, 1918.

If the newspapers and the theaters are indecent it is because readers and audiences are eager to pay for indecency, or are tolerant of it. Indecency is profitable because it is desired by many and not sufficiently condemned by a robust and wholesome public sentiment.—*New York Law Review.* 5:87. *March* 1927.

Congress shall make no law respecting an establishment of religion, or prohibiting the free exercise thereof; or abridging the freedom of speech, or of the press; or the right of the people peaceably to assemble, and to petition the Government for a redress of grievances.—*United States Constitution. First Amendment.*

The best-oiled and smoothest-running publicity and anti-publicity machine operated in the United States during the twentieth century has been that controlled by the Board of Directors of the Mother Church, the First Church of Christ, Scientist, in Boston, Massachusetts.—*Henry R. Mussey. Nation.* 130:147. *February* 5, 1930.

Fundamental liberties, like those of free speech, free press, and the right of assemblage, become specially valuable when some authority attempts to deny them, for that happens only when somebody uses them in the way that they were meant to be used. Liberties do not exist when they are merely exalted as an abstract ideal.

—*Forrest Bailey. World Tomorrow.* 11:55. *February* 1928.

A legal censorship, under which a single individual tries to apply in a haphazard way an uncertain standard, is an abomination in the sight of God and man. It is now thoroughly discredited, and recent history has shown that it cannot be made to work. It is a form of tyranny that is worthy only of the middle ages, and should have no place in this country.—*Flora W. Seymour. Literary Digest.* 77:28. *June* 23, 1923.

There is not and cannot be any definite and universally accepted standard by which may be decided what is decent and clean and what is indecent and obscene. Under our system of laws the issue must be determined by judges and juries and upon the trial of an indictment for indecency all twelve of the jurors must agree as to the quality of the act charged, or no guilt can be established. —*New York Law Review.* 5:86. *March* 1927.

Control of propaganda, through muzzling the press, censoring of books, theatres, and movies, and regulation of the expression of teachers, is the sure method of putting propaganda eventually in the hands of the strongly organized and socially destructive powers of selfishness. If we wish to conserve the possibility of fighting for the right, we must first of all conserve and guarantee the power to fight.—*Knight Dunlap. Social Psychology.* p. 257.

The absurdity of censorship lies mainly in its application. Only the highest quality of intellect and understanding is capable of acting as a censor, and it is obvious that no man or woman of fine intelligence will act in any way as a censor of the arts. Therefore such activity is left in the power of those individuals who have little if any sense of value in literature, drama, and art generally. —*Horace B. Liveright. Independent.* 110:192. *March* 17, 1923.

Any new discovery or pronouncement in science, politics, ethics, art, or any other field is upheld, to begin with, by only a small minority. The overwhelming majority always opposes it. The triumph of censorship means the end of experiment, discovery, innovation, argument on controversial subjects. It means that in our thinking we must stay where we are. Free and open treatment of all subjects is the only way of human advancement.—*Nelson A. Crawford. Debunker.* 12:32. *June* 1930.

I am very doubtful about the whole value of censorship of books, plays, pictures, or anything else. It is not easy to commit to a few people, selected as they must be, the privilege or right or duty of deciding in advance in these doubtful questions that are generally the subject of censorship. We are safer in a great free republic with carefully prepared laws on these matters and the action of the courts bringing to justice those who violate the law.—*William I. Haven. Literary Digest.* 77:28. *June* 23, 1923.

The disseminator of wrong ideals is altogether more dangerous to society than the disseminator of wrong opinions. Investigators and thinkers, working in the sphere of opinion, may safely be left free to speak and print, because their errors will spread slowly and will likely be overtaken by the truth before they get very far. Moreover, opinion does not shape conduct so much as is generally supposed. But artists, working in the sphere of personal ideals, may not be left entirely uncensored, seeing that any poison they emit circulates so rapidly.—*Edward A. Ross. Social Psychology.* p. 133.

Censorship must be considered not only in the light of its immediate effects, but also with regard for the future developments which will arise from the situation which is thus generated. Censorship of one public undertaking is the opening wedge that may lead to the stifling of all public activity. If it is right to censor one thing it is right to censor all things. We cannot draw a line between the realms of the censorable and the uncensorable. There is too much overlapping for that. We must either do without any official censorship, or run the risk of total censorship. There is no half-way mark.—*Howard B. Morris. Law Notes.* 32:99. *August* 1928.

The conclave which compiles the Index of the Roman Catholic Church is the most august, ancient, learned, famous, and authoritative censorship in Europe. Is it more enlightened, more liberal, more tolerant than the comparatively infinitesimal office of the Lord Chamberlain? On the contrary, it has reduced itself to a degree of absurdity which makes a Catholic university a contradiction in terms. All censorship exists to prevent anyone from challenging current conceptions and existing institutions. All progress is initiated by challenging current conceptions and executed by supplanting existing institutions. Consequently the first condition of progress is the removal of censorships. There is the whole case against censorships in a nutshell.—*Bernard Shaw Author's Apology.* p. 40-1.

That strange mixture of tyranny and freedom which has characterized every popular form of government nowhere presents more instructive contrasts than in Massachusetts. Boston has a play censor and a literary censor, and dramas and books which are received elsewhere without visible deteriorating effect on the people are there forbidden. But Boston has also a State House where any citizen, even one temporarily resident in an asylum or a prison, may petition the Legislature and demand, and obtain, a committee hearing on the bill which his petition outlines. The results include a lot of useless declamation and documentation; time is wasted terribly; and the Legislature, which meets yearly, holds sessions two and three times as long as those in most other States.—*Editorial. New York Times. February* 10, 1930.

Never in history has censorship worked properly. Censorship, as practiced in modern societies, serves neither morals nor art. Censors are never, even when they are not appointed for obscure political reasons, fit for their job. No one who is fit for the job is ever willing to be a censor. The things that get by are as absurd as the things that are held up. Censorship, properly managed, demands an immense store of knowledge, long experience of literature and art, extremely wise judgment, entire lack of prejudice, and a profound acquaintance with human psychology. In all these gifts [sic] professional reformers are rather notoriously lacking.—*Katharine F. Gerould. Saturday Evening Post.* 194:12. *April* 8, 1922.

The policy of censorship has been exercised with reference to many activities at various times, and by a variety of social agencies. Such dominant institutions as the church and state have often attempted control of speech, the fine arts, and the press by repressive measures. At best their success has been questionable; at worst the policy has been both tyrannical and abortive. Repression has generally proved dangerous regarding either emotions or opinions. When crushed in one form they seek expression in another, most frequently on a lower plane. In general, the idea of censorship has so conflicted with enlightenment and truth seeking that many of the struggles of higher civilization have centered about freedom of opinion, freedom of speech, and freedom of the press. So successful have these struggles been that such freedoms are now recognized as cardinal principles of democracy. Nevertheless there are continued irruptions of reform crusades for censorship of literature, painting, the drama, and even of speech and the press. This is particularly true during times of stress as in the case of war.—*Walter R. Smith. Principles of Educational Sociology.* p. 306.

The long chapter of folly and failure which records the history of restrictive and prohibitive law-making is highly instructive in its teachings, and its lessons have to be learned anew through bitter experience by every new generation. In matters of purely intellectual concern, it gives us warning examples in the form of trials for heresy, actions against sedition, and all kinds of restraints upon the press, the pulpit, and the platform. The very idea of censorship has become suspect, so uniformly has the practice been associated with the suppression of ideas that had far better been left free to find vent. And yet, if the question is pressed home, there is probably no individualist so confirmed as to deny the social necessity of setting some limits to freedom of expression. Society cannot, considering its own safety, permit open incitement to what is universally recognized as crime, or open encouragement to what all but the hopelessly perverted will admit to be dangerous immorality.—*Dial.* 48:137. *March* 1, 1910.

The attempt to draw a line between what is dangerous to a community in words or pictures or symbols, that is, what is dangerous in ideas, has never succeeded. A good many generations have tried it, but the really thoughtful know that it cannot be done. It is safe to say there never has been a book or a play or a newspaper which somebody did not want suppressed. The whole history of civilization might be written in terms of the failure of censorship of one sort or another to distinguish between the good and the bad. All well-informed persons know that. But apparently some very estimable persons have never stopped to reflect on it. If they had they would realize that there is no immediate test of ideas, which, when applied, has not done harm. There is only one way to discover the truth about an idea. That way is to set it free to fight for its life with other ideas. One idea can destroy another; nothing else can. But a dangerous idea is doubly dangerous for being suppressed. There are superstitions which have persisted for ages simply because they have never been permitted to come out in the open and be destroyd.—*Lucian Cary. Current Opinion.* 56:299. *April* 1914.

Russia grants the franchise on a strict class basis, and for the first time in history possession of property is regarded as a disqualification for voting. The Communist party, with perhaps 1,000,000 followers out of Russia's nearly 150,000,000 people, is not simply one of the political parties of Russia; it is the only political party permitted to exist there, and it is held together by iron discipline. The Communist party does not believe in the right of private property, or the right of religion, of free press, of free speech, of free assembly, nor does it believe in the Governments of the world as they exist outside of Russia. The Communist Party monopolizes political power in Russia. This it is able to do, for it disfranchises propertied classes, gives greater representation to the cities where Communist sentiment abides than to the rural districts, conducts a system of indirect instead of direct elections thus weeding out all possible non-Communist officials, sets aside local elections which may return those out of sympathy with the party and its practices, denies hostile factions all means of carrying on propaganda against the regime of the party, and maintains rigid discipline.—*World News. February* 2, 1930.

To withstand this flood of impiety the papal government established two institutions, (1) the Inquisition, (2) Auricular confession—the latter as a means of detection, the former as a tribunal for punishment. In general terms the commission of the Inquisition was to extirpate religious dissent by terrorism, and surround heresy with the most horrible associations. This necessarily implied the power of determining what constitutes heresy. The criterion of truth was thus in possession of this tribunal, which was charged "to discover and bring to judgment heretics lurking in towns, houses, cellars, woods, caves, and fields." With such savage alacrity did it carry out its object of protecting the interests of religion, that between 1481 and 1808 it had punished 340,000 persons, and of these nearly 32,000 had been burnt. [alive]. In its earlier days, when public opinion could find no means of protesting against its atrocities, "it often put to death, without appeal, on the very day that they were accused, nobles, clerks, monks, hermits, and lay persons of every rank." In whatever direction thoughtful men looked, the air was full of fearful shadows. No one could indulge in freedom of thought without expecting punishment.—*John W. Draper. History of the Conflict between Religion and Science.* p. 207.

The most ominous sign of our time, as it seems to me, is the indication of the growth of an intolerant spirit. It is the more dangerous when armed, as it usually is, with sincere conviction. It is a spirit whose wrath must be turned away by the soft answers of a sweet reasonableness. It can be exercised only by invoking the Genius which watched over our infancy and has guided our development, a good Genius, still potent let us believe, the American spirit of civil and religious liberty. Our institutions were not devised to bring about uniformity of opinion: if they had been, we might well abandon hope. It is important to remember, as has well been said, that the essential characteristic of true liberty is, that under its shelter many different types of life and character and opinion and belief can develop unmolested and unobstructed. Nowhere could this shelter be more necessary than in our own country with its different racial stocks, variety of faiths, and the manifold interests and opinions which attest the vigor and zeal of our intellectual life. Some of the most menacing encroachments upon liberty invoke the democratic principle and assert the right of the majority to rule. The interests of liberty are peculiarly those of individuals, and hence of minorities, and freedom is in danger of being slain at her own altars if the passion for uniformity and control of opinion gathers head.—*Charles E. Hughes. Report of the American Bar Association.* 1925. p. 186-7.

Democracy depends upon free thought, free public discussion, a free press, free assemblage, and free selection of public policies and public leaders. That rational like-mindedness which is both the basis and the motive power of a democracy is only possible through the free interchange of ideas and opinions, however diverse and apparently dangerous they may be. For a democracy is a consensus of all ideas and opinions, and all should be given play in the final decision. As soon as freedom of thought and of public discussion are abridged the whole machinery of adjustment in a group will be hampered; it will be impossible to compare ideas, and to come to a rational judgment regarding group policies; stagnation, social inertia, inbreeding of ideas and prejudices, degeneration of thought and institutions occur. It is only through free discussion and the formation of a public opinion, untrammeled either by the prejudices and emotions of the whole group, or by the interests and power of some special class, that democracy can be a safe and efficient means of social control. Censorship, or any denial of free speech, press, and assemblage in a democracy is, according to the theory of democracy, actually class control or oligarchy. As such it sets in motion those processes that are the constant worries of class states and oligarchies, viz., unrest and revolution. Discussion brings about a sifting process whereby the weaknesses of "that which is" are determined. It is a safety valve for accumulating unrest, and assurance of social amity and continuity. Those who try to do away with this complete freedom of discussion on the ground that criticisms of existing conditions and discussions of possible changes are subversive of democracy, either do not understand the implications of democracy, or have no confidence in the ability of the people to exercise their constitutional rights. The failures of government have almost always been failures of free public opinion—mostly of public opinion that was ill-formed, that was denied the facts, or that was misguided by self-constituted masters. The latter, too, will always remain one of the greatest menaces.—*Joyce O. Hertzler. Social Progress.* p. 378-9.

PART II

CENSORSHIP OF SPEECH

BRIEF

SUPPRESSION OF PROPAGANDA FOR THE OVERTHROW OF THE UNITED STATES GOVERNMENT[1]

AFFIRMATIVE

I. Introduction.
   A. There exists in the United States today the Communist Party, an active, well-organized, well-directed, well-financed minority which is increasingly successful.
      1. This party is an actual menace to our Government
         a. In its ultimate aim of destroying the established government of the United States.
         b. In its immediate program for achieving its objective.
   B. There is a fundamental distinction between advocating Bolshevism to be substituted by peaceful means for our present form of government, and organized propaganda inciting men to this change by force and violence.
      1. It is against force and violence that the Affirmative are urging suppressive measures.
   C. This propaganda is not being checked at present.

[1] Yale University Briefs. Report from *University Debaters' Annual.* vol. 6. p. 294-9. 1920.

1. Existing legislation which might handle the situation is not applied.
2. Certain dangerous phases of the situation are not covered by present legislation.

D. It is the duty of Congress to pass enforcing measures applying existing general laws and also to adopt whatever new legislation is necessary.

II. It is the organized propaganda of the Communist Party which has brought into existence and is increasing the acute danger to our governmental institutions that has been mentioned.

A. The organization of this party in Chicago in 1919 brought all the radical elements, I. W. W.'s, syndicalists, anarchists, nihilists, etc., into one united body.

B. The Official Manifesto and Program of the party declares the intention of this body to conquer and destroy the power of the state by force and violence.

C. In the immediate program for achieving this purpose, there are outlined four methods of attack.

1. The stimulation and exploitation of industrial unrest.
   a. Some of our industrial strikes of the last few months were due to the clever propaganda of these Communist leaders.
   b. The party plans to exploit the industrial strike and turn it into political mass action to overthrow the entire government.
      (1) This was partly accomplished in the recent Seattle strike.
2. Agitation among the negroes of the country.

- a. Racial strife is fomented with the idea of developing social hatred into political revolution.

3. Terrorization of public officials.
   - a. Such outrages as the recent attacks on Attorney-General Palmer, Senator Hardwick, and Ole Hanson are an essential part of this party program.
4. Exploitation of the great mass of foreigners in the cities of our country.
   - a. There is no tool which gives more promise than this great, inert, ignorant foreign population, of our cities, with no part in American life because of inability to speak and read English.

D. The problem is rendered more difficult by the powerful support which the party receives from Russia.

III. This propaganda cannot be permitted to continue because it has not only pernicious aims, but immediately pernicious results.

A. Those who lack faith in democracy are spreading the contagion of the idea that grievances can be redressed only by overthrow of government.

B. The extreme statements of radicals produce fierce reaction in conservatives, and as the breach widens, mutual suspicion grows.

1. As a result, considered opinion is impossible.

IV. Governmental measures can suppress this propaganda.

A. Bad ideas have been suppressed in the past.

1. Our own Civil War testifies to the suppression of two bad ideas—by force.

B. In this case it is proposed to suppress not opinions nor ideas but merely a method of propagating opinion.

C. Public opinion will support measures to suppress this propaganda.
   1. The American people have already approved the principle of suppression of certain forms of propaganda, under existing laws.

V. Such measures are entirely in accord with the principles on which the Constitution is based, and constitute a legitimate defence of the State against attack.
   A. Any State has two functions.
      1. It must erect as good a system of government as possible and protect that government from any attacks made upon it.
      2. It must contain within itself every possible means for its alteration, growth and development.
   B. The program of the Affirmative would accomplish both these functions.
      1. It is only taking a logical step in self-defense by stamping out propaganda inciting to violent overthrow of our institutions.
      2. It does not interfere with the possibility of national and governmental development thru the expression of new ideas.
         a. The Constitution of the United States has made ample provision for amendment and alteration.
   C. Such a program does not abrogate freedom of speech, it merely recognizes the distinction between liberty and license.

NEGATIVE

I. Every idea should have an opportunity for expression.
   A. Then, if it is bad, it can be overcome and neutralized in the competition of ideas in the open market.

B. This principle has always been the basis of liberal government everywhere.

C. Our own government has always been based on it.

   1. Our government has continually proved successful and has attained a place of preeminence among the nations.

   2. We have been faced with such propaganda as is being disseminated today in many forms before and over a long period of time.

      a. At the time of the Lawrence textile strike, the membership of the I. W. W. increased from 6,000 to 100,000 in a year.

      b. By 1917 membership had again decreased to 7,000.

      c. Anarchistic propaganda has been preached freely in this country for seventy years.

D. European countries have attempted to suppress such propaganda in the past.

   1. As a result anarchism, syndicalism and communism have spread much faster in Europe than in the United States.

II. There is no danger at present of a revolution in this country.

A. The crux of the danger has been met and passed.

   1. At the time the armistice was signed, our industries had to be readjusted to peace pursuits and much hardship resulted.

      a. Thousands were thrown out of work.

      b. Prices were advanced without limit.

B. The situation has been much relieved since then.

C. Industrial unrest is subsiding.
   1. Industrial unrest is the natural accompaniment of a transition period when prices advance more rapidly than wages.
   2. Wages have now been increased generally and the Government has successfully prevented prices from continuing to advance at such a fearful rate.

III. If there were danger of a revolution now, for the government to adopt the Affirmative plan would be national suicide.
   A. Existing legislation defines and provides punishment for any form of direct incitement to violence.
   B. What the Affirmative are urging is laws for the punishing of indirect incitement to violence, i. e., the holding of unfavorable opinions toward the government.
   C. Suppression of opinion invariably defeats its own purpose.
      1. Ideas can be met only by ideas and defeated by their own intrinsic weakness—oppression invariably strengthens them.
   D. Suppression of opinion is dangerous and inimicable to our continued existence as a nation for several reasons.
      1. Men punished for their opinions are considered martyrs to a cause.
         a. Martyrs create sympathy.
      2. Suppression of opinion arouses hatred toward the government.
      3. It lends credence to the claims of the agitator that the government is autocratic.
      4. It drives radical propaganda under the surface where the light of reason cannot reach it.
         a. The logical outcome will be a federal spy system.

b. All the history, traditions and ideals of the American people are against any such system.

IV. There is danger that if laws are enacted as the Affirmative suggest, they will be used to cover offenses for which they were never intended, and so become a weapon of terrorization.

A. Freedom to criticize the government in any way will be exercised only at the constant peril of indictment.

B. The history of such laws in other lands shows that, under the jurisdiction of those who administer them, they are invariably stretched to cover cases for which they were never intended.

C. The protection of jury trial is no relief in cases of this sort.

1. It was designed for the defense of the majority of people against tyranny, not for the defense of a minority against a majority.

D. Almost any opinion can be twisted by a prosecutor into a dangerous meaning.

1. That is why the fathers of our country insisted on absolute freedom of press and of speech.

V. The passage of such laws in the United States will breed suspicion and discontent.

A. Labor will fear that they will be used to prevent strikes.

B. People generally will suspect such legislation.

1. They know it is against the spirit and letter of the Constitution.

C. Its passage would be due to a blind fear of radicalism and revolution, rather than to the dictates of reason and common sense.

BIBLIOGRAPHY

Bibliographies

American Civil Liberties Union. List of books, pamphlets, and leaflets on civil liberty. 100 Fifth Ave. N.Y.

Chafee, Zechariah, jr. Freedom of speech. Harcourt, Brace and Howe. N.Y. '20.

Bibliography on freedom of speech, p. 377-405.

Library of Congress. List of references on freedom of the press and speech and censorship in time of war (with special reference to the European war). Ap. 20, '17.

Phelps, Edith M. Civil liberty. Reference Shelf. vol. 4. no. 9. H. W. Wilson. N.Y. '27.

Briefs, bibliography, and articles.

Phelps, Edith M. University debaters' annual. vol. 6. H. W. Wilson. N.Y. '20.

Suppression of propaganda for the overthrow of the United States government, p. 293-372. Two debates. Briefs. Bibliography.

Phelps, Edith M. University debaters' annual. vol. 10. H. W. Wilson. N.Y. '24.

California criminal syndicalism law, p. 57-100. Brief. Bibliography. Debate.

Phelps, Edith M. University debaters' annual. vol. 15. H. W. Wilson. N. Y. '29.

Freedom of speech, p. 231-79. Briefs, bibliography, and speeches.

Schroeder, Theodore Albert. Free speech bibliography. H. W. Wilson. N.Y. '22.

General References

Books and Pamphlets

Burdick, Charles K. Law of the American constitution. Putnam. N.Y. '22.

Freedom of speech, p. 344-73.

Chafee, Zechariah. Freedom of speech. Harcourt, Brace. N.Y. '20.

Chafee, Zechariah. Inquiring mind. Harcourt, Brace. N.Y. '28.

Cooley, Thomas M. Constitutional limitations. 8th ed. Little, Brown. Boston. '27.

Vol. 2, p. 876-959. Liberty of speech and of the press.

Police and the radicals: what 88 police chiefs think and do about radical meetings. 11p. American Civil Liberties Union. N.Y. '21.

War-time prosecutions and mob violence involving the rights of free speech, free press, and peaceful assemblage. 55p. National Civil Liberties Bureau. N.Y. '19.

Periodicals

*American Bar Association Journal. 13:658-9. N. '27. Our courts and free speech. Thomas J. Norton.

American City. 30:559-61. My. '24. Restriction by city government on freedom of speech.

American Law Review. 55:695-721. O. '21. Freedom of speech and the espionage act. Henry W. Taft.

†American Political Science Review. 18:712-36. N. '24. Freedom of speech during and since the civil war. R. H. Eliel.

American Sociological Society. Papers and Proceedings. 9:46-66. D. '14. Reasonable restrictions upon freedom of speech. James B. Reynolds and others.

*American Sociological Society. Publications. 18:121-6. '24. Intolerance: causes and lessons. John A. Ryan.

Annals of the American Academy. 78:194-204. Jl. '18. Freedom of discussion in war time. Norman Angell.

Atlantic Monthly. 120:811-19. D. '17. Threatened eclipse of free speech. J. H. Robinson.

Bellman. 24:287-8. Mr. 16, '18. Problem of free speech.

California Law Review. 10:512-18. S. '22. Criminal syndicalist act.

Case and Comment. 22:455. N. '15. Free speech and its limits. R. P. Falkner.

Case and Comment. 22:461-5. N. '15. Freedom of speech in public streets, parks, and commons. John D. Chamberlain.

Case and Comment. 22:466-70. N. '15. Freedom of speech in industrial controversies. A. G. Shepard.

Case and Comment. 22:471-5. N. '15. Free speech and its enemies. James F. Morton, jr.

Columbia Law Review. 21:526-37. Je. '21. Free speech in war time. James P. Hall.

Congressional Digest. 9:38-41. F. '30. Freedom of communication in America: Growth and development of free speech in the colonial period. Leon Whipple.

Current Opinion. 68:9-13. Ja. '20. Congress grapples with the question of Bolshevism and Anarchism.

Everybody's Magazine. 25:717-20+. N. '11. An answer and an answer. Lincoln Steffens and Erman J. Ridgway.

Harper's Magazine. 147:371-80. Ag. '23. With the I.W.W. in the wheat lands. D. D. Lescohier.

Harper's Magazine. 155:397-406. S. '27. Our courts and free speech. John T. Flynn.

Harvard Law Review. 23:413-40. Ap. '10. Freedom of public discussion. Van Vechten Veeder.

Harvard Law Review. 32:932-73. Je. '19. Freedom of speech in war time. Zechariah Chaffee, jr.

Harvard Law Review. 41:525-8. F. '28. Present status of freedom of speech under the federal constitution.

†Illinois Law Review. 19:124-47. N. '24. What is free speech under the constitution? a debate. Sveinbjorn Johnson and Roger N. Baldwin.

Illinois Law Review. 22:541-5. Ja. '28. Criminal syndicalism. E. F. Albertsworth.

Independent. 55:2940-1. D. 10, '03. Liberty of opinion defined.

Independent. 100:244-5. D. 20, '19. Still after the reds.

Independent. 101:99-100. Ja. 17, '20. Raids on the reds.

Independent. 101:100-1. Ja. 17, '20. Anti-Bolshevik laws.

Independent. 106:48-9. Ag. 6, '21. Red dictionary.

*Independent. 114:583-5. My. 23, '25. On being on the air. H. V. Kaltenborn.

Independent. 116:646-7. Je. 5, '26. Free speech and the schools.

Indiana Law Review. 4:445-55. Ap. '29. Freedom of speech and of the press. Hugh E. Willis.

Literary Digest. 55:11. O. 20, '17. Limits of free speech.

Literary Digest. 64:18. Ja. 24, '20. Drastic sedition laws.

Literary Digest. 64:11-13. F. 7, '20. Alien and sedition bills of 1920.

Literary Digest. 64:17-19. Mr. 6, '20. Dead-line of sedition.

Literary Digest. 65:42. Ap. 3, '20. Friends' plea for free speech.

Literary Digest. 66:48-53. Jl. 17, '20. Tomcat vibrators, Hamlets, and ordinary reds.

†Literary Digest. 74:32. Ag. 19, '22. A document on liberty. William Allen White.

Literary Digest. 77:38-46. Ap. 28, '23. Some bright red communists and spy K 97.

Literary Digest. 77:12. My. 19, '23. A blue day for the reds.

Literary Digest. 77:10-12. Je. 16, '23. Free speech and jailed speakers.

*Literary Digest. 85:9-10. Je. 20, '25. Free speech, limited.

Literary Digest. 93:9-10. My. 28, '27. California's anti-Red law upheld.

Massachusetts Law Quarterly. 11:25-8. Ag. '26. A few historical reminders as to the importance of the right of free speech.

Monthly Labor Review. 10:812-15. Mr. '20. Opinion of the Secretary of Labor with regard to membership in the Communist Party.

Monthly Labor Review. 14:803-12. Ap. '22. Criminal syndicalism and sabotage. Daniel F. Callahan.

Monthly Labor Review. 16:471-3. F. '23. Membership in the I.W.W. a criminal offense under California statute.

Nation. 105:219-20. Ag. 30, '17. Freedom of speech in war time. Herbert L. Stewart.

Nation. 105:342-3. S. 27, '17. Mr. Warner Fite on free speech and democracy. Herbert L. Stewart.

Nation. 110:425-7. Ap. 3, '20. Constitution by candle-light. Lewis S. Gannett.

†Nation. 110:587-9. My. 1, '20. Why freedom disappears. Will Durant.

Nation. 116:170-1. F. 14, '23. Arbuckle and the I.W.W. Catherine Hofteling.

Nation. 117:381-2. O. 10, '23. Pennsylvania justice.

Nation. 122:473-5. Ap. 28, '26. Radio censorship and the listening millions. M. L. Ernst.

*Nation. 123:7-8. Jl. 7, '26. Great American tradition. Charles A. Beard.

Nation. 123:344-5. O. 13, '26. Free speech in Cincinnati. Mary D. Brite.

Nation. 123:523. N. 24, '26. Are teachers muzzled?

New Republic. 12:204-7. S. 22, '17. Public opinion in war time.

New Republic. 19:42-5. My. 10, '19. Mr. Burleson, Espionagent. William Hard.

New Republic. 20:377-83. N. 26, '19. Espionage act interpreted.

New Republic. 27:350-1. Ag. 24, '21. On the advantages of censorship and espionage. Charles A. Beard.

New Republic. 52:251-2. O. 26, '27. Can the radio be rescued?

New Republic. 57:345-6. F. 13, '29. Land of the free: 1928. R. Lowood.

*Open Forum. 1:2-3. Je. '20. Nature and limits of free speech. M. C. Harrison.

Outlook. 88:813-15. Ap. 11, '08. Right of free speech.
*Outlook. 107:230-1. My. 30, '14. Free speech.
*Outlook. 123:569-70. D. 31, '19 Rights and the crimes of speech.
*Outlook. 125:610-11. Ag 4, '20. The red peril and the red hysteria. Frederick M. Davenport.
Outlook. 126:181-2. S. 29, '20. Talking red and seeing red.
Outlook. 133:786. My. 2, '23. What is criminal syndicalism?
Overland. 83:117-18. Mr. '25. California Syndicalist Act—strong or wobbly? A. B. Reading.
Public. 22:236-7. Mr. 8, '19. History and free speech. J. H. Dillard.
Quarterly Review. 117:519-39. Ap. '65. Libel and the freedom of the press.
Radio Broadcast. 9:375-6. S. '26. Broadcasting is not a public utility.
Review. 1:468-9. O. 11, '19. As to deporting undesirables. Sydney Reid.
Review. 1:634-5. D. 6, '19. Issue of free speech.
Review. 1:636-7. D. 6, '19. Justice Holmes dissents.
Southwestern Political Science Quarterly. 3:287-305. Mr. '23. Philosophy of Justice Holmes on freedom of speech. Tully Nettleton.
Survey. 43:422-3. Ja. 17, '20. Aliens and sedition in the New Year. Kate H. Claghorn.
Survey. 43:493. Ja. 31, '20. Espionage in peace times.
†Survey. 44:232-3. My. 15, '20. A closed town remains closed.
†Survey. 50:79-81. Ap. 15, '23. Free speech in Logan. Heber Blankenhorn.
Survey. 50:81-2. Ap. 15, '23. Free speech and a fair wage.
Virginia Law Review. 14:49-55. N. '27. Freedom of speech.

Weekly Review. 4:528. Je. 4, '21. A petty tyranny ended.

World Today. 51:484. Ap. '28. Wireless speechifying.

World Tomorrow. 11:55-7. F. '28. Free speech, limited. Forrest Bailey.

World's Work. 39:341-5. F. '20. On the trail of the Reds. Samuel Crowther.

Affirmative References

Books and Pamphlets

House of Representatives. Hearings before a special committee to investigate communist activities in the United States. 71st Congress, 2d Session. '30.

*Roosevelt, Theodore. Message to Congress. D. 3, '01.

Ryan, John A. and Millar, M. F. X. State and the church. Macmillan. N.Y. '22.
Freedom of speech, pages 16, 55, 239-43.

United States. Supreme Court. Abrams et al v. United States. 250 U.S. 616. N. 10, '19.

United States. Supreme Court. Debs v. United States. 249 U.S. 211. Mr. 10, '19.

United States. Supreme Court. Fiske v. Kansas. 274 U.S. 380. My. 16, '27.

United States. Supreme Court. Frohwerk v. United States. 249 U.S. 204. Mr. 10, '19.

*United States. Supreme Court. Gitlow v. People of New York. 268 U.S. 652. Je. 8, '25.

United States. Supreme Court. Schaefer v. United States. 251 U.S. 466. Mr. 1, '20.

*United States. Supreme Court. Schenck v. United States. 249 U.S. 47. Mr. 3, '19.

United States. Supreme Court. Sugarman v. United States. 249 U.S. 182. Mr. 3, '19.

*United States. Supreme Court. Whitney v. California. 274 U.S. 357. My. 16, '27.

Periodicals

Catholic World. 106:577-88. F. '18. Freedom of speech in war time. John A. Ryan.

*Congressional Record. 72:5502-3. Mr. 18, '30. Freedom of speech. Park Trammell.

†Current History. 16:761-8. Ag. '22. I.W.W. menace self-revealed. Harry Hibschman.

Current History. 18:419-22. Je. '23. Real strength of American communism. Edward T. Bullock.

Forum. 56:5-7. Jl. '16. Abusing freedom of speech. R. B. Wood.

†Forum. 81:293-6. My. '29. Limits of liberty. Archibald E. Stevenson.

Green Bag. 13:461-3. O. '01. Nation and the anarchists. Eugene Wambaugh.

Journal of the American Institute of Criminal Law and Criminology. 10:71-5. My. '19. Free speech and the espionage act. G. P. Garrett.

Literary Digest. 62:27-8. Jl. 5, '19. Rounding up the parlor reds.

*Literary Digest. 62:45-6. Jl. 5, '19. Immoral right to free speech.

Literary Digest. 63:15-16. N. 8, '19. Red threats of revolution here.

Open Shop Review. 22:3-9, 54-9, 94-8, 199-203, 238-44, 281-6. Ja.-Jl. '25. Bolshevism in the United States. Jacob Spolansky.

Outlook. 112:364-5. F. 16, '16. Free speech and law.

Outlook. 112:879-80. Ap. 19, '16. Americanism and free speech.

Outlook. 124:99-100. Ja. 21, '20. Remedy for radicalism.

Outlook. 124:104-6. Ja. 21, '20. Revolutionary menace. James B. Bocock.

Outlook. 132:643-4. D. 13, '22. Case of the millionaire communist.

Outlook. 146:145-6. Je. 1, '27. Limits of free speech.

Review of Reviews. 61:161-6. F. '20. Reds in America. Arthur W. Dunn.

University of Cincinnati Law Review. 4:211-16. Mr. '30. Limiting freedom of speech by suppressing the advocacy of direct action. Edward L. Coyle.

Unpopular Review. 2.223-35. D. '14. Some free speech delusions.

Negative References

Books and Pamphlets

American Civil Liberties Union. Fight for civil liberty 1927-1928. 71p. N.Y. '28.

American Civil Liberties Union. Free speech 1925-1926. 47p. N.Y. '26.

American Civil Liberties Union. Free speech 1926. 42p. N.Y. '27.

Angell, Norman. Why freedom matters. 62p. W. B. Lloyd. Chicago. n.d.

*Bagehot, Walter. Physics and politics. Appleton. N.Y. '73.

Benefits of discussion, p. 161-6.

Baldwin, Roger N. and De Silver, Albert. Fight for free speech. 31p. American Civil Liberties Union. N.Y. '21.

Chafee, Zechariah, jr. Freedom of speech. Harcourt, Brace and Howe. N.Y. '20.

De Silver, Albert. Supreme Court or civil liberty: dissenting opinions of Justices Brandeis and Holmes. 8p. American Civil Liberties Union. N.Y. '21.

Freeman, Alden. Fight for free speech. 34p. '09.

†Holmes, John H. Freedom of speech and of the press. 30p. National Civil Liberties Bureau. N.Y. '18.

Lippmann, Walter. American inquisitors. Macmillan. N.Y. '28.

Russell, Bertrand. Free thought and official propaganda. B. W. Huebsch. N.Y. '22.

Schroeder, Theodore. Constitutional free speech defined and defended. Free Speech League. N.Y. '19.

Schroeder, Theodore. Free speech case of Jay Fox. 10p. Free Speech League. N.Y. n.d.

Schroeder, Theodore. Meaning of free speech. 16p. Free Speech League. N.Y. '17.

Whipple, Leon. Story of civil liberty in the United States. Vanguard Press. N.Y. '27.

Periodicals

*Advocate of Peace. 85:408-9. D. '23. Theory of the freedom of speech up to date. Ernest M. Hopkins.

†Arena. 39:694-9. Je. '08. Lawless suppression of free speech in New York. Theodore Schroeder.

†Arena. 39:737-41. Je. '08. Sinister assault on the breastworks of free government. B. O. Flower.

Atlantic Monthly. 124:616-27. N. '19. What modern liberty means. Walter Lippmann.

Atlantic Monthly. 125:116-18. Ja. '20. Price of intolerance. Graham Wallas.

Century. 105:797-800. Mr. '23. Al. Smith pardons Jim Larkin. Glenn Frank.

Christian Century. 45:277-8. Mr. 1, '28. American Legion and free speech. Sherwood Eddy.

*Collier's Weekly. 70:3. N. 4, '22. Let the people know the truth. Henry E. Jackson.

Everybody's Magazine. 25:796-9. D. '11. Free speech vs. censorship. Lincoln Steffens.

Forum. 60:670-6. D. '18. Your right to speak freely. Miles Poindexter.

Forum. 75:232-5. F. '26. Free speech in the pulpit. G. A. S. Kennedy.

Forum. 81:290-3+. My. '29. Democracy's safety valve. Arthur G. Hays.

Harper's Magazine. 151:440-7. S. '25. New fight for old liberties. Oswald G. Villard.

Harper's Magazine. 155:397-406. S. '27. Our courts and free speech. John T. Flynn.
Harper's Magazine. 157:529-40. O. '28. What the blue menace means. Oswald G. Villard.
Independent. 114:683-4. Je. 20, '25. Overloading the constitution.
Journal of the American Institute of Criminal Law and Criminology. 10:71-5. My. '19. Free speech and the Espionage Act. George P. Garrett.
Journal of the American Institute of Criminal Law and Criminology. 11:181-90. Ag. '20. Free trade in ideas. George P. Garrett.
Nation. 105:243-4. S. 6, '17. Free speech and democracy. Warner Fite.
Nation. 111:684-6. D. 15, '20. In the wake of the Espionage Act. Walter Nelles.
Nation. 112:211-13. F. 9, '21. Oases of freedom. Norman Hapgood.
Nation. 114:364-5. Mr. 29, '22. Fiat lux—but no Red rays. Arthur Warner.
Nation. 117:8. Jl. 4, '23. Free speech: the vital issue. William E. Borah.
Nation. 117:87. Jl. 25, '23. Anyhow Debs spoke in Cincinnati.
*Nation. 118:105-6. Ja. 30, '24. Sanity creeps back.
Nation. 120:347-8. Ap. 1, '25. Count Karolyi and America. Charles A. Beard.
Nation. 123:240-1. S. 15, '26. I believe in free speech, but—. Harbor Allen.
Nation. 124:30. Ja. 12, '27. What does the war lord mean?
*Nation. 124:414. Ap. 20, '27. Free speech and the American Legion.
Nation. 127:292-3. S. 26, '28. The way of Boston. Gardner Jackson.
Nation. 127:604-5. D. 5, '28. How to win free speech. Ruben Levin.

New Republic. 13:17-18. N. 3, '17. In explanation of our lapse. John Dewey.

†New Republic. 17:66-9. N. 16, '18. Freedom of speech. Zechariah Chafee, jr.

New Republic. 18:102-4. F. 22, '19. Freedom of speech: whose concern?

New Republic. 19:13-15. My. 3, '19. Debs case and freedom of speech. Ernst Freund.

New Republic. 19:151-2. My. 31, '19. Debs case.

New Republic. 19:379-85. Jl. 23, '19. Legislation against anarchy. Zechariah Chafee, jr.

†New Republic. 20:360-2. N. 26, '19. Call to toleration.

New Republic. 21:50-2. D. 10, '19. What is left of free speech? Gerard C. Henderson.

New Republic. 21:249-52. Ja. 28, '20. Red hysteria.

New Republic. 21:253-4. Ja. 28, '20. Advocacy of force and violence.

New Republic. 21:303-5. F. 11, '20. Freedom of opinion and the clergy.

New Republic. 21:313-16. F. 11, '20. Perhaps the turn of the tide. William Hard.

New Republic. 22:316-17. My. 5, '20. Freedom of thought and work. John Dewey.

New Republic. 25:259-62. Ja. 26, '21. Freedom of speech and states' rights.

New Republic. 25:344-6. F. 16, '21. Freedom of speech and press. Ernst Freund.

New Republic. 30:160-2. Ap. 5, '22. Free speech, but— Bruce Bliven.

New Republic. 43:141-2. Jl. 1, '25. Gitlow case.

New Republic. 49:126-7. Old fashioned free speech.

New Republic. 51:34-5. Je. 1, '27. Why freedom of speech?

New Republic. 51:41-4. Je. 1, '27. California ashamed and repentant. David W. Ryder.

New Republic. 51:194-6. Jl. 13, '27. Free speech for the army. Harry F. Ward.

New Statesman. 10:228-9. D. 8, '17. Free speech.
North American Review. 206:673-7. N. '17. Must we all go to jail?
Outlook. 129:507. N. 30, '21. Birth control and free speech.
Outlook. 146:100. My. 25, '27. Syndicalism and the Supreme Court.
*Outlook. 152:99. My. 15, '29. Do you believe in free speech? Edmund B. Chaffee.
Public. 22:236-7. Mr. 8, '19. History and free speech. James H. Dillard.
Radio Broadcast. 10:277. Ja. '27. Why censorship of programs is unfortunate.
Scribner's Magazine. 77:582-7. Je. '25. How free is free speech? Robert W. Winston.
Toledo City Journal. 4:134. Mr. 1, '19. Free speech in Memorial Hall. Cornell Schreiber.
World Tomorrow. 9:156-9. O. '26. Altars of freedom. John N. Sayre.
World Tomorrow. 11:55-7. F. '28. Free speech. Forrest Bailey.

GENERAL DISCUSSION

FREE SPEECH—ITS VALUE AND ITS PERILS[1]

Bismarck tells in his memoirs of a certain General von Canitz who used to deliver lectures at the Military School on the campaigns of Napoleon. Whenever a young officer asked him why Napoleon omitted this movement or that movement, the lecturer was wont to exclaim: "Well, you see just what this Napoleon was; a really good-hearted fellow, but stupid."

There is a school of Junker thought in this country which holds a similar opinion in regard to the men who framed the Government of the United States. The Fathers of the Republic were really good-hearted fellows, but stupid, and being stupid, they did not know what they were doing when they imposed their rigid limitations on the Federal authority in order to safeguard the liberty of the individual.

There seems to be a wide-spread belief that radicalism was born yesterday and that incendiary speech is an invention of the Bolsheviki, and that, such phenomena being quite without precedent in the history of the human race, we should proceed to improvise methods of dealing with them which will, somehow, make the punishment fit a new and peculiarly heinous crime that is obviously inspired by the devil for the corruption of what would otherwise be an earthly paradise.

As it happens, radicalism and incendiary speech are just as old as the institution of government, however old that may be—perhaps a day or two younger, for we must

[1] By Frank I. Cobb. From *Cobb of "The World,"* edited by John L. Heaton. p. 150-61.

allow a reasonable time for discontent to get its bearings in relation to the status quo.

The men who drafted and ratified the Constitution of the United States had no abiding faith in the infallibility of government. They had had much experience of government themselves, and knew something of the abuses to which it was subject. Jealous of their rights and jealous of their liberties, they undertook to protect themselves against all invasion, even an invasion of the majority. Although they omitted the Bill of Rights from the original draft of the Constitution, they did this because, having established a government of enumerated and delegated powers, they believed that this government had no power to set aside any of the guaranties of the Bill of Rights. As Hamilton expressed it:

> For why declare that things shall not be done which there is no power to do? For instance, should it be said that the liberty of the press shall not be restrained when no power is given by which restrictions shall be imposed?

Nevertheless the American people were not disposed to take anything for granted, and as a condition of ratification they insisted that the Bill of Rights be made a part of the Constitution, by way of assurance that there would be no encroachments upon Fundamental rights.

The safeguards to human liberty thus embedded in the Constitution and the Bill of Rights represented everything that had been won throughout long centuries in resistance to tyranny and despotism and arbitrary government. The privilege of the writ of habeas corpus was not to be suspended except in cases of rebellion or invasion, when the public safety might require. No bill of attainder or ex post facto law was to be passed. The trial of all crimes, except in cases of impeachment, was to be by jury. Congress was to make no law respecting an establishment of religion or prohibiting the free exercise thereof, or abridging the freedom of speech or of the press or the right of the people to assemble peacefully and petition for a redress of grievances. The right of the people to be secure in their persons, houses, papers and effects against unreasonable searches and seizures was affirmed, and no warrant was to issue except on probable cause supported by oath.

In nothing was their inherent distrust of government more strikingly revealed than in the clause relating to treason. They left nothing to chance. "Treason against the United States," they said, "shall consist only in levying war against them, or in adhering to their enemies, giving them aid and comfort. No person shall be convicted of treason unless on the testimony of two witnesses to the same overt act, or on confession in open court."

My excuse for reciting these ancient formulæ is that they were written into the organic law of the United States by men who believed that they were worth fighting for and worth dying for—by men who had themselves gone down into the valley of the shadow of death in order to give these principles an eternal life.

In one form or another, it has been said many times that what we learn from history is that men learn nothing from history; but there are usually exceptions to every rule. We need go back only a century and a quarter to find in our own annals a complete parallel to the present situation in respect to radicalism and freedom of speech, but whether we are prepared to learn anything from it is another matter.

The clamor for sedition laws, for the deportation of aliens who advocate communistic theories of government, for the expulsion of socialists from legislative bodies on the ground that their platform is inimical to the best interests of the state, for the stern repression of all utterance and opinion which can be twisted into a plea for resistance by forcible means to established economic and political institutions—all this is a reaction from the Russian Revolution.

There was a similar reaction in the United States from the French Revolution. The radicals hailed it as the dawn of a new emancipation for mankind. The conservative classes regarded it as a saturnalia of the anti-Christ. The specter of the guillotine haunted them; the possibility that their own property would be confiscated by the mob terrorized them.

The country was soon divided into two parties, one the champions of the French Revolution, the other profoundly antagonistic to it in all its manifestations. Washington struggled desperately to maintain the balance, and that part of his Farewell Address which is held in such austere veneration by every opponent of the League of Nations was in reality a plea to his hysterical fellow-countrymen not to permit their pro-French sympathies or their pro-British sympathies to wreck the Federal Republic that they had succeeded in establishing.

In Adams's administration, the quarrel between the United States Government and the Directory brought the issue to a head. The Anti-Federalists were vehement in their support of the French and were commonly denounced as Jacobins by the Federalists. The Federalists were in control of the Government in all its branches; they were the party of property and their leaders decided that it was time to set the heel of the Federal authority upon the neck of this godless French radicalism which was ruining the United States.

The result was the Alien and Sedition laws, and the result of the Alien and Sedition laws was the utter destruction of the Federalist party which enacted them.

Except slavery no other issue in the United States ever bred such a bitter and impassioned political contest as the French Revolution, or one which so greatly affected the history of the country. Yet when we come to examine the actual influence that the doctrines of the French Revolution exerted upon the American institutions we cannot find a trace.

The attempt to smother freedom of speech and of the press in order to protect the American people from the infection of French radicalism brought about the annihilation of the responsible Federalist party; it made

Thomas Jefferson President of the United States, and John Marshall was disposed to class Jefferson with the "absolute terrorists," yet the radicals who followed the leadership of Jefferson never adopted a single policy of the French Revolution, a fact that might profitably be considered by all the timid souls who are panic-stricken lest the American people go over to Bolshevism bag and baggage if they are permitted to talk about it except in terms of fevered denunciation.

An eminent American historian has compared the enactment of the Alien and Sedition laws to the momentary hysteria of the persecution of Salem witchcraft, and we are going through another period of witchcraft hysteria in consequence of the Russian Revolution which has appealed to the imagination of certain groups in much the same manner that the French Revolution appealed, although it has awakened the enthusiastic support of a very much smaller fraction of the population.

Gentlemen who modestly describe themselves as 100 per cent Americans and conduct themselves in the manner of 150 per cent Americans, have set themsleves up as the guardians of the country against political and economic heresy, yet I often wonder who gave them their credentials and signed their commissions.

Whatever defects the American people may have, lack of patriotism is not one of them. In all history there is no record of a more devoted and passionate loyalty than that which the American people voluntarily gave to their Government during the recent war. In spite of the heterogeneous mixture of races, in spite of the fact that to millions of men and women the conflict between the United States and the Central Powers took on all the attributes of a civil war, with brother battling against brother, the patriotism of the American people was almost religious in the fervor of its passion. No request of the Government was ever denied. No sacrifice was ever shirked.

Now that the war is won we are asked to believe that

all this militant patriotism has suddenly turned to passive treason, and that the American people are ready to destroy their own institutions because certain economically discontented elements of the population have become infatuated with the Russian Revolution as some of our ancestors were with the French Revolution.

I have been asked tonight to discuss the perils as well as the value of free speech. Most of the perils lie in repression. There is likely to be far more danger in the limitations than in the free speech itself, however foolish and intemperate the speech may be. If there were any virtue in repression, the Bourbons would still be on the throne of France, the Romanoffs would still be on the throne of Russia, Spain would still be a great empire, the Hapsburgs would still rule a Holy Roman Empire, and the Federalist party might still be in power in Washington.

I am well aware that unrestricted freedom of speech in respect to political and economic matters may often be a nuisance and may sometimes be a menace, but life is filled with nuisances and menaces, and clumsy attempts to cure them by drastic remedies have uniformly proved worse than the disease. The punishment of opinion is always dangerous. If we have not learned that, we have indeed learned nothing from history.

It is true that freedom of speech may be easily abused. It is true that fanatics and demagogues not infrequently appeal to violence. But appeals to violence, even the most reckless and sinister appeals, do not necessarily produce violence. In fact they rarely produce violence, and when they do, the instigator is no less guilty than the actual participants in the crime itself.

The extent to which Congress may, under the Constitution, interfere with free speech was long ago declared by a unanimous Supreme Court in these words:

> The question in every case is whether the words are used in such circumstances, and are of such a nature as to create a clear and present danger that they will bring about the sub-

stantive evils that Congress has a right to prevent. It is a question of proximity and degree.

It is a safe rule in every case that the evil must be real, the danger must be an actual danger, "a clear and present danger" as the Court said, not a remote or conjectural danger, and when that danger exists there is no lack of law to meet the situation. But when Government attempts to infer from an opinion, and then punish the intent as a criminal act, it is engaged in a highly hazardous proceeding. It would not be difficult to maintain the thesis that the amount of violence which has resulted from incendiary speech is infinitesimal when compared with the amount of violence that has resulted from the efforts of Government to suppress manifestations of discontent.

There can be no hard and fast test of what is a proper public utterance and what is an improper utterance. It all depends upon circumstances, and if men were never allowed to speak unless they spoke wisely, a great silence would brood upon the earth.

The punishment of political offenses, even those that by their nature compel punishment, has always been one of the most hazardous occupations in which Government can engage. There is no other enmity that persists so long as that which these punishments engender. There is no other thirst for revenge that remains so long unquenched. As Froude so dramatically phrased it, "the grass soon grows over blood shed upon the battlefield, but never over blood shed upon the scaffold."

In that very remarkable book, *The Emancipation of Massachusetts,* written by a great-grandson of the President who signed the Alien and Sedition bills, Brooks Adams summed up the long struggle for human freedom in these words:

Freedom of thought is the greatest triumph over tyranny that brave men have ever won. For this they fought the wars of the reformation, for this they left their bones to whiten upon unnumbered fields of battle, for this they have gone to the dungeon, the scaffold and the stake. We owe to their heroic devotion the most priceless of our treasures, our perfect liberty of thought and speech.

Five years ago no American would have thought of disputing the truth of that eloquent opinion. Yet if it was true then, it is true now. No fundamental principle of human freedom has been changed as a result of the war. Liberty is still liberty, and it is no less desirable now than it was the day before Lenin and Trotski executed the *coup d'état* which made Bolshevism both the Government and the religion of a prostrate Russia.

The capacity for self-government does not depend upon written constitutions or upon Congresses and legislatures or upon armies and policemen. It is something that is inherent in the people themselves. They either have it or they do not have it. It can be developed by education but it cannot be created by fiat of law. The best definition of free institutions of which I have knowledge was made many years ago by Elihu Root in a lecture at Yale University when he said that "Popular government is organized self-control." If we have that organized self-control, we need not be seriously disturbed by the vehemences of soap-box orators and the revolutionary utterances of the preachers of a new political and economic dispensation. If we lack that organized self-control, sedition laws will not save us, nor will governmental restrictions upon the freedom of speech.

There can be no question that the American people have emerged from the clash of arms in a state of perplexity and confusion. The general condition of unrest and discontent is one manifestation of it. The fate of the treaty of peace will serve as an example. Whatever mistakes President Wilson has ever made, the United States under his leadership came out of a victorious war with a power and a prestige that no other nation in all history had ever attained. The American people were not only the dominant political and economic force in the world, but they were the moral masters of civilization, with the opportunity to mould it mightily to their ideals. Having gained this commanding and unique eminence they at once proceeded to abandon it. The President having affronted a powerful element in the Senate, the leadership of the United States in the world was wantonly sacrificed by way of rebuking the President. We fell to playing school-boy politics with the mightiest international issue ever known to man.

The Senatorial dignity has now been salved, the President has been rebuked, but in the meantime the United States has lost every friend that it ever had and nobody in Europe, Asia, Africa or South America believes in the honesty of our purpose or the integrity of our professions, or trusts us, or is likely soon to trust again.

While we were engaged in destroying our political and moral influence throughout the world, we were likewise engaged in destroying our personal liberty at home, in wrecking police powers of the States, in nullifying self-government and in establishing the Federal authority as the supreme arbiter over what men shall eat and what they shall drink, and what the family doctor may prescribe for the influenza. From that to the complete extinguishment of freedom of opinion is only a step; it is a step which all the demogogues of reaction are urging the country to take. Yet in spite even of the blind stupidity and folly of the New York Assembly there are signs that the pendulum is swinging back toward sanity.

We are naturally a conservative people. The form of government established by the Constitution of the United States is now the oldest government in the world. All the others have been revolutionized since Washing-

[a] The "folly" to which Mr. Cobb here refers is the expulsion of the five Socialist members from the New York Assembly and, perhaps, the law requiring the licensing of private schools. There is no question whatever of the power of the legislature to do either of these things, but the advisability of doing them may be very seriously questioned. It is not a question of agreement or disagreement with the doctrines of the Socialist members; the fact remains that they have the same right to hold the views they hold, as do their opponents to hold different views. Both groups have the right to attempt to secure followers by peaceful and orderly means.

ton first took the oath of office. Of all nations, we are the most reluctant to experiment, and the most resentful of political and economic innovation. If Bolshevism were finally to prevail in the world, we should be the last country to go over to it. We take kindly to any improvised religion, but we are distrustful of everything that tends to disturb business.

It is inevitable that Americans of settled occupation and habit should be startled and terrified whenever a new and radical political idea suddenly shoots across the horizon. They are never quite sure whether it is a meteor or whether it means that the end of the world has come and the heavens are being rolled up like a scroll. Whenever these untoward events begin to disturb the routine of our daily life, there is an immediate demand for the intervention of government. No other people on earth flout government so consistently as we do; no other people are so habitually contemptuous of law; yet no other people have such a superstitious regard for statutes as a bulwark of civilization. The same childlike faith that has made us the chief consumers of patent medicine also leads us to believe that an act of Congress will cure anything.

Yet while these first impulses of the American people are very likely to be wrong, the sober second thought of the American people is almost certain to be right. They often make serious mistakes about men; but in the long run they make few mistakes about measures, and especially about measures that bear a vital relation to the life of the community. When they are confronted with a definite issue which they have had the time and opportunity to discuss in all its aspects they make few blunders at the ballot box.

They have yet to go to the ballot box on any of the questions that are now agitating the nation, but when they do it will be found that their inherent common sense will be a surer security against the excesses of radicalism than all the politicians and professional patriots who are now bedevilling the country. Our liberties to-day are in far greater danger from the fools and fanatics of reaction than from the fools and fanatics of radicalism.

The war is destined to produce mighty changes, not only politically but economically. Some of these changes have already taken place. Dynasties have been overthrown. Empires have crumbled. New theories of the relation of the individual to property are asserting themselves. Civilization is passing through one of its great periods of fermentation or as that splendid soldier-statesman from South Africa, Jan Smuts, visualized it, "the tents have been struck and the great caravan of humanity is once more on the march."

We need not wander blindly into the desert of the unknown and the uncertain. The compass is still true to the pole. The stars have not shifted in their courses. The old landmarks have not been destroyed, and we can still take our direction from them—remembering, if you please, that the people do not belong to the government, but the government belongs to the people—remembering, too, that no problem can be intelligently solved in a representative democracy without the fullest and freest discussion, and that in the end we must rely for our political and economic stability, for the permanence of our institutions—not upon the prosecuting attorney and the jailer, but upon that organized self-control which is both the substance and the soul of popular government.

THE NATURE AND LIMITS OF FREE SPEECH[a]

"Free speech" is a misnomer. No one, unless he is a philosophical anarchist believes that there is, or ought to be, unlimited free speech. That may sound like treason to some liberals; yet a moment's reflection ought to make

[a] By M. C. Harrison. *Open Forum.* June 1920.

it obvious. For "free speech" is, in fact, one of those ambiguous catch-words, which mean much or little or nothing, according to one's viewpoint, and is just indefinite enough to make a splendid battle-cry for extreme partisans who are bored, and even irritated, with the nicer distinctions which careful study tends to suggest. Such people like the easy contrasts of absolute right and absolute wrong.

A more accurate term, to commence with, is "freedom of opinion." It may be granted that every man has this right, without any qualification or limitation. As Jefferson expressed it "Almighty God has created the mind free. All attempts to influence it by temporal punishment, or by civil incapacities, tend only to beget habits of hypocrisy and meaness."

But "freedom of opinion" does not always involve freedom of public expression of that opinion. The editor of the Chicago *Tribune* has a perfect right to the opinion that Henry Ford is an ignorant fool, and a contemptible anarchist into the bargain; but when he states that opinion in public he will not be heard to set up his right of "free speech" in defense. Nor can a man stand beneath my window, making the night hideous with abusive and profane language, and then hold himself immune because of his right to "free speech."

The fact of the matter is that the mere saying of words constitutes an act—an act which may be just as important as the pulling of a trigger. Last year a mob of blood-thirsty ruffians were gathered about the Omaha city jail where a miserable colored man was confined, awaiting trial. A man jumps upon a box and shouts, "Smash in the doors—let's get the nigger." The crowd surges in—gets the man—and hangs him. Is there anyone who will deny that the man who urged on the mob, actually lynched that poor colored man just as much as did the man who put the noose about his neck? There was no moral difference in responsibility. Why should there be a legal distinction? If a bully says "Sic'em" to his dog, and thereby sets it upon some victim, who will listen to his plea of "free speech"?

The whole question of immunity for public speech is too extensive to permit of careful analysis here and only two or three fundamental principles may be suggested.

In the first place, there is no immunity under the guise of "free speech" to one who directly and intentionally incites to unlawful action. Thus, in the case already stated, one has the right to the opinion that all colored men, charged with assault, should be lynched at sunrise. One has the further right, no doubt, to state that opinion in public, and to attempt to convert others to that point of view. But the one who gets up in the midst of a mob, and directly incites to an immediate lynching, is a common criminal and should be dealt with as such. Direct incitement to crime may be restrained as properly as the crime itself. Otherwise we should find ourselves in the ludicrous position of attempting to restrain a criminal act, but impotent to reach the one who planned and directly counselled its commission.

The second basic fact to be kept in mind is that all governments have the undoubted power to determine how near to or how remote from immediate incitement to crime the law will take cognizance of spoken words. And all governments have the undoubted power to pass laws which seem unwise and savage, to an enlightened minority; and to enforce them. The recent war prosecutions illustrate this fact. Some of the noblest men and women in this country are in prison for speaking words which were honestly said, and truly said; but which were, nevertheless, unlawful. Scandalous and shameful as it is, there is no good in mere endless repetition that their imprisonment is in direct violation of the right of free speech. Many of them violated the law; intentionally and defiantly violated the law. All honor to stiff necked heroes who walk in the light of their conscience, and snap their fingers at what they deem unrighteous laws.

But let us not deceive ourselves with phrases. It is simply another case of weak and ignorant men enacting unwise and foolish laws; and brave and proud men refusing to be bound by them.

Finally, what we call "free speech," is a misnomer because it implies that every person has it as a natural right. It is conceived of as a very law of nature. The fact is that the extent of free speech, or better, the amount of social tolerance to minority opinion, depends directly upon the general sense of security. In wartime, this margin of safety contracts. The public mind becomes hysterical and apprehensive; and a very considerable part of this social tolerance—this so called right of free speech, disappears. In any time of stress and strain, tempers become shorter, and the margin of tolerance shrinks accordingly. This may be apparent in the laws, or not; but it will certainly be obvious in everyday life. No law is needed to prevent freedom of speech in favor of negro rights, in the South. This is lamentable, no doubt, but it is a fact. The memory of carpet bagger days leaves no sense of security, and no margin of tolerance for the expression of the minority view. It may be taken as an axiom, that whenever a minority, thru public discussion, threatens the sense of security in the dominant class, tolerance for that opinion and its public expression will immediately disappear. That, too, is lamentable, but it is a fact; and a fact which renders the discussion of "freedom of speech" about as academic as debates upon the amount of standing room for angels upon the point of a needle.

To sum up, "free speech," is an ambiguous and misleading expression, and the constant emphasis upon it as an assumed right, tends to confuse the realities of the situation. If a man directly incites to crime, he will be dealt with as a criminal, and the right of free speech will not give him immunity. Ignorant lawmakers will sometimes make silly laws in the attempt to prevent what they deem criminal; and the saying of words will thereby be made unlawful which sensible men know could have no possible causal connection to crime. Nevertheless, so long as government rests upon the shoulders of stupid men, we must expect a great deal of stupid legislation. The solution of the ills that arise from this unfortunate fact cannot be sought through parrot-like repetition of the catchword, "free speech," but must be found in the education of the general mass of society; for it seems to be a safe generalization, that government cannot be more wise or more tolerant than the mass of the people it represents.

RADIO CENSORSHIP[4]

The radio speaker on current events must be very careful not to give offense. He must be generous, broad-minded, and tactful. The moment he intrudes a sharply accented personal point of view, he creates irritation. The radio audience is just as quick to blame as to praise. There is resentment at anything in the way of propaganda. Intelligent advertisers who use the radio are careful not to overdo the mention of their product in connection with their entertainment offerings. New York City's powerful broadcasting station has lost very much in popular esteem because Mayor Hylan uses it to advance his personal political fortunes.

Cranks and bigots listen in eagerly and delight to indulge in epistolary abuse of those speakers who may offend a particular prejudice. When I spoke with some enthusiasm of the elevation to the high rank of prince of the Catholic Church of a poor lad from the East Side of New York City, I received a flood of mail from people who honestly believed that the Pope was seeking by this means to become the chief governing authority in the United States.

My chief troubles in radio broadcasting have arisen

[4] **By H. V. Kaltenborn. *Independent.* 114:583-5. May 23, 1925.**

out of my disagreement with the State Department on the recognition of Soviet Russia. I have no sympathy with communism or with the Soviet Government, but I feel that the best way to help the Russian people to a better government is by granting recognition. I cautiously expressed this belief through Station WEAF in New York City, linked up at the time with Station WCAP in Washington. There was an immediate explosion in high places. Just what happened, I do not know. The *Brooklyn Eagle's* contract was unceremoniously canceled without any explanation. Since that time, despite my continued popularity as a speaker through other radio stations and on numerous public platforms, the American Telephone and Telegraph Company has barred me from its station. Several times the *Brooklyn Eagle* has offered to pay the current rate of $10 a minute to put me back "on the air" through Station WEAF, but without avail.

It is quite possible that if the *Brooklyn Eagle* were a Republican newspaper, whose editors could be counted on to give general support to most Administration policies, I would still be *persona grata.* Broadcasting stations need the cooperation of Federal authorities. They wish to remain on good terms with the powers at Washington. The Department of Commerce allocates and withdraws wave lengths and broadcasting rights. A corporation controlling broadcasting stations in various parts of the country would be foolish to prejudice its interests by antagonizing those in high places. No one out of tune with generally accepted principles or policies is apt to be welcomed "on the air." That is why the Unitarians complain of discrimination, and why the Catholics, through the Paulist Fathers, are erecting a powerful New York City broadcasting station for their own purposes.

Unknown to the general public, there is a thorogoing radio censorship already in effect. It operates quietly and efficiently through a process of exclusion.

Those who are excluded have thus far had the recourse of opening stations of their own, but this will soon be cut off. Federal policy from now on will oppose the erection of an unlimited number of high-powered stations in congested districts. Before long, we are likely to witness a legal battle to compel broadcasting stations, which make a practice of selling time, to sell it to all comers on equal terms. "Freedom of the air" will come to have a meaning akin to "free speech" or "freedom of the press." Broadcasting is as much of a public service and convenience as the telephone, and ultimately must be subject to the same kind of regulation and control.

Radio audiences are not only sensitive to what is said, but they are peculiarly sensitive to a speaker's manner and method. Slovenly speech is much more offensive on the air than on the platform. Speakers who have been guilty of certain mispronunciations all their lives are likely to hear about them for the first time when they address an invisible audience. "What is your authority for slighting the first *n* in government?" queried an irate school ma'am from Paducah, Kentucky, after my radio début. "Please pronounce Los Angeles correctly," a resident of that city telephoned after hearing me use the soft, instead of the hard, *g*.

BRIEF EXCERPTS

Freedom of discussion breaks the ancestral spell.—*Edward A. Ross. Social Psychology. p.* 234.

Free speech is less in need of guarding in this country than the truth.—*Thomas J. Norton. American Bar Association Journal.* 13:659. *November* 1927.

How to preserve both liberty of speech and the peace of the community is a difficult problem.—*Outlook.* 123:570.*December* 31, 1919.

The right of free speech is a bulwark of freedom

and progress.—*Thomas Templeton. Encyclopedia of Religion and Ethics. vol.* 3. *p.* 305.

The United States Supreme Court has held freedom of speech and of the press are protected against state action by the due process clause of the Fourteenth Amendment.—*Hugh E. Willis. Indiana Law Review.* 4:445. *April* 1929.

One may not counsel or advise others to violate the law as it stands. Words are not only the keys of persuasion, but the triggers of action, and those which have no purport but to counsel the violation of law cannot by any latitude of interpretation be a part of that public opinion which is the final source of government in a democratic state.—*Judge Learned Hand.* 244 *Federal Reporter* 540.

The most widespread attempt to curtail freedom of speech has been through state laws. Thirty-four states and the two territories now have criminal syndicalist or sedition or anarchy laws. Most of them have been passed since the Armistice, the largest crop being in 1919 and showing a remarkable similarity of language.—*Harry F. Ward. Publications of the American Sociological Society.* 18:130. 1924.

In England, under the blasphemy laws, it is illegal to express disbelief in the Christian religion. It is also illegal to teach what Christ taught on the subject of non-resistance. Therefore, whoever wishes to avoid becoming a criminal must profess to agree with Christ's teaching, but must avoid saying what that teaching was. —*Bertrand Russell. Free Thought and Official Propaganda. p.* 5.

The American Legion, through its national and departmental commanders, has successfully brought pressure to bear and prevented my speaking in several cities in the south recently. The Legion seems to have inaugurated a policy of endeavoring to dictate who shall speak in various communities and of preventing pacifists and others who do not agree with their views from having a hearing. I saw their policy applied to other speakers as well, such as Dr. Cadman and Will Durant.—*Sherwood Eddy. Christian Century.* 45:277. *March* 1, 1928.

The most elementary condition, if thought is to be free, is the absence of legal penalties for the expression of opinions. No great country has yet reached to this level, although most of them think they have. The opinions which are still persecuted strike the majority as so monstrous and immoral that the general principle of toleration cannot be held to apply to them. But this is exactly the same view as that which made possible the tortures of the Inquisition. There was a time when Protestantism seemed as wicked as Bolshevism seems now.—*Bertrand Russell. Free Thought and Official Propaganda. p.* 6-7.

There exists no moral right to make false statements or to advocate wrong doctrines. Freedom of expression is not an end in itself. It is merely a means. It is reasonable only when the end that it seeks is reasonable, and when it promotes that end in a reasonable way. Obviously no reasonable end is served by the utterance or advocacy of doctrines or theories that are contrary to the truth. If it is wrong to practice polygamy or industrial sabotage, it is likewise wrong to advocate the theories that support and provoke these actions. A man has no more right to say what he pleases than to do what he pleases.—*Rev. John A. Ryan. Catholic World.* 106:577-8. *February* 1918.

To the moneyless and unfortunate are refused those freedoms which the well-to-do exercise as a matter of course. The poor may not freely assemble and freely speak. Their talk leaders, grievance-bearers, agitators, organizers, and walking delegates are suppressed by eleventh-hour ordinances made to corporation orders, by blanket statutes that would prohibit even neighbors meeting round a common board and toasting one another, provided some plutocrat thought it a dangerous practice, or by any other means that may work. Every labor strike causes liberty of speech and of assemblage to be restricted virtually to the capitalist and his sympathizers. The laborer who dares assert his rights is clubbed and jailed.—*Newill L. Sims. Ultimate Democracy and its Making. p.* 92.

The personal liberties guaranteed by the Constitution were not created by that instrument. They were liberties of long standing recognition, which were simply preserved there against future forgetfulness. They came to us by way of inheritance. Other rights even more fundamental were inherent in the compact, which were so clearly implied in the nature of society as to require no covenant. One of the very first of these is expressed by the maxim *Alterum non laedere.* Injure not another. The right of freedom of speech must be read in consonance with this other principle upon which the Constitution was reared. Therefore, the guaranty is that we shall be secure in freedom to use such speech as does not injure the rest of the community.—*G. P. Garrett. Journal of the American Institute of Criminal Law and Criminology.* 10:73-4. *May* 1919.

After the Thirty Years' War bands of marauding soldiers wandered around Europe terrorizing the inhabitants of every town and village to which they could gain access, and something of that sort is going on now [1920] in the United States. Bands of propagandists are wandering around terrorizing public opinion and trying to frighten it into submission to theories of government that are strange to American institutions. Some of the marauders represent radicalism and some reaction, but there is a striking similarity in their methods. Radicalism appeals to violence against reaction, and reaction appeals to violence against radicalism. One menaces with threats of the torch and the bomb, and the other with threats of the rope and the rifle. Both profess to be champions of human freedom. Radicalism pretends to be engaged in restoring human liberty to its primitive simplicity, and reaction, wrapped in the Stars and Stripes, is ready to have everybody else die for the Constitution as it thinks the Constitution ought to be interpreted.—*Frank I. Cobb, Editorial Writer, New York World. Senate Document* 175, 66 *Congress, 2d Session. January* 10, 1920. *p.* 5.

"Congress shall make no law abridging the freedom of speech or of the press." That this amendment was intended to secure to every citizen an absolute right to speak or write or print whatever he might please, without any responsibility, public or private, therefor, is a supposition too wild to be indulged by any rational man. This would be to allow to every citizen a right to destroy at his pleasure the reputation, the peace, the property, and even the personal safety of every other citizen. A man might out of mere malice and revenge, accuse another of the most infamous crimes; might excite against him the indignation of all his fellow citizens by the most atrocious calumnies; might disturb, nay, overturn all his domestic peace, and embitter his parental affections; might inflict the most distressing punishments upon the weak, the timid, and the innocent; might prejudice all a man's civil and political and private rights; and might stir up sedition, rebellion, and treason even against the government itself, in the wantonness of his passions, or the corruption of his heart. Civil society could not go on under such circumstances. Men would then be obliged to resort to private vengeance to make up for the deficiences of the law; and assassinations and savage cruelties would be perpetrated with all the frequency belonging to barbarous and brutal communities. It is plain, then, that the language of this amendment imports no more than that every man shall have a right to speak, write, and print his opinions upon any subject whatsoever, without any prior restraint, so always, that he does not injure any other person in his rights, person, property, or reputation; and so always, that he does not thereby disturb the public peace, or attempt to subvert the government. It is neither more nor less than an expansion of the great docrine recently brought into operation in the law of libel, that every man shall be at liberty to publish what is true, with good motives and for justifiable ends. And with this reasonable limitation it is not only right in itself, but it is an inestimable privilege in a free government. Without such a limitation, it might become the scourge of the republic, first denouncing the principles of liberty, and then by rendering the most virtuous patriots odious through the terrors of the press, introducing despotism in its worst form.—*Joseph Story. Commentaries on the Constitution of the United States. vol.* 2. *p.* 597-8. *Section* 1880.

AFFIRMATIVE DISCUSSION

THE GITLOW CASE[1]

The indictment was in two counts. The first charged that the defendants had advocated, advised, and taught the duty, necessity, and propriety of overthrowing and overturning organized government by force, violence, and unlawful means, by certain writings therein set forth, entitled, *The Left Wing Manifesto*; the second, that the defendants had printed, published, and knowingly circulated and distributed a certain paper called *The Revolutionary Age,* containing the writings set forth in the first count, advocating, advising, and teaching the doctrine that organized government should be overthrown by force, violence, and unlawful means.

. . . It was admitted that the defendant signed a card subscribing to the Manifesto and Program of the Left Wing which all applicants were required to sign before being admitted to membership; that he went to different parts of the state to speak to branches of the Socialist party about the principles of the Left Wing, and advocated their adoption; and that he was responsible for the Manifesto as it appeared, that "he knew of the publication, in a general way, and he knew of its publication afterwards, and is responsible for its circulation."

There was no evidence of any effect resulting from the publication and circulation of the Manifesto.

No witnesses were offered in behalf of the defendant.

Extracts from the Manifesto are set forth in the margin. Coupled with a review of the rise of Socialism,

[1] Decision of the United States Supreme Court. 268 U. S. 652, 655-72. June 8, 1925.

it condemned the dominant "moderate Socialism" for its recognition of the necessity of the democratic parliamentary state; repudiated its policy of introducing Socialism by legislative measures; and advocated, in plain and unequivocal language, the necessity of accomplishing the "Communist Revolution" by a militant and "revolutionary Socialism," based on "the class struggle" and mobilizing the "power of the proletariat in action," through mass industrial revolts developing into mass political strikes and "revolutionary mass action," for the purpose of conquering and destroying the parliamentary state and establishing in its place, through a "revolutionary dictatorship of the proletariat," the system of Communist Socialism. The then recent strikes in Seattle and Winnipeg were cited as instances of a development already verging on revolutionary action and suggestive of proletarian dictatorship, in which the strike workers were "trying to usurp the functions of municipal government"; and Revolutionary Socialism, it was urged, must use these mass industrial revolts to broaden the strike, make it general and militant, and develop it into mass political strikes and revolutionary mass action for the annihilation of the parliamentary state.

. . . The sole contention here is, essentially, that, as there was no evidence of any concrete result flowing from the publication of the Manifesto, or of circumstances showing the likelihood of such result, the statute as construed and applied by the trial court penalizes the mere utterance, as such, of "doctrine" having no quality of incitement, without regard either to the circumstances of its utterance or to the likelihood of unlawful sequences; and that, as the exercise of the right of free expression with relation to government is only punishable "in circumstances involving likelihood of the substantive evil," the statute contravenes the due process clause of the Fourteenth Amendment. The argument in support of this contention rests primarily upon the following propositions: first, that the "liberty" protected by the Fourteenth Amendment includes the liberty of speech and the press; and second, that while liberty of expression "is not absolute," it may be restrained "only in circumstances where its exercise bears a causal relation with some substantive evil, consummated, attempted, or likely"; and as the statute "takes no account of circumstances," it unduly restrains this liberty, and is therefore unconstitutional.

The precise question presented, and the only question which we can consider under this writ of error, then, is whether the statute, as construed and applied in this case by the state courts, deprived the defendant of his liberty of expression, in violation of the due process clause of the Fourteenth Amendment.

The statute does not penalize the utterance or publication of abstract "doctrine" or academic discussion having no quality of incitement to any concrete action. It is not aimed against mere historical and philosophical essays. It does not restrain the advocacy of changes in the form of government by constitutional and lawful means. What it prohibits is language advocating, advising or teaching the overthrow of organized government by unlawful means. These words imply urging to action. Advocacy is defined in the Century Dictionary as: "1. The act of pleading for, supporting, or recommending; active espousal." It is not the abstract "doctrine" of overthrowing organized government by unlawful means which is denounced by the statute, but the advocacy of action for the accomplishment of that purpose. . . .

The Manifesto, plainly, is neither the statement of abstract doctrine nor, as suggested by counsel, mere prediction that industrial disturbances and revolutionary mass strikes will result spontaneously in an inevitable process of evolution in the economic system. It advocates and urges in fervent language mass action which shall progressively foment industrial disturbances, and, through political mass strikes and revolutionary mass action, overthrow and destroy organized parliamentary government. It concludes with a call to action in these words: "The proletariat revolution and the Communist reconstruction of society—*the struggle for these*—is now indispensable. . . The Communist International calls the proletariat of the world to the final struggle!" This is not the expression of philosophical abstraction, the mere prediction of future events: it is the language of direct incitement.

The means advocated for bringing about the destruction of organized parliamentary government, namely, mass industrial revolts usurping the functions of municipal government, political mass strikes directed against the parliamentary state, and revolutionary mass action for its final destruction, necessarily imply the use of force and violence, and in their essential nature are inherently unlawful in a constitutional government of law and order. That the jury were warranted in finding that the Manifesto advocated not merely the abstract doctrine of overwhelming organized government by force, violence, and unlawful means, but action to that end, is clear.

For the present purposes we may and do assume that freedom of speech and of the press—which are protected by the First Amendment from abridgment by Congress—are among the fundamental personal rights and "liberties" protected by the due process clause of the Fourtenth Amendment from impairment by the states. . . .

It is a fundamental principle, long established, that the freedom of speech and of the press which is secured by the Constitution does not confer an absolute right to speak or publish, without responsibility, whatever one may choose, or an unrestricted and unbridled license that gives immunity for every possible use of language, and prevents the punishment of those who abuse this freedom. 2 Story, Const. 5th ed. section 1580, page

634. . . Reasonably limited, it was said by Story in the passage cited, this freedom is an inestimable privilege in a free government; without such limitation, it might become the scourge of the republic. That a state, in the exercise of its police power, may punish those who abuse this freedom by utterance inimical to the public welfare, tending to corrupt public morals, incite to crime, or disturb the public peace, is not open to question. . . Thus it was held by this court in the Fox case, that a state may punish publications advocating and encouraging a breach of its criminal laws; and, in the Gilbert case, that a state may punish utterances teaching or advocating that its citizens should not assist the United States in prosecuting or carrying on war with its public enemies.

And, for yet more imperative reasons, a state may punish utterances endangering the foundations of organized government and threatening its overthrow by unlawful means. These imperil its own existence as a constitutional state. Freedom of speech and press, said Story (supra), does not protect disturbances of the public peace or the attempt to subvert the government. It does not protect publications or teachings which tend to subvert or imperil the government, or to impede or hinder it in the performance of its governmental duties. . . . It does not protect publications prompting the overthrow of government by force; the punishment of those who publish articles which tend to destroy organized society being essential to the security of freedom and the stability of the state. . . . And a state may penalize utterances which openly advocate the overthrow of the representative and constitutional form of government of the United States and the several states, by violence or other unlawful means. . . . In short, this freedom does not deprive a state of the primary and essential right of self-preservation, which, so long as human governments endure, they cannot be denied. . . .

By enacting the present statute the state has

determined, through its legislative body, that utterances advocating the overthrow of organized government by force, violence, and unlawful means, are so inimical to the general welfare, and involve such danger of substantive evil, that they may be penalized in the exercise of its police power. That determination must be given great weight. Every presumption is to be indulged in favor of the validity of the statute. . . . That utterances inciting to the overthrow of organized government by unlawful means present a sufficient danger of substantive evil to bring their punishment within the range of legislative discretion is clear. Such utterances, by their very nature, involve danger to the public peace and to the security of the state. They threaten breaches of the peace and ultimate revolution. And the immediate danger is none the less real and substantial because the effect of a given utterance cannot be accurately foreseen. The state cannot reasonably be required to measure the danger from every such utterance in the nice balance of a jeweler's scale. A single revolutionary spark may kindle a fire that, smoldering for a time, may burst into a sweeping and destructive conflagration. It cannot be said that the state is acting arbitrarily or unreasonably when, in the exercise of its judgment as to the measures necessary to protect the public peace and safety, it seeks to extinguish the spark without waiting until it has enkindled the flame or blazed into the conflagration. It cannot reasonably be required to defer the adoption of measures for its own peace and safety until the revolutionary utterances lead to actual disturbances of the public peace or imminent and immediate danger of its own destruction; but it may, in the exercise of its judgment, suppress the threatened danger in its incipiency. . . .

We cannot hold that the present statute is an arbitrary or unreasonable exercise of the police power of the state, unwarrantably infringing the freedom of speech or press; and we must and do sustain its constitutionality.

This being so it may be applied to every utterance—not too trivial to be beneath the notice of the law—which is of such character and used with such intent and purpose as to bring it within the prohibition of the statute. . . . In other words, when the legislative body has determined generally, in the constitutional exercise of its discretion, that utterances of a certain kind involve such danger of substantive evil that they may be punished, the question whether any specific utterance coming within the prohibited class is likely, in and of itself, to bring about the substantive evil, is not open to consideration. It is sufficient that the statute itself be constitutional, and that the use of the language comes within its prohibition.

It is clear that the question in such cases is entirely different from that involved in those cases where the statute merely prohibits certain acts involving the danger of substantive evil, without any reference to language itself, and it is sought to apply its provisions to language used by the defendant for the purpose of bringing about the prohibited results. There, if it be contended that the statute cannot be applied to the language used by the defendant because of its protection by the freedom of speech or press, it must necessarily be found, as an original question, without any previous determination by the legislative body, whether the specific language used involved such likelihood of bringing about the substantive evil as to deprive it of the constitutional protection. In such cases it has been held that the general provisions of the statute may be constitutionally applied to the specific utterances of the defendant if its natural tendency and probable effect were to bring about the substantive evil which the legislative body might prevent. And the general statement in the Schenck case that the "question in every case is whether the words are used in such circumstances and are of such a nature as to create a clear and present danger that they will bring about the substantive evils"—upon which great reliance is placed in the defendant's argument—was manifestly intended, as shown by the context, to apply only in cases of this class, and has no application to those like the present, where the legislative body itself has previously determined the danger of substantive evil arising from utterances of a specified character. . . .

And finding, for the reasons stated, that the statute is not in itself constitutional, and that it has not been applied in the present case in derogation of any constitutional right, the judgment of the court of appeals is affirmed.

IN THE NAME OF FREE SPEECH[1]

Invoking the sacred right of liberty of speech the Bolsheviki are busily engaged destroying liberty itself, and the federal and state authorities, to preserve the first, seem oblivious to the slow destruction of the other. A Methodist bishop, Richard J. Cooke, in calling attention to this anomalous state of public morals, quotes in support of his diagnosis the farewell remark of the Austrian Ambassador Dumba, who was the first of our undesirable aliens helped out of the country. "Good-by," he said, "to the land where everybody does as he pleases." This characterization, points out the bishop, in *Zion's Herald* (Boston), "seems exactly to express the opinion which undesirable aliens and the motley element of propagandists, from university professors down to the dregs of anarchy, seem to have of this country, its institutions, and its laws." What amazes the bishop is the length to which the federal and state authorities allow the enemies of social order to go before any attempt is made to curtail their seditious propaganda. He fears that here as in England, the "wide margin left for the play of political-social eccentricities" may be over-stept, "and when patience has done its perfect work" that the people will

[1] *Literary Digest.* 62:45-6. July 5, 1919.

suddenly "accept the Bolshevik idea of this country themselves and play Bolshevik to the Bolsheviki with terrible results." He warns us that:

Such explosions of long-restrained, pent-up wrath are not unknown in this country, as many unfortunate instances during the war in such widely separated states as Colorado, Montana, Idaho, testify. The danger is they may become all too frequent. What intensifies the resentment of our people, and makes them so sanguinary in their reprisals, is not that traitors, anarchists, and radicals of all brands should hold opinions antagonistic to our social system, but that they should have the cowardly audacity to shelter their crimes and to beg for mercy and protection under the very laws and institutions they seek to destroy.

During a Senatorial inquiry January 10 last, into alleged pro-German activities of the newspaper man, W. R. Hearst, a pro-German professor in one of our greatest universities so persistently referred to what the Constitution in his opinion permitted or did not permit our government to do, that, rebuking him, Senator Sterling said, "You have a very unfortunate habit of citing the Constitution as justification for everything pro-German." Such double dealing is so revolting to every instinct of honor and justice that, in the thoughts of many, vengeful violation of the law is justified by the nature of the offense. This, of course, is subversive of all law and is condemnable. It makes unwilling Bolsheviki of loyal citizens who abhor every sign and symbol of barbarism and ruin. But if the fundamental laws of our country are to be so interpreted that almost every attack upon government and society can justify itself under the plea of freedom of speech, what are you going to do about it? Liberty of speech is a poor compensation for the destruction of all liberty.

We need have no fear of Bolshevism as such spreading among the American people, the bishop declares, "providing the government will protect loyalty as carefully as it guards the freedom of disloyalty." Change the emphasis in public opinion, he urges, on the meaning of constitutional freedom, and it will "bring to memory the forgotten fact that the American Constitution was made for the American government for the benefit of the American people, and not for the protection of the enemies of both." He writes:

Behind the letter of law is the natural law of self-preservation. This law is as applicable to society as it is to the individual. When these enemies of order, or traitors to this government, though now naturalized citizens, landed on these shores they took an oath of allegiance to this government, or were admitted on oath that they were not antagonistic to our form of government. Had they not done so they would not have been permitted to remain here, or to acquire the rights of citizenship.

Can such undesirables remain citizens and at the same time violate that oath? That is, has any one the right to the benefits of his perjury? The logical answer leads without any circumlocution to their speedy deportation and the confiscation of their property after due process of law. Moral justice demands that whoever allows Bolshevik principles or conspires in any way or fulminates, not against officials of government, or methods of government, but against the nature of the government itself, in such a manner as would destroy the government and substitute for it another kind of government, that criminal should not be permitted to live in the United States under the protection of the government. The Bolshevik has neither moral nor political right in this country to the benefits of his violated oath.

The amazing contention, however, on the part of these agents of destruction, is that they have the right to come here, and that being here they have the constitutional right to freedom of speech. They spare themselves the fatigue of ascertaining what freedom of speech means, but either through ignorance or contempt for the country where everybody does as he pleases, they read into it license without limit to spread the propaganda of Bolshevism.

Does the Constitution protect the Bolshevik until he has destroyed the Constitution? asks the bishop, adding another query. "When does the Constitution begin to protect the State?"

FREE SPEECH AND ANARCHY[8]

The Congress assembles this year under the shadow of a great calamity. On the sixth of September, President McKinley was shot by an anarchist while attending the Pan-American Exposition at Buffalo, and died in that city on the fourteenth of that month.

Of the last seven elected Presidents, he is the third who has been murdered, and the bare recital of this fact is sufficient to justify grave alarm among all loyal American citizens. Moreover, the circumstances of this, the

[8] By President Theodore Roosevelt. *Message to Congress*, December 3, 1901.

third assassination of an American President, have a peculiarly sinister significance. Both President Lincoln and President Garfield were killed by assassins of types unfortunately not uncommon in history; President Lincoln falling a victim to the terrible passions aroused by four years of civil war, and President Garfield to the revengeful vanity of a disappointed office-seeker. President McKinley was killed by an utterly depraved criminal belonging to that body of criminals who object to all governments, good and bad alike, who are against any form of popular liberty if it is guaranteed by even the most just and liberal laws, and who are as hostile to the upright exponent of a free people's sober will as to the tyrannical and irresponsible despot.

It is not too much to say that at the time of President McKinley's death he was the most widely loved man in all the United States; while we have never had any public man of his position who has been so wholly free from the bitter animosities incident to public life. His political opponents were the first to bear the heartiest and most generous tribute to the broad kindliness of nature, the sweetness and gentleness of character which so endeared him to his close associates. To a standard of lofty integrity in public life he united the tender affections and home virtues which are all-important in the make-up of national character. A gallant soldier in the great war for the Union, he also shone as an example to all our people because of his conduct in the most sacred and intimate of home relations. There could be no personal hatred of him, for he never acted with aught but consideration for the welfare of others. No one could fail to respect him who knew him in public or private life. The defenders of those murderous criminals who seek to excuse their criminality by asserting that it is exercised for political ends inveigh against wealth and irresponsible power. But for this assassination even this base apology cannot be urged.

President McKinley was a man of moderate means,

a man whose stock sprang from the sturdy tillers of the soil, who had himself belonged among the wage-workers, who had entered the Army as a private soldier. Wealth was not struck at when the President was assassinated, but the honest toil which is content with moderate gains after a lifetime of unremitting labor, largely in the service of the public. Still less was power struck at in the sense that power is irresponsible or centered in the hands of any one individual. The blow was not aimed at tyranny or wealth. It was aimed at one of the strongest champions the wage-worker has ever had; at one of the most faithful representatives of the system of public rights and representative government who has ever risen to public office. President McKinley filled that political office for which the entire people vote, and no President—not even Lincoln himself—was ever more earnestly anxious to represent the well thought-out wishes of the people; his one anxiety in every crisis was to keep in closest touch with the people—to find out what they thought and to endeavor to give expression to their thought, after having endeavored to guide that thought aright. He had just been re-elected to the Presidency because the majority of our citizens, the majority of our farmers and wage-workers, believed that he had faithfully upheld their interests for four years. They felt themselves in close and intimate touch with him. They felt that he represented so well and so honorably all their ideals and aspirations that they wished him to continue for another four years to represent them.

And this was the man at whom the assassin struck! That there might be nothing lacking to complete the Judas-like infamy of his act, he took advantage of an occasion when the President was meeting the people generally; and advancing as if to take the hand outstretched to him in kindly and brotherly fellowship, he turned the noble and generous confidence of the victim into an opportunity to strike the fatal blow. There is no baser deed in all the annals of crime.

The shock, the grief of the country, are bitter in the minds of all who saw the dark days, while the President yet hovered between life and death. At last the light was stilled in the kindly eyes and the breath went from the lips that even in mortal agony uttered no words save of forgiveness to his murderer, of love for his friends, and of unfaltering trust in the will of the Most High. Such a death, crowning the glory of such a life, leaves us with infinite sorrow, but with such pride in what he had accomplished and in his own personal character, that we feel the blow not as struck at him, but as struck at the Nation. We mourn a good and great President who is dead; but while we mourn we are lifted up by the splendid achievements of his life and the grand heroism with which he met his death.

When we turn from the man to the Nation, the harm done is so great as to excite our gravest apprehensions and to demand our wisest and most resolute action. This criminal was a professed anarchist, inflamed by the teachings of professed anarchists, and probably also by the reckless utterances of those who, on the stump and in the public press, appeal to the dark and evil spirits of malice and greed, envy and sullen hatred. The wind is sowed by the men who preach such doctrines, and they cannot escape their share of responsibility for the whirlwind that is reaped. This applies alike to the deliberate demagogue, to the exploiter of sensationalism, and to the crude and foolish visionary who, for whatever reason, apologizes for crime or excites aimless discontent.

The blow was aimed not at this President, but at all Presidents; at every symbol of government. President McKinley was as emphatically the embodiment of the popular will of the Nation expressed through the forms of law as a New England town meeting is in similar fashion the embodiment of the law-abiding purpose and practice of the people of the town. On no conceivable theory could the murder of the President be accepted as due to protest against "inequalities in the social order," save as the murder of all the freemen engaged in a town meeting could be accepted as a protest against that social inequality which puts a malefactor in jail. Anarchy is no more an expression of "social discontent" than picking pockets or wife-beating.

The anarchist, and especially the anarchist in the United States, is merely one type of criminal, more dangerous than any other because he represents the same depravity in a greater degree. The man who advocates anarchy directly or indirectly, in any shape or fashion, or the man who apologizes for anarchists and their deeds, makes himself morally accessory to murder before the fact. The anarchist is a criminal whose perverted instincts lead him to prefer confusion and chaos to the most beneficent form of social order. His protest of concern for workingmen is outrageous in its impudent falsity; for if the political institutions of this country do not afford opportunity to every honest and intelligent son of toil, then the door of hope is forever closed against him. The anarchist is everywhere not merely the enemy of system and of progress, but the deadly foe of liberty. If ever anarchy is triumphant, its triumph will last for but one red moment, to be succeeded for ages by the gloomy night of despotism.

For the anarchist himself, whether he preaches or practices his doctrines, we need not have one particle more concern than for any ordinary murderer. He is not the victim of social or political injustice. There are no wrongs to remedy in his case. The cause of his criminality is to be found in his own evil passions and in the evil conduct of those who urge him on, not in any failure by others or by the State to do justice to him or his. He is a malefactor and nothing else. He is in no sense, in no shape or way, a "product of social conditions," save as a highwayman is "produced" by the fact that an unarmed man happens to have a purse. It is a travesty upon the great and holy names of liberty and freedom to permit them to be invoked in such a cause.

No man or body of men preaching anarchistic doctrines should be allowed at large any more than if preaching the murder of some specified private individual. Anarchistic speeches, writings, and meetings are essentially seditious and treasonable.

I earnestly recommend to the Congress that in the exercise of its wise discretion it should take into consideration the coming to this country of anarchists or persons professing principles hostile to all government and justifying the murder of those placed in authority. Such individuals as those who not long ago gathered in open meeting to glorify the murder of King Humbert of Italy perpetrate a crime, and the law should ensure their rigorous punishment. They and those like them should be kept out of this country; and if found here they should be promptly deported to the country whence they came; and far-reaching provision should be made for the punishment of those who stay. No matter calls more urgently for the wisest thought of the Congress.

The Federal courts should be given jurisdiction over any man who kills or attempts to kill the President or any man who by the Constitution or by law is in line of succession for the Presidency, while the punishment for an unsuccessful attempt should be proportioned to the enormity of the offense against our institutions.

Anarchy is a crime against the whole human race; and all mankind should band against the anarchist. His crime should be made an offense against the law of nations, like piracy and that form of manstealing known as the slave trade; for it is of far blacker infamy than either. It should be so declared by treaties among all civilized powers. Such treaties would give to the Federal Government the power of dealing with the crime.

A grim commentary upon the folly of the anarchist position was afforded by the attitude of the law toward this very criminal who had just taken the life of the President. The people would have torn him limb from limb if it had not been that the law he defied was at once invoked in his behalf. So far from his deed being committed on behalf of the people against the Government, the Government was obliged at once to exert its full police power to save him from instant death at the hands of the people. Moreover, his deed worked not the slightest dislocation in our governmental system, and the danger of a recurrence of such deeds, no matter how great it might grow, would work only in the direction of strengthening and giving harshness to the forces of order. No man will ever be restrained from becoming President by any fear as to his personal safety. If the risk to the President's life became great, it would mean that the office would more and more come to be filled by men of a spirit which would make them resolute and merciless in dealing with every friend of disorder. This great country will not fall into anarchy, and if anarchists should ever become a serious menace to its institutions, they would not merely be stamped out, but would involve in their own ruin every active or passive sympathizer with their doctrines. The American people are slow to wrath, but when their wrath is once kindled it burns like a consuming flame.

BRIEF EXCERPTS

During a war liberty disappears as a community feels itself menaced.—*Walter Lippmann. Liberty and the News.* p. 29.

Free speech is not an absolute right, and when it or any right becomes a wrong by excess is somewhat elusive of definition.—*United States Supreme Court.* 251 *U. S.* 474.

It is not the duty of the nation to assume that the tongue can commit no crimes, nor to leave the public or the individual unprotected from crimes which the tongue commits.—*Outlook.* 123:570. *December* 31, 1919.

What is too often ignored is the fact that a belief in

communism as an ideal is not at all incompatible with good citizenship.—*Editorial. Brooklyn Daily Eagle. March* 18, 1930.

History admonishes us that truth and error can exist side by side for centuries, the latter as well as the former continuously winning new adherents.—*John A. Ryan. The State and the Church.* p. 57.

"Mere poppycock," is all our talk of free speech, says the Brooklyn *Citizen,* meaning that "there are limits to free speech and those limits have been recognized in all civilized countries."—*Literary Digest.* 85:9. *June* 20, 1925.

No one will question the fact that freedom of speech can be abused. No one will question the fact that a sufficient abuse of the freedom of speech should be punished.—*Hugh L. Black. Congressional Record.* 71: 4468. *October* 11, 1929.

Freedom of speech is guaranteed to the individual and newspaper by the Constitution. It is, however, the use and not the abuse of free speech and free press that is guarded by the fundamental law as sacred.—*Supreme Court of Missouri.* 230 *Missouri* 629.

It is the duty of the government to protect the community and every individual in the community from speech the purpose of which is, the effect of which will be, to incite the hearers to acts of lawless violence or to crimes of any description.—*Outlook.* 123:570. *December* 31, 1919.

No society can afford to let its members say or publish or exhibit what they please. The ordered sex relation is, perhaps, man's greatest achievement in self-domestication. Common sense forbids that the greed of purveyors of suggestive plays, pictures, or literature be suffered to disturb it.—*Edward A. Ross. Social Psychology. p.* 126.

That a state in the exercise of its police power may punish those who abuse this freedom by utterances inimical to the public welfare, tending to incite to crime, disturb the public peace, or endanger the foundations of organized government, and threaten its overthrow by unlawful means, is not open to question.—*United States Supreme Court.* 268 *U.S.* 652.

Although the rights of free speech and assembly are fundamental, they are not in their nature absolute. Their exercise is subject to restriction, if the particular restriction proposed is required in order to protect the state from destruction or from serious injury, political, economic, or moral.—*Justices Brandeis and Holmes.* 274 *U.S.* 373.

To justify suppression of free speech there must be reasonable ground to fear that serious evil will result if free speech is practiced. There must be reasonable ground to believe that the danger apprehended is imminent. There must be reasonable ground to believe that the evil to be prevented is a serious one.—*Justices Brandeis and Holmes.* 274 *U.S.* 376. *May* 16, 1917.

It is a mistake to assume that the right of free speech is unlimited. It is obvious that a speaker who should urge unlawful violence, such as an assassination or the burning of a court house, commits a criminal act. The provision of the Federal Constitution, assuring its citizens right to life, liberty, and property, does not apply to unlawful acts.—*Editorial. Outlook.* 146:145. *June* 1, 1927.

The communists, who are perpetually complaining that their own right of free speech is interfered with, take great pains to prevent the same right from being exercised by their critics. In the course of an extended interchange of letters the Civil Liberties Union has been unable to secure from the party authorities any promise that its members will not continue to howl down unfriendly critics.—*New Republic.* 43:164. *July* 8, 1925.

Mother Jones is reported to have said in a public speech in Gary that she intended to raise hell in America. This is not an idle threat. Not sulphurous flames in the centre of the earth, but the passions of envy, jealousy, and hate in the hearts of men, are the fires of hell. It is not difficult for men to kindle them. It is the duty of the government to protect the community from all such fire fiends.—*Outlook.* 123:570. *December* 31, 1919.

Governments have been overthrown, as the example of Russia shows, by a handful of audacious conspirators. The conspiracy of Malet in 1812, while Napoleon was with the Grand Army in Russia, came within an ace of succeeding. The revolt of a few sailors at Kiel in November 1918 overthrew the German monarchy. Gitlow's conviction was merited and when he comes out of prison, he should be instantly deported.—*Brooklyn Citizen. Literary Digest.* 85:10. *June* 20, 1925.

There is a good deal of nonsense uttered in our time about free speech. There is no reason why the tongue should be any freer than the hand; no reason why society should not punish a man who uses his tongue to injure his neighbor as it punishes the man who uses his hand to injure his neighbor; no reason why it should not take necessary protective measures to guard against wrongdoing by the tongue as it takes necessary protective measures to guard against wrongdoing by the hand.—*Editorial. Outlook.* 107:230. *May* 30, 1914.

The first Amendment, while prohibiting legislation against free speech as such, cannot have been and absolutely was not intended to give immunity for every possible use of language. We venture to believe that neither Hamilton nor Madison, nor any other competent person then or later, ever supposed that to make criminal the counselling of a murder within the jurisdiction of Congress would be an unconstitutional interference with free speech.—*United States Supreme Court.* 249 *U. S.* 206.

We have had too many severe lessons to take threats against the Government lightly. A mere handful of men with the proper weapons could destroy in a day the vital machinery of a city. It is useless to argue that their fiery language does not mean what it says. It does, and only the opportunity is lacking to allow the rude proof of it. Theories are all right but not much use to a man with a gun pointed at his head. He isn't likely to theorize on whether it is loaded or not.—*Boston Post. Literary Digest.* 85:9-10. *June* 20, 1925.

The existence in the United States of various groups and organizations which advocate the overthrow of organized government by direct force and the setting up of a new government according to their ideas, has led to the passage of numerous acts by Congress and state legislatures, declaring the advocacy of such doctrines to be criminal. The courts have generally held it to be within the power of Congress and the states to pass such statutes.—*Edward L. Coyle. University of Cincinnati Law Review.* 4:211-12. *March* 1930.

No thoughtful person believes in unlimited freedom of speech. No government permits unlimited freedom of speech. Inasmuch as a man can injure his neighbors by the written or spoken word quite as effectively, even though not quite so directly, as by physical violence, speech cannot logically or rightfully be left unrestrained by the civil law. Therefore, the issue is one of rational limitation, of such limitation as permits the largest freedom which is consistent with the welfare of the neighbor. —*John A. Ryan. Publications of the American Sociological Society.* 18:121. 1924.

Simple as the [espionage] law is, perilous to the country as disobedience to it was, offenders developed and when it was exerted against them, challenged it to decision as a violation of the right of free speech assured by the Constitution of the United States. A curious spectacle was presented: that great ordinance of government and orderly liberty was invoked to justify the activities of anarchy or of the enemies of the United States, and by a strange perversion of its precepts it was adduced against itself.—*United States Supreme Court.* 251 *U.S.* 477.

Freedom of expression carried so far as to include the

utterance of doctrines which are false and injurious to human welfare is not a rational freedom, since the end which it promotes is irrational. Consequently there exists no such natural right, any more than there exists a natural right of a manufacturer to adulterate food. Of the two forms of adulteration that which injures mind and character is frequently more deadly than that which harms only the body. Therefore, the natural right of freedom of expression extends only to those opinions and doctrines which are true and righteous.—*John A. Ryan. The State and the Church.* p. 55.

That the freedom of speech which is secured by the Constitution does not confer an absolute right to speak, without responsibility, whatever one may choose, or an unrestricted and unbridled license giving immunity for every possible use of language and preventing the punishment of those who abuse this freedom; and that a state in the exercise of its police power may punish those who abuse this freedom by utterances inimical to the public welfare, tending to incite to crime, disturb the public peace, or endanger the foundation of organized government and threaten its overthrow by unlawful means, is not open to question.—*United States. Supreme Court.* 274 *U.S.* 371. *May* 16, 1927.

Free speech does not mean that any man may propose to a group of his fellow-men to put the Constitution, or the laws under that Constitution, at defiance. It does not mean that he may libel or slander any of his fellow-citizens—not even those who have been elected to public office by popular suffrage. Free speech does not mean the right to misrepresent the Constitution or the laws or the administration of those laws. It does not mean the right to blaspheme religion or by falsehood to inflame the passions of the mob against the institutions either of religion or of the state or of industry. It does not mean the right to incite the individual, the group, or the crowd to crimes and violence.—*Outlook.* 123:570. *December* 31, 1919.

It undoubtedly was a well-pondered reliance with them [the Secessionists] that in their own unrestricted effort to destroy Union, Constitution, and law, all together, the government would, in large degree, be restrained by the same Constitution and law from arresting their progress. Their sympathizers pervaded all departments of the government and nearly all communities of the people. From this material, under cover of liberty of speech, liberty of the press, and habeas corpus, they hoped to keep on foot amongst us a most efficient corps of spies, informers, suppliers, and aiders and abettors of their cause in a thousand ways.—*Abraham Lincoln. Letter to Erastus Corning et al. June* 12, 1863. *Nicolay and Hay. Complete Works of Abraham Lincoln. vol.* 8. *p.* 302.

Two recent events challenge the attention of those concerned by the spread of communism in the United States. March 15th soviet sympathizers broke up a meeting in the Garrick Theatre in Chicago because the speaker was exposing the awful plight of men and women exiled to Siberia for expressing opinions contrary to sovietism. The other event was the breaking up of a meeting in Town Hall in New York when the speaker began giving the facts about soviet rule in Russia. That is how free speech fares when the reds are in control, yet they demand for themselves freedom to preach anarchy and treason. It would be interesting to hear how these who advocate the recognition of soviet Russia defend such actions. It would be equally interesting to learn who is supplying the money to maintain the paid agitators who organize these riots.—*Open Shop Review.* 22:141. *April* 1925.

Alexander Stoklitzky, a Russian sent here for propaganda purpose, was the guiding spirit of the meeting. He later became secretary of the Russian Federation of the Communist Party of America. This man had been sent here by Trotzky for the express purpose of spreading propaganda and furthering the communist idea throughout America. He had been sent here to work up class hatred, to create unrest in the labor classes, and by any means possible to generate a feeling of hatred against the government among the working classes to such a point that revolution would result. Stoklitzky stayed for a time in New York, moving in the latter part of 1918 to Chicago. He was later arrested in Detroit, where charges of spreading revolutionary propaganda were brought against him, ending in deportation to Russia, where he now holds office as head of the emigration department.—*Jacob Spolansky. Open Shop Review.* 22:4-5. *January* 1925.

Pope Leo explicitly rejects the doctrine of unlimited freedom of expression. The logic of his argument is unassailable. Speech and writing are not ends in themselves. They are only means to human welfare. The chief constituents of welfare are virtue and truth: the chief obstacles, vice and error. Any action or institution which exposes men to the latter is contrary to human welfare, to social welfare, and, so far as possible, should be prohibited by the state. As a matter of fact, this principle is to some extent recognized in the laws of every enlightened people. False statements injurious to the neighbor, teaching the young immoral practices, publishing and distributing indecent literature,—are scarcely anywhere recognized as legitimate liberties. No peculiar sacredness inheres in the vocal organs or in the faculties which produce the written or printed page. There is no more reason for permitting a man to say or write what he pleases than for permitting him to exercise any other set of muscles according to his unregulated pleasure and regardless of social welfare.—*John A. Ryan. The State and the Church.* p. 55.

We have heard a good deal in the discussion about freedom of the press and freedom of speech. There is no greater adherent than myself to the policy of freedom of the press and freedom of speech. These policies have been the very bulwark upon which our country has succeeded and prospered and grown and maintained its high standard of ideals and purposes down through the ages and which, too, have brought us to this happy hour in the life of our Nation. But, my friends, freedom of the press and freedom of speech do not mean a license to destroy our Government, nor do they mean a license to destroy our homes and blight the future of the youth of the land. Never since the days of our patriotic forefathers has freedom of speech and the press been carried to such unreasonable extent. The communists and anarchists are attempting to prey on this country. That might be minimized by some. Some might rise here and in the interest of so-called freedom of speech plead in behalf of the communists that they be allowed to come here and carry on their devilish teachings with perfect immunity, and this not only among the adults of the land but that they should be allowed to come with perfect freedom into our schools and there teach the overthrow and the destruction by force of our American form of government, that they might there teach atheism and all kinds of evils contrary to our American ideals. In this country we have felt that our ideals are along correct lines. Certainly under the wise policies of the Nation our Republic has prospered and succeeded and preserved the most wonderful citizenship on the globe. So far as I am concerned, I would try to perpetuate it against any and all corrupting influences.—*Park Trammell. Congressional Record.* 72:5502. *March* 18, 1930.

The defendants were found guilty on all the counts. They set up the First Amendment to the Constitution forbidding Congress to make any law abridging the freedom of speech, or of the press, and bringing the case here on that ground have argued some other points. . . But it is said, suppose that that was the tendency of this circular, it is protected by the First Amendment to the Constitution. Two of the strongest expressions are said to be quoted respectively from well-known public men. It well may be that the prohibition of laws abridging the freedom of speech is not confined to previous restraints, although to prevent them may have been the main purpose. We admit that in many places and in ordinary times the defendants in saying all that was said in the circular would have been within their constitutional rights. But the character of every act depends upon the circumstances in which it is done. The most stringent protection of free speech would not protect a man in falsely shouting fire in a theatre and causing a panic. It does not even protect a man from an injunction against uttering words that may have all the effect of force. The question in every case is whether the words used are used in such circumstances and are of such a nature as to create a clear and present danger that they will bring about the substantive evils that Congress has a right to prevent. It is a question of proximity and degree. When a nation is at war many things that might be said in time of peace are such a hindrance to its effort that their utterance will not be endured so long as men fight and that no Court could regard them as protected by any constitutional right. It seems to be admitted that if an actual obstruction of the recruiting service were proved, liability for words that produced that effect might be enforced. The statute of 1917 in paragraph 4 punishes conspiracies to obstruct as well as actual obstruction. If the act (speaking, or circulating a paper), its tendency and the intent with which it is done are the same, we perceive no ground for saying that success alone warrants making the act a crime.—*United States. Supreme Court.* 249 *U. S.* 52.

NEGATIVE DISCUSSION

FREE SPEECH A SOCIAL NECESSITY[1]

The formation of a sound, rational public opinion requires that the bulk of the people must be in a position to determine of their own knowledge, or by weighing evidence, a substantial part of the facts required for a rational decision. For this free speech, free public criticism, a free press, and free discussion and free assemblage are absolutely necessary. As Walter Bagehot pointed out, the discovery and spread of truth is possible only through absolutely unlimited discussion. In the first amendment to our Federal Constitution we have a recognition of the importance of free public discussion as a factor in arriving at substantial social conclusions and policies. Not only is freedom of speech guaranteed to us as a right; it is also necessary in order to rationalize and stabilize public opinion. In the words of Bagehot, "It gives a premium to intelligence." It puts a premium on sound argument rather than unsound. It insures honesty of purpose and effort. It provides the opportunity for the cooperative working of the intelligence of the whole group in building up new social habits, ideals, and institutions. Through discussion the richest results of experience can be brought to bear on a given situation, and there is the greatest chance of a wise rational solution. Free discussion enables men to discover the truth by contest or argument. Or, as Justice Holmes said in a dissenting opinion, "The best test of the truth is the power of the thought to get itself accepted in the competition of the market." The late Frank I. Cobb in commenting on this statement said, "That will always

[1] By Joyce O. Hertzler. *Social Progress.* p. 253-5.

remain the best test of truth, and we cannot afford to tamper with it, however strong the immediate provocation may be, nor can we afford to suppress that competition." It also enables men to adopt the wisest course of action, and carry it out in the wisest way. As Professor Chafee points out, free speech is more than a personal or individual interest; it is a great social interest and value; a fundamental social need that is never to be abridged as an individual interest or value, because its purpose is to discover and spread the truth. Of course, freedom of speech, press, and assemblage does not guarantee sound public opinion. Truth is not spontaneous and self-evident. But it does make possible the unobstructed sway of truth, and as Milton said in Areopagitica, "Who ever knew Truth put to the worse in a free and open encounter?" In the free competition of opinions the truth will always win if you allow the competition to extend over a sufficiently long time.

Freedom of speech and thought is the best way to forbid social institutions to dictate beliefs and standards; it is the best protection against the whims or desires of the powerful; it is the best preservative against the excesses of either radicalism or conservatism; it is the great searchlight which the group uses to illuminate its problems.

For the best public opinion is needed the broadest possible freedom of intercommunication, of interstimulation, and response. This demands the fullest development of all the mechanisms of free intercommunication, including both the abolition of all social barriers, and the improvement of all the mechanical aids. For only in this way does that desirable selection and gradual association and combination of ideas that we call the formation of public opinion occur.

In the last analysis freedom of discussion is a wonderful aid to social progress. Among those people where it has been free and untrammeled, social development has been normal and uninterrupted.

There are many who would shackle the freedom of speech, press and assemblage. These are mainly vested interests of one kind or another who profit by ignorance, or at least ignorance along certain lines which they are careful to maintain. Hence they take their stand against incisive and untrammeled political, economic, or religious utterance. But they do more; they acquire possession of governmental machinery and use it as a means of repression. By their denial of free speech they make public opinion a factory product. Needless to say such social repression of variations means stagnation, social inertia, and probable extermination, for in the long run social inbreeding brings degeneration and death. Such tactics of course encourage unrest and sooner or later result in social revolution.

If those who shackle free speech, press, and assemblage are not prompted by such motives, they are of the group who feel the very foundations of morality will fall if certain things are discussed. As such they have the viewpoint of the heresy hunters and hounders of scientists three centuries ago when social life was at low ebb. Anything unorthodox was dangerous. If a man said the earth went around the sun, he was not trusted anywhere. But it turned out that the orthodox were wrong in that case, as in most of their stands. How then can they be so sure they are right today? It is doubtless true that the very groups who advocate, or resort to, attempts to thwart or repress free speech, or press, or assemblage would be the most active and vociferous in their objections to any curtailment of their own efforts to preach or convert. This is because they are usually interested, not in a better and more rational public opinion, or in scientific objectivity, but in maintaining inherited creeds, dogmatism, and special interests at any cost, even by intimidation. We are beginning to see today that the cause that ducks, slinks, or applies the gag ought to rest under suspicion. Conversely, a noble social cause is very likely to court publicity and discussion.

There are, of course, justifiable limits set by government to the degree of freedom of speech and press. Freedom along these lines does not mean license; it does not give a person the right to spread salacious or obscene ideas, or ruthlessly to destroy other valuable social products. In general, the group does not have difficulty in setting the limits. An absence of the agents which now tend to corrupt or contaminate public opinion is needed.

BENEFITS OF DISCUSSION[3]

A government by discussion, if it can be borne, at once breaks down the yoke of fixed custom. The idea of the two is inconsistent. As far as it goes, the mere putting up of a subject to discussion, with the object of being guided by that discussion, is a clear admission that that subject is in no degree settled by established rule, and that men are free to choose in it. It is an admission, too, that there is no sacred authority,—no one transcendent and divinely appointed man whom in that matter the community is bound to obey. And if a single subject or group of subjects be once admitted to discussion, erelong the habit of discussion comes to be established, the sacred charm of use and wont to be dissolved. "Democracy," it has been said in modern times, "is like the grave; it takes, but it does not give." The same is true of "discussion." Once effectually submit a subject to that ordeal, and you can never withdraw it again; you can never again clothe it with mystery, or fence it by consecration; it remains forever open to free choice, and exposed to profane deliberation.

The only subjects which can be first submitted, or which till a very late age of civilization can be submitted to discussion in the community, are the questions involving the visible and pressing interests of the community; they are political questions of high and urgent

[3] By Walter Bagehot. *Physics and Politics.* p. 161-6.

import. If a nation has in any considerable degree gained the habit, and exhibited the capacity, to discuss these questions with freedom, and to decide them with discretion, to argue much on politics and not to argue ruinously, an enormous advance in other kinds of civilization may confidently be predicted for it. And the reason is a plain deduction from the principles which we have found to guide early civilization. The first prehistoric men were passionate savages, with the greatest difficulty coerced into order and compressed into a state. For ages were spent in beginning that order and founding that state; the only sufficient and effectual agent in so doing was consecrated custom; but then that custom gathered over everything, arrested all onward progress, and stayed the originality of mankind. If, therefore, a nation is able to gain the benefit of custom without the evil,—if after ages of waiting it can have order and choice together,—at once the fatal clog is removed, and the ordinary springs of progress, as in a modern community we conceive them, begin their elastic action.

Discussion, too, has incentives to progress peculiar to itself. It gives a premium to intelligence. To set out the arguments required to determine political action with such force and effect that they really should determine it, is a high and great exertion of intellect. Of course, all such arguments are produced under conditions; the argument abstractedly best is not necessarily the winning argument. Political discussion must move those who have to act; it must be framed in the ideas, and be consonant with the precedent, of its time, just as it must speak its language. But within these marked conditions good discussion is better than bad; no people can bear a government of discussion for a day, which does not, within the boundaries of its prejudices and its ideas, prefer good reasoning to bad reasoning, sound argument to unsound. A prize for argumentative mind is given in free states, to which no other states have anything to compare.

Tolerance, too, is learned in discussion, and, as history shows, is only so learned. In all customary societies bigotry is the ruling principle. In rude places to this day any one who says anything new is looked on with suspicion, and is persecuted by opinion if not injured by penalty. One of the greatest pains to human nature is the pain of a new idea. It is, as common people say, so "upsetting"; it makes you think that after all, your favorite notions may be wrong, your firmest beliefs ill founded; it is certain that till now there was no place allotted in your mind to the new and startling inhabitant, and now it has conquered an entrance, you do not at once see which of your old ideas it will or will not turn out, with which of them it can be reconciled, and with which it is at essential enmity. Naturally, therefore, common men hate a new idea, and are disposed more or less to ill-treat the original man who brings it. Even nations with long habits of discussion are intolerant enough. In England where there is on the whole probably a freer discussion of a greater number of subjects than ever was before in the world, we know how much power bigotry retains. But discussion, to be successful, requires tolerance. It fails wherever, as in a French political assembly, any one who hears anything which he dislikes tries to howl it down. If we know that a nation is capable of enduring continuous discussion, we know that it is capable of practising with equanimity continuous tolerance.

The power of a government by discussion as an instrument of elevation plainly depends—other things being equal—on the greatness or littleness of the things to be discussed. There are periods when great ideas are "in the air," and when, from some cause or other, even common persons seem to partake of an unusual elevation. The age of Elizabeth in England was conspicuously such a time. The new idea of the Reformation in religion, and the enlargement of the moenia mundi by the discovery of new and singular lands, taken together, gave an impulse to thought which few, if any, ages can equal. The discussion, though not wholly free, was yet far freer than in the average of ages and countries. Accordingly every pursuit seemed to start forward. Poetry, science, and architecture, different as they are, and removed as they all are at first sight from such an influence as discussion, were suddenly started onward. Macaulay would have said you might rightly read the power of discussion "in the poetry of Shakespeare, in the prose of Bacon, in the oriels of Longleat, and the stately pinnacles of Burleigh." This is, in truth, but another case of the principle of which I have had occasion to say so much as to the character of ages and countries. If any particular power is much prized in an age, those possessed of that power will be imitated; those deficient in that power will be despised. In consequence an unusual quantity of that power will be developed, and be conspicuous. Within certain limits vigorous and elevated thought was respected in Elizabeth's time, and, therefore, vigorous and elevated thinkers were many; and the effect went far beyond the cause. It penetrated into physical science, for which very few men cared; and it began a reform in philosophy to which almost all were then opposed. In a word, the temper of the age encouraged originality, and in consequence original men started into prominence, went hither and thither where they liked, arrived at goals which the age never expected, and so made it ever memorable.

In this manner, all the great movements of thought in ancient and modern times have been nearly connected in time with government by discussion. Athens, Rome, the Italian republics of the Middle Ages, the communes and states-general of feudal Europe, have all had a special and peculiar quickening influence, which they owed to their freedom, and which states without that freedom have never communicated. And it has been at the time of great epochs of thought—at the Peloponnesian War, at the fall of the Roman Republic, at the Reformation, at the French Revolution—that such liberty of speaking and thinking have produced their full effect.

A BRIEF FOR FREE SPEECH[a]

Let the "people know the truth," said Abraham Lincoln, "and the country is safe." This country is not safe today. For we are threatened with denial of the means of discovering the truth. We had supposed that the Constitution guaranteed to us the right not only to think our thoughts, but to express them. This right of free speech is the very basis of social and political progress. Yet today this basic right stands in jeopardy. This has been clearly shown by such recent acts as those of Attorney General Daugherty at Chicago, and the arrest of William Allen White.

These are danger signals of one of the nation's gravest perils. The time has come for every lover of democratic ideals to take the offensive.

Is free speech a right, or is it not? Is it a right with reservations? If so, what are they? And how shall they be enforced? Who is to determine the limits upon liberty of speech?

I here submit a lawyer's brief in behalf of free speech. Let those who disagree answer it if they can.

1. It Is the Wise Method

If you deny to anyone else the right to say what you think is wrong, it will not be long before you will lose the right to say what you think is right. Defence of the freedom of others is self-defense. Voltaire stated this fact as a genius can: *"I wholly disagree with what you say and will contend to the death for your right to say it."*

2. It Is the Safe Method

When men are emotionally stirred over real or supposed wrongs, they need the safety valve which speech gives them. It may be dangerous to permit certain opinions to be expressed: it is *more dangerous not to* permit them to be expressed. The attempt to prevent an ex-

[a] By Henry E. Jackson. *Collier's Weekly.* 70:3. November 4, 1922.

plosion in the boiler by sitting on the safety valve is obviously futile and foolish. It invites disaster. Suppression is the seed of revolution. *"No abuse of a free press,"* said George William Curtis, *"can be so great as the evil of its suppression."*

3. It Is the Preventive Method

All that most mental diseases, like physical ones, need for their cure is exposure to the fresh air and sunshine. The weakness of wrong opinions stands exposed when submitted to the test of open discussion. They will thus be made harmless. But the merit of right opinions is revealed in the same way. To reject the bad and accept the good, from whatever source they come, is our aim. A democratic policy recognizes the people's right to learn by making mistakes. Free speech may cause temporary disturbance, as it did on a notable occasion once in the open forum at Nazareth. *But Truth is more desirable even than Peace.*

4. It Is the Conservative Method

A community can operate only on the basis of the lowest common denominator. It can undertake only those activities which public opinion will support. Since, therefore, each proposed measure must go through the process of securing public opinion for its support, discussion is a conservative safeguard against hasty action. This is what gives merit to a freeman's inalienable right to trial by jury. It prevents hasty or unjust action through enforced open discussion of his case by his fellow citizens. Those who value this right at its full worth are willing to agree with the drastic statement of Wendell Phillips, that *"The community which does not protect its worst and most hated member in the free utterance of his opinions, no matter how hateful, is only a gang of slaves."*

5. It Is the Democratic Method

It stimulates respect for opinions other than our own. "A decent respect for the opinions of mankind" is a necessary safeguard against the illusion that we are infallible—the danger against which Oliver Cromwell warned the members of Parliament: *"I beseech you, gentlemen, by the mercies of Christ, to remember that it is possible for you to be mistaken."*

6. It Is the Logical Method

The task of correcting wrong opinion is a spiritual process and requires a spiritual weapon. That is what discussion is. An idea is a thing which cannot be organized. Therefore the limits for its discussion cannot be determined. You cannot exterminate an idea with a club; you only *scatter* it. It must be met on its own ground. The only antidote to a wrong opinion is a right opinion. Hence, Jefferson's great dictum, *"Error of opinion may be tolerated, if reason is free to combat it."*

7. It Is the Workable Method

There are only two ways to govern a nation; by the sword, or by public opinion—by force, or by reason. If we adopt the method of reason, then freedom of speech must be complete, not partial. The function of law is to deal with overt acts, not with opinions. If a man's speech results in an actual *deed* intended to hurt the community, then and then only is it a guilty act subject to law. But dogmatically to predetermine what opinions will be helpful or harmful is impossible. Where are the men wise enough to say what subjects citizens may or may not discuss? *"Abuses of freedom of speech ought to be suppressed,"* said Benjamin Franklin, *"but to whom dare we commit the care of doing it?"*

8. It Is the Successful Method

The history of attempts to combat opinion with force instead of reason is a wearisome tale of monotonous failures. It was the method used by the Czar, by the Kaiser, by Lenin. That we, in the face of these failures, should go on repeating them, is amazingly stupid. It directly promotes the cause it seeks to destroy. *The Christian religion owes Nero an immense debt of gratitude for the advertising he gave it by his persecution.*

9. It Is the Progressive Method

Unless there is freedom to discuss and criticize things as they are, there is no chance to help make them what they ought to be. It is the only method which makes improvement possible. Mark Twain clearly stated this necessity when he said: *"My kind of loyalty was loyalty to one's country, not to its institutions. The country is the real thing, the eternal thing. Institutions are extraneous, they are its mere clothing, and clothing can wear out, become ragged. To be loyal to rags, that is a loyalty to unreason. It belongs to monarchy; let monarchy keep it. The citizen who thinks he sees that the commonwealth's clothes are worn out, and yet holds his peace and does not agitate for a new suit, is disloyal; he is a traitor."*

10. It Is the Lawful Method

Any American citizen who attempts to discourage freedom of discussion, violates the organic law of our nation. The first amendment to the Federal Constitution bluntly says that freedom of speech must not be abridged. Ours is a government by public opinion; its prosperity depends on the freedom of forces which mold public opinion.

All public officials or private citizens who suppress free speech are law-breakers and should be treated as such. If there be any who disagree with the First Amendment, it is their right to agitate for its repeal through our regular and orderly method of making changes in the government.

The strange wave of fear and hysteria and organized panic, which during and since the war has been causing disobedience to the first amendment to the Constitution, is relieved by a touch of a sad sort of humor. For these law-breakers pose as patriots. It is these gentlemen most of all who need to be Americanized. They are tragically mistaken about America's ideals, and they are pitifully ignorant of human nature.

More than 90 per cent of all social, industrial and political disputes could be settled in short order, if the parties to them would meet in the same room, put their feet under the same table, look into one another's faces, and be honest.

If the same fairness, tolerance, affection, willingness to differ in opinion without differing in feeling which is employed in fraternal orders were extended to the citizen-members of America as a society, social unrest would cease. It would mean the prevention of an incalculable loss of life, money, and good will, if America would now heed Jefferson's plea: *"Let us restore to social intercourse that harmony and affection, without which liberty and even life itself are but dreary things."*

DO YOU BELIEVE IN FREE SPEECH?[4]

Do you believe in free speech? You probably honestly think you do but has your faith ever been tested? This faith is part of our conventional Americanism. It is written into our Federal Constitution and the constitutions of our several States. But not one in a hundred really believes in it. Indeed Constitutional guaranties have been abrogated and interpreted away whenever powerful interests or public opinion were against the ideas seeking expression. But this has been so, not because the laws passed to maintain freedom of opinion were weak, but because only an insignificant number of individuals have ever really believed in freedom of expression. Such an attitude is a high, moral achievement, attained to by but few. The overwhelming majority of us are for free speech only when it deals with those subjects concerning which we do not feel strongly, about which we have no intense convictions.

[4] By Edmund B. Chaffee. *Outlook.* 152:99. May 15, 1929.

A vivid illustration of the superficiality of a good deal of the homage paid to the principle of freedom of expression was reported in the daily press a few weeks ago. Among those who have been most insistent on this traditional American right of free speech and have fought heroically to maintain it, no group has been more conspicuous than our social radicals. In recent years no group of them has been more bitterly and persistently assailed than the Communists. They have been hated by authorities and citizens alike. Their meetings have been broken up; their speakers have been clubbed; their leaders have been thrown into prison. They, like many other groups whose rights have been invaded, have appealed to the Civil Liberties Union and other agencies seeking to maintain the Constitutional rights of all. Again and again their defense has been "Free Speech." Here, surely, one would think, were men who believed in the right of every man to say what he wished on the great issues of the day. But note the sequel:

A few months ago there began to be dissension in the ranks of the Workers' (Communist) Party here in the United States. The party, as a reflection of the Communist Party of Russia, had a Trotskyist opposition. But the American Communist Party was controlled by the Stalin faction. Following Stalin's method, they began to force all Trotsky sympathizers out of their places of leadership within the party and in some cases out of the party itself. One of these Trotsky adherents, James P. Cannon, could not be silenced. He and his followers issued a paper, "The Militany," in which they presented their side of the struggle. They were forced to do this as the regular party press was in the hands of the Stalin group. Then they began to hold public meetings both in New York City and elsewhere.

Here the real trouble began. The usual places for holding Communist meetings were not open to them. In this situation, they appealed to Labor Temple, an institution of the Presbyterian Church, which has ministered especially to the industrial workers. Ever since its organization this Church at Fourteenth Street and Second Avenue, New York, has steadily maintained the right of all groups to be heard, no matter how unpopular those groups might be. Mr. Cannon and his aides secured permission to hold their meeting at Labor Temple.

It was held but there was a deliberate attempt on the part of the Stalin group to break it up by force. A near riot ensued and the police were called in. They were quite prepared to protect the meeting, but the Trotsky group were unwilling to speak under the protection of the "Capitalist Police," so the meeting was adjourned.

But neither Mr. Cannon nor the committee in control of Labor Temple was content to let the matter drop at that point. Another meeting was therefore scheduled. Arrangements were made by the Labor Temple management for ample police protection. Rumors were rife for days in advance that this second meeting would be attacked vigorously. The Civil Liberties Union was appealed to and sent representatives to the meeting, as did also the I. W. W. After several disturbers had been ejected from the hall, and the police had battled vigorously to keep the streets in front clear, the meeting was called to order. Only the continuous presence of the police prevented the Stalin group in control of the official Communist Party from attacking en masse.

The whole incident revealed how little one group cared for the principle of free speech when that principle threatened its supremacy. And it led the executive officer of the Civil Liberties Union, which has defended many a Communist, to ask the Communist Party if that is the official Communist method of disposing of meetings which contravene their wishes.

However, in this incident most of us can see ourselves. We believe in free speech in the abstract, but we believe in it in the concrete only when the subject discussed does not interest or concern us unduly. The conservative is ready to stop the radical when the latter's utterances are at all effective; and the radical will silence the conservative when he has the power. The men and women who are ready to give a respectful hearing to all opinions, even those with which they do not agree, are very, very few.

The men and women who are ready to protect the preacher of doctrines they detest in his right to preach them are still fewer. There are few Voltaires who can say "I hate what you say, but I will defend with my very life your right to say it." But until some such spirit becomes the rule rather than the exception, there will be no such thing as free speech in any critical time, or on any critical subject. Laws will not bring this about. There are laws enough on this subject already. On all our great social questions there must come the same candid search for truth which now marks the realm of physical science. Real progress along these lines will be snail-like until men can have deep convictions without losing the capacity to hear and consider their opposite. Free speech is a legal principle. In a far deeper sense it is a spiritual triumph.

DISSENTING OPINION: GITLOW CASE[8]

Mr. Justice Brandeis and I are of opinion that this judgment should be reversed. The general principle of free speech, it seems to me, must be taken to be included in the Fourteenth Amendment, in view of the scope that has been given to the word "liberty" as there used, although perhaps it may be accepted with a somewhat larger latitude of interpretation than is allowed to Congress by sweeping language that governs, or ought to govern, the laws of the United States. If I am right, then I think that the criterion sanctioned by the full court in Schenk *v.* United States, 249 U. S. 47, 52,

[8] **Dissenting opinion of Justices Holmes and Brandeis. 268 U.S. 672-3.** June 8, 1925.

applies: "The question in every case is whether the words used are used in such circumstances and are of such a nature as to create a clear and present danger that they will bring about the substantive evils that [the state] has a right to prevent." It is true that in my opinion this criterion was departed from in Abrams *v.* United States, 250 U. S. 616, but the convictions that I expressed in that case are too deep for it to be possible for me to believe as yet that it and Schaefer *v.* United States, 251 U. S. 466, have settled the law. If what I think the correct test is applied, it is manifest that there was no present danger of an attempt to overthrow the government by force on the part of the admittedly small minority who shared the defendant's views. It is said that this Manifesto was more than a theory, that it was an incitement. Every idea is an incitement. It offers itself for belief, and, if believed, it is acted on unless some other belief outweighs it, or some failure of energy stifles the movement at its birth. The only difference between the expression of an opinion and an incitement in the narrower sense is the speaker's enthusiasm for the result. Eloquence may set fire to reason. But whatever may be thought of the redundant discourse before us, it had no chance of starting a present conflagration. If, in the long run, the beliefs expressed in proletarian dictatorship are destined to be accepted by the dominant forces of the community, the only meaning of free speech is that they should be given their chance and have their way.

If the publication of this document had been laid as an attempt to induce an uprising against the government at once, and not at some indefinite time in the future, it would have presented a different question. The object would have been one with which the law might deal, subject to the doubt whether there was any danger that the publication could produce any result; or, in other words, whether it was not futile and too remote from possible consequences. But the indictment alleges the publication and nothing more.

BRIEF EXCERPTS

It is more dangerous to suppress opinion than to permit its expression.—*Independent.* 116:647. *June* 5, 1926.

Many people make foolish speeches, but the constitution leaves them free to talk, holding them responsible for what they say.—*Clarence Darrow. City Club Bulletin. Chicago.* 11:188. *June* 3, 1918.

The prevention of terrorism is to be found in greater freedom of speech, and more earnest and honest efforts to discover and remove legalized injustice.—*Theodore Schroeder. Arena.* 39:699. *June* 1908.

Freedom of opinion, of speech, and of press is our most valuable privilege, the very soul of republican institutions, the safeguard of all other rights.—*William E. Channing. Works.* 11*th ed. vol.* 6. *p.* 149.

Repression and censorship never work within an intellectually alert group of boys such as constitute the college.—*Ernest M. Hopkins. Advocate of Peace.* 85: 408. *December* 1923.

The best remedy for foolish proposals is free discussion. Repression does not suppress. Twice America has tried it and failed.—*Outlook.* 123:570. *December* 31, 1919.

No pupil will be ousted from the public schools of the city because of communist beliefs or participation in communist demonstrations.—*William J. O'Shea. Brooklyn Daily Eagle. March* 18, 1930.

It is the ferment of ideas, the clash of disagreeing judgments, the privilege of the individual to develop his own thought and shape his own character, which makes progress possible.—*Calvin Coolidge. Address before the American Legion. October* 6, 1925.

Fear of serious injury cannot alone justify suppression of free speech and assembly. Men feared witches and burnt women. It is the function of speech to free men from the bondage of irrational fears.—*Justices Brandeis and Holmes.* 274 *U.S.* 376.

There is no more unhappy tendency in our contemporary American life than that to persecute those individuals and those doctrines with which we may not ourselves happen to agree.—*Nicholas Murray Butler. Nation.* 118:105. *January* 30, 1924.

If there be any among us who would wish to dissolve this Union or to change its republican form, let them stand undisturbed as monuments of the safety with which error of opinion may be tolerated where reason is left free to combat it.—*Thomas Jefferson. First Inaugural Address.* 1801.

A fundamental principle of free government is that while the majority must rule, the minority must be heard, so as to have a chance to convert the majority. There can be neither freedom nor progress without free discussion.—*Willis M. West. The American People. p.* 589.

The British Empire claims to be the most liberal on earth with regard to freedom of speech. That claim is probably true. The English have learned that it is a good policy to let the people vent their feelings by giving expression in words.—*J. F. Rutherford. Freedom for the Peoples. p.* 55.

Any attempt at suppressing free speech and free thought is bad for the nation in the same way as the attempt of the Turks to cover up their mines and not allow the gold and silver to be extracted is bad for Turkey.—*Israel Zangwill. Report of the Joint Select Committee on Stage Plays. p.* 331.

Preserve inviolate the right of free inquiry. No institution may rightfully claim immunity from scrutiny and test. Nothing should be held so sacred that it may not be criticized by a competent person at the proper time and in a seemly manner.—*Edward A. Ross. Principles of Sociology.* p. 509.

The Tennessee Legislature may yet prove to be an important friend of the human race. By seeking to make the theory of evolution illegal, it has made it exciting; the people will imbibe more bootleg knowledge in a month than they would absorb under usual circumstances in a decade.—*New Republic.* 43:111. *June* 24, 1925.

If we except religion, England probably has the greatest freedom of speech of any country in the world, and it is almost the only one in which there have been no plots to assassinate its rulers. In Russia we have the most active censorship over political opinion, and the greatest number of assassinated officers.—*Theodore Schroeder. Arena.* 39:695. *June* 1908.

It is the worst policy in the world to drive people to secret meetings and plottings. Let them speak in the open and you will have no secret plottings, throwing of bombs and assassinations. It is hard to make the little pin-head in authority understand this in this free country, where of all the world it should be understood.—*William J. Gaynor. Arena.* 39:737. *June* 1908.

The cry has been that war is declared, and all opposition should therefore be hushed. A sentiment more unworthy of a free country could hardly be propagated. If the doctrine be admitted rulers have only to declare war and they are screened at once from scrutiny. . . In war, then, as in peace, assert the freedom of speech and of the press. Cling to this as the bulwark of all your rights and privileges.—*William E. Channing. Works.* 11th *ed. vol.* 6. *p.* 149.

The Plain Dealer went after Director Barry, and Director Barry went after Chief Graul, and Chief Graul went after the inspectors, and the inspectors went after the captains, and the captains went after the officers on the beats, who should themselves have rooted out the "policy" gambling rackets without any inspiration from above. The police can stand seeing a lot of sharpers take poor folks' money, but they can't stand publicity.—*Editorial. Cleveland Press. February* 5, 1930.

Those who won our independence believed that the final end of the state was to make men free to develop their faculties. They believed that freedom to think as you will and to speak as you think are means indispensable to the discovery and spread of political truth; that without free speech and assembly discussion would be futile; that with them discussion affords ordinarily adequate protection against the dissemination of noxious doctrine.—*Justices Brandeis and Holmes.* 274 *U.S.* 375.

Once more the American Legion looms up as a menace to the liberties of the country. Once more it has proved how completely the spirit of Prussianism, which its members once set out to conquer, has entered into their own minds and possessed them. The West Chester, Pennsylvania, post has now dared to lay down the law in Pennsylvania, that there shall be no criticism of the government or its policies in any institution which is maintained by public money in that state.—*Nation.* 124: 414. *April* 20, 1927.

It is now hundreds of years since Voltaire, skeptic and philosopher, declared to one who opposed him, "I disagree with everything you say, but I will fight to the death for your right to say it." Today, in various parts of the United States, notably North Carolina, Voltaire's words are paraphrased to read, "I disagree with everything you say, and I will fight to the death to prevent you from saying it." This is the most democratic country in the world so far as its form of government goes, but it has a lot to learn yet about the right of free speech.—*Chicago Herald and Examiner. September* 25, 1929.

The wireless telephone, which has in it the potentiality of a wizard's wand, can broadcast the ribald song, the obscene jest as well as a noble hymn or recitation. Shall this new and marvelous invention be used to carry to the silencc of the farm the vile reek of the New York dance hall? Must this agency also be censored? Undoubtedly it must ultimately come under some control. Its possibilities of communication are illimitable, for evil as well as for good. It is not merely a question of instruction in vice and crime, it is a question of vulgarizing, cheapening, standardizing life.—*Hamlin Garland. Literary Digest.* 80:28. *January* 19, 1924.

No matter whose the lips that would speak, they must be free and ungagged. Let us believe that the whole of truth can never do harm to the whole of virtue; and remember that in order to get the whole of truth you must allow every man, right or wrong, freely to utter his conscience, and protect him in so doing. Entire unshackled freedom for every man's life, no matter what his doctrine—the safety of free discussion no matter how wide its range. The community which dares not protect its humblest and most hated member in the free utterance of his opinions, no matter how false or hateful, is only a gang of slaves. If there is anything in the universe that can't stand discussion, let it crack.—*Wendell Phillips.*

There can be no question which is the more dangerous to society, the spouting of Communist dogma by a campaign orator or the forcible suppression of such oratory by the public authority. No community can afford to deny candidates of any party their rights as citizens to freedom of speech. Several recent instances of deplorable officiousness in this direction indicate that some communities at least have not recovered from the hysteria of war. The governmental system of this country has far more to fear from the flouting of its laws by officials sworn to enforce them than from a few discontented persons who find a safety valve in spouting revolutionary theories.—*Editorial. Cleveland Plain Dealer. October* 25, 1928.

Arkansas will vote next month on an anti-evolution law, which would prohibit the teaching of the theory of evolution in tax-supported schools. Charles Smith, president of the American Association for Advancement of Atheism, went to Little Rock, Ark., to open an office and fight the proposed law. He was promptly arrested on a charge of breach of the peace, and he went to jail to serve out a fine of $25 and costs. "No atheist will be permitted to maintain headquarters in Little Rock, Ark., if I can prevent it," Mayor Charles E. Moyer declared. Arkansas has apparently made up its mind not only to prevent the teaching of scientific truths in her schools, but also to deny her people the right to hear both sides of the question before they vote on the law.—*Editorial. Cleveland Press. October* 24, 1928.

Our government is based on the agreement both tacit and implied, that the minority shall always have the rights of free speech, of free press, and of free agitation, in order to convert itself if possible from a minority into a majority. As soon as these rights of the minority are denied, it will inevitably resort to secret meetings, conspiracies and finally force. In times of stress, it may be extremely embarrassing for the majority to be hampered in quick, decisive action by an obstinate minority; but nevertheless the recognition of the right of the minority is our sole bond of unity. For this reason, I repeat that any attempt to interfere with the rights of free speech and free press is a blow at the very foundations of our government.—*Franklin H. Giddings. On the Espionage Bill,* 1917.

The greatest truths are often the most unpopular and exasperating; and were they to be denied discussion till the many should be ready to accept them, they would never establish themselves in the general mind. The progress of society depends on nothing more than on the exposure of time-sanctioned abuses, which cannot be touched without offending multitudes, than on the promulgation of principles which are in advance of public sentiment and practice, and which are consequently at war with the habits, prejudices, and immediate interests of large classes of the community. The right of free discussion is therefore to be guarded by the friends of mankind with peculiar jealousy. It is at once the most sacred and most endangered of all our rights. He who would rob his neighbor of it should have a mark set on him as the worst enemy of freedom.—*William E. Channing. Works.* 11th *ed. vol.* 2. *p.* 160-1.

It is essential to the intelligent conduct of society that radical groups, however small and unpopular, should develop and express their views. Their proposals do good by forcing the discussion of principles and so leading to an illumination otherwise impossible. The large and moderate parties have a conforming tendency and usually differ but little in principles, if indeed they are conscious of these at all. But the radical program is a challenge to thought, and can hardly fail to be educative. For some time past the Socialists have been of the utmost service in this way, and round their searching theories of human betterment discussion has largely centred. Such theories are like the occupation of an advanced post by a detachment of an army; they push forward the line of battle even if the position occupied does not, in the long run, prove tenable. We easily overlook the fact that an honest project is seldom wholly wrong, and that even if it is there may be profit in discussing it.—*Charles H. Cooley. Social Progress.* p. 368.

PART III

CENSORSHIP OF NEWSPAPERS AND MAGAZINES

BRIEF

RESOLVED: *That the Minnesota Nuisance Law should be adopted by every state in the Union.*

INTRODUCTION

I. The meaning of the question.
   A. The Minnesota Nuisance Law of 1925 declares that any newspaper, magazine, or other periodical is a public nuisance if it is:
      1. Obscene, lewd, and lascivious, or
      2. Malicious, scandalous, and defamatory.
   B. It provides that any such publication may be suppressed, either temporarily or permanently, by injunction of a District Court.
      1. It does not grant any court the power to enjoin any one single libel, defamation, or obscenity.
      2. No newspaper or periodical may be suppressed or suspended because of any one particular article or any one issue or number.
      3. Only those newspapers and periodicals which customarily and regularly engage in the publication of matter forbidden by the statute may be declared to be a public nuisance and may be enjoined as such either temporarily or permanently.

C. The County Attorney, the Attorney General, or any citizen of the county may institute and maintain a suit for this purpose.

D. A permanent injunction can be issued only after a formal trial with pleadings, evidence, and arguments.

II. The importance of the question.

A. One of the nation's greatest problems is the dilemma of the press.

1. How can we maintain the freedom of the press and at the same time free ourselves from the blighting abuses of its more degenerate forms.

B. Every other industry or undertaking is under some legal or moral restraint, save only the press.

1. The *Nation* has said in an editorial, "The characteristic of the yellow papers is that they are an irresponsible force. Every other influence in the community, not openly criminal, acknowledges some sort of restraint." (66:336. May 5, 1898.)

C. The Minnesota Nuisance Law is the greatest forward step ever taken towards solving this problem.

III. The first amendment to the Federal Constitution has no bearing on the question in any way.

A. It has no possible application to the state governments.

B. It is a limitation of the powers of Congress, and nothing more.

Affirmative

I. There is urgent need for some remedy for the evils produced by the low grade newspapers and the vicious magazines.

A. American journalism has greatly deteriorated in the last forty years.
   1. There are no longer any professional editors, men whose ideas, ideals, and personality are expressed by their newspapers.
      a. There is no editor of the type of Horace Greeley in all America today.
      b. Henry Watterson was the last professional editor in America.
      c. Editors do not now write their own opinions and convictions, but those of the owners of the paper for which they work. (R. C. Brooks. *Corruption in American Politics and Life.* p. 122-3.)
   2. American journalism is now debased by commercialism.
      a. All newspapers cater to circulation.
         (1) Many of them publish a great deal of filth and drivel, claiming to believe that this is what the people want.
      b. They also cater to advertisers.
         (1) No news unfavorable to department stores can be published.
         (2) Emory S. Bogardus says, "The advertisers are the censors of the news and editorials." (*Introduction to Sociology*. p. 306.)
      c. Most newspapers and magazines publish advertisements they know to be dishonest, fraudulent, or harmful.
         (1) They continually publish the advertisements of fraudulent patent medicines.
         (2) They often publish advertisements of worthless stocks and

d. Practically all the newspapers publish as news the propaganda prepared by publicity agencies employed by selfish private interests to mislead the public.

(1) Among the selfish private interests that desire and seek to mislead and deceive the general public are the liquor interests, the power trust, the steel strike of 1919, the manufacturers of firearms and battleships, various promotion schemes, and various fanatical interests.

(2) Emory S. Bogardus says, "The highest social usefulness of the newspaper has been compromised by commercialism." (*Introduction to Sociology*. p. 305.)

3. Yellow journalism is a serious evil, a menace to America.

a. It began in the late eighties and has spread over the whole country.

b. It regularly prints as news rumors, opinions, propaganda, and deliberate falsehoods.

(1) One never knows when to believe what he reads in most of the newspapers.

(2) Thirty years ago the *Nation* said in an editorial, "Nothing so disgraceful as the behavior of two of these newspapers in the past week has ever been known in the history of American Journalism. Gross misrepre-

sentation of facts, deliberate invention of tales calculated to excite the public, and wanton recklessness in the construction of headlines which outdid even these inventions, have combined to make the issues of the most widely circulated newspapers firebrands scattered broadcast throughout the community." (66:139. February 24, 1898.)

c. It plays up crime, criminal trials, and executions.
   (1) Often a large part of the first page is devoted to crime.
   (2) The most gruesome details are published in full.

d. Scandals, divorces of rich or prominent people, and other trivial matters are presented as the leading news items of the day.

e. Prize fights and other sports are always given undue importance.

f. Pictures of vicious criminals, prize fighters, and bathing beauties generally take up a great deal of space.

g. Jingoism, ill-will towards other nations, is an important feature of yellow journalism.

h. Ballyhoo, drivel written up and printed as if it were important news, together with the policy of suppressing or slighting the important news of the day, are the regular policies of yellow journalism.

(1) It makes a newspaper to fit the tastes, ideals, and mentality of morons and pool room loafers.

(2) Silas Bent has said, "The Sunday papers are a little lower than the fourteen year old might be brought to enjoy." (*Independent.* 119:409. October 22, 1927.)

(3) Ted Robinson, a prominent newspaper man, has said, "The newspaper must, to survive, appeal to the average intelligence. The paper whose contents cannot be readily apprehended and enjoyed by the thirteen-year-old intelligence will soon be bankrupt." (*Cleveland Plain Dealer. May* 13, 1930.)

i. Sob stuff, the sickly emotional and sentimental stories and editorials, are an important part of yellow journalism.

j. The worst part of yellow journalism is that it develops a public appetite for more yellow journalism.

(1) It is a habit-forming social poison, like alcohol and the narcotic drugs.

(2) Felix Frankfurter has said, "A low tone, emotionalism, off-emphasis, irrelevance, and neglect are, we submit, the outstanding sources of newspaper shortcomings. These qualities of news matter fashion the mind of the public. The public,

in its turn, is stimulated to want this kind of news." (*Criminal Justice in Cleveland.* p. 524.)

4. For forty years yellow journalism has been a power pulling all American newspapers down to a lower level.
   a. Many of the old high-grade newspapers have been unable to survive the competition and have combined or gone out of business.
      (1) There are fewer high-grade newspapers in this country today than there were forty years ago, when the population was not half what it is now.
   b. Many high-grade and reputable newspapers have met the competition of yellow journalism by lowering their standards and adopting some of the methods and policies of yellow journalism.
      (1) Some have used larger headlines.
      (2) Almost all of them publish a great deal more crime news.
      (3) Prize fights and sports are given more space and more prominence.
      (4) Scandals among society people are written up as news.
      (5) Many pictures of bathing beauties, criminals, and prize fighters are published.
      (6) Much sob stuff is published.
      (7) Drivel makes up a large part of the Sunday papers.
      (8) Jingoism is often resorted to.

(9) A page or two a day, and many more on Sundays, are devoted to comics.

(10) Important news is slighted or suppressed entirely.

(11) A promotion staff is employed.

B. The vicious magazines have become a menace to America.

1. They have multiplied like rats in a granary.
   a. Hundreds of them are now being published.
   b. New ones are continually being started.
2. They circulate and carry their poison virus throughout the country.
   a. They are on sale at almost every newstand in the country.
   b. They carry their filth to every village and hamlet in America.
   c. They are so cheap as to be within the reach of almost every school child.
3. They are poisoning the minds of the young.
   a. They are filled with sex smut and love slop.
      (1) Prof. Edward A. Ross has said, "The ordered sex relation is man's greatest achievement in self-domestication. No society can afford to let its members say or publish or exhibit what they please. Common sense forbids that the greed of purveyors of suggestive plays, pictures, or literature be suffered to disturb it." (*Social Psychology.* p. 126.)

b. They publish immoral and indecent stories.
c. They often publish obscene and indecent pictures.
d. They use lewd and vulgar language.

4. They become a terrible danger to society in the hands of children, the weak, and the feebleminded.
a. They make crime attractive.
b. They picture as heroes the vilest and most vicious criminals.
c. They are filled with suggestive vice.

C. The yellow newspapers and vicious magazines have lowered the character, ideals, and standard of citizenship of the American people.

1. By continuously publishing drivel and suppressing important news, the newspapers have enfeebled the minds of the American people, developing the shallow, flighty, imaginative mind. (Edward A. Ross. *Social Psychology.* p. 85-6, and *Ladies Home Journal.* 26:5. January 1909.)
a. Most people will not read serious editorials, worth-while magazines, or the best books.
b. Many insist that all of their reading must be for vulgar entertainment.
c. Many people have never learned the difference between humor and filth.
d. The yellow newspapers and the vicious magazines have made this short skirt jazz age.
e. A few years after the beginning of the yellow newspaper the *Nation* said in an editorial, "There appears to be hardly a clergyman, statesman, or

lawyer in the country who does not denounce the yellow journals and deplore their influence on the young." (*Nation.* 66:336. May 5, 1898.)

2. By playing up prize fights, sports, scandals, and bathing beauties they have caused many people to lose interest in public affairs.
   a. The majority of the persons eligible to vote no longer do so.
      (1) In the national election of 1924 only 48 per cent of the people voted, in 1928 only 52 per cent did so.
      (2) In city and local elections often not over 25 per cent vote.
      (3) In primary elections the percentage sometimes falls as low as 10 per cent.
      (4) This condition has steadily grown worse.
   b. Most people will no longer attend political meetings or listen to serious discussions of public questions.
      (1) Even college debaters find it difficult now to secure an audience.
3. By defamation and libel of public officials they keep most of the best men and women entirely out of public life.
   a. Today there are few statesmen among our forty-eight governors, and within the past twenty years several have been impeached or convicted of crime.
   b. There is scarcely a first class executive serving as the mayor of an American city.

c. Bosses and political machines rule everywhere.

d. Bribery and corruption prevail on all sides.

e. Incompetence, inefficiency, and extravagance are the general rule in governmental matters.

f. The attitude of most of the better class of American people has become that uttered by H. G. Wells when he said, "I would as soon go to live in a pen in a stockyard as into American politics." (*The Future in America.* p. 130.)

4. By continually suppressing, coloring, and falsifying the news and by regularly publishing as news the propaganda of private interests, the low grade newspapers have poisoned the wells of democracy at their source.

a. The propaganda of private interests, published as news or as editorials, is deceiving the nation on important public matters.

(1) Silas Bent says, "More than half the reading matter in metropolitan newspapers is of interested origin." (*Ballyhoo: the Voice of the Press.* p. 121.)

(2) The general public was completely deceived by the press in regard to the nature of the Steel Strike of 1919. (Commission of Inquiry of the Interchurch World Movement. Report on

the Steel Strike. p. 242-3, and Public Opinion and the Steel Strike.)

(3) The *Review of Reviews* has recently said, "Readers in our large cities should be warned that the metropolitan press has seriously misled the public by its method of dealing with the prohibition question." (74:125. August 1926.)

(4) Philip P. Parsons says, "The boasted free press has become largely the mouthpiece of interests, commercial, industrial, political, even fanatical. The use of the free press for purposes of vicious propaganda is as criminal as the use of the mails to defraud. (*Crime and the Criminal.* p. 376.)

b. The most vicious and corrupt political bosses and rings have had strong newspaper support.

(1) B. O. Flower has said, "One of the chief sources of the strength of the Tweed Ring was found in the subserviency of the daily press. (*Arena.* 33:274. March 1905.)

(2) James M. Lee says, "During the days when Tweed controlled New York, it is asscrted that eighty-nine newspapers were on his payroll and that after the exposure of the Ring by the New York *Times,* twenty-seven of these papers, which had de-

pended upon city plunder for existence, were compelled to suspend. (*History of American Journalism*. p. 330.)

c. Great wars have sometimes been caused by newspapers which degenerate into jingoism and foster international misunderstanding and illwill.
   (1) Bismarck maintained a Reptile Press for this purpose.
   (2) The Spanish war was caused by the yellow newspapers of the United States.
   (3) Walter Williams has said, "In one sense this hideous war (the world war) was made by the world's press." (*Public*. 20: 1012. October 19, 1917.)

5. By constantly playing up crime, publishing in full the gruesome details of crimes and criminal trials, and by presenting as heroes even the most vicious criminals, the newspapers have increased disrespect for law and have made the United States the most criminal of all civilized nations.
   a. The American people were originally a nation of pure and lofty ideals, formed by a blending of the principles of the Puritans, the Cavaliers, the Calverts, and the Quakers.
      (1) Through the colonial period and for two generations afterwards this country was one of the most law-abiding of nations.
   b. In the late eighties yellow journalism and the vicious magazines began to undermine American ideals.

c. Today the United States has more crime, in proportion to its population, than any other civilized nation in the world.

(1) We have twice as much murder in proportion to our population as Italy, four times as much as Australia or South Africa, eight times as much as New Zealand, Ireland, or Spain, nine times as much as Norway, fifteen times as much as Ontario, seventeen times as much as Great Britain, eighteen times as much as Scotland, twenty-four times as much as Holland, and thirty-six times as much as Switzerland.

(2) Chicago has twenty-five times as high a murder rate as London; Detroit has twice as high a rate as Chicago; and Memphis has three times as high a rate as Detroit.

(3) Cleveland has more crime each year than Great Britain, with forty times its population.

(4) The Prohibition Law is not a cause, but its violation is one more evidence of this condition.

(5) Dr. Frederick L. Hoffmann has said, "Deaths from homicide in American cities reached the highest rate on record during 1924. The rate for twenty-eight American cities almost exactly doubled the rate for 1900, or

twenty-five years ago." (*Spectator*. New York. 114:3. May 21, 1925.)

d. These conditions have been produced in considerable measure by the newspapers and magazines.

(1) They have continually advertised crime and sometimes made it appear attractive, especially to the weak and feebleminded.

(2) The publicity given to crime has interfered with the detection, apprehension, and conviction of criminals. (*Criminal Justice in Cleveland*. p. 521 et seq.)

(3) Lombroso, everywhere recognized as one of the great authorities on crime, has said that the newspapers are a "cause of crime by inciting criminals to emulation and imitation." (*Crime: its Causes and Remedies*. p. 54.)

(4) George W. Kirchwey has said, "With the automatic gun to paralyze the victim and wayfarers and the automobile at the curb to ensure a quick get-away, is there any wonder that the young dare-devils of the criminal profession are attracted to the game? With the newspapers reporting and dramatizing every detail of every hold-up of this character, the wonder is that more of them don't go in for it. It is cer-

tainly made to look like easy money with a minimum of risk." (*Survey.* 55:593. *March* 1, 1926.)

(5) The Christian Science *Monitor* has said in an editorial, "Expert surveys add further corroboration to the evidence that crime news engenders crime. The persistent glorification of criminals in the press, the publication of their portraits, the use of laudatory or at least striking nicknames, and the growing practice of feature writers of spreading the views and exploits of criminals all over the Sunday papers, stimulate, encourage, and increase crime. (*November* 20, 1926.)

e. Newspapers have sometimes made the weak excuse that they publish what the people want, but what they mean is that they try always to publish what they think will sell the most papers.

(1) Nobody believes that the people want crime waves manufactured for their reading.

(2) President Roosevelt declared that the demand for crime news and moral filth no more justified its publication than did demand justify the proprietor of an opium den or the peddler of morphine.

(3) This very lame excuse is inconsistent with the claim of newspapers that it is their duty to mold public opinion.

6. The newspapers have aided and developed the great national vice of gambling.
   a. They regularly publish race track records.
   b. Every newspaper publishes stock reports.
   c. They publish facts about the great derbies.
   d. They always publish spectacular accounts of the people who have won in these gambling contests.
7. The newspapers are the greatest detriment to the use of good English, the greatest handicap to the schools in their efforts to teach good English.
   a. They continually use coarse, vulgar, disgusting slang words.
   b. Their vocabulary is crude and very limited.
   c. Their short, choppy paragraphs are always pointed out by every teacher of English as an excellent example of the way not to do it.

D. There is no other remedy.
   1. The reading public is powerless to protect itself against these frightful abuses.
      a. The great majority of the people are unable to select the best, or even the good, in newspaper and magazine reading matter.
         (1) Philip P. Parsons says, "The public is no more capable of choosing its reading matter than

it is of choosing clean drinking water or clean milk." (*Crime and Criminals.* p. 376.)

2. Ordinary censorship, restraint in advance of publication, is so complicated as to be impracticable and almost impossible.
   a. It was not even used in this country during the World War.
   b. To have a government censor read every newspaper and magazine in advance of publication, and delete every falsehood, exaggeration, indecency, obscenity, and impropriety is impracticable.
      (1) It would require an enormous staff of well-paid and highly-trained censors.
      (2) It would mean delay in publication.
      (3) It could not prevent newspapers and magazines being distributed to subscribers through the mail from publishers outside of the state.
3. Legal action for redress in the courts has utterly and completely failed as a remedy.
   a. Criminal actions have almost always been fruitless.
      (1) Judges and prosecutors are often unduly influenced by or seek to curry the favor of the newspaper publishers.
      (2) Such actions do not prevent a recurrence of the crime.
      (3) The Supreme Court of Minnesota has said, "It is a matter of common knowledge that prose-

cutions under the criminal libel statutes do not result in efficient repression or suppression of the evils of scandal." (174 Minn. 457.)

(4) Charles Whibley has said, "It is clear that the law of libel has sunk into oblivion." (*Blackwood's Magazine.* 181:533. *April* 1907.)

b. Civil actions for damages accomplish nothing as a rule.

(1) Such an action can be taken only after the harm has been done.

(2) It does not prevent a repetition of the offense.

(3) The publicity given to the trial sometimes makes it do more harm than good.

(4) The delays in courts often exhaust both the patience and the resources of the injured party.

(5) The expense of trials and appeals puts this remedy entirely out of the reach of all except the rich.

(6) The damages awarded are often trivial.

II. The Minnesota Nuisance Law is a wise and desirable remedy for these evils.

A. It is a complete and adequate remedy.

1. It can be applied promptly.

2. It will completely remedy the evils.

a. Obscenity and indecency can be stopped at once.

b. Defamation can be brought to a sudden and abrupt end.

c. The publication of scandal can be ended completely.

d. The continual publication of drivel can be discouraged.

e. The publication of falsehood and propaganda can be checked.

3. No one can oppose the adoption of this law except those who favor the publication of moral filth or criminal libel.

B. It will have a great potential power and influence.

1. It will put a feeling of responsibility into the minds of those newspaper and magazine men who have seemed to think that they were above all law.

2. It will put fear into the criminal element among writers and publishers.

3. It will encourage and give the advantage to the reputable and high grade newspapers and magazines.

C. It will protect and safeguard every proper right.

1. Reputable and legitimate newspapers, magazines, and news agencies will not be interfered with.

2. The complete freedom of the press will not be impaired.

a. The freedom of the press has never been an absolute right.

b. Freedom of the press has never meant license to publish scandalous, malicious, obscene, or indecent matter.

c. The first amendment to the Federal Constitution does not guarantee the freedom of the press.

(1) It does not in any way limit the power of the state governments.

(2) It is merely a limitation on the power of Congress.

(3) Every state may properly regulate its own newspapers, magazines, and news agencies, restraining their abuses and criminal acts, under its police power, its inherent right to protect the health, safety, and morals of its people.

3. It is due process of law.

a. It has twice been so held by the Supreme Court of Minnesota.

b. Every person or newspaper accused has his day in court, his chance to be heard in his own behalf, his right to be represented by counsel, to summon witnesses in his behalf, and every other right to defend himself.

III. The Minnesota Nuisance Law is a practicable remedy for one of the greatest evils of this generation.

A. It has worked well in Minnesota.

1. It has been in effect since 1925 and has given general satisfaction, except to those who want to violate both it and the laws against libel, scandal, obscenity, and indecency which have been on the statute books for many years, and which they had formerly violated with impunity.

a. Their opposition to it merely illustrates the old adage: "No rogue e'er felt the halter draw with good opinion of the law."

2. It has been used only in extreme and exasperating cases.

a. Only two small weekly papers have been suppressed.
b. One has had many hearings in court, its case having been carried to the Supreme Court of the state three different times.

3. It has done no harm to the reputable newspapers or magazines of the state.
4. The general tone of journalism of the state has been improved.
   a. The competition of the lowest level has been removed.
5. Efforts in the legislature to force the repeal of the law have been unsuccessful.
   a. The New York *Times* has said in an editorial that there is more anxiety about the law outside of Minnesota than in it.

B. The principle is the same as that used by the Federal Government during the World War.
   1. The Government did not then attempt to censor all newspapers and magazines in advance.
   2. It did completely and entirely suppress every treasonable and disloyal paper and magazine.

C. It is the natural and logical remedy.
   1. It brands as a public nuisance that which most obviously is a public nuisance.
   2. It applies in abatement of the nuisance the remedy that has been used for that purpose from time immemorial.

D. It is the most practicable form of remedy for the evil.
   1. It is a complete and adequate remedy.
   2. It may be applied promptly.
   3. It is economical and inexpensive.

   a. It calls for the creation of no new legal or administrative machinery, no additional officials, bureaus, or commissions.
   b. It creates no new principles and no new systems of law.
4. It is simple to operate.
   a. It is merely a matter of filing a suit in equity and holding a hearing thereon.
5. It preserves the freedom of the press.
   a. It punishes by suppression only after repeated violations of long existing laws against malicious libel or obscene and indecent matter.

E. It is in perfect harmony with American institutions.
   1. It has twice been held constitutional and a proper remedy by the Supreme Court of Minnesota. (State v. Guilford. 174 Minn. 457. 219 N.W. 770. 58 A.L.R. 607. May 25, 1928, and 179 Minn. 40. 228 N.W. 326. December 20, 1929.)
   2. It is not in violation of the Federal Constitution.
   3. If a similar law should be declared unconstitutional in any other state, that defect could be remedied by an amendment to the state constitution.
      a. This method has often been used to secure needed reform, as illustrated by the abolition of slavery, the Federal income tax, and the abolition of the saloon.

F. It has been endorsed in principle by many of the best minds.

1. Edward A. Ross has said, "No society can afford to let its members say or publish or exhibit what they please." (*Social Psychology.* p. 126.)
2. The *Nation* has said, "It is a crying shame that men should work such mischief simply in order to sell more papers, and the first impulse of every right-minded person is to wish that journalism of this sort might be suppressed by the hand of the law." (66: 139. February 24, 1898.)
3. The *New York Times* has said in an editorial, "For the passage of such a law, and its sympathetic reception by any court, the blame must be left on the doorsteps of the sensational press. To such jackals of journalism no morsel is inedible. Decent newspapers everywhere sympathize with the public resentment which takes form in such laws as that passed in Minnesota." (December 24, 1929.)

Negative

I. The Minnesota Nuisance Law is un-American in principle.
   A. It is contrary to all precedent in this country.
      1. Never before was any law passed empowering one judge to suppress a newspaper or magazine permanently.
         a. This law is an application of the padlock principle.
      2. Never before was the power of injunction to abate a public nuisance extended to include the press.
   B. It is contrary to the spirit of American institutions.

1. It is contrary to the spirit of the Federal Constitution.
    a. The first amendment says, "Congress shall make no law abridging the freedom of the press."
    b. The fourteenth amendment says, "Nor shall any state deprive any person of life, liberty, or property without due process of law."
2. It is contrary to the spirit of the constitution of every state in the Union.
    a. All of the state constitutions contain a provision designed to perpetuate and safeguard the freedom of the press.
    b. The Constitution of Minnesota says, "The liberty of the press shall forever remain inviolate, and all persons may freely speak, write, and publish their sentiments on all subjects, being responsible for the abuse of such right."
        (1) Either these words mean what they say, or they do not mean anything.
        (2) For a District Court using the power vested in it by this law, to forbid a periodical to publish another number, is a plain violation of the clause which says that all persons may freely publish their sentiments on all subjects, being responsible (that is, afterwards) for the abuse of such right.

C. It is contrary to all American traditions and policy.

1. Complete freedom of the press, with no censorship or other restraint in advance of publication, has always been the American policy.
    a. The few deviations from this established historical policy have been in time of war or when there was imminent danger of war.
2. The American policy has been to leave all persons free to write and publish their thoughts, opinions, beliefs, and convictions on all subjects, but to hold them responsible after publication, either in civil action for damages, or in criminal action, if what they uttered was false, defamatory, and malicious, or if it was obscene, immoral, and indecent.

D. The Minnesota law is Russian, rather than American, in principle.

II. There is no necessity for the general adoption of the Minnesota Nuisance Law.

A. There is no social danger in a free press.

1. No harm has ever been done our country or our institutions by the freedom of the press.
    a. It has not caused the increase in crime.
        (1) In naming the causes of crime the recognized authorities on the subject have seldom mentioned the publication of crime news as one of them.
        (2) No real evidence has ever yet been presented to show that the publication of crime news is even a contributing cause of crime.

(3) Snapshot opinions of persons who are not expert criminologists are of no real value.

(4) It is more reasonable to suppose that reading about crimes and criminal trials and executions would turn people away from crime, rather than lead them to such a life.

(5) Several recent authorities on crime have declared the newspaper accounts of crime have practically no effect in increasing crime. (Healy. *The Individual Delinquent.* p. 302. Brason. *The Elements of Crime.* p. 166-7.)

b. Newspaper vilification does not keep the best men and women out of public life.

(1) Politics is very distasteful to many excellent men and women.

(2) The greater opportunities and the greater rewards in private business are a far greater influence than newspaper abuse.

(3) James Bryce, in his *American Commonwealth,* in the chapter entitled, "Why great men do not become President," does not mention newspaper vilification as a cause.

2. Newspapers do not exert as great an influence on the general public as is sometimes supposed.

a. There have been quite a number of cases where a man was elected mayor of an American city although he was opposed by all the newspapers.

3. Even newspapers and magazines advocating socialism, communism, syndicalism, and anarchy have never done any real harm.
   a. Their circulation is very limited.
   b. No one of them has ever made many converts to their cause.
   c. They have merely served as agencies of protest against the obvious injustice of the established social order.
   d. They may have done real good by setting some dreamers actually to thinking.

B. The newspapers and magazines have done great and lasting good to the country.

1. William B. Munro has said, "There are probably more newspapers and periodicals printed in the United States than in all the countries of Europe put together" (with four times our population.) (*Current Problems in Citizenship*. p. 84.)
   a. Such a mass of periodical literature must have a great educational benefit upon the country.
2. They instruct and entertain practically all the people.
   a. They have taught millions of people to do some systematic reading.
   b. There are some of the features of the daily newspaper that are interesting to practically every person in the country.

3. They safeguard our institutions and our liberties.
    a. They are prompt to expose and attack an abuse or wrong.
4. They have purified and elevated our politics.
    a. They have exposed every great wrong by the national government or its officials.
        (1) They exposed the Credit Mobilier scandal of the Grant administration, in which one later President owned stock.
        (2) They exposed the theft of Teapot Dome and Elk Hills, which led to the conviction of one cabinet officer.
    b. They have opposed the wrongs and crimes committed by state officials.
        (1) They opposed and secured the repeal of the Fifty Year Franchise steal in Ohio.
        (2) They exposed the Ninety-nine Year Franchise Bill in Illinois.
    c. The great improvement in American city government since 1900 has been due very largely to the work of the newspapers and magazines.
        (1) It was *Harper's Weekly* and the *New York Times* that brought about the fall of the Tweed Ring, the worst and most corrupt political machine in our history.
        (2) The articles on the shame of the cities in *McClure's Magazine* by Lincoln Steffens in the early

years of the century did much to better city government.

(3) James Bryce said, "The American press may not be above the moral level of the average good citizen, but it is above the level of the machine politicians in the cities. In the war waged against these worthies, the newspapers of New York, Boston, Philadelphia, and Chicago have been one of the most efficient battalions." (*American Commonwealth.* 3d ed. vol. 2. p. 275-6.)

C. There are laws in every state that provide ample safeguards and remedies for all evils and abuses that now exist or may hereafter arise.
   1. Libel is a crime in every state, and is punishable by a fine or by imprisonment.
   2. Libel is also a tort, a wrong for which the injured party may recover damages by a civil action.

D. The recent changes in journalism have been for the best in their permanent results.
   1. Many of them have been the natural consequences of progress and development.
      a. News is now collected by great news-gathering agencies whose scope is world wide.
      b. Papers are now printed in a great plant, which uses much expensive machinery.
      c. It is now uneconomical and impractical for one city of a hundred thousand people to have eight or ten daily newspapers, as was the case fifty years ago.

(1) It means a duplication of effort.
(2) Consolidation is the tendency of the time in all industrial undertakings.

2. The changes in the nature of the news published and of the other reading matter in the newspapers has been a natural development.
   a. Now the newspapers are being read by enormous numbers of people who did not do so even fifty years ago.
   b. Any newspaper must publish what its readers want.
3. The newspapers and magazines are better now than they ever were before.
   a. The news is published more fully and more accurately than it was in previous generations.
   b. Other features, instructive and entertaining to certain classes, makes them fit the public needs much better than was formerly the case.
   c. Innumerable mechanical improvements have made them neater, more attractive, better printed and illustrated, than ever before.
4. There is continual improvement in both the newspapers and the magazines.
   a. Colleges of journalism, most of which are of recent origin, are continually turning out better trained reporters, editors, feature writers, correspondents, and critics.
   b. The use of the periodicals and magazines in the public schools shows that many of them are very satisfactory and beneficial.

III. The Minnesota Nuisance Law is unwise and undesirable.
   A. It is wrong in principle.
      1. It seeks completely to prevent some people from publishing their thoughts and opinions.
      2. Any law relating to the press should seek to improve and better it, not to suppress and destroy it.
   B. It involves grave dangers to the state.
      1. It is always a dangerous thing for a government to stifle or suppress the free publication of thought.
         a. Free publication serves as a social safety valve, for it lets the agitators blow off steam before the danger point is reached.
         b. Official suppression only drives the agitators into secret channels, into cellars and sewers.
         c. Suppression has always embittered agitators and made them desperate.
            (1) It leads to plots and conspiracies, to violence and uprisings, and sometimes to assassinations.
      2. This law might be only the entering wedge for the enactment of even more drastic and unwise legislation.
         a. Political rings and machines, feeling a sense of security and relief from the criticism of the press they had silenced, would next seek the enactment of a similar law curtailing the freedom of speech.
         b. They would naturally seek for other legislative means of perpetuating themselves in office.

C. It is open and liable to serious abuses.
   1. It gives too much and too arbitrary power to one man.
      a. Judges are only human.
         (1) That they are liable to err is shown by the number of decisions of the lower courts that are reversed when appealed to the higher courts.
         (2) They are liable to be influenced by their prejudices and their partisanship.
         (3) They may be vindictive towards political opponents.
         (4) They may be controlled or influenced by party bosses or political machines.
      b. There have been many cases of abuse of judicial power in the past.
         (1) There has been nation-wide abuse of the power of injunction, especially in times of labor disputes.
         (2) There has been since the beginning serious abuse of the power of contempt of court.
         (3) Some judges have been impeached for corruption or other reasons and removed from office.
   2. There is danger that a newspaper might be suppressed simply because it has fought a corrupt and entrenched political machine.
      a. According to this law the plain truth is illegal, if it is uttered with malice.

b. It is an easy matter for any court to see malice in almost any criticism a newspaper could publish of a political machine.

D. An absolutely free press is absolutely necessary to a democracy.

1. It was essential to the beginning of a democracy.

a. All authorities agree that it was the free press that made real democracy possible.

(1) James Bryce has said, "It is the newspaper press that has made democracy possible in large countries." (*Modern Democracies.* vol. 1. p. 92.)

(2) David Lawrence says, "It is the constitutional freedom of the press that has made America a democracy in fact as well as in name." (*Annals of the American Academy.* 72:114. July 1917.)

2. It is essential to the functioning of a democracy.

a. A democracy is a government where the thoughts and opinions of everybody are freely uttered and published.

b. Democracy is a condition where all opinion is pooled and action results from considering every point of view.

c To the extent that opinion is suppressed democracy ceases to exist.

3. It is essential to the preservation of a democracy.

a. Joyce O. Hertzler says, "The failures of government have almost always been failures of free opinion, mostly of public opinion that was ill-formed, that was denied the facts, or that was misguided by self-constituted masters." (*Social Progress.* p. 378.)

4. It is essential to the improvement of democracy.
   a. If plain and sharp criticism is silenced it would be impossible to better conditions or to remedy abuses.
      (1) James A. Garfield once said, "Without a free press the established order of things can nowhere be improved." (*Works.* vol. 2. p. 579.)
   b. In proportion as criticism is silenced, in just such proportion will improvement be impossible.

IV. The Minnesota Nuisance Law is entirely impracticable.
   A. It has not even worked well in Minnesota.
      1. It has not accomplished what was so positively claimed for it.
         a. In this respect it is like most of the recent social or political reforms.
         b. Overzealous reformers, imbued with a pet hobby, can always make promises with the sky as a limit.
      2. Although it has been in effect since 1925, it has not improved journalism in the state.
         a. There has been no noticeable change for the better in the newspapers or magazines of Minnesota as compared with those of other states.

3. It has been used only to suppress two small weekly papers which were vicious in their criticisms of certain politicians.
    a. This action was a matter of personal spite on the part of the county attorney whom they had opposed.
    b. It has no connection with and no influence upon the bulk of the newspapers and magazines of the state.

B. It cannot remedy the evils in the newspaper press.
1. It cannot even be enforced against any large or powerful newspaper.
    a. No such attempt has ever been made in Minnesota.
2. There is nothing in the law to prevent any newspaper from publishing columns of mere drivel.
    a. Insipid editorials do not violate the law.
    b. Comics and word puzzles are legal.
    c. Pictures of bathing beauties and prize fighters are entirely lawful.
    d. Fiction serials full of sentimental love slop do not violate this law.
    e. Advice to the lovelorn, often in the form of fake questions and answers, is not contrary to the law.
3. The law does not even attempt to prevent the publication of too much crime news or giving it the most prominent place in the paper.
4. The law makes no attempt to prevent the publication of news or pictures of prize fights, nor giving too much space to sports.

5. The law does not make illegal the publication as news matter of the paid propaganda of selfish financial, political, commercial, industrial, or fanatical interests.
6. It does not make any provision against the continual publication of false statements, unless they are defamatory or malicious.
7. It does not prevent the complete suppression of important news.
8. It makes no attempt to prevent the coloring or distorting of important news.
9. It does not make unlawful the publication of advertisements of fraudulent medicines or worthless stocks.

C. There are already too many unenforced and unenforcible laws on the statute books of every state.
   1. The enactment of a multitude of ill-considered and unenforcible laws is one of the worst evils in America.
      a. Any law that does not clearly reflect and represent the will of a considerable majority of the people is unenforcible.
   2. District judges and county attorneys might much better devote their energies to enforcing the multitude of existing laws that are now "more honored in the breach than in the observance."
      a. There is an urgent need for better enforcement of the laws against all the major crimes, such as murder, burglary, robbery, kidnapping, etc.
      b. The liquor laws are nowhere in America honestly and effectively enforced.

        c. The laws against prize fights, gambling, adulteration of foods and medicines, libel, and slander are nowhere adequately enforced.

D. All history and all experience teach that only harm is done by legally limiting the freedom of the press.
    1. Most such attempts in any free government have been soon abandoned.
    2. None of them has ever done any good.
    3. All of them have done serious harm.

E. It has met with general opposition and distrust.
    1. The principle of this law has been opposed by the best minds for three hundred years.

BIBLIOGRAPHY

Bibliographies

Library of Congress. List of references on freedom of the press and speech and censorship in time of war. Ap. 20, '17.

Matson, Henry. References for literary workers. A. C. McClurg. Chicago. '11.

Should the liberty of the press be left by the government unrestricted? p. 167-8.

New York Public Library. Bulletin. 27:658-71, 675-80. Ag. '23. Liberty of the press. Military censorship. Carl L. Cannon.

American Journal of Sociology. 32:806-13. Mr. '27. The American newspaper. R. E. Park.

Denney, J. V., Duncan, C. S., and McKinney, F. C. Argumentation and debate. American Book Co. N.Y. '10.

p. 101-3. Freedom of the press. Specimen brief. Negative.

General References

Books and Pamphlets

Belloc, Hilaire. The free press. George Allen and Unwin. London. '18.

*Bent, Silas. Ballyhoo: the voice of the press. Boni, Liveright and Co. N.Y. '27.

*Cooley, Thomas M. Constitutional limitations. 8th ed. Little, Brown and Co. Boston. '27.

Vol. 2. p. 876-959. Liberty of speech and of the press.

Dawson, Samuel A. Freedom of the press. Columbia University Press. N.Y. '24.

Duniway, Clyde A. Development of freedom of the press in Massachusetts. Longmans, Green and Co. '06.

Floyd, William. Social progress: a handbook of the liberal movement. Arbitrator. N.Y. '25.

p. 155-62. Newspaper bias.

*Holt, Hamilton. Commercialism and journalism. Houghton, Mifflin Co. N.Y. '09.

*Lee, James M. History of American journalism. Houghton Mifflin Co. Boston. '17.

*Lippmann, Walter. Liberty and the news. Harcourt, Brace and Howe. N.Y. '20.

†New York. Report of the Crime Commission. '27.

p. 307-26. A study of the relation of the daily press to crime and the administration of justice.

Ross, Edward A. Changing America. Century. N.Y. '12.

p. 109-36. The suppression of important news.

Salmon, Lucy M. The newspaper and authority. Oxford University Press. N.Y. '23.

Sinclair, Upton. Brass check: a study of American journalism. Pasadena, Cal. '20.

Story, Joseph. Commentaries on the Constitution of the United States. Little, Brown and Co. Boston. '73.

Vol. 2. p. 609-19. Sections 1880-92. Liberty of the press.

Periodicals

Academy of Political Science. Proceedings. 7:360-74. Jl. '17. A plea for an uncensored press. Frederick R. Martin et al.

†American Bar Association Journal. 13:390-7. Jl. '27. Relation of daily press to crime and the administration of justice.

†American Law Review. 62:13-93. Ja. '28. The effects of news of crime and scandal upon public opinion. R. D. Highfill.

American Sociological Society. Papers and Proceedings. 9:67-116. D. '14. Freedom of the press in the United States. Henry Schofield.

American Sociological Society. Papers and Proceedings. 9:117-32. D. '14. Reasonable restrictions upon freedom of the press. Charles H. Grasty et al.

Arena. 34:150-5. Ag. '05. Significance of yellow journalism. Lydia K. Commander.

Atlantic Monthly. 137:761-9. Je. '26. Journalism and morality. Silas Bent.

Bellman. 25:325-6. S. 21, '18. Censorship of the press. J. M. Lee.

Bookman. 52:116-21. O. '20. Democracy and a free press. H. L. West.

Case and Comment. 22:476-7. N. '15. What is liberty of the press? Lenn J. Oare.

Century. 112:41-7. My. '26. Unfortunate necessity: freedom of the press and public confidence. G. W. Johnson.

Clevelander. 2:8-10+. O. '27. Do the newspapers give 'em what they want? Erie C. Hopwood.

Collier's Weekly. 81:26+. Mr. 24, '28. The dirt disher. Walter Davenport.

Contemporary Review. 114:177-83. Ag. '18. Freedom of the press in the United States. Lindsay Rogers.

Current Opinion. 65:250-1. O. '18. Hilaire Belloc's hope for the free press in England.

English Review. 22:261-72. Mr. '16. Press censorship.

*Fortnightly Review. 85:528-36. Mr. '06. The press in war-time.

Fortnightly Review. 123:813-20. Je '25. Should divorce cases be reported? J. H. Richardson.

Forum. 7:503-12. Jl. '89. Ethics of journalism. W. S. Lilly.

*Harper's Magazine. 155:485-94. S. '27. Art of ballyhoo. Silas Bent.

Harvard Law Review. 16:55-6. N. '02. Restrictions on the freedom of the press.

Harvard Law Review. 27:27-44. '13. The extension of federal control through the regulation of the mails. Lindsay Rogers.

International Journal of Ethics. 38:191-203. Ja. '28. Ethics and the press. H. C. Lehman.

†International Review. 3:479-91. Jl. '76. The newspaper press and the law of libel. David D. Field.

Johns Hopkins University Studies. 34:246-71. '16. Limitations on the Postal power. Lindsay Rogers.

†Journal of the American Institute of Criminal Law and Criminology. 17:40-103. My. '26. The effects of news of crime and scandal upon public opinion. R. D. Highfill.

†Journal of the American Institute of Criminal Law and Criminology. 20:6-59, 246-93. My.-Ag. '29. Crime and the press. Joseph L. Holmes.

Literary Digest. 55:19. Jl. 28, '17. Post office censors under fire.

Literary Digest. 55:12. O. 6, '17. Mr. Burleson to rule the press.

Literary Digest. 55:20. D. 15, '17. Where the censor might halt.

Literary Digest. 84:34-5. Mr. 14, '25. Crime and the newspapers.

Literary Digest. 90:9. Ag. 14, '26. Fight for freedom of the press.

Literary Digest. 93:12-13. My. 14, '27. The President asks the press to be American.

Literary Digest. 98:30. Ag. 4, '28. The press not yellow.

*Literary Digest. 104:13. F. 1, '30. War on the Minnesota "Gag Law."

Living Age. 298:769-74. S. 28, '18. Freedom of the press in the United States. Lindsay Rogers.

Marquette Law Review. 13:1-8. D. '28. Restraints on freedom of the press. Walter J. Mattison.

Nation. 76:4-5. Ja. 1, '03. Silencing the press.

Nation. 107:336-7. S. 28, '18. The nation and the post office.
†Nation. 116:458. Ap. 18, '23. Admiral Sims's challenge to our press.
Nation. 116:598-600. My. 22, '26. Bunking trustful readers.
Nation. 124:34-6. Ja. 12, '27. Mussolini chokes the press. Gaetano Salvemini.
Nation. 128:576. My. 15, '29. Myth of a free press.
*Nation. 130:241-3. F. 26, '30. Freedom of the press. Henry Raymond Mussey.
New Republic. 23:sup.1-42. Ag. 4, '20. A test of the news. Walter Lippmann and Charles Merz.
North American Review. 155:694-705. D. '92. A blow at the freedom of the press. Hannis Taylor.
North Carolina Law Review. 4:24-38. F. '26. Restrictions on a free press. Robert H. Wettach.
*Outlook. 90:891-2. D. 26, '08. The right to a good name.
*Outlook. 91:415-16. F. 27, '09. Is criminal libel freedom of the press?
*Outlook. 94:275. F. 5, '10. Criminal libel and freedom of the press.
Outlook. 98:333-4. Je. 17, '11. A bribe to the press.
*Outlook. 116:56-7. My. 9, '17. War and a free press.
Quarterly Review. 234:132-46. Jl. '20. Censorship of the press. Cecil Headlam.
Review of Reviews. 75:257-61. Mr. '27. Divorce publicity here and abroad. J. C. Welliver.
Review of Reviews. 75:406-10. Ap. '27. What is the press doing? Civic and community service. John E. Drewry.
Spectator. 115:649. N. 14, '15. Duty of newspapers.
Survey. 38:245-6. Je. 9, '17. Censorship as finally enacted.
Survey. 43:222-4. D. 13, '19. New varieties of censorship.

Survey. 57:731-3. Mr. 1, '27. Eyes and ears of democracy. William Bolitho.

Welfare Magazine. 18:557-69. My. '27. Influence of the newspaper. W. A. N. Dorland.

Woman Citizen. n.s. 4:782-8. Ja. 31, '20. Press and public opinion. Frank I. Cobb.

World Tomorrow. 11:154-7. Ap. '28. Our American press—the bright side. Oswald G. Villard.

World's Work. 34:243-4. Jl. '17. Public confidence and the censor.

World's Work. 48:29-40. My. '24. How Carl Magee broke Fall's New Mexico ring. William G. Shepherd.

World's Work. 48:585-6. O. '24. Justice in New Mexico.

Yale Law Journal. 23:559-79. '14. Federal interference with the freedom of the press. Lindsay Rogers.

Yale Law Journal. 27:550-3. F. '18. Judicial review of administrative determinations.

Affirmative References

Books and Pamphlets

*Minnesota Supreme Court. State v. Guilford. 174 Minn. 457. 219 N.W. 770. 58 A.L.R. 607. My. 25, '28.

Minnesota Supreme Court. State v. Guilford. 179 Minn. 40. 228 N.W. 326. D. 20, '29.

Periodicals

†American Bar Association Journal. 13:574-5. O. '27. Technique of misquotation.

*American Catholic Quarterly Review. 48:68-71. Ja. '23. Liberty of the press. John E. Fagan.

†Annals of the American Academy. 16:56-92. Jl. '00. The American newspaper: a study in social psychology. Delos F. Wilcox.

*Arbitrator. 9:4. Ja. '27. The dangerous press.

*Arena. 38:170-80. Ag. '07. Menace of irresponsible journalism.

Arena. 38:318-19. S. '07. How the reactionary daily press poisons the public mind by deliberate misrepresentations.

Atlantic Monthly. 91:145-51. F. '03. Sensational journalism and the law. George W. Alger.

*Blackwood's Magazine. 181:531-8. Ap. '07. The yellow press. Charles Whibley.

Bookman. 24:396-403. D. '06. Tainted news as seen in the making.

*Century. 72:317-18. Je. '06. A danger to American democracy.

*Century. 83:631-3. F. '12. A curb for the sensational press.

*Christian Century. 42:148-9. Ja. 29, '25. An editorial open letter to the newspaper proprietors of Chicago.

*Christian Century. 42:273-5. F. 26, '25. Should newspapers tell the truth?

*Christian Century. 42:358. Mr. 12, '25. Holds crime increased by newspapers.

Collier's Weekly. 38:24-5. F. 23, '07. Tainted news.

†Collier's Weekly. 39:13-15. My. 4, '07. Tainted news.

Current Literature. 41:517-18. N. '06. Are newspapers weakening our national fiber?

Current Literature. 45:630-3. D. '08. Sounding the doom of the comics.

Fortnightly Review. 88:919-31. D. 2, '07. Significance of Mr. Hearst. Sydney Brooks.

*Independent. 61:946. O. 18, '06. The scandal of criminal journalism.

*Independent. 61:1068-9. N. 1, '06. Faked cable news.

*Independent. 84:44-5. O. 11, '15. The partiality of the press.

*Independent. 84:55-6. O. 11, '15. Peace and the press. Jane Addams.

*Independent. 116:264-6. Mr. 6, '26. Those terrible tabloids. Samuel T. Moore.

*Independent. 119:407-9. O. 22, '27. The mother of yellow journalism. Silas Bent.

†Ladies' Home Journal. 26:5. Ja. '09. A crime against American children.

Law Notes. 33:15. Ap. '29. Newspapers as nuisance.

Lippincott's Magazine. 45:267-70. F. '90. The newspaper and the individual: a plea for press censorship. A. E. Watrous.

*McClure's Magazine. 26:450-2. F. '06. Manufacturing public opinion.

McClure's Magazine. 26:535-49. Mr. '06. How railroads make public opinion. Ray S. Baker.

Minnesota Law Review. 14:787-98. Je. '30. Power of the state to enjoin publication of a newspaper as a public nuisance.

*Nation. 66:139. F. 24, '98. Disgraceful behavior of two New York newspapers.

*Nation. 66:336-7. My. 5, '98. New political force.

*Nation. 73:238-9. S. 26, '01. Responsibility for yellow journalism.

*Nation. 104:518-19. My. 3, '17. For a sensible censorship.

*New Republic. 45:350-2. F. 17, '26. Gutter literature. Ernest W. Mandeville.

North American Review. 190:587-93. N. '09. Sensational journalism and the remedy. S. W. Pennypacker.

Outlook. 65:947. Ag. '25, '00. Shades of yellow in journalism.

Outlook. 85:276-7. F. 2, '07. Lessons in crime fifty cents per month.

Outlook. 91:510-11. Mr. 6, '09. Why I believe in the kind of American journalism for which the Outlook stands. Theodore Roosevelt.

Putnam's Monthly. 4:343-7. Je. '08. What we put up with. Anna A. Rogers.

Virginia Law Review. 5:178-89. D. '17. Military censorship and freedom of the press. T. J. O'Donnell.

*Westminster Review. 166:617-18. D. '06. Should not the publishing of false news be by law a misdemeanour? Mark H. Judge.

†World's Work. 7:4567-70. Mr. '04. Why people disbelieve the newspapers. Edward Bok.

Negative References

Books and Pamphlets

Baldwin, Roger N. Fight for free speech. 31p. American Civil Liberties Union. N.Y. '21.

Belloc, Hilaire. Free press. Allen and Unwin. London. '18.

Cobb, Frank I. Public opinion. 12p. Senate document 175. 66 Congress, 2 session, 1920.

Schroeder, Theodore. Our vanishing liberty of the press. 7p. Free Speech League. N.Y.

Whipple, Leon. Story of civil liberty in the United States. Vanguard Press. N.Y. '27.

Perodicals

Academy of Political Science. Proceedings. 7:360-4. Jl. '17. Plea for an uncensored press. F. R. Martin.

Academy of Political Science. Proceedings. 7:365-8. Je. '17. Value of a free press. J. T. Graves.

American Law Review. 34:321-41. Je. '00. Liberty of the press. H. B. Brown.

*Annals of the American Academy. 72:139-41. Jl. '17. International freedom of the press essential to a durable peace. David Lawrence.

Arena. 41:218-19. F. '09. The freedom of the press as viewed by Roosevelt, Jefferson, and de Tocqueville.

Atlantic Monthly. 124:779-87. D. '19. Liberty and the news. Walter Lippmann.

Century. 112:41-7. My. '26. An unfortunate necessity. Gerald W. Johnson.

Chicago Tribune. Mr. 6, '29. Free speech in Minnesota. Editorial.

Chicago Tribune. Mr. 19, '29. Monkey state candidate. Editorial.

*Chicago Tribune. Mr. 28, '29. Minnesota joins the monkey states. Editorial.

*Chicago Tribune. Mr. 11, '30. Minnesota nuisance law. Editorial.

Commonweal. 3:16-17. N. 11, '25. Good news and bad. Agnes Repplier.

Current Opinion. 68:378-80. Mr. '20. Liberty and the news.

English Review. 21:490-6. D. '15. The public and the press. Charles Dawbarn.

Independent. 55:1371-5. Je. 11, '03. Press, its liberty and license. C. E. Smith.

Independent. 62:785-6. Mr. 29, '00. The other side of yellow journalism.

Journal of Criminal Law and Criminology. 11:181-90. Ag. '20. Free trade in ideas. George P. Garrett.

*Law Notes. 30:162. D. '26. Press and criminal trials.

Lawyer and Banker. 22:1-2. Ja. '29. Law of the tyrant.

Lawyer and Banker. 22:133-4. My. '29. Minnesota nuisance law.

Nation. 96:198-9. F. 27, '13. Slander made easy.

Nation. 104:424-5. Ap. 12, '17. Censorship and suppression.

Nation. 105:361-2. O. 4, '17. Censorship of the press.

Nation. 112:422. Mr. 23, '21. Supreme Court strikes at the press.

Nation. 123:142. Ag. 18, '26. Lese majeste.

Nation. 130:241-3. F. 26, '30. Christian Science censor. Henry R. Mussey.
New Republic. 49:344-5. F. 16, '27. Is the censor coming?
New York Times Magazine. Ja. 27, '18. p. 9. Free criticism a fine thing for nation at war. Louis Marshall.
North American Review. 208:702-9. N. '18. Freedom of the press. Richard Barry.
North American Review. 209:795-802. Je. '19. Lynching of public opinion. G. R. Brown.
Ohio Law Bulletin and Reporter. 31:394-412. Mr. 24, '30. Full text of the Cleveland newspaper contempt case. Court of Appeals for Cuyahoga county.
Outlook. 102:831. D. 21, '12. The freedom of the press.
Outlook. 121:18-19. Ja. 1, '19. Shall we have a free press? Charles Kerr.
*Outlook. 150:1283. D. 5, '28. A blow at freedom.
Public. 20:1011-12. O. 19, '17. International free press. Walter Williams.
Survey. 24:365-8. Je. 4, '10. Freedom of the press.
Survey. 38:358. Jl. 21, '17. Protest against a muzzled press.
Survey. 43:301-2. D. 27, '19. Justice Mintern dissents.
Virginia Law Review. 16:1-39. N. '29. Mining and sapping our Bill of Rights. Sterling E. Edmunds.
Woman Citizen. 4:389-90. S. 20, '19. For freedom of the press.

GENERAL DISCUSSION

THE AMERICAN NEWSPAPER[1]

The newspaper is the agent par excellence in the formation of public opinion, and, in this connection, its ultimate social function and its first duty, as stated by Frank I. Cobb, the eminent late editor of the New York *World,* is to furnish the raw materials for it and the tools for its information."

IMPORTANCE OF THE NEWSPAPER

Sixty years ago the American newspaper was quite different from the type we know today. It then was a publication which was intended to appeal to grown men only, and men of staid habits at that, for it made no pretense of providing light or easy reading. But as the result of the efforts of such men as James Gordon Bennett, Charles A. Dana, Joseph Pulitzer, and William Randolph Hearst, the newspaper has developed an appeal for everybody, —mature thinking men, the rank and file, women of all classes, immigrants, and children. Consequently the circulation of newspapers has increased to such an extent that we are today a nation of newspaper readers and have the largest number of newspapers and the greatest circulation per unit of population of any people under the sun. The newspaper is now read by nearly the whole family among all classes. In the past ten years the circulation of the daily newspapers of the United States has grown two and one-half times as fast as population as a whole. Its power is more decisive and irresistible than any other agency; consequently it overshadows them all in importance. With a few exceptions

[1] By Joyce O. Hertzler. *Social Progress.* p. 257-65.

the same trends are noticeable among all the peoples affected by the Industrial Revolution. The influence of the lecture room, the pulpit, the public meeting, the pamphlet, the book, has faded into insignificance as compared with the newspaper as a factor in the formation of public opinion.

All of us today have come to be almost altogether dependent upon the newspaper for our knowledge of widely interesting events. As the organization of society has become more complex and far-reaching, the newspaper's importance in the acquisition and distribution of knowledge has inevitably increased. It has come to be for our society what sight and hearing are for the individual, and as such is one of the most indispensable factors in modern life. It is the one certain daily influence on the minds of the majority of the people. "It is the only serious book most people read. It is the only book they read every day."

A few are in a position to read journals of opinion, critical journals, scholarly journals, and so on, as supplements or correctives to their newspaper reading; but not the great mass of plain people, the people who render the decision on all questions in the last analysis. They are almost exclusively newspaper readers only, for that is all that they can afford, or all they have been taught or encouraged to read. For these masses the newspaper is their chief educational, informational, and recreational agency, —their chief contact with the unseen environment; what it publishes they tend to believe as the gospel truth. Furthermore, they, like most of us, are willing to let others do their thinking for them; ready-made opinions appeal to them.

Suggestive Power of the Newspaper

We are largely shaped by what comes to us in the form of suggestions. Reading is today one of the main sources of suggestions and reading affects the habits of thought, and habits of thought give rise to habits of action, and these two together are the essence of character. It has been wisely said, "Tell me what you read and I will tell you what you are." This is especially true of the non-intelligent and non-cultured reader. Thus the newspapers have a power to suggest to the people what they should think and do. Even those who do not take their opinions direct from the newspaper have their intellectual standards and their method of reasoning influenced by it. The average person is tremendously affected by the newspaper. "If he is in the habit of reading that which is ugly, vulgar, and low, he himself will form habits that are ugly, vulgar, and low. If a man's reading is confined to the nonsensical and the brutal he ceases to be able to detect brutality and nonsense. If he reads nothing but what is ugly and tasteless he loses his sense of beauty and his taste."

When it is remembered that the great mass of readers are highly sensitized young people, and plain people whose minds are little disciplined, one realizes even more the potency of the press. When to this is added the fact that the newspapers use mass suggesion and constant reiteration, both multiplying the power of suggestion, it becomes even more obvious. By their persistent, never-ceasing, and powerful suggestion they work their will on their readers.

Thus the newspaper is a powerful director and moulder of public opinion, —a powerful means of creating general attitudes of thought and feeling. It is a gigantic force in the community capable of doing almost anything with it, —elevating its tastes and standards, its wants and desires, or dragging them in the dust. The newspapers are coming more and more to be the principal organs through which public tastes are formed and appeals to public intelligence made.

Herein also lies the opportunity of the newspapers, of becoming a powerful influence in the body politic for good. They could enormously accelerate our rate of national and individual progress toward a reign of equity and reason if they would. On the other hand, if they follow the course of least resistance or if they become the deliberate tools for manipulating the public in the interests of certain groups or classes, they can become agents of defilement and even retrogression. No other human institution has such potentialities for good or evil.

Condition of the Newspaper Press

There still are newspapers that seek to be inciters to intelligent opinion, that frankly and impartially present all the available facts in connection with public questions, that try to serve as culture media, that present news in a socially responsible manner, and in general seek to give their readers as complete and accurate a picture of their daily world as they can, but they are few and seem to be diminishing. There also are a large number of independent small-city dailies, and village and county weeklies and biweeklies that are entirely neutral. They do very little that is notably unbuilding; but neither are they a particularly sinister influence.

There has been a tendency, however, for the newspapers with the largest circulations to allow their news disseminating function to disintegrate to the point where it borders on a public menace. William Allen White, himself an editor of prominence, described the present state well on the editorial page of his Emporia Gazette:

> Take a look at any first page, even the best of papers, and what do you find? Sex, crime, and piffle. That's the whole of it. Apparently the newspaper reading public is composed of a lot of cheap, idle-minded morons. Serious questions are puzzling the world. Great events are stirring in a dozen centres of news. In America we are going into a new era. We are mapping out new courses of action in business, politics, and religion. The world is full of big things, happening quite outside the newspapers, which either ignore the big things or misunderstand them. Instead, they smear sex, crime, or piffle over the newspapers, and write inane editorials about nothing in particular. All because the people want this sort of daily pabulum. The newspapers are creating the demand, educating the morons, and then feeding them intellectual swill. Cheap, cheap, cheap! How long, Oh Lord, how long?

The most influential portion of the press is essentially sensational, commercial, and partisan. It tends in the direction of stimulating a love of sensation and an interest in purely superficial and material things. The astonishing, the bizarre, the shocking, the non-essential is the preponderant suggestive influence. It is not to be inferred that such material gets the bulk of the space always, but it makes up a sufficiently large part of the content to make its suggestion potentially the most outstanding influence. The following are among the commonest faults of the contemporary newspaper when considered as a factor in the formation of public opinion.

1. *Distortion, coloring, exaggeration, and suppression of news.* This seems to be done in a servile attempt to protect the private interests of persons controlling the paper, or advertisers using it, business associations or business in general, or the class represented by the paper or controlling it. The Pittsburgh papers, not wanting the steel strikers to win, gave a distorted account of the steel strike of 1919; the news syndicates, because of the nature of their control, felt justified in garbling and misrepresenting news about Russia. Again, the newspapers may err in exaggerating news. Any item of news that appears to favor the policy of the paper is seized upon, written up, and enlarged beyond its importance. Now, the personal equation of the writer cannot be eliminated, and obviously, the suppression of certain news is necessary, but there is so much distortion and suppression along certain lines where these are not socially necessary that one is forced to conclude that it is done as a matter of deliberate policy in order to withhold certain information from the public.

2. *Propaganda.* Propaganda is the opposite of suppression. It is over-emphasizing of facts. Dominant interests, political parties, nationalistic or imperialistic groups have always used or sought to use the press as a means of control. The propaganda of the press is the most dangerous kind; it is the covert, unproclaiming type.

The press is apparently impartial, and therefore not recognizable as propaganda. The newspaper stands before the community as a public teacher, and the first qualification of a public teacher is that he shall be sincere and disinterested.

3. *Sensationalism, muck, and sports.* The effort is constantly made today among many of our papers to search out and emphasise those incidents and occurrences that can be sensationalized. Not many years ago one of the most prominent newspaper editors in this country in an address to members of his profession declared it to be his aim to produce such a paper that every reader on first sight every morning would involuntarily exclaim, "My God!" Charles A. Dana once said, "News is anything that will make people talk." It is said of one of the most successful newspaper managers of St. Louis a generation ago that he was the man who best knew where hell was going to break out next, and had a reporter on the spot five minutes ahead of time. Today it is occasionally true that "when hell shows no signs of eruption, the successful newspaper manager sends a reporter to raise it." News, according to this standard, is hell breaking loose. American and British journalism, —perhaps not the majority, but certainly far too great a portion of it, —has to a distressing extent surrendered to this kind of an ideal. It has achieved a facility in playing up the sordid and startling aspects of our common life that has not been reached in any other field. Muck mongering has also come to be a huge vested interest. The result is a section of our press whose principal figures are persons of bad or questionable or at least unwholesome repute, and whose influence is suggestively to focus the minds of people upon the cancerous and malodorous portions of society. Murders, thefts, suicides, accidents, debaucheries, divorces, night-clubs, escapades of notorious actors and actresses, prize fighters, and so on receive more than their share of attention. Day after day, not consciously

perhaps, the press seems to be operating on the basis that a penetration to the lowest depths of our life, in order that the dregs may be displayed, is one of its chief functions. The kind of story that many a city editor today tries to develop further with investigation, surmise, interview, and illustration is a breach of social order, while the constructive event is finished in one day's telling. There seems to be an affinity between many of the newspapers and the unclean and morbid.

A long time ago one of the deepest students of the human mind who ever lived stated that the road to communal decency lies through fixing the attention on "Whatsoever things are true, whatsoever things are honorable, whatsoever things are just, whatsoever things are pure, whatsoever things are lovely, whatsoever things are of good report." As Prof. John Wright Buckham says, "It is becoming increasingly the purpose of too many American newspapers to fix the attention of their readers on whatsoever things are foul, whatsoever things are criminal, whatsoever things are ugly, whatsoever things are of ill-report, admonishing them that if there be any scandal, and if there be any shame, they shall think on these things."

More and more the newspapers today tend to affect the morale of the community along the lines of its vices, rather than its virtues. Such have in fact become a medium for the persistent pandering to the primitive love of sensation. The public is being taught that the sordid, the insane, the unbalanced, the antisocial is the relish and chief end of life. By this never-ending process of suggesting the trivial and morbid, the public mind is becoming unable to distinguish the important from the insignificant, it becomes incapable of serious thought, and does not possess the ripe common sense which gives man stability and charm and the qualities necessary for intelligent and dynamic citizenship. The newspapers also devote large sections to sports. While this is not positively harmful, it concentrates attention on the superficial and unimportant, and distracts attention from the real business of living.

4. *Syndicated and standardized news and editorials.* The formation of free opinion in this country is further

endangered by what has been called "canned journalism." Never before has so small a proportion of the contents of the daily been produced in its own office. Most of the state, national, and world news is provided for the individual newspapers by great news-gathering associations. To this must be added syndicated features, fillers, cartoons, comics, photographs, and special features. Even the local news is increasingly in large part identical in competing journals. In the larger cities the local reporting staff is supplemented and increasingly superseded by a city news association which reports local happenings for simultaneous publications. In recent years even editorials have been syndicated, not only in the form of those written by some hired editorial writer for a chain of commonly owned papers, but those now turned out by editorial "canning factories," which provide any type of editorial for any kind of newspaper. The big danger in this latter form of canned editorial service is that it may be dishonest and manipulated, furnishing disingenuous propaganda in place of honest comment.

5. *Concentration of ownership.* There is a general tendency toward local, sectional, and even nation-wide combination of papers. There has been a trend for several decades toward the combination of scattered newspapers into a chain controlled by a single person or corporation, but in recent years competing local newspapers have been absorbed one by one by some single paper until many of our cities have only one or two dailies left. Here again the power of monopoly and manipulation is tremendous.

Reasons for these Conditions

1. *The newspaper is a profit making business.* The modern newspaper is strictly a business proposition. The first consideration of its owners is that it make money. If run in a certain way its operation is very lucrative. Hence the newspaper manager feels that his

first duty is to make profits. Advertising is the most lucrative source of revenue, providing from 70 to 85 per cent of the average newspaper's income. The advertisers pay the highest rates to the papers with the largest circulation. Therefore the course of the newspaper publisher is obvious. In order to reach the largest possible number of readers, the newspaper's content is adjusted to the general level of information and intelligence, and that is not high, for about 70 per cent of the average newspaper's reading public is frankly uneducated, being composed of those classes who a century ago did not and could not read newspapers, and who today cannot intelligently read newspapers like the *Christian Science Monitor* or the Boston *Transcript* or the New York *Times.* Thus the type and quality of the news has to be adjusted to the marginal reader, that is, the reader with just enough intelligence and literacy to be able to read the sheet. This accounts also for the widespread sensationalism, the elementary and inadequate presentation of serious national and international news, the frequent piffling and asinine editorials, and the various moronic "features." It is actually true that the best newspapers in America today from the point of sobriety, intelligence, and impartiality, with a few exceptions, have the smallest circulation, while the newspaper with the largest circulation, (over 1,000,000 daily) is a moronic tabloid.

The profitableness of newspaper combinations, of course, arises out of the advantages of monopoly and the economics of large-scale production.

2. *Many newspapers are consciously or unconsciously instruments of control in the hands of the large-propertied classes.* The newspapers cannot live without the support of the propertied classes, either as stock-holders or advertisers. The men who own them are usually connected with other large interests or are sympathetic with them, and naturally want them protected; even the most remote contingencies must be prepared for. They are

often stockholders and perhaps directors of railways and banks and vast industrial concerns doing a national and even international business. Since the propertied classes have fixed policies and interests, the newspaper tends to become the voice of these classes or an instrument of control in their interests. Thus the actual fact is that the power of shaping public judgments and educating the masses is in the control of the people who have vast private and class interests at stake. In many newspapers this accounts both for what we see and what we do not see. These stockholders and directors are connected with corporations which are seriously affected by many public movements. For example, the public may demand certain reform measures that would disturb certain business interests involved; hence, news is omitted or perverted, and arguments are twisted so as to give the appearance of public spirit without its real presence. News is published, or suppressed, or modified, according to the manner in which it suits the interests of the proprietors or their associates. The newspaper may actually build up a certain sort of public opinion favorable to the ends or interests of those controlling them, as in the case of tariffs, presidential candidates, or in international affairs. It is true that in many cases the lurid accounts of crime and vice, the broadsides sports, the columns of jazzy piffle, are presented to discourage thought and draw attention away from economic, social, or political questions, the discussion of which might intimidate the interests involved. Where this is impossible, as in some international situations, biased news is resorted to. Thus some newspapers at least are wilful agents of public be wilderment, obfuscation, and debasement.

The Newspaper of the Future

One of the difficulties that must be faced is that most newspaper readers do not want the truth bad enough to protest when they do not get it. We tend to want to read what we care about or know about, or what fits in with the preconceptions or stereotypes, as Lippmann calls them, that have been developed in us. Furthermore, the quality of the marginal readers must be improved. Thus, if the newspapers are to be agents of public opinion of high quality, we need among many other things, a rank and file having high literacy, superior interests, a sense of moral responsibility, a critical attitude, and an appreciation of honest information. Until this is done the present dominant type of newspaper will be able to work its way among us.

The future of the newspaper a generation hence is quite uncertain. Under any circumstances it will be widely changed. The motion picture combined with the radio is likely to make the dissemination of the news quite different from what it is today. It is quite possible that twenty-five years from now we will have news machines installed in our homes, as we now have the telephone, that will give us the news at regular intervals illustrated by pictures transmitted by wireless. Then, of course, we will have new problems.

FREEDOM OF THE PRESS DEFINED[2]

The first Amendment to the Constitution of the United States provides, among other things, that Congress shall make no law abridging the freedom of speech or of the press. The privilege which is thus protected against unfriendly legislation by Congress, is almost universally regarded not only as highly important, but as being essential to the very existence and perpetuity of free government. The people of the states have therefore guarded it with jealous care, by provisions of similar import in their several constitutions, and a constitutional principle is thereby established which is supposed to form a shield of protection to the free expression of opinion in every part of our land.

[2] By Thomas M. Cooley. *Constitutional Limitations.* 8th ed. Vol. 2. p. 876-86.

It is to be observed of these several provisions, that they recognize certain rights as now existing, and seek to protect and perpetuate them, by declaring that they shall not be abridged, or that they shall remain inviolate. They do not assume to create new rights, but their purpose is to protect the citizen in the enjoyment of those already possessed. We are at once, therefore, turned back from these provisions to the pre-existing law, in order that we may ascertain what the rights are which are thus protected, and what is the extent of the privileges they undertake to assure.

At the common law, however, it will be found that liberty of the press was neither well protected nor well defined. The art of printing, in the hands of private persons, has, until within a comparatively recent period, been regarded rather as an instrument of mischief, which required the restraining hand of the government, than as a power for good, to be fostered and encouraged. Like a vicious beast it might be made useful if properly harnessed and restrained. The government assumed to itself the right to determine what might or might not be published; and censors were appointed without whose permission it was criminal to publish a book or paper upon any subject. Through all the changes of government [in England] this censorship was continued until after the Revolution of 1688, and there are no instances in English history of more cruel and relentless persecution than for the publication of books which now would pass unnoticed by the authorities. To a much later time the press was not free to publish even the current news of the day where the government could suppose itself to be interested in its suppression. Many matters, the publication of which now seems important to the just, discreet, and harmonious administration of free institutions, and to the proper observation of public officers by those interested in the discharge of their duties, were treated by the public authorities as offenses against good order, and contempts of their authority. By a fiction not very far removed from the truth, the Parliament was supposed to sit with closed doors. No official publication of its debates was provided for, and no other was allowed. The brief sketches which found their way into print were usually disguised under the garb of discussions in a ficticious parliament, held in a foreign country. Several times the Parliament resolved that any such publication, or any intermeddling by letter-writers, was a breach of their privileges, and should be punished accordingly on discovery of the offenders. For such a publication in 1747 the editor of the Gentleman's Magazine was brought to the bar of the House of Commons for reprimand, and only discharged on expressing his contrition. The general publication of parliamentary debates dates only from the American Revolution, and even then was still considered a technical breach of privilege.

The American Colonies followed the practice of the parent country. Even the laws were not at first published for general circulation, and it seemed to be thought desirable by the magistrates to keep the people in ignorance of the precise boundary between that which was lawful and that which was prohibited, as more likely to make them avoid all doubtful actions. The magistrates of Massachusetts, when compelled by public opinion to suffer the publication of general laws in 1649, permitted it under protest, as a hazardous experiment. For publishing the laws of one session in Virginia, in 1682, the printer was arrested and put under bonds until the King's pleasure could be known, and the King's pleasure was declared that no printing should be allowed in the Colony.[8] There were not wanting instances of the public burning of books, as offenders against good order. Such was the fate of Elliot's book in defense of unmixed principles of popular freedom, and Calef's book against Cotton Mather, which was given to the flames at Cambridge. A single printing press was introduced into the

[8] **Hildreth.** *History of the United States.* p. 561.

Colony as early as 1639, but the publication even of state documents did not become free until 1719, when, after a quarrel between Governor Shute and the House, he directed that body not to print one of their remonstrances, and, on their disobeying, sought in vain to procure the punishment of their printer. When Dongan was sent out as Governor of New York in 1683, he was expressly instructed to suffer no printing, and that Colony obtained its first press in 1692, through a Philadelphia printer being driven thence for publishing an address by a Quaker, in which he accused his brethren in office of being inconsistent with their principles in exercising political authority. As late as 1671 Governor Berkeley of Virginia expressed his thankfulness that neither free schools nor printing were introduced in the Colony, and his trust that these breeders of disobedience, heresy, and sects would long be unknown.

The public bodies of the united nation did not at once invite publicity to their deliberations. The Constitutional Convention of 1787 sat with closed doors, and although imperfect reports of the debate have since been published, the injunction of secrecy upon its members was never removed. The Senate for a time followed this example, and the first open debate was had in 1793, on the occasion of the controversy over the right of Mr. Gallatin to a seat in that body. The House of Representatives sat with open doors from the first, tolerating the presence of reporters, over whose admission, however, the speaker assumed control, and refusing in 1796 the pittance of two thousand dollars for full publication of debates.

It must be evident from these historical facts that liberty of the press, as now understood and enjoyed, is of very recent origin; and commentators seem to be agreed in the opinion that the term itself means only that liberty of publication without the previous permission of the government, which was obtained by the abolition of the censorship. In a strict sense, Mr. Hallam says, it consists merely in exemption from a licenser. A similar view is expressed by De Lolme. "Liberty of the press," he says, "consists in this, that neither courts of justice, nor any other judges whatever, are authorized to take notice of writings *intended* for the press, but are confined to those which are actually printed." Blackstone also adopts the same opinion, and it has been followed by American Commentators of standard authority as embodying correctly the idea incorporated in the constitutional law of the country by the provisions in the American Bills of Rights.

It is conceded on all sides that the common law rules that subjected the libeler to responsibility for the private injury, or the public scandal or disorder occasioned by his conduct, are not abolished by the protection extended to the press in our constitutions. The words of Chief Justice Parker of Massachusetts on this subject have been frequently quoted, generally recognized as sound in principle, and accepted as authority. Speaking of his own state, he says:

> Nor does our constitution or declaration of rights abrogate the common law in this respect, as some have insisted. The sixteenth article declares that "liberty of the press is essential to the security of freedom in a state; it ought not, therefore, to be restrained in this Commonwealth." The *liberty* of the press, not its *licentiousness*: this is the construction which a just regard to the other parts of that instrument, and to the wisdom of those who founded it, requires. In the eleventh article it is declared that "every subject of the Commonwealth ought to find a certain remedy, by having recourse to the law, for all injuries or wrongs which he may receive in his person, property, or character," and thus the general declaration in the sixteenth article is qualified. Besides, it is well understood and received as a commentary on this provision for the liberty of the press, that it was intended to prevent all such *previous restraints* upon publications as had been practiced by other governments, and in early times here, to stifle the efforts of patriots towards enlightening their fellow subjects upon their rights and the duties of rulers. The liberty of the press was to be unrestrained, but he who used it was to be responsible in case of its abuse; like the right to keep firearms, which does not protect him who uses them for annoyance or destruction.

But while we concede that liberty of speech and of the press does not imply complete exemption from responsibility for everything a citizen may say or publish, and complete immunity to ruin the reputation or business of others so far as falsehood and detraction may be able to accomplish that end, it is nevertheless believed that the mere exemption from previous restraints cannot be all that is secured by the constitutional provisions, inasmuch as of words to be uttered orally there can be no previous censorship, and the liberty of the press might be rendered a mockery and a delusion, and the phrase itself a byword, if, while every man was at liberty to publish what he pleased, the public authorities might nevertheless punish him for harmless publications.

An examination of the controversies which have grown out of the repressive measures resorted to for the purpose of restraining the free expression of opinion will sufficiently indicate the purpose of the guaranties which have since been secured against such restraints in the future. Except so far as those guaranties relate to the mode of trial, and are designed to secure to every accused person the right to be judged by the opinion of a jury upon the criminality of his act, their purpose has evidently been to protect parties in the free publication of matters of public concern, to secure their right to a free discussion of public events and public measures, and to enable every citizen at any time to bring the government and any person in authority to the bar of public opinion by any just criticism upon their conduct in the exercise of the authority which the people have conferred upon them. To guard against repressive measures by the several departments of the government, by means of which persons in power might secure themselves and their favorites from just scrutiny and condemnation, was the general purpose; and there was no design or desire to modify the rules of the common law which protected private character from detraction and abuse, except so far as seemed necessary to secure to accused parties a fair trial. The evils to be prevented were not the censorship of the press merely, but any action of the government by means of which it might prevent such free and general discussion of public matters as seems absolutely essential to prepare the people for an intelligent exercise of their rights as citizens.

The constitutional liberty of speech and of the press, as we understand it, implies a right freely to utter and publish whatever the citizen may please, and to be protected against any responsibility for so doing, except so far as such publications, from their blasphemy, obscenity, or scandalous character, may be a public offense, or as by their falsehood and malice they may injuriously affect the standing, reputation, or pecuniary interests of individuals. Or, to state the same thing in somewhat different words, we understand liberty of speech and of the press to imply not only liberty to publish, but complete immunity from legal censure and punishment for the publication, so long as it is not harmful in its character, when tested by such standards as the law affords. For these standards we must look to the common law rules which were in force when the constitutional guaranties were established, and in reference to which they have been adopted.

DEFINING FREEDOM OF THE PRESS[4]

The Supreme Court of Minnesota, in a recent opinion which should interest newspaper readers, states clearly the difference between liberty and license of the press. The opinion upholds a statute providing that any person who publishes regularly or customarily a malicious, scandalous, and defamatory newspaper is guilty of a nuisance.

At least one vigorous protest against the law has been heard outside the state, but most of the newspapers in Minnesota seem undisturbed by the new statute.

Publishers who recognize the problem of eliminating

[4] Editorial. *Christian Science Monitor.* August 8, 1929.

the scandalmonger from journalism may be divided into three groups: 1. Those who oppose any additional restraints, legal or professional. 2. Those who prefer to let newspaper men themselves remove the difficulty. 3. Those who are willing to sponsor more rigid professional rulings, or, if necessary, new laws directed against the offenders.

Editors have argued convincingly that malpractices by a few papers tend to undermine public confidence in the press as a whole. Mindful of the long struggle by which the press gained its liberty, however, publishers usually look with misgivings on any proposal which may be interpreted as a censorship. The Minnesota Court's decision attempts to set at rest any such apprehensions about the state law in question. It says in part:

> The constitutional protection meant the abolition of censorship, and that government permission or license was not to be required; and, indeed, our constitution, like the first amendment to the United States Constitution, effectually struck down the ancient system or method of fettering the press by a licensor and gave the individual freedom to act—but to act properly or within the legal rules of propriety. In Minnesota no agency can hush the sincere and honest voice of the press, but our constitution was never intended to protect malice, scandal, and defamation when untrue or published with bad motives or without justifiable ends. It is a shield for the honest, careful, and conscientious press. He who uses the press is responsible for its abuse. A business that depends largely for its success upon malice, scandal, and defamation can be of no real service to society.

The Minnesota statute raises a question which is pertinent to other states. Naturally publishers prefer to regulate their own affairs. The court's decision should impress upon them, therefore, the need to work, within their societies and with their publications, for high professional standards. Such efforts might obviate the necessity for new laws elsewhere.

THE WAR ON THE MINNESOTA LAW[5]

The freedom of the press in Minnesota is reduced "to about the freedom of a strait-jacket."

[5] From *Literary Digest*. 104:13. February 1, 1930.

That is how it looks to the far-off editor of the Miami *News,* who remarks that life for a Minnesota editor is "now a lovely thing," and his morning prayer must be: "Grant that this day nothing that I may print may be in violation of the holy will of the district attorney, or of any judge to whom he may apply for a death-warrant against my paper!"

All American newspaperdom seems to be out with a club to smash the "gag law" that hampers the freedom of the Minnesota press.

The smashing, if any, will be done in the United States Supreme Court, and the bleachers, so to speak, already are packed with editors cheering for a victory by the American Newspaper Publishers' Association. The fight, we read, is being led by an association committee headed by Col. Robert R. McCormick, publisher of the Chicago *Tribune.* Waving the free-speech and free-press guaranty in the first article in the Bill of Rights of the Constitution,[6] the committee seeks to nullify the Minnesota law under which the *Saturday Press,* of Minneapolis, denounced by the county prosecutor as a "scandal sheet," was silenced in 1927 by court injunction. The injunction recently has been held valid by the Minnesota Supreme Court. The opposition faced by the publishers is sketched for us by an Associated Press dispatch:

> On the other side is an act of the legislature of Minnesota, four decisions of its minor and major courts, a county attorney who obtained an injunction against the paper which criticized him, and the idea of a legislator who five years ago sought to silence a now deceased editor who was attacking him.
>
> The *Saturday Press,* which was suspended under the law, was published in Minneapolis in 1927 by J. M. Near and Howard A. Guilford. It attacked what it alleged was a gambling and general "racket" business in Minneapolis, and declared that this situation was being tolerated by the city administration and law-enforcement heads.
>
> Floyd Olson, county attorney, whom the paper included in its attack, obtained a writ of injunction under what opponents

[6] Of course any child old enough to read won't be fooled by this statement. He will know that the First Amendment has nothing at all to do with the matter.

described as the "gag" statute, silencing the paper. The writ later was upheld by the district court, and recently by the Minnesota Supreme Court. The *Saturday Press*, which suspended publication immediately after the first injunction, has not been published since.

The "gag law" was introduced by a legislator from the Iron Range country in northern Minnesota, in 1925, to silence an editor in his constituency, who had attacked him, but the editor died before action could be taken.

The Minnesota Supreme Court, in upholding the injunction, found that the law does not violate the Constitutional provision guaranteeing the freedom of the press, and that "presumably an evil, inimical to the public welfare, existed in this State which the legislature intended to remedy." Furthermore: "No claim is advanced that the method and character of the operation of the newspaper in question was not a nuisance if the statute is constitutional. It was regularly and customarily devoted to malicious, scandalous, and defamatory matter."

But American newspaperdom most emphatically disagrees with this opinion. No matter what the provocation, suppression by injunction is held intolerable. In all parts of the country editors fairly shout their denunciation of the Minnesota law. It means "muzzling the press"; it is "a glaring infringement" of Constitutional rights, and another evidence of "the growing tendency to censor the press." The views of many editors are exprest succinctly by the New York *Herald Tribune*, which calls the law "a standing threat of instant death to any newspaper displeasing to officials in power, who find in its utterances any color of the 'nuisance' which the statute defines." Preparing for the Supreme Court fight, Colonel McCormick made clear the stand of the publishers' association:

> We have no wish to foster libelous publications. The general libel laws can be invoked against those if the charges are proven. Our fight is against allowing the truth to be suppressed and newspapers ruled out of existence by a single judge, without a jury trial.

"Legislation that hampers the newspapers in their work of placing facts before the people is pie for crooked politicians," warns the Philadelphia *Record.*

To the Houston *Post-Dispatch,* whose editorial bears the mournful caption, *Freedom of the Press Passing,* the Minnesota case "is indicative of the growing tendency on the part of the judiciary to attempt to censor the press." Continuing:

> During the past year editors and publishers of newspapers in various places have been committed to jail for contempt of court for refusing to divulge sources of news, or for criticizing court action, or for violating orders to refrain from printing accounts of proceedings in courts. In Texas there has been one instance of a judge ordering the press to refrain from publishing reports of a hearing in a murder case, the idea being that by keeping the testimony secret a change of venue could be avoided. If the present tendency in the judiciary continues, in due course of time the newspapers will find themselves being edited from the bench.

A somewhat different view of the situation is held by the *Christian Science Monitor,* which asserts that "if there be any menace to the freedom of the press in the United States to-day, it is a menace which comes from the unscrupulous within the ranks of the profession." Asserting that "responsible journalism, if it is to preserve its rights and protect its name, must repudiate the disreputable activities of the sensational, scandal-seeking newspaper." This editor concludes:

> Undoubtedly the law is capable of the most high-handed and arbitrary use. It places in the hand of a single judge the authority summarily to abolish an offending newspaper and reduces "due process of law" to an exceedingly slender right. But if the cure is potentially worse than the malady, it should be appreciated that the most flagrant and offensive violations of public decency and journalistic ethics have brought about its enactment. It seems to us that when journalism is able to defend itself from within, and when the American Society of Newspaper Editors, for example, is able to enforce a more effective respect for its own high code of newspaper ethics, then the danger of dogmatic censorship from without will be slight. Until that time, the very conditions which have invited the dangerous Minnesota statute will continue to recur, bringing in their wake more restrictions and more censorship. It is not enough merely to attack this law. The conditions which produced it must be minimized.

MINNESOTA NUISANCE LAW[1]

Text of the Statute

Any person who, as an individual, or as a member or an employee of a firm or association or organization, or as an officer, director, member, or employee of a corporation, shall be engaged in the business of regularly or customarily producing, publishing, or circulating, having in possession, selling or giving away (a) an obscene, lewd and lascivious newspaper, magazine, or other periodical, or (b) a malicious, scandalous and defamatory newspaper, magazine or other periodical, is guilty of a nuisance, and all persons guilty of such nuisance may be enjoined, as hereinafter provided.

Participation in such business shall constitute a commission of such nuisance and render the participant liable and subject to the proceedings, orders, and judgments provided for in this Act. Ownership, in whole or in part, directly or indirectly, of any such periodical, or of any stock or interest in any corporation or organization which owns the same in whole or in part, or which publishes the same, shall constitute such participation.

In actions brought under (b) above, there shall be available the defense that the truth was published with good motives and for justifiable ends, and in such actions the plaintiff shall not have the right to report to issues or editions of periodicals taking place more than three months before the commencement of the action.

Whenever any such nuisance is committed or is kept, maintained, or exists, as above provided for, the County Attorney of any county where any such periodical is published or circulated, or—(in the event of such County Attorney's failure or refusal to proceed upon written request in good faith of a reputable citizen of the State)

[1] *Minnesota Statutes.* Sections 10123-1 to 10123-3. *Mason's Minnesota Statutes.* 1927. vol. 2. p. 1992.

the Attorney General, or—(in the event of such Attorney General's failure or refusal to proceed upon written request in good faith of a reputable citizen of the state) any citizen of such county,—may commence and maintain in the District Court of said county, an action in the name of the State of Minnesota, upon the relation of such County Attorney or Attorney General or citizen, as the case may be, to perpetually enjoin the person or persons committing, conducting, or maintaining any such nuisance. In any such action, the court, or a judge thereof in vacation, may, upon such evidence as the court shall deem sufficient, taken in such form as the court shall require, grant a Writ of Temporary Injunction.

The defendant or defendants shall be served therein as in other actions, and the statutory provisions as to service by publication shall be applicable as in other cases. In the case of unknown persons having or claiming any ownership, right, title, or interest in any such periodical, or who may be participants in committing or maintaining such nuisance, such persons may be made parties to the action by designating them in the summons and complaint as "all other persons unknown claiming any ownership, right, title, or interest in the periodical affected by this action or participating in the commission or maintenance of any nuisance affected by this action," and services on such persons may be made by publishing the summons in the manner prescribed in Section 7737 of the General Statutes for 1913.

The defendant or defendants shall have the right to plead by demurrer or answer, and the plaintiff shall have the right to demur or reply as in other cases.

The action may be brought to trial and tried as in the case of other actions in such District Court, and shall be governed by the practice and procedure applicable to civil actions for injunctions.

After trial the court may make its order and judgment permanently enjoining any and all defendants found guilty of violating this act from further committing or continuing the acts prohibited hereby, and in and by such judgment, such nuisance may be wholly abated.

The court may, as in other cases of contempt, at any time punish, by fine of not more than $1,000 or by imprisonment in the county jail for not more than twelve months, any person or persons violating any injunction, temporary or permanent, made or issued pursuant to this act.

WAR AND A FREE PRESS[a]

The bill in Congress putting limits on the liberty of the press during the war has elicited heated protests from certain influential daily papers. We make no attempt to discuss the provisions of the bill because it is still subject to amendment and the questioned provisions may be altered before this number of the *Outlook* can reach our readers. But the occasion is fitting for a statement of general principles by which both Congress and the country should be guided.

The liberty of the press in a free country differs in no essential respect from other forms of liberty. Democracy assumes the truth of an aphorism attributed to Augustine, "Please to do right, and then do as you please." It assumes that most men please to do right, and it generally leaves them free to do as they please. But the country may define what is right, and may punish the individual or prevent him from doing what is wrong. He has liberty to use his hands as he pleases, but if he uses his fist to knock his neighbor down the law punishes him. He has liberty to use his tongue as he pleases, but if he uses his tongue to slander his neighbor the law punishes him. Liberty and anarchy are not synonyms. The country retains the right to define the limits within which the individual may do as he pleases.

[a] **Editorial.** ***Outlook.*** **116:56-7. May 9, 1917.**

The law of liberty recognizes the rights and interests of the public as well as of the individual. If the orator uses his tongue to incite a mob to ravage, plunder, and burn, or a printer uses his type to furnish obscene prints or obscene literature to school-boys, the law punishes the offender. The law protects the rights of both the individual and the public against any man who does not please to do right; and the community assumes the authority to define for the individuals in the community what is right.

There is preventive law, as there is preventive medicine. If a man threatens to assault his neighbor, the neighbor does not have to wait until he is assaulted. He may have his would-be assailant arrested and bound over to keep the peace. If a man purposes any act which will work an irreparable injury to his neighbor or to the community, neither the neighbor nor the community has to await the fulfillment of the evil purpose. The court will issue an injunction against the threatened wrong and enforce the prohibition by a summary process.

Apply these simple principles to the liberty of the press.

If a newspaper libels the President, the editor should be liable to punishment. An American citizen does not lose his right to the protection accorded to other American citizens because the Nation has made him its President.

If a newspaper incites a mob to violence, or if in time of war it publishes statements the obvious effect and probable purpose of which are to give aid and comfort to the enemy its editor should be liable to punishment. There is no sacredness in type which makes immune from punishment the men who use it for a criminal purpose.

Preventive law is legitimate in time of war as in time of peace. Whatever information is given by the newspapers to the country is also given to the enemies of the country. The great majority of newspapers will voluntarily refrain from such publication. But one newspaper which does not refrain may inflict on the country an irreparable injury. The country has a right to protect itself against this peril by prohibiting the publication of any information which will do injury to the country or give aid and comfort to its enemies. And it may take such measures as it deems wise for giving to the press and to the public the information which is consistent with the public interests, and may prohibit the publication of information which it regards as perilous to the Nation. Such prohibition is only the application to the newspapers in time of war of a principle long since recognized and acted upon in time of peace.

The saying attributed to Jefferson, "'Error is dangerless so long as truth is left free to combat it," is true. The press must be left free to give untrammeled expression to public opinion concerning public acts and public policies. It must be left free to criticise or condemn the public utterances and the public acts of the Government and its agents. They are the servants of the people; the master must be left free to criticise his servants. But that does not imply freedom to misreport those acts and utterances, or to asperse the motives of those servants, or to give those facts to the public which public safety requires should not be given to the enemies of the country. It will sometimes be difficult to draw the line between legitimate and illegitimate criticism. But honestly patriotic editors will rarely find it difficult to draw that line for themselves; and others must be content, as their fellow-citizens are content, to leave the line between the lawful and unlawful in doubtful cases to be defined for them by the courts.

In one important respect the censorship of the press in democratic countries will always differ from the censorship of the press in autocratic countries. In autocratic countries the few rulers, in democratic countries the people, are to be safeguarded. In autocratic countries the press is prohibited from any utterance which lowers the authority and lessens the power of the autocrat. In democratic countries the press is restrained from utterance which imperils the liberty and well-being of the people, and is encouraged in every utterance which protects their liberties and promotes their welfare. Free criticism of the rulers of the people is therefore discouraged or prohibited by autocracies; free criticism of the servants of the people is permitted and encouraged in democracies.

Congress ought to protect the right of the Administration to prevent the publication of news which it deems injurious to the public interest; and it ought to protect the right of the public through the press to criticise freely the public acts and public policies of the Administration.

CENSORED ADVERTISING[9]

The *New York Times* advertising censorship represents a careful endeavor to exclude whatever is fraudulent, misleading or "catchpenny." The *Times* declines tens of thousands of agate lines of advertising monthly. Its purpose is to protect the readers of the *Times.*

More significant than the unequalled volume of advertising in the *New York Times* is the high character of the announcements in its columns. The *Times* year by year and month by month holds supremacy among all New York newspapers in total volume of advertising. In 1928 this total was 30,736,530 agate lines, 11,002,817 more than any other New York newspaper.

The Times Advertising Index Expurgatorius

1. Fraudulent or doubtful advertisements.

2. Offers of something of value for nothing; advertisements that make false, unwarranted or exaggerated claims.

[9] This appeared as a full page advertisement in the *New York Times* on Saturday, May 18, 1929.

3. Advertisements that are ambiguous in wording and which may mislead.

4. Attacks of a personal character; advertisements that make uncalled-for reflections on competitors or competitive goods.

5. Advertisements holding out the prospect of large guaranteed dividends or excessive profits.

6. Bucket shops and offerings of undesirable financial firms.

7. Advertisements that are indecent, vulgar, suggestive, repulsive or offensive either in theme or treatment.

8. Matrimonial offers; fortune telling; massage.

9. Objectionable medical advertising and offers of free medical treatment; advertising that makes remedial, relief or curative claims, either directly or by inference, not justified by the facts or common experience.

10. Advertising of products containing habit-forming or dangerous drugs.

11. Want advertisements which request money for samples or articles.

12. Any other advertising that may cause money loss to the reader, or injury in health or morals, or loss of confidence in reputable advertising and honorable business, or which is regarded by the *Times* as unworthy.

The *Times* welcomes information from readers in aid of its efforts to keep its advertising columns clean. The *New York Times* will pay a reward of $100 to any one causing the arrest and conviction of a person or firm obtaining money under false pretenses through fraudulent advertising published in its columns.

THE CHRISTIAN SCIENCE CENSOR[10]

Constant dropping wears away the stone. The committees on publication and the loyal members of the Christian Science Church, in whatever nook and corner of the country they may be, are forever on the job.

[10] By Henry Raymond Mussey. *Nation.* 130:241-3. February 26, 1930.

Their zeal, earnestness, and discipline create the impression of large numbers, and consequently bring prompt results in newspaper, radio, and legislative fields. I report largely in the words of the committees on publication themselves, as published in the *Christian Science Sentinel.*

Starting at the top, the committees are carefully hand-picked all the way down. To give a single example, John M. Dean, First Reader of the church in Memphis, was appointed Committee on Publication for Tennessse for the year beginning October 1, 1923. Mr. Dean was not considered sufficiently "loyal," and his appointment was vetoed by the Board of Directors in Boston. The (local) assistant committees are similarly controlled. The general manager of committees in Boston, by means of regular bulletins and, when necessary, special communications, keeps in touch with the State committees and through them with the local ones. State committees, according to the manager, are required to correct impositions and injustices as provided in the Manual, "to guard the rights of Christian Scientists against restriction by public authority" (a duty prescribed by the directors under Article I, Section 6), and to perform any other duties required under the same by-law. The duties of assistant committees are similar.

Now for the actual work. Committees are constantly on the alert to secure the insertion in local newspapers of notices and reports of Christian Science lectures and other news valuable to the church, and to see that there is promptly published a "correction" of any unfavorable publicity of whatever character. How this result is accomplished it is well worth while to observe, for the methods at need often go far beyond the simple friendly request that constitutes a natural and proper first step. Christian Scientists are commonly well-to-do persons with good business connections. The committees therefore can, and do if necessary, bring valuable personal influence and advertising pressure to bear on the newspapers with surprisingly effective results. Such power is ordinarily exercised quietly, and on that account all the more effectively.

An unusually well-known example occurs in Washington, D. C. The District Committee on Publication is part owner of one of the large Washington department stores. Through his advertising power he holds in the hollow of his hand the *Herald* and the *Star,* which Washingtonians read in the morning and evening respectively. Some time ago the business manager of the *Star* told an interested inquirer that anything on the subject of Christian Science was always submitted to this man before publication, and that as his store was among the *Star's* largest advertisers, the paper could not afford to antagonize him. The advertising manager of the *Post* complained that the man concerned was going much too far in putting pressure on that paper through advertising power. An examination of these two papers over a period of nearly four years shows that they have published no news adverse to the Mother Church, while authorized Christian Science lectures, given in Washington every two or three weeks, have been reported to the extent of anywhere from half a column to the full text of the lecture.

The District Committee on Publication, officially reporting his activities for 1924, says:

> There was also a syndicated article, critical and adverse to Christian Science, which was withheld from publication in one of the local papers upon the request of your committee. The wisdom of Mrs. Eddy in establishing the activity of the Committee on Publication is becoming more apparent each year in a rapidly diminishing desire on the part of newspapers to print any criticism or incorrect statement concerning Mrs. Eddy or Christian Science.

What a model diminishing desire! Four years later the committee reports thus:

> No unfriendly sermons were advertised, but an objectionable advertisement from a counterfeit organization appeared. A reply was presented, but the publisher stated that he could not accept a correction to a paid advertisement. Upon the insistence

of your committee that something be done in the matter, the publisher in lieu of printing the correction agreed not to accept in future objectionable advertisements.

Desire is still diminishing, but presumably not department-store advertising.

News is not news in Washington alone. A rival Christian Science organization offered an advertisement to the Chicago *Tribune,* and elicited the two following telegrams from the advertising manager:

November 17, 1927.

Sorry publisher will not accept my recommendation to run your advertisement. Will write you regarding changes.

November 23, 1927

Cannot accept religious advertising controversial in character. This ruling prevents acceptance of your order. Revision is futile in view of your objective. Very sorry.

One advertising manager apparently learned a good deal in the course of a week. One may hazard a shrewd guess as to who was the teacher. At any rate, the Illinois Committee on Publications was able to report in 1925:

Many editors now refuse copy of a controversial nature and we are advised that any objectionable allusion to our religion reaching such well-guarded pages does so because of ignorance or oversight on the part of the newspaper employes.

The advertising departments of two of the largest daily newspapers firmly refuse advertising matter issued by false claimants of Christian Science.

The education of our journalistic brethren, however, cannot always be accomplished simply by "the sweet amenities of Love," as provided in the Manual, or even, it appears, by the sweet amenities of advertising, for in the report of the New York committee for 1925 we read:

It is seldom that the better papers quibble over printing a correction. To be sure, it is still necessary at times to emphasize the moral obligation and discreetly to point out the possible legal liability on the part of publishers in connection with the printing of statements misrepresenting the teachings and practice of Christian Science.

Note correction outrunning error in Michigan in 1927:

In August a press dispatch which quoted certain misstatements of Mrs. Eddy's teaching was printed in only one newspaper of this State, while fourteen newspapers printed a subsequent dispatch which quoted the Committee on Publication from New York in reply to the earlier statement.

The busy committees on publication, in their ceaseless pursuit of error, have much reading to do outside *Science and Health* and the newspapers.

A WORD FROM A PRISON[11]

The discussion of the relationship of newspaper reports to the spread of crime which the *Monitor* reprints in another column from the *Echo,* published by inmates of the Western Penitentiary of Pennsylvania, has somewhat the authority of expert testimony. In this respect it does not stand alone, for police and prison officials all over the land continually report a similar sentiment existent among those who come under their observation.

Expert surveys, like that which the Rockefeller foundation conducted in Cleveland, Ohio, add further corroboration to the evidence that crime news engenders crime. Indeed, any student of the responsiveness of the human mind to suggestion, however hurtful, needs little concrete evidence to convince him that the persistent glorification of criminals in the press, the publication of their portraits, the use of laudatory, or at least striking, nicknames, and the growing practice by "feature writers" of spreading the views and the exploits of criminals all over the Sunday papers stimulate, encourage and increase crime.

Certain New York newspapers at this moment are devoting from three to five pages daily to the publication of the verbatim testimony in a criminal trial in a neighboring state. For this there is not the common excuse offered for the publication of crime news. Nobody will claim that the search of that New Jersey court for truth is being aided by the publication of the testimony vividly

[11] Editorial. *Christian Science Monitor.* November 20, 1926.

decorated with comments and descriptive writing by practiced sensationalists of the daily press.

Elsewhere in the *Monitor* today will be found expressions of leading Chicagoans concerning the overemphasis of criminal news in their local papers. In no city is there greater intellectual activity than in Chicago. None has undertaken so great a work of beautification as the "Chicago plan." Nowhere are public benefactions more liberal, nor can such monuments to public enterprise as the Field Museum, the Wacker Drive, or the Rosenwald Museum, now in the early stage of development, be paralleled in many cities. Yet a great part of the press in Chicago finds its chosen field of activity in the vivid reporting of crimes of violence. The effect upon the reputation of the city throughout the world is little less than disastrous.

Newspaper editors and publishers all know and all are constantly declaring that the great problem of journalism is to find space for all the matters of interest which demand publication. In view of this, one can only wonder at the editorial judgment which selects a criminal trial as the most important news of the decade—for we can recall nothing else, not even the election, which has been "covered" with such minute particularity and to which space has been so lavishly allotted. Certainly nothing of an educational, religious, or economic nature has been thus dignified by the New York press.

The editors of the prison newspaper, which the *Monitor* quotes, say, "To speak of them as primers of crime would be mild. If we were seriously bent on compiling a handbook of crime for the use of criminals, all necessary material could be taken from our daily newspapers." True, from this general indictment three outstanding papers are omitted—one of which, we regret to say, gave twenty-four columns of small type yesterday to New Jersey's combination of vaudeville and criminal justice. But we believe that many papers other than those mentioned are beginning to question the value of crime news, or at any rate to compare in a spirit of doubt and inquiry the value of circulation obtained through it with that of circulation based on more important contributions to the knowledge and welfare of the community.

For the moment, there may seem to be great material prosperity ready to the hand of the publisher who is willing to purvey for profit the news of the gutter and the slum. But no enduring edifice of prosperity can ever be based upon crime—either upon its commission or its exploitation for profit.

BRIEF EXCERPTS

The advertiser tends to control the policy of the paper.—*Hamilton Holt. Commercialism and Journalism. p.* 34.

A newspaper may be a criminal as well as an individual.—*Outlook.* 91:416. *February* 27, 1909.

When war is declared the first casualties are free press and free speech.—*Nation.* 104:205. *February* 22, 1917.

Only rarely do newspapermen take the general public into their confidence.—*Walter Lippmann. Liberty and the News. p.* 16.

Liberty of circulating is as essential to that freedom [of the press] as liberty of publishing.—*United States Supreme Court.* 96 *U.S.* 733.

Commercialism is at present the greatest menace to the freedom of the press.—*Hamilton Holt. Commercialism and Journalism. p.* 98.

The department stores are seldom or never referred to unfavorably by the New York papers.—*Hamilton Holt. Commercialism and Journalism. p.* 68.

Practices of present day journalism constitute an important factor in the problem of crime.—*Report of New York State Crime Commission.* 1927. *p.* 324.

The newspaper is to society much what sight and hearing are to the individual.—*Delos F. Wilcox. Annals of the American Academy.* 16:56. *July* 1900.

One of the chief sources of the strength of the Tweed ring was found in the subserviency of the daily press.—*B. O. Flower. Arena.* 33:274. *March* 1905.

The *Daily Mirror*, published in New York, is barred from Canada under orders issued by the department of customs.—*Cleveland Plain Dealer. March* 3, 1926.

There are probably more newspapers and periodicals printed in the United States than in all the countries of Europe put together.—*William B. Munro. Current Problems in Citizenship. p.* 87.

It would be safe to say that the average man or woman does not read the hundredth part of what is printed in a daily newspaper.—*Willam B. Munro. Current Problems in Citizenship. p.* 88.

A national board of magazine censorship was proposed today in a bill by Representative Wilson of Mississippi.—*Cleveland Plain Dealer. December* 16, 1927. *Congressional Record.* 69:720. *December* 15, 1920.

No newspaper of considerable size can print nearly all the copy that comes to it. There must be a process of selection. Some news must be suppressed.—*Nelson A. Crawford. The Ethics of Journalism. p.* 56-7.

dissemination of knowledge has in the past year heaped up an indictment of itself that it will take much faithful service and honest effort to quash.—*Samuel Gompers. American Federationist.* 26:1134. *December* 1919.

The newspaper in its contemporary forms is incapable of providing more than a tithe of the information currently needed for intelligent participation in the affairs of a complex society.—*John Storck. Man and Civilization. p.* 269-70.

The newspaper is the creation of no one person, but that of many, who have given freely of themselves to carry enlightenment and understanding into every corner of life.—*Julia Traver. Proceedings of the Sixty-Fourth Annual Meeting of the American Education Association.* 1926. *p.* 76.

The American press may not be above the moral level of the average good citizen,—in no country does one either expect or find it to be so,—but it is above the level of the machine politicians in the cities.—*James Bryce. The American Commonwealth.* 3d *ed. vol.* 2. *p.* 275.

The newspapers are read more extensively than any other publication in the United States. Is it not an anomaly that in most schools, even most high schools and colleges, the newspaper is not mentioned from September to June?—*Nelson A. Crawford. The Ethics of Journalism. p.* 176.

Liberty of the press does not mean freedom from criminal responsibility. The law does not prevent in advance the free publishing of news and comment, but if a newspaper sees fit to smirch private character and steal reputation, it is as open to prosecution and punishment as if it stole property.—*Outlook.* 94:275. *February* 5, 1910.

Much of what appears in the news columns of city journals about the conduct of municipal business is altogether untrustworthy as a basis of judgment. The news columns are forced to present as actuality a great deal that is guesswork or gossip.—*William B. Munro. Principles and Methods of Municipal Administration. p.* 9.

The characteristics of the American journalist consist in an open and coarse appeal to the passions of his readers. He abandons principles to assail the characters of individuals, to track them into private life, and disclose all their weaknesses and vices. Nothing can be more deplorable than this abuse of the powers of thought. —*Alexis de Tocqueville. Democracy in America. vol.* 1. *p.* 187.

In discussing public opinion we should be much concerned about the low level on which it exists today. Why is it that on the whole the newspapers with the widest circulation are those which are the cheapest and least sincere? There are a few exceptions to this, but the exceptions only prove the rule.—*Everett Dean Martin. Psychology: What it has to teach you about yourself and your world. p.* 198.

Hearst, the man, has recently been correctly called "one of the most melancholy figures of our time." He has done more to degrade the entire American press than any one else in its history. He has achieved enormous material success—it is said that his net profits in 1922 amounted to $12,000,000—but he is without popular respect or regard.—*Oswald Garrison Villard. Some Newspapers and Newspaper Men. p.* 15.

There is a widespread prejudice against the newspapers, based on the belief that they cannot be trusted to report truly the current events in the world's life on account of incompetence or venality. But in spite of this distrust we are almost altogether dependent upon them for our knowledge of widely interesting events.—*Delos F. Wilcox. Annals of the American Academy.* 16:56. *July* 1900.

During the early history of this country newspaper censors were ever present who, clothed by the law with authority, never hesitated to annoy the poor printer whenever he put anything interesting in his paper. A jail sentence rather than a libel suit was the sword of Damocles which hung in every newspaper office should something be printed which reflected in any way upon the government.—*James M. Lee. History of American Journalism. p.* 28.

A newspaper or periodical may habitually and consistently practice a malign and slanderous untruthfulness. A paper of this stamp may exert a real influence for evil by the way in which it teaches young men of good education, whose talents should be at their country's service, that decent and upright public men are as properly subjects of foul attacks as the most debased corruptionist.—*Theodore Roosevelt. Outlook.* 91:511. *March* 6, 1909.

I doubt if there is a dramatist in England who would dream of putting into his work some of the stuff that is commonly and unashamedly put into newspapers. I have observed, without surprise, that the newspapers which are the most angry about immoral plays are precisely those whose columns stink with indecency. Perhaps they fear that the theatre may cut into their trade. —*St. John Ervine. Spectator.* 135:262. *August* 15, 1925.

The Minnesota law does not attempt to grant the power to enjoin a single libel or a single defamatory publication. It carefully lays down certain conditions which must exist before the publication may be declared to be a nuisance. Only newspapers customarily and regularly engaged in the publication of matter forbidden by the statute may be declared to constitute a nuisance and be enjoined as such.—*Minnesota Law Review.* 14: 797-8. *June* 1930.

It would be a great advantage to the American people if an editor and publisher of a libelous newspaper could be put behind prison bars, so the conviction could be brought home to irresponsible journalists that liberty of the press does not mean liberty maliciously to vilify any private citizen or public official who happens to have aroused the hostility of the newspaper or whose vilification appears to the editor to have a commercial value. —*Outlook.* 90:891-2. *December* 26, 1908.

The modern newspaper is almost forced by its readers to become a mere institutionalization of gossip. But few new journals of the nonsensational type succeed in establishing themselves in the larger cities nowadays, and many of the older papers have been forced to discontinue or to consolidate. The irresponsible yellow press constitutes a great force working to perpetuate ignorance, prejudice, and hysteria in public life.—*John Storck. Man and Civilization. p.* 270.

Wherever rich men abound the power of money is formidable in elections and in the press, and corruption more or less present. I will not say that wherever there is money there will be corruption, but true it is that Poverty and Purity go together. The two best administered democracies in the modern world have been the two poorest, The Orange Free State before 1899 and the Swiss Confederation.—*James Bryce. Modern Democracies. vol.* 2. *p.* 457-8.

What does the advertiser ask as a bonus in return for his business favor? Sometimes a whole change of editorial policy, as when the Pittsburgh newspapers were forced to support a candidate for the bench chosen by the department stores; more often the insertion of personal matter of no news value in itself; most often the suppression of news harmful to himself, his family, or his business associates.—*Will Irwin. Collier's Weekly.* 47:16. *May* 27, 1911.

During the last few years it has become lamentably evident that certain daily newspapers, certain periodicals, are owned or controlled by men of vast wealth who have gained their wealth in evil fashion, who desire to stifle or twist the honest expression of public opinion, and who find an instrument fit for their purpose in the guided and purchased mendacity of those who edit and write for such papers and periodicals.—*Theodore Roosevelt. Outlook.* 91:510. *March* 6, 1909.

The newspapers have followed the trend of the times toward mass production, consolidation, cooperative marketing, lower costs, high profits, mechanical progress and mental stupefaction. They used to spread ideas; they now only avoid making comparisons between the New York newspapers of twenty-five years ago and those of the present. But who can point out any improvement that is not wholly material?—*Gaylord M. Fuller. American Mercury.* 7:155. *February* 1926.

The news of the day as it reaches the newspaper office is an incredible medley of fact, propaganda, rumor, suspicion, clues, hopes, and fears, and the task of selecting and ordering that news is one of the truly sacred and priestly offices in a democracy. For the newspaper is in all literalness the bible of democracy, the book out of which a people determines its conduct. It is the only serious book most people read. It is the only book they read every day.—*Walter Lippmann. Liberty and the News.* p. 47.

The papers of the South seldom betrayed the movements of Confederate troops in such a way as to give valuable information to the North. This condition was due to the fact that most of the papers in that section of the country received their war news through an official press association. By means of this organization the

Confederacy was better able to control what appeared in the newspapers than was the Government at Washington, in spite of its censorship.—*James M. Lee. History of American Journalism. p.* 290.

James M. Lee, head of the School of Journalism at New York University, thinks news of informational value, instead of concentration on paid sports, screen stars, aviators, and channel swimmers, could be made to pay. "Crowded as is the New York field," he writes, "it would, in my opinion, support a newspaper which adopted as its motto, *All the news that's important.*" The experiment of producing a paper living up to that motto has never been made in the United States.—*Silas Bent. Harper's Magazine.* 155:494. *September* 1927.

In our country the newspapers and the cheap and popular magazines, which sell by the hundreds of thousands, are largely supported by the money paid for the advertisements which they contain, and it will be noticed that the advertisements receive as much or more attention than the reading matter. This enables the publishers to sell the newspapers and magazines for far less than would otherwise be possible, for the price received from the buyer would often not even pay for the paper used.—*James H. Robinson and Charles A. Beard. History of Europe: Our Own Times. p.* 515.

One wonders whether anything can be devised to meet that great evil of the press, the lie which, once under way, can never be tracked down. The more scrupulous papers will, of course, print a retraction when they have unintentionally injured someone; but the retraction rarely compensates the victim. The law of libel is a clumsy and expensive instrument, and rather useless to private individuals or weak organizations because of the gentlemen's agreement which obtains in the newspaper world. After all, the remedy for libel is not money damages, but an undoing of the injury. —*Walter Lippmann. Liberty and the News. p.* 73.

The public's taste for manufactured commodities has been widened by advertising. Its literary taste has been debased and narrowed as a result of the advertisers' demand for bigger but not better circulation. Formerly we worried along with almost no intelligence of sport stars and master minds in crime: now we have a saturnalia of gunmen, divorcees and boxers. There is a *noblesse oblige* between the press and Big Business. The newspaper editor may hark back with pride to the Palladium of Liberty, but that palladium is crumbling. He has sold his birthright for a mess of advertising.—*Silas Bent. Ballyhoo: the Voice of the Press. p.* 225.

The history of the struggle for the freedom of the press discloses that at different times freedom of the press had distinctly different meanings. Indeed, as is the case in the determination of many constitutional questions, changing social and economic conditions render statutes constitutional which a generation ago would have been considered unconstitutional. As stated by Mr. Justice Holmes, "The provisions of the Constitution are not mathematical formulas having their essence in their form; they are organic living institutions transplanted from English soil."—*Minnesota Law Review.* 14:790. *June* 1930.

Experience has shown that most political, social, and scientific advances have been fostered and encouraged by permitting an unfettered inquiry for truth. On the other hand, the state's interest in maintaining the public safety, morals, and general welfare of the public is bound to be interfered with by an unrestricted and absolute freedom of publication. The clash is inevitable, but "like the course of heavenly bodies, harmony in national life is a resultant of the struggle between contending forces." Recent adjudications by the Federal Supreme Court reveal an attempt by that body to distinguish between those publications dangerous to the general welfare of the state and those not possessed of that quality.—*Minnesota Law Review.* 14:791. *June* 1930.

A generation or two ago the influence of money upon journalism was smaller than it is today. Year by year the subservience of the editorial to the business policy of the newspaper becomes more apparent. It is a matter of common knowledge, reinforced by much direct evidence, that many journals will not print news adverse to local department stores. Public franchise corporations, banks, railroads, and other great undertakings enjoy a lesser, though still considerable, immunity. In publicity, as in politics, bought demagogues had their place and office, and were not without their reward.—*Walter E. Weyl. The New Democracy. p.* 123 *et seq.*

Secrecy is of the essence of successful warfare. Publicity is of the essence of successful journalism. How is a common ground to be found or manufactured between these abrupt opposites? How are we to prevent the publication of naval and military movements, the disclosure of which may fatally impair chances of victory? How are we to reconcile the freedom of an uncensored and irresponsible press with the concealments, the disguises, and the false scents on which may depend not merely the fortunes of a campaign, but the fate of the nation?—*Fortnightly Review.* 85:528. *March* 1906.

The Hearst newspapers, as the outstanding examples of socalled "yellow journalism," have often been given credit for originating the distinctive characteristics that became associated with them. As a matter of fact, however, the Hearst papers were not pioneers in developing new features. . . . The advent of a Hearst newspaper in a city often resulted in the adoption of Hearst methods by rival papers. . . . The influence of the Hearst type of journalism on the form and contents of American newspapers has been as great as that of any other single force.—*Silas Bent. Ballyhoo! the Voice of the Press. p.* 386-8.

That the bulk of the contents of the newspaper is of the nature of gossip may be seen by noting three traits which together seem to make a fair definition of that word. It is copious, designed to occupy, without exerting, the mind. It consists mostly of personalities and appeals to superficial emotion. It is untrustworthy, except upon a few matters of moment which the public are likely to follow up and verify. It fosters superficiality and commonplace in every sphere of thought and feeling, and is, of course, the antithesis of literature and of all high or fine spiritual achievement.—*Charles H. Cooley. Social Organization. p.* 84-5.

The admitted function of newspapers is to convey to the public the objective facts of current events. The public is convinced that the newspapers are not fulfilling this function. The articulate part of the public charges that news is manufactured, suppressed, distorted, and colored. The reasons for these offenses it holds generally to be that the publishers of newspapers are subsidized for propaganda purposes, are influenced by the demands of advertisers, are seekers for circulation even at the cost of honesty, and through interlocking directorates and other relationships are closely tied to various private business interests.—*Nelson A. Crawford. Nation.* 115: 249. *September* 13, 1922.

During the controversy [in the General Court, i.e. Legislature, of Massachusetts in 1634] a pamphlet by Israel Stoughton of Dorchester attacked the claim of the Assistants with what Winthrop calls "many weak arguments." The Assistants called Stoughton before them, forced him to recant, ordered his book burned, probably not for its "weak arguments," deprived him of his elective office of deputy, and forbade him to hold any office for three years. Winthrop had written a pamphlet in favor of the veto power, [the other side of the question] and the magistrates saw no wrong in public argument on that side.—*Willis M. West. The American People. p.* 61-2.

The publishing and reading of salacious magazines in America have increased to such an extent that this country bids fair to take the lead in lewd literature away from France. Some scores of short story magazines are exploiting strictly sex emotions with a libidinous appeal that constitutes a grave social problem. The combined yearly circulation of twenty of the largest magazines which devote their pages to exploiting sex comes to the large total of 55,560,000. The average copy sold is read by four persons, according to the opinion of large distributors. There are in all human probability 222,240,000 readings of sex-thrill magazines in the United States each year.—*Literary Digest.* 86:33. *September* 19, 1925.

More than half the "reading matter" in metropolitan newspapers is of interested origin. It arises from, and on occasion is created by, agencies which have a special stake in its presentation. Yet it is presented as though it were an impartial and colorless statement of fact on which the reader may with security base an opinion. Sometimes it is mere trivia, and does no more harm than to intrude worthless material into our field of thought. Sometimes it is important and legitimate news, which takes the form of the publicity handout because the press is too indolent or too niggardly to gather such news for itself. Sometimes it is propaganda of the sinister sort.—*Silas Bent. Ballyhoo: the Voice of the Press. p.* 121.

Hideous yellow journalism deifies the cult of the mendacious, the sensational, and the inane, and, throughout its wide but vapid field, does as much to vulgarize and degrade the popular taste, to weaken the popular character, and to dull the edge of the popular conscience, as any influence under which the country can suffer. These men sneer at the very idea of paying heed to the dictates of a sound morality; as one of their number has cynically put it, they are concerned merely with selling the public whatever the public will buy—a theory of conduct which would justify the existence of every keeper of an opium den, of every foul creature who ministers to the vices of mankind.—*Theodore Roosevelt. Outlook.* 91:510. *March* 6, 1909.

I learned, years ago, that some people are always complaining about how bad the newspapers are, and that it would be impossible to fix up a newspaper to suit such people. Newspapers cannot be perfect. If they were, their circulations would be too small to pay running expenses. Newspapers have to depend for the bulk of their circulation upon a class of people that never reads anything else but the papers. The newspaper must, to survive, appeal to the average intelligence. And statistics gathered by means of country-wide intelligence tests show that the average mental age is thirteen. So that the paper whose contents cannot be readily apprehended and enjoyed by the thirteen-year-old intelligence will soon be bankrupt.—*Ted Robinson. Cleveland Plain Dealer. May* 13, 1930.

American journals were, early in their career, if not at its very beginning, written for the bulk of the people. They had attained no high level of literary excellence when some forty years ago an enterprizing man of unrefined taste created a new type of "live" newspaper, which made a rapid success by its smartness, copiousness, and variety, while addressing itself entirely to the multitude. Other papers were almost forced to shape themselves on the same lines, because the class which desired something more choice was still relatively small; and now the journals of the chief cities have become such vast commercial concerns that they still think first of the mass and are controlled by its tastes, which they have themselves done so much to create.—*James Bryce. The American Commonwealth.* 3d *ed. vol.* 2. *p.* 775.

What is to be done about our new literature? There has probably never been so wide a distribution of this sort of thing as is now made possible by modern publishing methods. But a special censorship, usually the first glib suggestion, whether federal or state, should be unthinkable. We already have laws against obscenity which serve in many states, and the censorship of the Post Office Department is steadily at work. In his field the Postmaster General is supreme. The courts will not interfere to control any executive official in the discharge of a duty involving the exercise of judgment and discretion. Since the publications under consideration are delivered through other channels than the mail, the question arises as to what further steps shall be taken.—*Oswald Garrison Villard. Atlantic Monthly.* 137:397. *March* 1926.

More than one writer has remarked, in recent years, on the striking changes which are being brought about in journalism through the increasing reliance upon syndicated material. Nearly all telegraphic news is nowadays supplied by one or another of the great agencies; routine local news in the large cities is gathered and distributed in the same way by cooperative bureaus; comic strips, cartoons, photographs, fillers, uplift essays for the editorial page, household hints, "columns," book reviews, Sunday magazine sections, all are turned out by the cubic yard in New York and published simultaneously in Oshkosh and Omaha, Kankakee and Keokuk, Minneapolis and Miami. Cut off their title-lines and the most loyal native son cannot tell the *Bingville Bugle* from the *Gallopolis Gazette.*—*Silas Bent. Ballyhoo: the Voice of the Press.*

Certain types of story magazines drew attention yesterday from public officials all over Ohio as Attorney General C. C. Crabbe threw the weight of the state behind the crusade by listing 22 publications as obscene and lascivious. Other parts of the country were absorbed with the subject yesterday. Twenty magazines have been barred in Spokane. At Omaha the state prosecutor referred complaints to federal authorities. Assistant United States Attorney O'Regan of Chicago recommended to Postmaster General New that twenty publications be taken out of the mails. District Attorney Gordon of Washington was continuing his campaign against objectionable periodicals after ten had been withdrawn from the news stands at his request. Yesterday he added 16 more.—*Cleveland Plain Dealer. May* 21, 1925.

During the days when Tweed controlled New York, it is asserted that eighty-nine newspapers were on his pay roll and that after the exposure of the ring by the *New York Times,* twenty-seven of these papers, which had depended upon city plunder for existence, were compelled to suspend. The records showed that messages of the mayor which the reading public accepted as news were really paid advertisements charged to the city at the rate of one dollar a line. During the Tweed regime some of the smaller evening papers received an annual subsidy of one thousand dollars a month. Unsettled newspaper claims from various papers totaled over two millions. A remarkable thing connected with the Tweed control was the fact that two hundred dollars a year was voted by the Aldermen to reporters for omitting to report the activities of the Aldermen.—*James M. Lee. History of American Journalism. p.* 330.

The second condition of political liberty is the provision of an honest and straightforward supply of news. Those who are to decide must have truthful material upon which to decide. Their judgment must not be thwarted by the presentation of a biased case. We have learned, especially of late years, that this is no easy matter. A statesman cannot seldom be made what the press chooses to make him. A policy may be represented as entirely good or bad by the skilful omission of relevant facts. Our civilization has stimulated the creation of agencies which live deliberately on the falsification of news. It would, indeed, not be very wide of the mark to argue that much of what had been achieved by the art of education in the nineteenth century had been frustrated by the art of propaganda in the twentieth. A people without reliable news is, sooner or later, a people without the basis of freedom.—*Harold J. Laski. A Grammar of Politics. p.* 147-8.

The Minnesota nuisance statute was invoked for the first time in the case of two Minneapolis weekly newspapers—the *Twin City Reporter* and the *Saturday Press.* They had been conducting a somewhat lurid campaign against vice conditions and officials in Hennepin county. Instead of protecting himself and his colleagues through libel action, the district attorney of Hennepin county had the papers silenced under the section of the 1925 measure providing for the suppression of publications engaged in printing malicious, scandalous, or defamatory matter. The *Twin City Reporter* did not resist the decision, but the case of the *Saturday Press* was taken to the Minnesota Supreme court, which upheld the constitutionality of the newspaper injunction law. Convinced that the Minnesota statute contravenes the fundamental constitutional guaranty of freedom of the press, the *Tribune* has arranged to have the law tested by the United States Supreme court.—*Editorial. Chicago Tribune. March* 6, 1929.

The dominant section of the press is obviously a phase of commercial enterprise. It thrives as such on large circulations and voluminous advertising. Circulation is promoted by giving readers what they want or at least what they like after they try it. They largely want news, real or alleged, of divorce scandals, atrocious crimes, sports events and other sensational occurrences, besides comic strips, advice to the lovelorn and other special features. Many, perhaps most, readers also want a modicum of news on important developments in business, industry, politics and public affairs. Newspapers in general do not present a balanced, comprehensive account of really important happenings in the world, because it would not be good business to do so. The news and editorial articles of almost all are colored, selected, or biased, in various degrees, and as a consequence do not supply altogether reliable information on the events they are supposed to report or interpret.—*Seba Eldridge. The New Citizenship. p.* 252-3.

The summer of 1871. Tweed was at that time in complete control of the city government. The Democratic machine throughout the state was his to direct. While matters were in this shape a bookkeeper in one of the departments of the city government had gradually collected evidence that the public was being robbed on a large scale. He offered this evidence to one New York paper after another. Incredible as it may now seem, one paper after another refused it. The newspapers of that day were afraid to publish facts which the party machine preferred to keep quiet. Finally the *New York Times* undertook the campaign of publicity. I am told that it did so with much reluctance.—*Arthur T. Hadley. Undercurrents in American Politics. p.* 156.

President Jackson, in his inaugural message, advocated the right of Federal supervision of newspapers. This recommendation by President Jackson was referred by the Senate to a committee of which the chairman was John C. Calhoun, of South Carolina. Speaking for the committee, Calhoun reported on February 14, 1826, [sic] that it was not up to Congress to decide when newspapers were incendiary, for they might also decide they were not, and thus laden the mails of the South with papers advocating abolition. He insisted that it belonged to Southern States and not to Congress to determine what newspapers should circulate in that section. He also proposed that it should not be lawful for any postmaster in any state or territory of the United States knowingly to deliver to any person any newspaper touching the subject of slavery. Calhoun's recommendations were put in a bill which was ordered to a third reading in the Senate by a vote of 18 to 16, but it failed to pass.—*James M. Lee. History of American Journalism. p. 227.*

The constitution does not protect a publisher from the consequences of crime committed by the act of publication. It does not shield a printed attack on private character. It does not permit the advertisement of lotteries. It does not permit the publication of blasphemous or obscene articles. It places no restraint upon the power of the legislature to punish the publication of matter which is injurious to society according to the standard of the common law. It does not deprive the state of the primary right of self-preservation. It does not sanction unbridled license, nor authorize the publication of articles prompting the commission of murder or the overthrow of government by force. All courts and commentators contrast the liberty of the press with its licentiousness, and condemn as not sanctioned by the constitution of any state appeals designed to destroy the reputation of the citizen, the peace of society, or the existence of the government.—*New York Court of Appeals.* 171 *N.Y.* 423. *June* 10, 1902.

There is no constitutional right to publish every fact or statement that may be true. Every citizen has an equal right to use his mental endowments, as well as his property, in any harmless occupation or manner; but he has no right to use them so as to injure his fellow citizen or to endanger the vital interests of society. Immunity in the mischievous use is as inconsistent with civil liberty as prohibition of the harmless use. The liberty protected is not the right to perpetrate acts of licentiousness, or any act inconsistent with the peace and safety of the state. Freedom of speech and press does not include the abuse of the power of tongue or pen, any more than freedom of other action includes an injurious use of one's occupation, business, or property. The notion that the broad guaranty of the common right to free speech and free thought, contained in our constitution, is intended to erect a bulwark or supply a place of refuge in behalf of the violaters of laws enacted for the protection of society from the contagion of moral diseases belittles the conception of constitutional safeguards and implies ignorance of the essentials of civil liberty.—*Supreme Court of Errors of Connecticut. 73 Conn.* 18. 1900.

Every newspaper attaining a given circulation should pay for the most valuable of all franchises and give a guaranty for its share in the exercise of the greatest of all powers, by placing certain space in every issue at the disposal of each of the four political parties that cast the largest votes in the preceding state election. It is likely that, with such a law in force, each party would employ its ablest advocates to plead its cause before the bar of public opinion in the space thus placed at its disposal. Misrepresentation would be checked because if it occurred, it would be exposed in parallel columns or in the succeeding issue. Men who now refuse to have an organ of the opposing party in their homes would be impelled by curiosity to read contrasting arguments. The deadliest of all monopolies, monopoly of access to the mind, would be overthrown, and a habit of the public would be developed which in itself might solve the unsolved problems of the technique of democracy, prevent revolution, and insure orderly progress.—*Edward C. Hayes in Seba Eldridge's Political Action. p.* xv-xvi.

Dr. Charles Harrington, an admirable health officer, turned his attention to the Massachusetts breweries. He found by analysis that much of the beer and ale sold in his state was adulterated, contrary to law, with salicylic or fluoric acid. In the course of six weeks the grand jury indicted a dozen brewery companies and many bottling houses for this offense. It was important news. Did the *Transcript* or the *Globe* or the *Post* publish the fact? They did not. Red Fox Ale was on the list of indictments. Red Fox Ale had a small advertisement in the *Transcript*. When the Grand Jury returned its findings in that case the *Transcript* published a list of the day's indictments, but omitted this highly important one.

The grind of justice reached Harvard Beer, a heavy advertiser. The Harvard Brewing Company was indicted. Most of the evening papers, including the *Transcript,* ignored this important piece of news. "Harvard Beer, 1000 Pure," appeared in the pages of the *Transcript* as a half page advertisement.—*Will Irwin. Collier's Weekly.* 47:16. *May* 27, 1911.

There is literal and absolute freedom of the press in its relations with the federal government in so far as any actual, implied, or attempted control over what is written in Washington is concerned. This means that every Washington correspondent may write at any time anything that impresses him as legitimate news, subject only to those confidences which he must respect and subject to certain rules which may be laid down, e.g., as to a direct quotation of the President. Neither Congress nor the administration has any right, nor presumes to have any, to discipline any correspondent, except when one of these rules is violated. His report may be objected to and protested against on the floor of Congress. Or a statesman, on occasion, may take matters in his own hands and physically assault the journalist who has given offense. This has happened many times, but without serious casualty. The point I make, however, is that no censorship in any form is applied, and none could be enforced, were it attempted.—*J. Frederick Essary. American Political Science Review.* 22:903-4. *November* 1928.

The press in most communities, and particularly in Pittsburgh, led the workers there to the belief that the press lends itself instantly and persistently to strike breaking. They believed that the press immediately took sides, printed only the news favoring that side, suppressed or colored its records, printed advertisements and editorials urging the strikers to go back, denounced the strikers and incessantly misrepresented the facts. All this was found to be true in the case of the Pittsburgh papers, as analyzed in a subreport. Foreign language papers largely followed the lead of the English papers. The average American-born discriminating citizen of Pittsburgh could not have obtained from his papers sufficient information to get a true conception of the strike; basic information was not in those papers. The steel-worker reader, moreover, gave attention not only to the commissions of the press but to commissions plainly directed against the strike. In the minds of workingmen outside steel areas the newspapers' handling of the steel strike added weight to the conviction that the press of the country is not the workingman's press.—*Commission of Inquiry. The Interchurch World Movement. Report on the Steel Strike of* 1919. *p.* 242-3.

To-day, man has a cinematographic brain. A thousand images are impressed daily upon the screen of his consciousness, but they are as fleeting as moving pictures in a cinema theater. The American press prints every year over 29,000,000,000 issues. No one can question its educational possibilities, for the best of all colleges is potentially the University of Gutenberg. If it printed only the truth, its value would be infinite; but who can say in what proportions of this vast volume of printed matter is the true and the false? The framers of the Constitution had few books and fewer newspapers. Their thoughts were few and simple, but what they lacked in quantity they made up in unsurpassed quality. Before the beginning of the present mechanical age, the current of living thought could be likened to a mountain stream, which though confined within narrow banks yet had waters of transparent clearness. May not the current thought of our time be compared with the mighty Mississippi in the period of a spring freshet? Its banks are wide and its current swift, but the turbid stream that flows onward is one of muddy swirls and eddies and overflows its banks to their destruction.—*James M. Beck. The Constitution of the United States. p.* 191-2.

The first amendment to the Constitution of the United States provides that "Congress shall make no law abridging the freedom of speech or of the press." This amendment is confined to laws passed by Congress. There is nothing in this amendment nor in the Constitution itself that prohibits the various states from passing laws restricting the right of newspapers to publish anything unless such laws become repugnant to the fourteenth amendment of the Constitution of the United States. Outside of this very limited restriction, the states can legislate on the subject in any way each individual state sees fit unless absolutely restricted or limited by the constitution of the state affected. We gather from this, in the first place, that the Federal Constitution does not guarantee the freedom of the press. Further, the constitutional provisions restricting Congress from making laws abridging the freedom of the press must likewise be construed in the light of other constitutional provisions. Freedom of the press is a relative term, somewhat analogous to that of liberty. While we secure certain rights as to liberty under the Constitution, such liberty is subject to other restraints contained in the Constitution, designed to safeguard the rights and liberties of others. Congress therefore has the right to pass laws which effectually restrain the freedom of the press where public necessity requires such restraint.—*Walter J. Mattison. Marquette Law Review.* 13:1. *December* 1928.

Prophylactics against mob mind: avoidance of the sensational newspaper. The howling dervishes of journalism propagate crazes and fads by distorting the significance of the moment. The valuable news is, in fact, but a slender fringe along the vast expanse of the valuable old. It is a hundred to one that the old classic is worth more than the book of the month. Old wit, condensed into homely maxims about cleanliness, avoiding draughts, keeping the feet warm and the head cool, save a thousand lives where the new wrinkles in medicine or surgery, which make newspaper copy, save a dozen. Now, this static side of life is ignored by the yellow press. By exaggerating the news it presents things in a false perspective. It can capture the public's pennies by exploiting the unique, the startling, even the imaginary. Therefore, to keep readers on the tiptoe of expectation, it promises something extraordinary which is always just on the eve of happening—but doesn't happen. So the jaded nerves are kept on the perpetual thrill, and, looking always for something wonderful to turn up, the deluded reader goes on and on like a donkey reaching for the sheaf of oats tied to the end of his wagon pole. Moreover, the constant flitting from topic to topic brings upon the confirmed newspaper reader what we may call *paragraphesis,* i.e., inability to hold the mind on a subject for any length of time. Reading so inimical to poise, self-control, and mental concentration as the sensational newspapers should be cut down to a minimum.—*Edward A. Ross. Social Psychology. p.* 85-6.

Shortly before the war the newspapers of New York took a census of the press agents who were regularly employed and regularly accredited and found that there were about 1,200 of them. Many of the direct channels to news have been closed, and the information for the public is first filtered through publicity agents. The great corporations have them, the banks have them, the railroads have them, all the organizations of business and of social and political activity have them, and they are the media through which news comes. Even statesmen have them. They are essentially attorneys for their employers. Their function is not to proclaim the truth, the whole truth, and nothing but the truth, but to present the particular state of facts that will be of the greatest benefit to their clients—in short, to manipulate the news. A great deal of the confusion of public opinion today is the direct product of that system. Take, for example, a great industrial disturbance, like the coal strike. What are the essential merits of it? Do you know? If you do, you are very fortunate. I don't, although I have spared no effort to get at the facts, many of which lie further underground than the coal itself. The reason none of us can get at the basic truth is very simple. The coal operators meet in secret, and through their publicity agent they give out a statement of their side of the case. The leaders of the miners meet in secret, and they give out a statement of their side of the case. Either statement by itself is plausible and believable. The two of them, taken together, are wholly irreconcilable and simply add to the sum total of human ignorance. The more of that kind of publicity we have the less we know, the less certain we can be of anything.—*Frank I. Cobb. Editorial Writer, New York World. Senate Document No.* 175, *Sixty-sixth Congress. Second Session. p.* 4-5. *January* 10, 1920.

The most destructive form of untruth is sophistry and propaganda by those whose profession it is to report the news. The news columns are common carriers. When those who control them arrogate to themselves the right to determine by their own consciences what shall be reported and for what purpose, democracy is unworkable. Public opinion is blockaded. For when a people can no longer confidently repair "to the best fountains for their information," then anyone's guess and anyone's rumor, each man's hope and each man's whim become the basis of government. All that the sharpest critics of democracy have alleged is true, if there is no steady supply of trustworthy and relevant news. Incompetence and aimlessness, corruption and disloyalty, panic and ultimate disaster, must come to any people which is denied an assured access to the facts. Statesmen may devise policies; they will end in futility, as so many have recently ended, if the propagandists and censors can put a painted screen where there should be a window to the world. Few episodes in recent history are more poignant than that of the British Prime Minister protesting that he cannot do the sensible thing in regard to Russia because a powerful newspaper proprietor has drugged the public. That incident is a photograph of the supreme danger which confronts popular government. All other dangers are contingent upon it, for the news is the chief source of the opinion by which government now proceeds. So long as there is interposed between the ordinary citizen and the facts a news organization determining by entirely private and unexamined standards, no matter how lofty, what he shall know, and hence what he shall believe, no one will be able to say that the substance of democratic government is secure. In so far as those who purvey the news make of their own beliefs a higher law than truth, they are attacking the foundations of our constitutional system. There can be no higher law in journalism than to tell the truth. —*Walter Lippmann. Liberty and the News. p.* 10-12

AFFIRMATIVE DISCUSSION

THE NUISANCE LAW UPHELD[1]

The word "nuisance" is sufficiently comprehensive to include the alleged unlawful business which necessarily works harm, injury, and prejudice to the individual and is prejudicial to the public welfare. Since it annoys, injures, and endangers the comfort and repose of a considerable number of persons it is a nuisance. Perhaps it also endangers safety within the meaning of the statute. Moreover, the people speaking through their representatives in the legitimate exercise of the police power have declared such acts a nuisance. Our legislature has declared the following to be nuisances: places where intoxicating liquor is illegally sold, houses of prostitution, dogs [that habitually worry, chase, or molest teams or persons traveling peaceably on the public road], malicious fences, itinerant carnivals, lotteries, and noxious weeds. This legislative power has been used as to various things constituting nuisances.

We are not here concerned with the power of equity to enjoin libel or otherwise to protect personal rights. The statute is directed at an existing nuisance arising out of a continued and habitual indulgence in malice, scandal, and defamation. Such is the declared purpose of the statute. Equity has always had jurisdiction to enjoin and abate public nuisances. Even sports may sometimes be enjoined as private nuisances.

In the exercise of the police power of the state the legislature must resort to measures which tend to accom-

[1] Decision of the Supreme Court of Minnesota in the case of State ex rel. Floyd B. Olson v. Howard A. Guilford and another (174 Minn. 457. May 25, 1928. 219 N. W. 770, 58 A. L. R. 607.) sustaining the constitutionality of the Newspaper Nuisance Law. Condensed and citations omitted.

plish the desired purpose, and on the other hand must not exceed the reasonable demands of the occasion. Police power involves the imposition of such restraints upon private rights as are practically necessary for the general welfare, that is, the public interest, and it must be limited to such matters. The police power is a governmental right in the state which authorizes it to prohibit all things harmful to the comfort, safety, and welfare of society. It is to the public what the law of necessity is to the individual.

The constituent elements of the declared nuisance are the customary and regular dissemination of a newspaper which finds its way into families, reaching the young as well as the mature, of a selection of scandalous and defamatory articles treated in such a way as to excite attention and interest so as to command circulation. The business at which the statute is directed involves more than libel. Mere libel under the statute does not constitute the nuisance. The statute is not directed at threatened libel but at an existing business which, generally speaking, involves more than libel. The distribution of scandalous matter is detrimental to public morals and to the general welfare. It tends to disturb the peace of the community. Being defamatory and malicious, it tends to provoke assaults and the commission of crime. It has no concern with the publication of the truth, with good motives and for justifiable ends. There is no constitutional right to publish a fact merely because it is true. It is a matter of common knowledge that prosecutions under the criminal libel statutes do not result in efficient repression or suppression of the evils of scandal. Men who are the victims of such assaults seldom resort to the courts. This is especially true if their sins are exposed and the only question relates to whether it was done with good motives and for justifiable ends.

This law is not for the protection of the person attacked nor to punish the wrong doer. It is for the protection of the public welfare. The courts have uniformly sustained the constitutionality of statutes conferring upon courts of equity power to restrain public nuisances although the acts constitute crime and the plaintiff's property rights are not involved. The inherent nature of the business bears such a relation to the social and moral welfare that we hold that the legislature was in the legitimate exercise of the police power when it declared such business to be a public nuisance. The right to do this was forced upon the state in the exercise of its functions, or rather duty, to preserve that equilibrium of relative right which must be preserved in organized society.

"The liberty of the press shall forever remain inviolate, and all persons may freely speak, write, and publish their sentiments on all subjects, being responsible for the abuse of such right." (Minnesota Constitution, Article 1, section 3.)

The liberty of the press consists in the right to publish the truth with impunity, with good motives and for justifiable ends; liberty to publish with complete immunity from legal censure and punishment for the publication, so long as it is not harmful in its character when tested by such standards as the law affords. The constitutional protection meant the abolition of censorship and that governmental permission or license was not to be required; and indeed our constitution, like the first amendment to the United States Constitution, effectually struck down the ancient system or method of fettering the press by a licenser and gave the individual freedom to act—but to act properly or within legal rules of propriety. In fact such was the rule of common law when our constitution was adopted. Our constitutional provisions intended to prevent the restraints upon publications which had been practiced by other governments.

In Minnesota no agency can hush the sincere and honest voice of the press; but our constitution was never intended to protect malice, scandal, and defamation when untrue or published with bad motives or without justifiable ends. It is a shield for the honest, careful, and conscientious press. Liberty of the press does not mean that an evil-minded person may publish just anything any more than the constitutional right of free assembly authorizes and legalizes unlawful assemblies and riots. There is a legal obligation on the part of all who write and publish to do so in such a manner as not to offend against public decency, public morals, and public laws. Otherwise our statute of criminal libel would not be valid. In making the publisher responsible for the abuse of the press the legislature is authorized to make laws to bridle the appetites of those who thrive upon scandal and rejoice in its consequences.

It was never the intention of the constitution to afford protection to a publication devoted to scandal and defamation. He who uses the press is responsible for its abuses. He may be required by legislation to have regard for the vital interests of society. Immunity in the mischievous use of the press is as inconsistent with civil liberty as prohibition of its harmless use. The constitutional rights of the individual are as sacred as the liberty of the press. Newspaper proprietors have no claims to indulgence. They have the same rights that the rest of the community has, and no more. It is the liberty of the press that is guaranteed—not the licentiousness. The press can be free and men can freely speak and write without indulging in malice, scandal, and defamation; and the great privilege of such liberty was never intended as a refuge for the defamer and the scandalmonger. Defendants stand before us upon the record as being regularly and customarily engaged in a business of conducting a newspaper sending to the public malicious, scandalous, and defamatory printed matter. Obviously indulgence in such publications would soon deprave the moral taste of society and render it miserable. A business that depends largely for its success upon malice, scandal, and defamation can be of no real service to society.

It is not a violation of the liberty of the press or of the freedom of speech for the legislature to provide a remedy for their abuse. Nor does the constitutional guaranty of the liberty of the press deprive the state of its police power to enact additional laws for the welfare of society such as hereinbefore stated.

The constitutional right of free speech is not violated by a law prohibiting public addresses on public grounds. A statute making a publication of a false report of the proceedings of any court a contempt does not violate such constitutional guaranty of liberty of the press. Nor is a criminal libel statute in derogation of the freedom of the press. A law making it a crime to publish an article inciting or encouraging crime is not violative of the freedom of the press. The constitutional guaranty of a free press cannot be made a shield for the violation of criminal laws. The statute prohibiting the mailing of obscene matter is not in derogation of the liberty of the press. The press cannot justify doing evil on the theory that good may result therefrom. It is the use and not the abuse of the liberty of the press that is guarded by our fundamental law. Liberty of the press and freedom of speech under the constitution do not mean the unrestrained privilege to write and say what one pleases at all times and under all circumstances.

The due process clause in our constitution was never intended to limit the subjects on which the police power of the state may lawfully be exerted. This guaranty has never been construed as being incompatible with the principle, equally vital because essential to peace and safety, that all property is held under the implied obligation that the owner's use of it shall not be injurious to the community. Indeed the police power of the state includes the right to destroy or abate a public nuisance. Property so destroyed is not taken for public use, and therefore there is no obligation to make compensation for such taking. The rights of private property are subservient to the public right to be free from nuisances which may be abated without compensation. The statute involved does not violate the due process of law guaranty.

THE NUISANCE LAW AGAIN UPHELD[2]

Appeal from District, Hennepin County. Mathias Baldwin, Judge. Action by the State, on the relation of Floyd B. Olson, against Howard A. Guilford, J. M. Near, and others. From an adverse judgment defendant Near appeals.

The action was to abate a nuisance, arising out of the operation of a newspaper business, as authorized by Laws 1925, C. 285. The cause has been here before. 174 Minn. 457. Presumably an evil, inimical to the public welfare, existed in this state which the Legislature intended to remedy. No claim is advanced that the method and character of the operation of the newspaper in question was not a nuisance if the statute is constitutional. It was regularly and customarily devoted largely to malicious, scandalous, and defamatory matter.

The claim is advanced that the statute is in contravention of article 1, section 3, of our state constitution, relating to the liberty of the press, and also that it violates the due process clause of both article 1, section 7, of our state constitution, and the Fourteenth Amendment to the Constitution of the United States. In our opinion the Laws of 1925, c. 285, violate neither the state nor the Federal Constitution. The record presents the same questions upon which we have already passed. Our former opinion will disclose other grounds urged by the appellant, and such grounds have been urged in this appeal, although we do not discuss them in detail.

The argument is made that the judgment goes too far, and literally prevents the defendants from publishing any kind of newspaper, and thereby deprives them of their means of livelihood and the legitimate use of their property. It is sufficient to say that the assignments of error do not go to the form of the judgment. The lower court has not been asked to modify the judgment. We see

[2] Decision of the Supreme Court of Minnesota. State ex rel. Olson v. Guilford et al. 179 Minn. 40. December 20, 1929. 228 N. W. 326.

no reason, however, for the defendants to construe the judgment as restraining them from operating a newspaper in harmony with the public welfare to which all must yield. The case has now been tried. The allegations of the complaint have been found to be true. Though this is an equitable action, defendants have in no way indicated any desire to conduct their business in the usual and legitimate manner.

SHOULD NEWSPAPERS TELL THE TRUTH[8]

It is a characteristic of American journalism as a whole that it has achieved a facility in playing up the sordid aspects of our common life that it has not reached in any other field. It has done this largely because of a definition of news that seems to us to have been essentially false, and certainly has been divorced from any recognition of moral responsibility. The outcome, in terms of social disintegration, is such that the entire press will be forced shortly to answer an aroused public opinion as to the basis on which it is proceeding.

What is news? No question is more debated; on none is there less agreement. The legend in many newspaper offices would make news a dog story—"If a dog bites a man, that is not news; if a man bites a dog, that is." News, by such a standard, is the bizarre. The influence of the theory is to be seen in the majority of American dailies. More attention is given to a second legend, that a good newspaperman is "one who knows where hell is going to break loose, and gets there five minutes ahead of time." News, by this standard, is hell breaking loose, and the influence of *this* theory is to be seen in the majority of American dailies.

The most serious attempt ever made by an American to answer the question has been that of the chief of the editorial page of the World, Walter Lippmann, in his book on *Public Opinion*. In his chapter on *The*

[8] Editorial. *Christian Century*. 42:273-5. February 26, 1925.

Nature of News, Mr. Lippmann arrives at a conclusion that is hard to summarize, but that may be expressed somewhat as follows: News is not coextensive with truth. It is the course of events projecting itself into an easily definable shape that lends itself to reporting. In most instances the newspaper must depend for its understanding of basic causes on the interpretation supplied by extra-newspaper agencies. Limitations of time, staff and public interest are bound to center the attention of the newspaper on the objective, the concrete.

While we await a final answer to the question, it should at least be possible to affirm one thing that news is *not.* News is not lying. Yet that is exactly what many newspapers are doing. By their methods of dealing with the sordid, these newspapers are impressing on their readers a community and world view that, however accurate it may be in some of its details, is, in its sum, a lie. No community can continue in safety while its light is such darkness.

Some of the comment inspired by our open letter (entitled *An editorial open letter to the newspaper proprietors of Chicago* and published on January 29, 1925) reads as though it had been suggested that the newspapers cease to publish reports of wrongdoing. No such proposal has been made. The words used were clear: "What is desired is that the sordid side be scaled by the life of a great city and a great country and given only the attention that it proportionately merits and that it proportionately has in real life." There is no lie more tricky and misleading than the lie of perspective. The paid manipulator of opinion spends his time affirming that mountains are mole-hills, and mole-hills are mountains. Thus, in the case of a steel strike, the public is urged to forget that thousands of men are wearing their lives out in a 12-hour day, and to remember that a strike leader once wrote a radical pamphlet.

The newspapers constantly commit this lie by smearing across their pages bestiality in such a way as to create the impression that bestiality is the focus of the city's life. Where it is not done by means of spectacular treatment, it may be done by means of constant iteration. It is at this point that the *World's* test of a newspaper by a single front page fails. It is not the single front page that fixes the impact of a newspaper, but the run of interests in a city editor's assignment book. What kind of story is it that a city editor always notes for further development, adding investigation to surmise, interview to testimony, illustration to discovery? The question answers itself. It is this determination to run down a breach of social order to its ultimate indecency, while dismissing constructive events as finished with a day's telling, that feeds the false view of the world foisted on many.

More devasting is the lie in the glamour that the newspaper casts about crime and bestiality. Not alone in headlines, but in articles, where no excuse of straitened space can be admitted, thieves are no longer thieves, but bandits; murderers are not murderers, but gunmen; adulterers are not adulterers, but proprietors of love nests. The surest method of becoming a hero of public attention is to commit crime. Kill your mother, and tomorrow the press will be devoting more space to your slightest word than to that of the President of the United States. It will photograph and interview you; compete without financial limit for such diaries, letters or other written material as you may desire to market; and will follow you to acquittal, prison or the gallows itself with the fanfare of fame. A few weeks ago a man on trial for a double murder in the state of Illinois insisted on taking the witness stand in the face of the protests of his counsel. Why? He had "always wished to appear as the star witness in a murder trial!" Where did the brain get that twist? What made the central position in a murder trial seem to that man a legitimate life ambition? Who was guilty of those two murders?

It is not necessary to speak of the way in which sections of the press, in its advertised purpose of giving the public what it wants, lie by a deliberate manufacture of bestiality. It is a criminal offense in England for the press to introduce into its reports of such matters elements that will not or cannot form a part of the official trial record. Should such a construction of the law for the protection of juries be applied in this country, it is safe to say that a large part of the press would stand in constant danger of prosecution.

To do the things that have been enumerated—to magnify wrongdoing until it overshadows the thought of a city, to give to the evil-doer a glamorous and romantic standing in the public eye, and even, on occasion, to manufacture sensation—is not to produce a newspaper. It is to propagate evil. It is to use the enormous machinery of publicity that is in the hands of the press to attack the subconscious defenses of public decency in the minds of the masses. It is to prostitute the profession of journalism.

A long time ago one of the deepest students of the human mind who ever lived stated that the road to communal decency lies through fixing the attention on "whatsoever things are true, whatsoever things are honorable, whatsoever things are just, whatsoever things are pure, whatsoever things are lovely, whatsoever things are of good report." As Professor John Wright Buckham says, it is becoming increasingly the purpose of too many American newspapers to fix the attention of their readers on whatsoever things are foul, whatsoever things are criminal, whatsoever things are ugly, whatsoever things are of ill report, admonishing them that if there be any scandal and if there by any shame, they shall think on these things. And this sort of prostitution, if long enough continued, will discredit the newspaper in any community.

Joseph Pulitzer—the man who made the *World*—knew that. Writing to one of his managing editors as to what the making of a newspaper required, Mr. Pulitzer put it this way: "Concentrate your brain upon these objectives: What is original, distinctive, dramatic, romantic, thrilling, unique, curious, quaint, humorous, odd, apt to be talked about, without shocking good taste or lowering the general tone, good tone, and above all without impairing the confidence of the people in the truth of the stories or the character of the paper for reliability and scrupulous cleanness." Theorists may take exception to this as a definition of what a newspaper is to carry in its columns. But in at least one respect Mr. Pulitzer was perfectly clear. There was to be nothing in the paper that he himself, a decent member of society, would not make the subject of his own regular attention. In the case of the proprietors of some of the newspapers to which our open letter was sent, and in the case of a good many other newspaper proprietors in the United States, that simply is not so. They would never dare by their conversation to spread about in their clubs, or repeat at their own dinner tables, the sort of filth that their papers continually contain. Not only would they not dare; they are the sort of gentlemen who would never think of so doing. By what moral standard, then, do they flaunt this viciousness in the face of the community at large?

"It is because they are compelled to act without a reliable picture of the world," Mr. Lippmann himself has written, "that governments, schools, newspapers and churches make such small headway against the more obvious failings of democracy." Nor is it disputed that the task of giving to the masses a reliable picture of the world is beyond complete accomplishment. But when newspaper proprietors refuse to do what they can to make the picture as reliable as possible, when they conduct papers that flout those tests of decency and good journalism enumerated by Mr. Pulitzer, when they deliver themselves to the propagation of evil, moral condemnation comes upon them that they cannot long escape.

The newspaper proprietors will not be able to abide

their present choice much longer. A mayor speaks in Boston, an independent editor in Buffalo, a nationally-known educator in Iowa—steadily the accusation moves across the country. The issue converges, for the moment, on Chicago. Already, the experienced eye can see in the Chicago press the influence of the open letter of the *Christian Century* and such agitation as has followed its publication. With just a little more emphasis, a little more determination, a little more pressing home to the proprietors of their personal responsibility, the changes that public decency demands will be ordered. The issue cannot be avoided. Those who recognize its importance —and especially those in the Chicago area—are under moral bonds to see that it is pressed home.

THE YELLOW NEWSPAPER[4]

If all countries may boast the press which they deserve, America's desert is small indeed. No civilised country in the world has been content with newspapers so grossly contemptible as those which are read from New York to the Pacific Coast. The journals known as yellow would be a disgrace to the Black Republic, and it is difficult to understand the state of mind which can tolerate them. Divorced completely from the world of truth and intelligence, they present nothing which an educated man would desire to read. They are said to be excluded from clubs and from respectable houses. But even if this prohibition were a fact, their proprietors need feel no regret. We are informed by the yellowest of editors that his burning words are read every day by five million men and women.

What, then, is the aspect and character of these yellow journals? As they are happily strange on our side the ocean, they need some description. They are ill-printed, over-illustrated sheets, whose end and aim

[4] By Charles Whibley. *Blackwood's Magazine.* 181:531-8. April 1907.

are to inflame a jaded or insensitive palate. They seem to address the half-blind eye and the sluggish mind of the imbecile. The wholly unimportant information which they desire to impart is not conveyed in type of the ordinary shape and size. The "scare" headlines are set forth in letters three inches in height. It is as though the editors of these sheets are determined to exhaust your attention. They are not content to tell you that this or that inapposite event has taken place. They pant, they shriek, they yell. Their method represents the beating of a thousand big drums, the blare of unnumbered trumpets, the shouted blasphemies of a million raucous throats. And if, with all this noise dinning in your ear, you are persuaded to read a yellow sheet, which is commonly pink in colour, you are grievously disappointed. The thing is not even sensational. Its "scare" headlines do but arouse a curiosity which the "brightest and brainiest" reporter in the United States is not able to satisfy.

Of what happens in the great world you will find not a trace in the yellow journals. They betray no interest in politics, in literature, or in the fine arts. There is nothing of grave importance which can be converted into a "good story." That a great man should perform a great task is immaterial. Noble deeds make no scandal, and are therefore not worth reporting. But if you can discover that the great man has a hidden vice, or an eccentric taste in boots or hats, there is "copy" ready to your hand. All things and all men must be reduced to a dead level of imbecility. The yellow press is not obscene—it has not the courage for that. Its proud boast is that it never prints a line that a father might not read to his daughter. It is merely personal and impertinent. No one's life is secure from its spies. no privacy is sacred. Mr. Stead's famous ideal of an ear at every keyhole is magnificently realised in America. A hundred reporters are ready, at a moment's notice, to invade houses, to uncover secrets, to molest honest citizens with indiscreet questions. And if their victims are unwilling to respond, they pay for it with public insult and malicious invention. Those who will not bow to the common tyrant of the press cannot complain if words are ascribed to them which they never uttered, if they are held guilty of deeds from which they would shrink in horror. Law and custom are alike powerless to fight this tyranny, which is the most ingenious and irksome form of blackmail yet invented.

The perfect newspaper, if such were possible, would present to its readers a succinct history of each day as it passes. It would weigh with a scrupulous hand the relative importance of events. It would give to each department of human activity no more than its just space. It would reduce scandal within the narrow limits which ought to confine it. Under its wise auspices murder, burglary, and suicide would be deposed from the eminence upon which idle curiosity has placed them. Those strange beings known as public men would be famous not for what their wives wear at somebody's else's "At Home," but for their own virtues and attainments. The foolish actors and actresses, who now believe themselves the masters of the world, would slink away into *entrefilets* on a back page. The perfect newspaper, in brief, would resemble a Palace of Truth, in which deceit was impossible and vanity ridiculous. It would crush the hankerers after false reputations, it would hurl the imbecile from the mighty seats which they try to fill, and it would present an invaluable record to future generations.

What picture of its world does the yellow press present? A picture of colossal folly and unpardonable indiscretion. If there be a museum which preserves these screaming sheets, this is the sort of stuff which in two thousand years will puzzle the scholars: "Mrs. Jones won't admit Wedding," "Millionaires Bet on a Snake Fight," "Chicago Church Girl Accuses Millionaire," "Athletics make John D. forget his Money." These are a few pearls hastily strung together, and they show what jewels of intelligence are most highly prized by the greatest democracy on earth. Now and again the editor takes his readers into his confidence and asks them to interfere in the affairs of persons whom they will never know. Here, for instance, is a characteristic problem set by an editor whose knowledge of his public exceeds his respect for the decencies of life: "What Mrs. Washington ought to do. Her husband Wall Street Broker. Got tired of Her and Deserted. But Mrs. Washington, who still loves him dearly, Is determined to win him back. And here is the Advice of the Readers of this Journal." Is it not monstrous—this interference with the privacy of common citizens? And yet this specimen has an air of dignity compared with the grosser exploits of the hired eavesdropper. Not long since there appeared in a Sunday paper a full list, with portraits and biographies, of all the ladies in New York who are habitual drunkards. From which it is clear that the law of libel has sunk into oblivion, and that the cowhide is no longer a useful weapon.

The disastrous effect upon the people of such a press as I have described is obvious. It excites the nerves of the foolish, it presents a hideously false standard of life, it suggests that nobody is sacred for the omnipotent eavesdropper, and it preaches day after day at the top of its husky voice the gospel of snobbishness. But it is not merely the public manners which it degrades; it does its best to hamper the proper administration of the law. In America trial by journalism has long supplemented, and goes far to supplant, trial by jury. If a murder be committed its detection is not left to the officers of the police. A thousand reporters, cunning as monkeys, active as sleuthhounds, are on the track. Whether it is the criminal that they pursue or an innocent man is indifferent to them. Heedless of injustice, they go in search of "copy." They interrogate the friends of the victim, and they uncover the secrets of all the friends and relatives he may have possessed. They care not how they prejudice the public mind, or what wrong they do to innocent men. If they make a fair trial impossible, it matters not. They have given their tired readers a new sensation, they have stimulated gossip in a thousand tenement houses, and justice may fall in ruins so long as they sell another edition. And nobody protests against their unbridled licence, not even when they have made it an affair of the utmost difficulty and many weeks to empanel an unprejudiced jury.

The greatest opportunity of the yellow press came a brief year ago, when a Mr. H. K. Thaw murdered an accomplished architect. The day after the murder the trial began in the newspapers, and it has been "run as a serial" ever since. The lives of the murderer and his victim were uncovered with the utmost effrontery. The character of the dead man was painted in the blackest colours by cowards, who knew that they were secure from punishment. The murderer's friends and kinsmen were all compelled to pay their tribute to the demon of publicity. The people was presented with plans of the cell in which the man Thaw was imprisoned while photographs of his wife and his mother were printed day after day that a silly mob might note the effect of anguish on the human countenance. And, not content with thus adorning the tale, the journals were eloquent in pointing the moral. Sentimental spinsters were invited to warn the lady typewriters of America that death and ruin inevitably overtake the wrongdoer. Stern-eyed clergymen thought well to anticipate justice in sermons addressed to erring youth. Finally, a *plébiscite* decided, by 2 to 1, that Thaw should immediately be set free. And when you remember the arrogant tyranny of the yellow journals, you are surprised that at the mere sound of the people's voice the prison doors did not instantly fly open.

You are told, as though it were no more than a simple truth, that the yellow press—the journals owned by Mr. Hearst—not merely made the Spanish-American War, but procured the assassination of Mr. McKinley. The statement seems incredible, because it is difficult to believe that such stuff as these should have any influence either for good or evil. The idle gossip and flagrant scandal which are its daily food do not appear to be efficient leaders of opinion. But it is the editorial columns which do the work of conviction, and they assume an air of gravity which may easily deceive the unwary. And their gravity is the natural accompaniment of scandal. There is but a slender difference between barbarity and sentimentalism. The same temper which delights in reading of murder and sudden death weeps with anguish at the mere hint of oppression. No cheek is so easily bedewed by the unnecessary tear as the cheek of the ruffian—and those who compose the "editorials" for Mr. Hearst's papers have cynically realised this truth. They rant and they cant and they argue, as though nothing but noble thoughts were permitted to lodge within the poor brains of their readers. Their favourite gospel is the gospel of Socialism. They tell the workers that the world is their inalienable inheritance, that skill and capital are the snares of the evil one, and that nothing is worth a reward save manual toil. They pretend for a moment to look with a kindly eye upon the Trusts, because, when all enterprises and industries are collected into a small compass, the people will have less trouble in laying hands upon them. In brief, they teach the supreme duty of plunder in all the *staccato* eloquence at their command. For the man whose thrift and energy have helped him to success they have nothing but contempt. They cannot think of the criminal without bursting into tears. And, while they lay upon the rich man the guilty burden of his wealth, they charge the community with the full responsibility for the convict's misfortune. Such doctrines, insidiously taught, and read day after day by the degenerate and unrestrained, can only have one effect, and that effect, no doubt, the "editorials" of the yellow press will some day succeed in producing.

The result is, of course, revolution, and revolution is being carefully and insidiously prepared after the common fashion. Not a word is left unsaid that can flatter the criminal or encourage the thriftless. Those who are too idle to work but not too idle to read the Sunday papers are told that the wealth of the country is theirs, and it will be the fault of their own inaction, not of the yellow press, if they do not some day lay violent hands upon it. And when they are tired of politics the yellow editors turn to popular philosophy or cheap theology for the solace of the public. To men and women excited by the details of the last murder they discourse of the existence of God in short, crisp sentences,—and I know not which is worse, the triviality of the discourse or its inappositeness. They preface one of their most impassioned exhortations with the words: "If you read this, you will probably think you have wasted time." This might with propriety stand for the motto of all the columns of all Mr. Hearst's journals, but here it is clearly used in the same hope which inspires the sandwichman to carry on his front the classic legend: "Please do not look on my back." But what is dearest to the souls of these editors is a mean commonplace. One leader, which surely had a triumphant success, is headed, "What the Bar-tender Sees." And the exordium is worthy so profound a speculation. "Did you ever stop to think," murmurs the yellow philosopher, "of all the strange beings that pass before him?" There's profundity for you! There's invention! Is it wonderful that five million men and women read these golden words, or others of a like currency, every day?

And politics, theology, and philosophy are all served up in the same thick sauce of sentiment. The "baby" seems to play a great part in the yellow morality. One day you are told, "A baby can educate a man;" on another you read, "Last week's baby will surely talk some day," and you are amazed, as at a brilliant discovery. And you cannot but ask, To whom are these exhortations addressed? To children or to idiots? The grown men and women, even of Cook County, can hardly regard such poor twaddle as this with a serious eye. And what of the writers? How can they reconcile their lofty tone, which truly is above suspicion, with the shameful sensationalism of their news-columns? They know not the meaning of sincerity. If they believed that "last week's baby would talk some day," they would suppress their reporters. In short, they are either blind or cynical. From these alternatives there is no escape, and for their sakes, as well as for America's, I hope they write with their tongue in their cheeks.

The style of the yellow journals is appropriate to their matter. The headlines live on and by the historic present, and the text is as bald as a paper of statistics. It is the big type that does the execution. The "story" itself, to use the slang of the newspaper, is seldom either humorous or picturesque. Bare facts and vulgar incidents are enough for the public, which cares as little for wit as for sane writing. One fact only can explain the imbecility of the yellow press: it is written for immigrants, who have but an imperfect knowledge of English, who prefer to see their news rather than to read it, and who, if they must read, can best understand words of one syllable and sentences of no more than five words.

For good or evil, America has the sole claim to the invention of the yellow press. It came, fully armed, from the head of its first proprietor. It owes nothing to Europe, nothing to the traditions of its own country. It grew out of nothing, and, let us hope, it will soon disappear into nothingness. The real press of America was rather red than yellow. It had an energy and a character which still exist in some more reputable sheets, and which are the direct antithesis of yellow sensationalism. The horsewhip and revolver were as necessary to its conduct as the pen and inkpot. If the editors of an older and wiser time insulted their enemies, they were ready to defend themselves, like men. They did not eavesdrop and betray.

They would have scorned to reveal the secrets of private citizens, even though they did not refrain their hand from their rivals. Yet, with all their brutality, they were brave and honourable, and you cannot justly measure the degradation of the yellow press unless you cast your mind a little farther back and contemplate the achievement of another generation.

The tradition of journalism came to America from England. *The Sun, The Tribune,* and *The Post,* as wise and trustworthy papers as may be found on the surface of the globe, are still conscious of their origin, though they possess added virtues of their own. The *New York Herald,* as conducted by James Gordon Bennett the First, modelled its scurrilous energy upon the press of our own eighteenth century. The influence of Junius and the pamphleteers was discernible in its columns, and many of its articles might have been signed by Wilkes himself. But there was something in *The Herald* which you would seek in vain in Perry's *Morning Chronicle,* say, or *The North Briton,* and that was the free-and-easy style of the backwoods. Gordon Bennett grasped as well as any one the value of news. He boarded vessels far out at sea that he might forestall his rivals. In some respects he was as "yellow" as his successor, whose great exploit of employing a man convicted of murder to report the trial of a murderer is not likely to be forgotten. On the other hand, he set before New York the history of Europe and of European thought with appreciation and exactitude. He knew the theatre of England and France more intimately than most of his contemporaries, and he did a great deal to encourage the art of acting in his own country. But above all things he was a fighter, both with pen and fist. He had something of the spirit which inspired the old mining-camp. "We never saw the man we feared," he once said, "nor the woman we had not some liking for." That healthy, if primitive, sentiment breathes in all his works. And his magnanimity was equal to his courage. "I have no objection to forgive enemies," he wrote, "particularly after I have trampled them under my feet." This principle guided his life and his journal, and, while it gave a superb dash of energy to his style, it put a wholesome fear into the hearts and heads of his antagonists.

One antagonist there was who knew neither fear nor forgetfulness, and he attacked Bennett again and again. Bennett returned his blows, and then made most admirable "copy" of the assault. The last encounter between the two is so plainly characteristic of Bennett's style that I quote his description in his own words. "As I was leisurely pursuing my business yesterday in Wall Street," wrote Bennett, "collecting the information which is daily disseminated in *The Herald,* James Watson Webb came up to me, on the northern side of the street—said something which I could not hear distinctly, then pushed me down the stone steps leading to one of the brokers' offices, and commenced fighting with a species of brutal and demoniac desperation characteristic of a fury. My damage is a scratch, about three-quarters of an inch in length, on the third finger of the left hand, which I received from the iron railing I was forced against, and three buttons torn from my vest, which my tailor will reinstate for six cents. His loss is a rent from top to bottom of a very beautiful black coat, which cost the ruffian $40, and a blow in the face which may have knocked down his throat some of his infernal teeth for all I know. Balance in my favour $39.94. As to intimidating me, or changing my course, the thing cannot be done. Neither Webb nor any other man shall, or can, intimidate me. . . . I may be attacked, I may be assailed, I may be killed, I may be murdered, but I will never succumb."

There speaks the true Gordon Bennett, and his voice, though it may be the voice of a ruffian, is also the voice of a man who is certainly courageous and is not without humour. It is not from such a tradition as that, that the yellow press emerged. It does not want much pluck to hang about and sneak secrets. It is the pure negation of humour to preach socialism in the name of the criminal and degenerate. And the yellow press owes its vices to none of its predecessors, but to its own inherent stupidity. To judge America by this product would be monstrously unfair, but it corresponds perforce to some baser quality in the cosmopolitans of the United States, and it cannot be overlooked. As it stands, it is the heaviest indictment of the popular taste that can be made. There is no vice so mean as impertinent curiosity, and it is upon this curiosity that the yellow press meanly lives and meanly thrives.

What is the remedy? There is none, unless time brings with it a natural reaction. It is as desperate a task to touch the press as to change the Constitution. The odds against reform are too great. A law to check the exuberance of newspapers would never survive the attacks of the newspapers themselves. Nor is it only in America that reform is necessary. The press of Europe, also, has strayed so far from its origins as to be a danger to the State. In their inception the newspapers were given freedom, that they might expose and check the corruption and dishonesty of politicians. It was thought that publicity was the best cure for intrigue. For a while the liberty of the press seemed justified. It is justified no longer. The licence which it assumed has led to far worse evils than those which it was designed to prevent. In other words, the slave has become a tyrant, and where is the statesman who shall rid us of this tyranny? Failure alone can kill what lives only upon popular success, and it is the old-fashioned, self-respecting journals which are facing ruin. Prosperity is with the large circulations, and a large circulation is no test of merit. Success is made neither by honesty nor wisdom. The people will buy what flatters its vanity or appeals to its folly. And the yellow press will flourish, with its headlines and its vulgarity, until the mixed population of America has sufficiently mastered the art of life and the

English tongue to demand something better wherewith to solace its leisure than scandal and imbecility.

GUTTER LITERATURE[5]

Have you looked over the wares displayed on an average news-stand lately? If not, there is a surprise in store for you. Within the last year or two a whole new type of periodical literature has sprung up in this country—most of it new in substance and all of it new in that it is now displayed openly where anyone, of any age, who possesses the requisite ten or twenty cents, may walk up and buy. The simplest, most accurate phrase by which to describe it is "gutter literature." Taken in the mass, it represents a social phenomenon of decided importance, which merits far more attention than it is getting.

The circulations of these new magazines run up into the millions; and some of them are still increasing, and rapidly. Fresh titles appear almost daily, seeking to outdo one another in sensationalism, vulgarity and often in obscenity, obscenity which either veils itself behind an affectation of smug moralizing, or openly and unashamedly appeals to the sex instinct at its worst—by which I mean, to passion without any hint of love, to casual promiscuity, which is described in terms of glitter and excitement as aphrodisiac as possible—and as false to the truth.

These magazines fall into various groups, which, while all more or less similar, should for the sake of clarity be discussed separately. One of the commonest is the risqué story group. It consists exclusively of fiction, corresponding more or less to what the "French farce" is on the stage. The formula on which these stories are based is well standardized, though variations in outcome are permissible. Let a woman be exposed to

[5] By Ernest W. Mandeville. *New Republic*. 45:350-2. February 17, 1926.

a sex danger, either at the hands of a brutal and unscrupulous male or under the excitation of her own overpowering and all-devouring passion. She may then either successfully resist the aforesaid dastardly male, or may succumb to the compelling passion. In either case (and here is the meat of the matter) the author must see to it that she emerges a better and nobler woman, who has been lifted to a new and almost excruciatingly fine moral plane because of the experience she has undergone.

To be sure, this formula is not original. It has been in use in literature of this general type for many years. Never, however, has it been brought to the pitch of perfection found to-day; and never have the authors and publishers been so brazen in the open distribution of their wares.

I do not know how I can describe the general tone of these magazines better than in the following words of one of their editors. The document quoted is his letter of instructions to his authors:

A Few Hints

I intend to keep—a sex magazine, but sex need not necessarily mean dirt. I want to stick to elementals, sex-elementals—the things closest to the heart of the average woman or girl, whatever her ignorance or sophistication. Above all, I mean to lift the moral tone of the magazine. I believe that to treat sex trivially is to diminish its dramatic value, while sober treatment enhances it. Characters may do anything they please but they must do it from some lofty, or apparently lofty, motive. If a girl falls, she must fall *upward.*

I am particularly partial to the story attacking conventional morals, exposing their hypocrisy and pointing to a higher standard. And the moral of a story need not be the conventional one: it can be personal, original, even weird, if it can be put over as superior to existent morality.

I also like stories of "bad" women who, judged by a higher standard, are really quite good.

The dramatization of some moral theme, of a moral standard, of a moral vogue, will always interest me.

In foreign stories, I mean to stick for the moment, to the type of story bringing out dramatically some point in which the foreign attitude towards sex differs from ours. In other words, how the French girl, for instance, meets her special sex problems and how these differ from the American girl's. Only foreign stories featuring the element, playing on the American girl's curiosity about Old World morality, as compared with her own, will interest me at the present time.

EDITOR.

The pressure on authors for sex stories instead of other material is evidenced by the following ingenuous statement by the Ten Story Book in the Writers' Market Department of a literary trade journal, the *Writers' Digest*:

We will, in the future, pay on acceptance for all sex stories and said acceptance will be made within a week of receipt of manuscript, or same will be returned to author. Non-sex stories, of which we are far less in need, will be paid for on publication as in the past.

A few titles from magazines of the risqué story group will indicate their general atmosphere better than any amount of description at second-hand:

RED EXPERIENCES WITH MODELS

ONE, TWO, THREE—OUT!

One man leads to another in the hectic life of the pretty flapper.

APHRODITE'S GUESTS

If you've forgotten your mythology, Aphrodite—more widely known as Venus—was the hot mamma of goddesses.

NONO STEPS OUT

JUST AN ICE GIRL

A sizzling pink phosphate or a cold gin fizz—what'll you have?

The ten chief exemplars of this sort of thing last year reached a combined circulation of a million copies of each issue. And they are still growing.

Another new and enormously popular type of periodical is the "confession" magazine. Its contents are invariably written in the first person. They are labeled genuine, though in reality they are, of course, produced professionally under formula. Since they are very easy to do, no plot technique or writing skill being necessary, a whole new crop of "authors" has sprung up to produce the grist for these hungry mills. Editorial advice from the office of one such journal, typical of all, is as follows:

> Here's a man, see? And his wife, see? And another man. Write about that. And let the shadow of a bed be on every page but never let the bed appear.

These magazines pride themselves—oh, so earnestly and incessantly!—on their morality. No matter how wicked a girl may be during the exciting days about which she confesses, she must always have reformed and learned her lesson before the final paragraph is reached. One of the organs of this type, lest in some unhappy instance the formula might fail, has a body of selected (sic) ministers pass upon every story before publication.

Once in a blue moon, of course, a genuine confession does find its way into these endless pages of turgid, sentimental slush. There is some justification, in fact, for the new proverb: "The wages of sin is a check from a confession magazine." Generally speaking, however, the standardized fictitious product proves more satisfactory to the editors than the real thing. Fiction is stranger than truth. Also, it is easier to get into the product which is manufactured on the premises just the right proportion of salaciousness, just the proper leering smirk, to be succeeded when the psychological moment arrives by the pious demureness of the brand clutched from the burning.

Take a look at the title page of a typical issue, and then see whether it is any wonder that shop girls cry for it:

WHAT A WOMAN WANTS

She feared to lose her girlish charms, then—

TWO WIVES AND ONE ROOF

Can a man love two women at the same time?

WHAT I NEVER EXPECTED

A familiar love story with a new final chapter.

The Cost of Cheating
He found the injury was to himself alone.

The Wages of Sin
Out of the depths came a nobler womanhood.

The Mother Heart
A soul that was torn between two loves.

Blind Love
She watched and prayed for his coming until—

Women With a Past
And the trick of fate that brought them together.

The Shadow of Her Sin
It returned to darken her late life.

Confessions of a Crook
A story of life in prison and out.

Murder Will Out
She thought her youth's secret forever hidden, but—

The Girl Between
Who almost shattered a young wife's happiness.

The Heart of a Hunchback
The tale of one who thwarted nature's cruelty.

Take Bond of Blood
Proving that it's a small world after all.

My Twice Wed Husband
Vows that were broken and mended again.

Love's Tragedy
What happened to the girl he left behind him.

The growth of magazines of this character is almost unbelievable. One of them started about four years ago with an initial print order of a little more than 100,000 copies. It has now passed the two million mark. There are several imitators, and while none has quite equalled this achievement, most of them have succeeded in attaining figures which in any other journalistic field would be regarded as phenomenally large.

Another distinct group which should not be overlooked is that which provides as its chief fare what might be called "smoking-car anecdotes." Barnyard humor, pleasantries of the high-school debauches, fly-specked, off-color jokes are the principal items. These publications are small in size, badly printed on cheap paper and very expensive, which facts do not prevent their having a sale which runs into many thousands.

Another important group is made up of straight-out imitations of the famous and naughty Vie Parisienne. The drawings are similar to those in the French original. This type of paper differs from most of the others under discusion in that its text is somewhat sophisticated, and a slight degree of intelligence on the part of the reader is necessary. On the whole, however, as the calculations show, there is more salacious excitement to be got from the pages of the purely home-grown product.

The newest and one of the most popular of the cycle of publications which base their appeal definitely on sex is the "art magazine." Of these we have had a deluge in the past year.

Their publishers are extremely moral men, and their only aim, according to their own editorial announcements, is "to bring reproductions of the old masters within the reach of the populace." However, even a low grade moron ought to be able, after glancing through the pages of a single issue, to realize that this is only camouflage; and I cannot imagine why this pretense is kept up unless it be for protection in case of court action. These magazines have one idea and one alone: the portrayal of nudity. Some of the pictures, it is true, are reproductions from art galleries; but just as many more are photographs of self-conscious chorus girls. In other words, the appeal of these periodicals is no more nor less than that in the old-fashioned "French picture postcards" which used to be offered for sale at two for a quarter—"mailed to you in a plain envelope."

Some time ago complaints were made against some of the periodicals of this character. The publicity in the papers promptly boosted the circulation until one of them, selling at a very high price, is now printing 200,000 copies of each issue.

Some of my readers may be surprised to know that a majority of all the publications I have been discussing are planned by their publishers for women readers. Rightly or wrongly, the editors believe that the ladies are more voluminous print-consumers than the men, even when it comes to stuff of this sort. While there are some of these periodicals which seek to interest men and boys, there are three times as many which do not.

Most of these journals, of course, and particularly the very popular confessional type, base their appeal on the fact that for the average man, and even more, for the average woman, leading the common existence in this country, only partially literate, with limited financial resources, real life is a drab, dull, and sordid affair. For such individuals the keenest pleasure, and almost the only pleasure, comes with temporary escape into a world of illusion and fantasy, wherein they can identify themselves with the imaginary heroes and heroines whose life experience is satisfactory in every point where their own is not. For this reason, the literature of escape which these magazines offer in such direct and simple form makes a powerful appeal, and one which it would be very difficult to break down. It is perhaps also for this reason that moral reformers, so busy with other aspects of our national life, have almost entirely ignored the growth of these new periodicals. After all, the malady does not lie in the willingness of publishers to pander nor that of readers to be pandered to. In part at least it is a malady of our civilization itself.

THOSE TERRIBLE TABLOIDS[6]

"Excuse me for a moment," said the young lady I had met by appointment in the Times Square subway station. "I simply can't get along without my daily installment of *Kraft-Ebbing*."

Whereupon she stepped over to a news stand and purchased a copy of one of New York's famous, or rather, infamous, tabloid newspapers. I mention the incident because it may help to explain the daily 1,250,000 circulation of Manhattan's picture press. It is difficult to believe that one-half of the population of the nation's greatest metropolis is one hundred per cent moron, but that is indicated by the circulation statistics of such an impartial organization as the Audit Bureau of Circulations. If a Rabelaisian sense of humor does not account for a large percentage of tabloid readers, then there is nothing to do but repeat the observation of Samuel Clemens that he certainly did love the human race, but there were times when he wished he had it concentrated in the Ark again—and he with an auger.

The picture newspaper made its bow to America immediately after the war. Its compactness as compared with the bulkiness of the standard newspapers, and its condensation of news items, were features copied from the *London Daily Mirror*. But there, at least so far as New York is concerned, the resemblance to the London paper ended. The amazing success of the pioneer tabloid inspired others to enter the field. In some cities these publications are edited with decency and constitute merely an interesting experiment in American journalism. In Manhattan they are an unholy blot on the fourth estate—bawdy, inane, and contemptible. To paraphrase the slogan of a noted newspaper, they carry "all the news that isn't fit to print." With the proverbial fine-tooth comb the world is curried for the salacious, intimate details of human nature

[6] By Samuel T. Moore. *Independent*. 116:264-6. March 6, 1926.

at its lowest. The sordid facts are distorted and then clothed in bromides and banalities of that school of fiction popularized by such writers as Laura Jean Libby and Bertha M. Clay.

There have been few protests against the deepening quagmire of journalistic muck and filth. Of all the legitimate metropolitan journals only the New York *World* has spoken out. The reason for the general silence is that the scurvy tabloids hide beneath the cloak of the constitutional guaranty, freedom of the press. The strategy succeeds, for every newspaper is bound by tradition to tolerate no compromise with that principle.

But there is one great danger inherent in the situation. Sound finances are an essential of any publication, and the pornographic press is a great success commercially. Will the dirty tabloids make such inroads on the reputable newspapers that the latter will be obliged to elaborate on the indecent and unsavory happenings of the day in order to hold their readers? God forbid!

Accuracy, the watchword of every reputable journal, has no place in the tabloid lexicon. Distortion, exaggeration, and undisciplined imagination are the trinity substituted therefor. Here is an example: An errand boy in a Bronx drug store is sent with a bottle of whiskey to an aged customer, a widow. He is perhaps seventeen years old and in every way a normal youth. To be sure he was a violator of the Volstead Act,—though an innocent one,—because the contraband was procured without a legal prescription. While he was making the delivery in the mean tenement, the recipient was fatally stricken with a cerebral hemorrhage and fell, striking her head against a table. The frightened boy summoned neighbors. The police responded, and and a detective decided to hold him for questioning. Such might be the actual facts of the tragedy.

It is a dull night in the editorial sanctums of the tabloids. True, that very day the Locarno pact may have been ratified, or the President may have sent a special message to Congress urging repeal of the tariff. But that is scarcely big news for a tabloid. The city news ticker revives hope for the morrow's edition as it brings the facts that a widow has been found dead somewhere in the Bronx and a boy is held for questioning. An army of "leg men" and photographers is dispatched to the scene, and

BOY BOOTLEG KING HELD IN DEATH PROBE

blares forth on the next edition of the tabloids.

The squalid room where the old woman died is described as "a love-nest of Oriental splendor and luxury." The pint of liquor is the excuse for making the unfortunate errand boy a member of criminal royalty. He is probably described as "a dapper, insouciant youth, dressed in the height of fashion and contemptuous of the serious charge overshadowing him."

Perhaps some energetic reporter learns that the boy often took the daughter of a neighbor to a motion-picture show or to a neighborhood dance hall. If the girl happened to be a graduate of a parochial school, and if her father was a postman, she is described as "the beautiful, charming, convent-bred daughter of a prominent government official." Without running foul of the libel laws, the reporter proceeds to develop the suspicion of intrigue, and the young woman is represented as "distracted by news of her fiancé's duplicity." There are pictures, too, of all the principals, and a staff artist is hastily commissioned to sketch a series of drawings showing how a career of crime never pays. Such is tabloid distortion.

The *Daily News,* pioneer in the field, is the property of the same men who own the *Chicago Tribune.* It was started in 1919, as a journalistic experiment, with earnings of the Tribune corporation which otherwise must have been paid to the Government as excess profits. The spectacular success attending the venture was noted by William Randolph Hearst, who after some none too encouraging preliminaries with the *Boston Ad-*

vertiser in tabloid form, launched the *Daily Mirror* in New York. He was quickly followed by that eminent exponent of physical culture, Mr. Bernarr MacFadden, whose fortunes have prospered in the manufacture and retailing of such paradoxical merchandise as "true fiction." His New York offering is the *Evening Graphic,* and he recently secured control of one of Philadelphia's tabloid papers.

In some ways the tabloids might be truthfully classified as a foreign-language press. *Homo sapiens* is invariably a "sheik," a "fiend," or a "magnate" of whatever commodity he deals in. Feminine figures in the tabloid news are always, "young and beautiful." If they are not "poor moths," "broken butterflies," or some rich man's "toy," they are, "shebas" or "red-hot mammas." Love is a hyphenated adjective in all-important headlines—as, for example, "love-pact," "love-nest," "love-child," "love-thief," "love-slayer," "love-cheat." Any social festivity is *ipso facto* an "orgy," and other favorite headline trimmings are the words "nude," "shame," "scarlet," and "probe."

The camera work takes on the same coloring, with effects that are often ludicrous. Ostensibly sorrowing women, victims of man's ruthless passions, must always be posed smiling, with their dresses elevated as far above the knees as possible—or, better still, in one-piece bathing suits or as semi-nude studies. When tragedy stalks a family the photographer and the "picture-hound" are dispatched on its trail. Miserable parents, grieving over the death or the disappearance of a child, suffer the disturbance of their privacy to pose with handkerchiefs at their eyes or to register sorrow before a photograph of the lost one.

Axes, pistols, and other implements of crime are highly esteemed as illustrations, and every captured criminal must be photographed chained to a detective or else posed in the embrace of some woman passionately declaring her loyalty. Another much prized expression of tabloid art lies in pictures of dead bodies on the street awaiting removal, or of bandage-swathed victims of accident or attack propped on their couches of pain. Perhaps the most sickening exhibition of this sort occurred in connection with a train wreck on Williamsburg Bridge. The photograph of a mere infant lying on a hospital cot carried a caption claiming high enterprise in journalistic efficiency—since the little victim died three hours after the picture was taken. But the 1925 medal for pornographic art was won by Mr. MacFadden's journal, which, during the Rhinelander annulment suit, reproduced by means of a composite picture the plight of the dusky bride standing all but naked before judge and jurors.

Criminals are frequently glorified; and when a woman is the central figure in a case the keenest sort of competition arises as to which of the tabloids will win "her own story"—the story being written by a staff reporter, with a reproduction at the top of the unfortunate's autograph.

But there is more in the tabloids than mere news and pictures. There are the most banal of "comic" strips, advice to the lovelorn, and chats about almost everything pertaining to the foibles of the gentler sex. There are daily "true fiction" stories and serials. I quote two titles from the paper before me: *The Love Cowards* and *Does Virtue Pay?* The literary quality is in keeping with the titles.

And then, the contests! Each of the tabloids is a prize-giving institution, and competition among the three is acrimonious and terrible. The *Mirror* boasts at present of running twelve contests simultaneously. Here they are:

First there is the "Look Like Mike" contest. "Mike" is a moving picture, and the girl who bears the closest resemblance to the heroine wins a cash prize. Next comes a "Comic Cipher" contest; "Ideal Marriages" is the third, the daily prize going to that reader who offers the best list of qualities for an ideal helpmeet. The "Red

Kimona" contest is another motion-picture exploitation stunt; the prize winners are those who put up the best arguments as to why a fallen woman may or may not become a useful member of society.

Havyer Got The Havyers?
Get 'Em And Win Cash

That is the editorial greeting over the next contest. The current first-prize winner wrote, "Havyer ever seen a barn swallowing?" So much for that. Others are "Embarrassing Moments," "Stingiest Persons," "Cutest Sayings," "Lafs," "Recipes," and "Dog Adoption." The majority of the offerings are personal anecdotes, and banality is obviously the measure of merit. The contests that are the most popular offer a stage career or chances for screen try-outs.

There are crusades, too. Mr. MacFadden's *Graphic* recently conducted an aggressive exposé of alleged fraud in the Atlantic City Bathing Girl Pageant. The bathing girls, of course, "ate it up." The *Mirror* is now waging a crusade with the slogan, "Why Don't You Get Married?" Before this it led a drive against the "subway sheiks," or alleged mashers. If memory serves aright there was also a movement to expel moral lepers from the city. If that campaign had been successful, what would have happened to the circulation of the tabloids?

There you have New York's picture papers. They are not friendly rivals; they constantly bicker and snap at one another in their editorials and news columns. Charges of bad faith and of poor taste in presenting "news" ring out in each issue along with boastful proclamations of exclusive triumphs in pornographic art and letters. If you have a good stout stomach, it sometimes amuses; generally, it nauseates.

There is one thing to be said for the tabloids. Never, so far as is known, have these purveyors of journalistic filth engaged in blackmail. But nobody, high or low, is immune from their peering and prying, and when they succeed in spotting an act of moral turpitude they fall upon it with cries of joy. Such is the postwar trend in Manhattan journalism; may common decency rise against it!

THE POWER OF YELLOW JOURNALISM[1]

The power of making war in a democracy must always, in the last resort, no matter what the constitutional arrangements may be, reside in the mass of the people. When war breaks out it is really brought about by the influences which have acted most powerfully on the popular mind in its favor. These influences are, in the main, the speaking and the writing which precede the war or bring it about. In default of other influences, the power of moulding opinion is passing,—in fact, has long since passed—into the hands of the press. As a strange fate would have it, too, the subject on which the very worst portion of the press exerts most influence is war. The fomenting of war and the publication of mendacious accounts of war have, in fact, become almost a special function of that portion of the press which is known as "yellow journals." The war increases their circulation immensely. They profit enormously by what inflicts sorrow and loss on the rest of the community. They talk incessantly of war, not in the way of instruction, but simply to excite by false news, and stimulate savage passions by atrocious suggestions. On some days they seem to have issued from an Iriquois village in war time, rather than from a Christian city. Read this clipped from a recent number of one of them, which claims a circulation of over a million copies every day:

Occasionally we hear croaks from peace men. "How sad to kill sons and fathers of sad-eyed women," they say. No sadder than to kill cousins and aunts of sad-eyed rattlesnakes. The man who would object to this [Spanish] war would object to the wholesale destruction of poisonous reptiles in India. And

[1] From the *Nation*. 66:336. May 5, 1898.

as for the American who has any feeling about the war other than a red-hot desire to hear of victories and Spanish ships sunk, all we can say is that he reminds us of the cannibal toad now on exhibition in the Paris Jardin d'Acclimation.

Now the characteristic of these papers, which so powerfully influence opinion, is that they are, for the first time in American history, an irresponsible force, and the only one in the state. Every other influence in the community, not openly criminal, acknowledges some sort of restraint. The gamblers and policy-dealers live in fear of the police. The vendors of obscene literature all have Anthony Comstock before their eyes. The dishonest business men live in dread of the loss of reputation or credit. Nearly every person prominent in any walk of life works under the control of something in the shape of conscience. There are some things he does, or does not do, because his own heart tells him they would be wrong. Even our Congressmen stand in awe of their constituents. Statesmen recoil from violating the constitution. Professional men dread the opinion of their professional brethren. It would be difficult to name any body of men, pursuing a calling not openly criminal, who do not live and labor under some sort of discipline, seen or unseen, which constantly reminds them that they, too, have duties which they must perform, or suffer in some way.

From every such discipline or restraint, except libel suits, the yellow journalist is absolutely free. His one object is to circulate widely and make money. And he does circulate widely. He treats war as a prize-fight, and begets in hundreds of thousands of the class which enjoys prize-fights an eager desire to hear about it. These hundreds of thousands write to their Congressman clamoring for war, as the Romans used to clamor for *panem et circenses;* and as the timid and quiet are generally attending only too closely to their business, the Congressman concludes that if he, too, does not shout for war, he will lose his seat.

This is an absolutely new state of things. In none of our former wars did anything like the modern press play any part. In the Mexican war we even had a powerful anti-slavery press fighting vigorously for peace and justice, and not to forget a great name, we had Lowell on the same side. The conservative, pro-slavery papers of that day, like the Washington *Intelligencer,* were gentlemanly, sober-minded sheets, still influenced by the old traditions of constitutional logic-chopping. In the Civil War, too, the great newspapers were serious publications. Our cheap press today speaks in tones never before heard out of Paris. It urges upon ignorant people schemes more savage, disregard of either policy or justice or experience more complete, than the modern world has witnessed since the French Revolution. It is true it addresses the multitude mainly or only. The wise and learned and the pious and industrious do not read it. But it is the multitude mainly, and not the wise and learned and industrious, who now set fleets and armies in motion, who impose silence and acquiesence on all as soon as the word "war" is mentioned, and insist successfully that they shall not be interfered with, by either voice or vote, until they have had their fill of fighting. They have already established a regime in which a blackguard boy with several millions of dollars at his disposal has more influence on the use a great nation may make of its credit, of its army and navy, of its name and traditions, than all the statesmen and philosophers and professors in the country. If this does not supply food for reflection about the future of the nation to thoughtful men, it must be because the practice of reflection has ceased.

It is hardly possible to drop the subject without a word about the way in which men supposed to be thoughtful and far-seeing help these very agencies which are robbing them every year more and more of their legitimate influence on the affairs of the nation. There appears to be hardly a clergyman, statesman, or lawyer in the country who does not denounce the yellow journals, and deplore their influence on the young and ignorant, and yet, whenever a yellow journal finds it desirable for advertising purposes to give itself a look of respectability, it does not find much difficulty in getting our prominent public teachers and moralists to comply with a request, fortified by a yellow check drawn on the proceeds of humbug and villainy, to sanctify their columns with discourses on morality, patriotism, and religion. This is due partly to fear and partly to vanity. The fear is that the yellow journal may, as it says, "alter its opinion about them"—that is, blackguard them vigorously and call them names for a week or two. The vanity comes from a delicious belief that anything which appears from their pens anywhere is sure to convince the yellow reader of his sin. It is very like a discourse of Marat from the Duc de la Rochefoucault, on "liberty, equality, and fraternity."

THE DANGEROUS PRESS [8]

The Hall-Mills case has again illustrated the mischief that can be done by an unscrupulous newspaper. The power of the press to injure individuals and deceive the public is stupendous and its immunity almost complete. Not a single daily can plead "not guilty" to the charge of misrepresenting facts. The substitution of opinion or sensation for news may be confined to trivial matters to make a good story, which even the dignified New York *Evening Post* justifies, or it may assume serious proportions like the transposed report of Senator La Follette's speech for which the Associated Press tardily apologized, or the fraudulent tales of atrocities admittedly fabricated by the editor of the *Providence Journal,* or the continued false reports from Russia by the *New York Times* after their errors had been exposed, or the anachronistic photographs deceitfully published by the *Chicago Tribune.*

News is often manufactured in editorial offices, usually around a foundation of actual occurrences but occasionally based only upon the desires of the pub-

[8] *Arbitrator.* 9:4. January 1927.

lishers. Everyone has observed the discrepancies in accounts of incidents that he has himself witnessed. It will not suffice to say, as editors and apologists do, that the errors are accidental, due to the haste with which papers must be prepared and the difficulty of fact-finding. Those accidental errors are forgivable and do comparatively little harm. The wonder is there are not more of them. It is the intentional deception by actual falsehood, by inference, by omission or coloration of news that causes unnecessary disaster.

The New York *Daily Mirror* was the chief offender by instigating the recent murder trial that cost Somerset County, New Jersey, $35,000; that held Harry Carpender incarcerated for four months awaiting a trial that never took place; that kept in jail Henry Stevens, charged with murdering a woman of whom he had never heard, and Willie Stevens who had done nothing to arouse suspicion; that persecuted Mrs. Hall with insinuations and publicity though no evidence was produced to show any knowledge on her part of the affair that cost her husband his life; and that necessitated the expenditure of a fortune by unjustly accused persons. All this agony and expense was suffered by innocent people because of false reports spread by the press.

That the *Mirror* planned the sensation to increase its circulation rather than to secure justice is probable in view of the methods employed. The only evidence produced since the failure of the Grand Jury to indict four years before was doctored evidence. The only eye-witness was the same pig woman whose identification by moonlight, or the flash of headlights, of persons at that time unknown to her was properly deemed impossible. The excuse for reviving the case was the statement of Diehl that his wife had said she had been bribed to keep silent. Though Mrs. Diehl promptly denied ever having made such a statement, the *Mirror* had Mrs. Hall arrested in the night so that it could have an exclusive beat in the next morning's edition. All the new evidence was merely rumor, false rumor fanned by the press until public suspicion was aroused and the Governor appointed a special prosecutor to prove that Jersey justice would not tolerate immunity bought by the rich. Alexander Simpson, the prosecutor, was a sensational man whose ambition run away with his common-sense. No jury could have credited the witnesses porduced by the State. No proof of guilt was forthcoming except a finger print on a card that had been found near the bodies of the murdered pair. That card had been in the possession of the *Mirror* for some time. Previously no finger print had been observed on it. Many papers during the trial insinuated guilt from evidence that did not warrant it and falsely reported statements made by witnesses.

As Hearst boasted to Frederic Remington that he could bring on the Spanish War, so some enterprising sheet may involve us in war with Mexico or Japan or England if steps are not taken to prevent the daily falsifications that become a habit and lead the press to extend its misrepresentations to political and international affairs.

Why not have a law making wilful misrepresentation of fact a misdeameanor? Proof of intentional fabrication would be simpler than in a libel suit. The district attorney could soon make it unprofitable for any paper to misrepresent the common occurrences of daily life, and a more truthful attitude would be adopted throughout the editorial world.

In other civilized countries people unjustly accused of crime are indemnified to a certain extent for the expense of their defense. The British Parliament has awarded as high as $25,000. Our states of Wisconsin and California allow an indemnity not to exceed $5,000 in any case of erroneous conviction of an innocent party. Our laws do not provide for compensation to those wrongly accused and rightly acquitted. The defendants in the Hall-Mills case propose to sue the *Daily Mirror* for libel.

BRIEF EXCERPTS

During a war liberty disappears as the commnutiy feels itself menaced.—*Walter Lippmann. Liberty and the News.* p. 29.

Propaganda is a terrible weapon.—*John A. Ryan. Publications of the American Sociological Society.* 18: 124. 1924.

One of the chief sources of the strength of the Tweed ring was found in the subserviency of the daily press.—*B. O. Flower. Arena.* 33:274. *March* 1905.

The irresponsible yellow press constitutes a great force working to perpetuate ignorance, prejudice, and hysteria in public life.—*John Storck. Man and Civilization. p.* 270.

The publication of false news is no more to be associated with freedom [of the press] than theft is to be associated with free exchange.—*Mark H. Judge. Westminster Review.* 166:618. *December* 1906.

Newspapers that were successful financially went after news aggressively, and on occasions made news, as my paper had done in the case of this illicit elopement.—*Silas Bent. Atlantic Monthly.* 137:762. *June* 1926.

Readers in our large cities should be warned that the metropolitan press has seriously misled the public by its method of dealing with the prohibition question.—*Review of Reviews.* 74:125. *August* 1926.

There is a prevalent feeling in newspaper offices that the public demands good stories and is not concerned much with their accuracy.—*Nelson A. Crawford. The Ethics of Journalism. p.* 80.

Legislation should be devised to provide for the punishment of a newspaper for publishing facts which might assist in the escape of criminals.—*Report of the New York State Crime Commission.* 1927. *p.* 325.

The American newspaper as an institution for the dissemination of knowledge has in the past year heaped up an indictment of itself that it will take much faithful service and honest effort to quash.—*Samuel Gompers. American Federationist.* 26:1134. *December* 1919.

In every country unscrupulous wealth can, by artificially "making opinion," mislead and beguile the people more easily and with less chance of detection than in any other way.—*James Bryce. Modern Democracies. vol.* 2. *p.* 486.

There can be no question that it is within the police power of the state to legislate against the publication of such malicious, scandalous, and defamatory material as is contemplated by the Minnesota statute.—*Minnesota Law Review.* 14:798. *June* 1930.

A questionnaire circulated among the inmates of the Elmira Reformatory in New York showed that sixty attributed their downfall to the alluring and romantic pictures of criminal life presented by the press.—*Silas Bent. Ballyhoo: the Voice of the Press. p.* 211.

A low tone, emotionalism, off-emphasis, irrelevance, and neglect are the outstanding sources of newspaper shortcomings. These qualities of news matter fashion the mind of the public. The public is stimulated to want this kind of news.—*Criminal Justice in Cleveland. p.* 524.

That there are in America daily and other periodicals which in different ways tend to weaken the brain, demoralize the spirit, and lower the tone of public opinion in the nation, any one may see.—*Century.* 72:317. *June* 1906.

The signs of the times are that the people are about ready to demand and support state and federal legislation regulating the newspaper and periodical business of the country.—*Henry Schofield. Papers and Proceedings of the American Sociological Society.* 9:116. *December* 1914.

Obviously this practice of trial by newspapers which precedes the judicial trial may have two serious results; first, exposing the prosecution's case, and secondly, creating a definite and wide-spread public opinion as to the merits of the case in anticipation of the trial.—*Criminal Justice in Cleveland. p.* 533.

American journalism is above all sensational journalism. If the facts reported are exact, so much the better for the paper; if not so much the worse for the facts. Beyond the date few statements are reliable. But the papers are always lively reading.—*Max O'Rell. Forum.* 7:510. *July* 1889.

Our great corporations include in their advertising bureaus well-equipped, secret departments for manufacturing public opinion favorable to themselves. . . . The publishing by the newspapers of these paid articles as reading matter is a pernicious business.—*McClure's Magazine.* 26:450, 452. *February* 1906.

Another evil creeping over American daily journalism concerns the growing volume of faked cable matter which is now appearing in many newspapers. Newspaper managers bespatter their pages with this cheap and fraudulent filling.—*Independent.* 61:1068-9. *November* 1, 1906.

The law, enacted by the 1925 legislature, gives a district judge sitting as a court of equity the power to suppress any publication printing "malicious, scandalous, and defamatory matter." A move to repeal the act in the last legislature failed.—*New York Times. December* 21, 1929.

When several hundred thousand dollars was subscribed by members of the New York trade unions for support of the steel strike at a meeting to which New York papers gave front page position, Pittsburgh newspapers omitted all reference to the subscriptions or the meeting.—*Nelson A. Crawford. The Ethics of Journalism. p.* 56.

The scientific temper is capable of regenerating mankind and providing an issue for all our troubles. The results of science, in the form of mechanism, poison gas, and the yellow press, bid fair to lead to the total downfall of our civilization. For us it is a matter of life and death.—*Bertrand Russell. Free Thought and Official Propaganda. p.* 55-6.

Anyone who has been interested in a huge strike or a similar social upheaval upon which public opinion naturally divides, must have been impressed with the ability of the press, whether capitalistic or labor, to select the occurrences which it wishes to record or headline and to ignore or suppress others.—*Jane Addams. Independent.* 84:55. *October* 11, 1915.

I confess that I do not entertain that firm and complete attachment to the liberty of the press which things, that are supremely good in their very nature, are wont to excite in the mind, and I approve of it more from a recollection of the evils it prevents than from consideration of the advantages it ensures.—*Alexis de Tocqueville. Democracy in America. Vol.* 1. *p* 181.

Frequently courts, in defining the limitations of the free press doctrine, have said that the constitutional guaranty protects the use rather than the abuse of the press. It is understood, of course, that freedom of the press does not imply a right to publish any and all matter under any and all circumstances. It is not an absolute right.—*Minnesota Law Review.* 14:790. *June* 1930.

There has been a considerable increase of deliberate lying in the British press since 1914, and a marked loss of journalistic self-respect. Particular interests have secured control of large groups of papers and pushed their particular schemes in entire disregard of the general mental well-being.—*H. G. Wells. The Salvaging of Civilization. p.* 188.

Year by year the subservience of the editorial to the business policy of the newspaper becomes more apparent. It is a matter of common knowledge, reenforced by much direct evidence, that many journals will not print news adverse to local department stores. Public franchise coporations, banks, railroads, and other great undertakings enjoy a lesser though still considerable immunity. —*Walter E. Weyl. The New Democracy. p.* 123.

So innate is the urge in political power to multiply and extend itself at the expense of the liberty of peoples, so prone is government everywhere and at all times to grasp new power and exercise it against all obstacles, that it remains the greatest unsolved problem of civilization, how to reconcile government with liberty.—*Sterling E. Edmunds. Virginia Law Review.* 16:1. *November* 1929.

It is the belief of Hilaire Belloc that the great modern press is essentially capitalistic in nature and that it is one of the most glaring evils of modern British society. Its function he asserts is really to vitiate and misinform opinion, and to place power into ignoble hands. We have and we must suffer the external consequences of so prolonged a regime of lying.—*Current Opinion.* 65:250. *October* 1918.

The false impression created by "waves" of crime news can be corrected if public agencies seek a better method of reporting crime data. At the present time such darkness exists in the realm of crime statistics that every prejudiced agency seems to be able to count upon this ignorance to protect it in publishing biased and incorrect accounts of the amount of crime.—*Report of the New York State Crime Commission.* 1927. *p.* 326.

When compared with the suppression of anarchy, every other question sinks into insignificance. The anarchist is the enemy of humanity, the enemy of all mankind, and his is a deeper degree of criminality than any other. No immigrant is allowed to come to our shores if he is an anarchist; and no paper published here or abroad should be permitted circulation in this country if it propagates anarchistic opinions.—*Theodore Roosevelt. Message to Congress. April* 9, 1908.

If Milton were living today he might indignantly protest against the great space given to frivolous and mostly inane details of sport news in our dailies, the flashy theatrical advertisements, the prurient scandals and police reports, the craze for novelties and for publishing sensational news, most of which is presented in such a way that grossly exaggerated inferences are drawn by the readers.—*John E. Fagan. American Catholic Quarterly Review.* 48:70. *January* 1923.

The Sunday paper is neatly adjusted to the American community. The screaming headlines of the main news section, the cheap emotionalism of the fiction, the slovenly English of the feature matter, the poverty of the literary, music, and art departments, the free publicity for stage and movie stars, the slang and slapstick of the funny-sides are a little lower than the fourteen-year-old might be brought to enjoy.—*Silas Bent. Independent.* 119:409. *October* 22, 1927.

The real offense of yellow journalism is that its pervading spirit is one of vulgarity, indecency, and reckless sensationalism; that it steadily violates the canons alike of good taste and sound morals; that it cultivates false standards of life, and demoralizes its readers; that it recklessly uses language which may incite the crack-brained to lawlessness; that its net influence makes the world worse. A force working to such ends surely ought to be restrained.—*Nation.* 73:238. *September* 26, 1901.

The scandal of a great deal of our American journalism has become too grievous to be borne tamely much longer. Neither the reputation of worthy men nor the virtue of pure women is any longer safe from the bloodhounds of a gang of newspaper thugs, fully half of whom are millionaires. It is disappointing that the victims of criminal journalism have thus far submitted so tamely to these outrages.—*Independent*. 61:946. *October* 18, 1906.

Except for the little news that it contains, which is to its managers a secondary consideration, the newspaper is simply an organ of deception. Every prominent newspaper is the defender of some interest and everything it says is directly or indirectly, and most-effective when indirectly, in support of that interest. There is no such thing at the present time [1903] as a newspaper that defends a principle.—*Lester F. Ward. Pure Sociology. p.* 487.

If the journalists prefer to disavow their constructive duty to society and deny that their activities are of public concern, as are those of the physician and lawyer, and like the shop-keeper, be guided only by their cupidity, at the same time hypocritically proclaiming the necessity of the freedom of the press, they must submit to regulation, as does he who engages in any other business which affects the public welfare.—*Joseph L. Holmes. Journal of the American Institute of Criminal Law and Criminology.* 20:293. *August* 1929.

No one,—no newspaper, certainly—denies that in this war a censorship is needed. In our Civil War the press had too great liberties in military matters, which it too frequently abused. Our war with Spain seemed sometimes to be a perfect revel of newspaper correspondents and sensational publications. If we had not learned something since then, and also taken to heart the lessons of the European war it would be much to our discredit. There is no real objection to a sensible censorship.—*Nation.* 104:519. *May* 3, 1917.

There is a type of newspaper that by exaggerating the importance of everything that the child does, or that happens to him, exploits him. Result—the part of the community that it serves has come to believe that a generation of headless, sinful, and carousing young people has arrived. But those of us who really know young people either in our own homes or in school know that this indictment is not true.—*Julia Traver. Proceedings of the Sixty-Fourth Annual Meeting of the National Education Association.* 1926. *p.* 73.

In one sense this hideous war was made by the world's press. If the journalism of Europe had been for a century free to publish the news uncolored by government influence or dictation, if it had been free to discuss in public the machinations of secret diplomacy this frightful strife would not have come. Certainly national antagonisms were increased and racial hatreds embittered by the international news served out from official or semi-official sources.—*Walter Williams. Public.* 20: 1012. *October* 19, 1917.

By means of clever, unscrupulous, and wholesale propaganda, nine-tenths of the American people were led to believe that the strike of the steel workers [in 1919] was revolutionary, bolshevistic, and aimed immediately at the overthrow of the government. As a matter of fact there was no more bolshevism in that contest than in any one of a dozen important industrial disputes that have occurred in the last ten years.—*John A. Ryan. Publications of the American Sociological Society.* 18:124. 1924.

The consequence of this press demoralization has been a great loss of influence for the daily paper. A diminishing number of people now believe the news as it is given them, and fewer still take the unsigned portions of the newspaper as written in good faith. The exploitation of newspapers by the adventurers of private enterprise in business has carried with it this immense depreciation in the power and honor of the newspaper.—*H. G. Wells. The Salvaging of Civilization. p.* 189.

The press, especially the daily newspaper, is at times an influence toward crime. The sensational advertising of crimes and the criminal becomes a suggestion of crime to many, particularly those who are uneducated or weak. That crime description forms too large a part of the daily news and that it is often made enticing or fascinating rather than repellent is a charge against irresponsible papers which has much truth in it. Immature and ignorant minds are particularly susceptible to such suggestion.—*Walter G. Beach. An Introduction to Sociology and Social Problems.* p. 319.

We are living in an atmosphere of slander. Our daily press reflects that atmosphere; our conversation reflects it. The newspapers daily display in large type and headlines the evils of men and women; the press makes much of some supposed charge against a man in high office. No one is immune from the slanderous tongue, the greatest of all the devil's works. Mere hearsay is the foundation of many of the statements made, hearsay that may be deliberate lying about others. —*Rev. Edward J. Sweeney, S. J. in a sermon at St. Patrick's Cathedral. New York Times. February* 3, 1930.

The press of the nation is the wellspring of general information. It is daily molding the thought of millions of people; but with the deadening of moral perceptions and sentiments of right and justice, which has advanced with the aggressive strides taken by the industrial autocracy, the press of the land has begun to fall under the moral blight of sordid greed and is becoming more and more the tool of the feudalism of privileged wealth which has already so largely corrupted government and degraded the business ideals of the nation.—*B. O. Flower. Arena.* 38:170. *August* 1907.

Civilization, by favoring the creation and dissemination of newspapers, which are always a chronicle of vices and crimes, and often are nothing else, has furnished a new cause of crime by inciting criminals to emulation and imitation. It is sad to think that the crime of Troppmann brought the circulation of the *Petit Journal* up to 500,000 and that of the *Figaro* to 210,000, and it was doubtless for this reason that this crime was imitated almost immediately in Belgium and in Italy.—*Cesare Lombroso. Crime: its Causes and Remedies. p.* 54-5.

He who robs one of his purse does not steal trash. He takes that which is the legitimate fruit of one's industry, the provision one has made for the support of himself and those dependent upon him, and the state is fulfilling one of its truest functions when giving its protection against theft. Should not the state in like manner protect one against the calumniator who tries by false witness to rob one of his good name? Surely one's character is entitled to at least the same consideration as is given to one's cash. Hardly a day passes but one reads false news in some newspaper.—*Mark H. Judge. Westminster Review.* 166:617. *December* 1906.

We know of no greater offense against the life and well being of a democracy than the distortion of news in the public print so that what is set forth as fact, is really an expression of an editor's or reporter's prejudice.

We call attention to this coloring of the news by an important American daily, not only because it violates the most important canon of conscientious journalism, but because it is a part of a dangerous and unpatriotic enterprise of trying to undermine the disarmament conference which certain American newspapers are carrying on.—*Editorial. Cleveland Press. February* 8, 1930.

The admitted function of newspapers is to convey to the public the objective facts of current events. The public is convinced that the newspapers are not fulfilling this function. The articulate part of the public charges that news is manufactured, suppressed, distorted, and colored. The reasons for these offenses it holds generally to be that the publishers of newspapers are subsidized for propaganda purposes, are influenced by the demands of advertisers, are seeking for circulation even at the cost of honesty, and through interlocking directorates and other relationships are closely tied to various private business interests.—*Nelson A. Crawford. Nation.* 115: 249. *September* 13, 1922.

Without doubt a newspaper, the most prominent feature of which is items detailing the immoral conduct of individuals, spreading out to public view an unsavory mass of corruption and moral degradation, is calculated to taint the social atmosphere, and, by describing in detail the means resorted to by immoral persons to gratify their propensities, tends especially to corrupt the morals of the young, and lead them into vicious paths and immoral acts. We entertain no doubt that the legislature has power to suppress this class of publications without in any manner violating the constitutional liberties of the press.—*Unanimous decision of the Supreme Court of Kansas.* 56 *Kansas* 242. 1895.

The fact that certain of the modern newspapers, particularly the so-called yellow variety, reach a strata of the population that probably never read newspapers in earlier days, is bringing to bear powerful influences upon certain persons whose mental age and characteristics permit them to be profoundly impressed and influenced by what they read. The power of suggestion is so great among these classes that they are being influenced in the direction of criminal practices much more than ever before. This danger is very difficult to deal with. It is unquestionably a public menace for newspapers to present the detail which they now print regarding the crimes and the divorce cases.—*Report of the New York State Crime Commission.* 1927. *p.* 324-5.

The [English] newspapers which give currency to false news are registered at the General Post Office, and are in consequence sent through the mails for less than the cost of transmission, in deference to the fetish that it is in the public interest for the state to afford facilities to the press irrespective of whether its news is true or false. Is this distribution by the state of what is known to be false news any less monstrous than it would be for the parcels department of the General Post Office to afford facilities for the transfer of property known to be stolen? The state gives due recognition to the command "Thou shalt not steal." Is it not time for the State to give a like recognition to the command "Thou shalt not bear false witness?"—*Mark H. Judge. Westminster Review.* 166:618. *December* 1906.

A more fundamental problem is involved in the character of some of the news published by the papers in recent months. No one who has read certain New York papers over the past years can doubt that there are being presented to the public at the present time more objectionable facts than ever before in history. Even the most ardent lover of freedom will question the lengths to which New York newspapers have gone in publishing such cases as the Browning divorce suit and the Hall-Mills trial. This is a plain case of public morals. We cannot avoid mentioning this tendency as one of the unquestioned forces that probably tend to injure the morals of the young and perhaps indirectly lead to disrespect for law and authority.—*Report of the New York State Crime Commission.* 1927. *p.* 326.

The industrial autocracy deliberately and systematically engages in sending out tainted news, news that is false and misleading and is sent out only for the purpose of advancing the secret ends which are inimical to the interests of the people or the cause of just and righteous government. So evident is it that the commercial feudalism has determined to poison the wells of the nation that it is of first importance that all thinking people be warned or put on their guard, for the most alarming feature of this poison campaign is found in the deceptive manner in which a large proportion of the reactionary press is disseminating the tainted news. Go where you will, you will find evidences in the press of this democracy-destroying influence.—*B. O. Flower. Arena.* 38:171. *August* 1907.

The most serious assaults upon the liberty of speech and press came with the Great War. A nation's supreme crisis is always despotism's chief opportunity. Immediately with its declaration, and simultaneously with a bill to conscript the whole man-power and subject it to military law, a new seditious libel law, the Espionage Act, was introduced in the Senate to curb all criticism of government on the part of those whose mouths were not effectively closed as military conscripts. Senator Chamberlain of Oregon offered a bill to make the whole United States a part of the zone of operations and to subject all citizens to martial law. Senator Walsh of Montana presented a measure for press censorship, which was beaten by the slim majority of six votes.—*Sterling E. Edmunds. Virginia Law Review.* 16:8. *November* 1929.

It must be acknowledged that the superficial reader of a newspaper, and that means nearly every reader, does not get a just and well-balanced idea of the course of events. This is due to the fact that each journal plays up the news to suit itself, and in some cases this is done in a way to convey an altogether erroneous impression of what has been done or said. This may be seen by comparing the accounts of the same event in two opposing newspapers. The body of the story may be much the same or even identical in language, but by arrangement and headlines it is made to convey very different impressions. It is chiefly in misproportion rather than by falsification or exclusion that our papers sin against the truth. Misproportion may, indeed, be called a form of misrepresentation, and hence should be avoided.—*Independent.* 84:44-5. *October* 11, 1915.

That a large portion of the American press is derelict in its duty to society in its handling of so-called crime news is the consensus of delegates to the American Prison Congress, in session here with approximately 1000 men and women from all parts of the United States in attendance. It is evident, according to delegates who have addressed the convention, that the press is overlooking constructive means of remedying the so-called crime situation, and is blinking its eyes at the task which confronts those responsible for the ends of justice being served. Delegates declared that the actual relation of a large part of the American press to crime is retrogressive to the ends of justice and that newspapers are "making a serious mistake" in featuring spectacular crimes and "directing sympathetic attention to criminals by coining names" which are calculated to make heroes of them among certain classes of newspaper readers.—*Christian Science Monitor. October* 18, 1926.

Students of civic life are openly declaring journalism's preoccupation with crime to be a major cause of much of the moral delinquency in our time. The man in the street is more inclined every day to believe that there is an unholy alliance between the newspaper and the crooked influences in politics and society. Along with this there grows a legend of an innate affinity between the newspapers and the unclean. We know that the apology often made for the vulgarity and scandal which bulks so large in the press is that this is the sort of thing the public wants. That there is some truth in this no one would deny; but you must concede that at least a considerable proportion of this demand is the creation of the press itself, which has fed the baser appetites of the public until it keeps asking for more and still more. Thus there has been set going a vicious circle of supply and demand.—*Editorial. Christian Century.* 42:148. *January* 29, 1925.

This danger of the yellow press, than which no greater threatens the democracy of our day and land, is the evil power of a sensational press to increase the evil sentiment on which it thrives. The periodicals that live on false witness, one-sided statements, doctored news, demagogic appeals; the loud calling of public attention to all the big or petty crimes in the calendar; that fan the vices by their constant parade of them; that are vindictive in their enmities; that are used to advance the selfish and impertinent ambitions of their owners; that exploit good causes for private emolument or personal advancement; that bring suspicion upon restrained, accurate, disinterested criticism of public men by their reckless attacks; that make reform odious by conscienceless imitations of its honest activities; that, in a word, live by cultivating the appetite for sensationalism; such periodicals are the parents of all the vulgarities.—*Century.* 72:318. *June* 1906.

In the past few years, since the money power has gained control of our industry and government, it controls the newspaper press. The people know this. Their confidence is weakened and destroyed. No longer are the editorial columns of newspapers a potent force in educating public opinion. The newspapers, of course, are still patronized for news. But even as to news, the public is fast coming to understand that wherever news items bear in any way upon the control of government by business, the news is colored; so confidence in the newspaper as a newspaper is being undermined. Cultured and able men are still to be found upon the editorial staffs of all great dailies, but the public understands them to be hired men who no longer express honest judgments and sincere conviction, who write what they are told to write, and whose judgments are salaried.—*Senator Robert M. La Follette, Sr. Address delivered at the Periodical Publishers Association, Philadelphia, February* 12, 1912.

Time was when character was regarded as a valuable part of a citizen's property, but today it would seem to be rather the property of such newspapers as choose to serve it up for the mercantile purpose of gaining or maintaining a circulation large enough to attract the advertisement of the honest merchant. Owing partly to the breaking down of the old standards of selfrespect and partly to the difficulty and expense of prosecuting for libel, the sensational newspapers have acquired virtually a free hand in the exploitation of degrading crime, alleged offenses against political and social usages, and the private affairs of persons who by reason of notoriety or prominence are objects of curiosity. As a consequence the largest part of the space of the most popular newspapers is divided on one hand between the activities of such vigorous contributors to human history as criminals, gamblers, and prize fighters, and on the other to the frailties and pastimes of the rich.—*Century*. 83:632. *February* 1912.

Newspapers frequently receive important pieces of news that lack the necessary details for presenting them with due dignity of length. It becomes necessary to supply the missing materials in the office. In not a few cases it becomes the duty of the reporter or editor to supply the missing materials from his inner consciousness, drawing upon his memory or his imagination. This kind of license has become absolutely necessary in writing the reports of events which will be past when the paper appears, but which must be described before they occur. Intense rivalry for the latest news long ago drove editors to the use of the journalistic imagination in such cases. The amount of matter that is prepared in this way, especially for evening papers, probably would surprise the average reader. The fact will account for many of the inaccuracies of the press, but on the whole it is cause for wonder that the newspapers can be as accurate as they are under the circumstances.—*Edwin L. Shuman. Practical Journalism. p.* 103-4.

In a sermon discussion of what he called crime sewerage, Dr. Allen Pastor of the Pilgrim Congregational Church, Oak Park, Ill., recently told his congregation that the newspapers are making the crime situation worse rather than better. He said that the enormous amount of space being given crime tends to make it attractive rather than repellant, that it constitutes psychological blunder on the part of the newspapers, and that the method of treatment is not remedial. "The public press of Chicago," Dr. Allen said, "has been asked by a great many organizations and individuals to play down crime, bestiality, and the sordid aspects of life, and play up those really significant events and constructive activities which make life worth living. Their answer for the most part has been to ignore the issue. There is a deep undercurrent of protest against the daily press as at present administered. This protest will find expression suddenly and some of our so-called newspapers will go out of business. Why rear another generation on the crime-sewerage of society?"—*Christian Century.* 42:358. *March* 12, 1925.

The editors and publishers of our daily press and our weekly and monthly magazines give the people what they —the editors and publishers—think the people want. What we find running through all this literature is the reiterated assumption that we are, in the matter of crime, facing an unprecedented situation. The expressions "crime wave" and "crime tide," originating in the picturesque imaginations of newspaper headline writers, have been accepted by all the propagandists and, from them, by the reading public as an accurate description of existing conditions. In the period of thirteen years, 1900-1913, there was a marked decrease of 37.7 per cent in general criminality in the United States in proportion to the population. The gain to the community from the downward trend of the general crime curve is obviously a matter for gratification. With the automatic gun to paralyze the victim and wayfarers and the automobile at the curb to ensure a quick get-away, is there any wonder that the young dare-devils of the criminal profession are attracted to the game? With the newspapers reporting and dramatizing every detail of every hold-up of this character, the wonder is that more of them don't go in for it. It is certainly made to look like easy money with a minimum of risk. The crime wave is a state of mind. Our more unbridled propagandists have drawn the long bow too hard. They have shot the community full of their own panicky state of mind.—*George W. Kirchwey. Survey.* 55:593-6. *March* 1, 1926.

The avidity with which all the particulars attending this horrid butchery, the murderer's trial, execution, and the confessions, real or manufactured, said to have fallen from his lips, have been collected, published, and read, evinces no less a depraved appetite in the community, than a most unprincipled and reckless disregard of consequences on the part of those who are willing, nay eager, for the sake of private gain, to poison the fountains of public intelligence, and fan into destroying flames the hellish passions which now slumber in the bosom of society. The moral guilt incurred and the violent hurt inflicted upon social order and individual happiness by those who have thus spread out the loathsome details of this most damning deed, are tenfold greater than those of the wretched miscreant himself. The guilt of murder may not stain their hands, but the fouler and more damning guilt of making murderers, of raising and training to their tasks men who will dare to strike the blow the fear of the law perhaps restrains themselves from giving, rests upon their souls and will rest there forever. —*Horace Greeley. New York Tribune. April* 19, 1841.

While the rise of the newspaper in recent decades has been meteoric and marvelous in many ways, the press has not become as dignified and constructive a social agency as might have been the case. In catering to the masses, crowd emotion, and the economic attitudes of advertisers, it has felt obliged to belittle its high calling. The highest social usefulness of the newspaper has been compromised by commercialization. The securing of large financial returns has become a dominant factor in the publishing of newspapers today. Therefore, the profit standard too often overrules the human welfare standard. A very large proportion of the total receipts in the newspaper business are [sic] derived from the sale of advertisements. The subscriptions represent a decreasing percentage. Advertising yields as high as two-thirds of the earnings of the daily newspaper; it may yield up to 90 per cent. The advertiser, rather than the subscriber, supports the newspaper. When news columns and editorials become of less importance than the sale of advertisements, it becomes true that the advertisers are the censors of the news and editorials. –*Emory S. Bogardus. Introduction to Sociology. p.* 305-6.

Free speech and a free press may be considered the bulwarks of democracy. But most of our speaking today is done in ignorance and the boasted free press has become largely the mouthpiece of interests, commercial, industrial, political, even fanatical. Most of the talking and the greater part of the printing of the present day are aimed at specific objectives, almost none of which is social. It is absurd to expect public opinion to be enlightened under these circumstances. Society has a right to insist that all speaking and all printing bearing on human relationships shall be socially sound, just as it has a right to insist upon clean amusements and clean streets. The public is no more capable of choosing its reading matter than it is of choosing clean drinking water or clean milk. The assertion that the average man has the opportunity to read everything and the capacity to detect the true among the false is balderdash. It is vicious and dangerous to teach such things to our children. The avenues of influencing public opinion are public property.

It is an unwise state which permits their prostitution in the interests of individuals or groups. The use of the free press for purposes of vicious propaganda is as criminal as the use of the mails to defraud.—*Philip P. Parsons. Crime and the Criminal. p.* 376.

There is no such thing in America as an independent press unless it is in the country towns. You know it and I know it. There is not one of you who dare express an honest opinion. If you express it, you know beforehand that it would never appear in print. I am paid $150 a week for keeping my honest opinions out of the paper I am connected with. Others of you are paid similar salaries for doing similar things. If I should permit honest opinions to be printed in one issue of my paper, like Othello, before twenty-four hours my occupation would be gone. The man who would be so foolish as to write honest opinions would be out on the street hunting for another job. The business of the New York journalist is to distort the truth, to lie outright, to pervert, to vilify, to fawn at the feet of Mammon, and to sell his country and race for his daily bread, or for what is about the same thing, his salary. You know this and I know it, and what foolery to be toasting an independent press. We are tools, and the vassals of rich men behind the scenes. We are jumping jacks. They pull the strings and we dance. Our time, our talents, our lives, our possibilities, all are the property of other men. We are intellectual prostitutes.—*John Swinton, in Robert C. Brooks's Corruption in American Politics and Life. p.* 122-3 *and in Lester F. Ward's Pure Sociology. p.* 487-8.

The admirable conduct of the government officials at Washington renders the course of the sensational press in this city [New York] the more shameful by contrast. Nothing so disgraceful as the behavior of two of these newspapers in the past week has ever been known in the history of American journalism. Gross misrepresentation of the facts, deliberate invention of tales calculated to excite the public, and wanton recklessness in the construction of headlines which outdid even these inventions, have combined to make the issues of the most widely circulated newspapers firebrands scattered broadcast throughout the community. It speaks well for the good sense of the masses that so little effect has been produced by all this stuff. It is evident that a large proportion of the public refuses to take the sensational newspapers seriously, and reads them only from motives of curiosity. At the same time there is abundant evidence that thousands of people are affected by such announcements in print as "War Sure," and that this sort of recklessness disturbs the public mind unnecessarily. It is a crying shame that men should work such mischief simply in order to sell more papers; and the first impulse of every right-minded person is to wish that journalism of this sort might be suppressed by the hand of the law.—*Nation.* 66:139. *February* 24, 1898.

The taking of testimony in a trial is hedged about with a thousand precautions derived from long experience of the fallibility of the witness and the prejudices of the jury. We call this, and rightly, a fundamental phase of human liberty. But in public affairs the stake is infinitely greater. It involves the lives of millions, and the fortune of everybody. The jury is the whole community, not even the qualified voters alone. The jury is everybody who creates public sentiment—chattering gossips, unscrupulous liars, congenital liars, feeble-minded people, prostitute minds, corrupting agents. To this jury any testimony submitted, is submitted in any form, by any anonymous person, with no test of reliability, no test of credibility, and no penalty for perjury. If I lie in a lawsuit involving the fate of my neighbor's cow, I can go to jail. But if I lie to a million readers in a matter involving war and peace, I can lie my head off, and, if I choose the right series of lies, be entirely irresponsible. Nobody will punish me if I lie about Japan, for example. I can announce that every Japanese valet is a reservist, and every Japanese art store a mobilization center. I am immune. And if there should be hostilities with Japan, the more I lied the more popular I should be. If I asserted that the Japanese secretly drank the blood of children, that Japanese women were unchaste, that the Japanese were really not a branch of the human race after all, I guarantee that most of the newspapers would print it eagerly, and that I could get a hearing in churches all over the country. And all this for the simple reason that the public, when it is dependent on testimony and protected by no rules of evidence, can act only on the excitement of its pugnacities and its hopes. The mechanism of the news-supply has developed without plan, and there is no one point in it at which one can fix the responsibility for truth.—*Walter Lippmann. Liberty and the News.* p. 39-41.

NEGATIVE DISCUSSION

A BLOW AT FREEDOM[1]

Self government can endure only as long as opinion, including the expression of it, is free. Any people who cannot by word or print freely make charges against those in authority are not self governing. They must be secure in their right of free speech and free press; otherwise they are not governing but are simply governed.

Freedom of speech and of the press involves freedom to make mistakes, freedom to express wrong as well as right opinions, freedom even to utter slanders and libels. This does not mean that people in a self-governing community shall not be held accountable for the way in which they exercise their freedom. On the contrary, the freer the people, the more responsible they are for the preservation of their freedom against abuse. Nor does freedom of speech or press mean license to disturb the public peace or obstruct the freedom of others. But it does mean that no one shall have the power to decide beforehand what any man shall think or say or publish. It is because this freedom is essential to self government that it is guaranteed by the Federal Constitution against interference by the Federal Government, and by every State Constitution,—so far as we know—against interference by the State.

Minnesota's Constitution puts the guaranty of a free press in the following words: "The liberty of the press shall forever remain inviolate, and all persons may freely speak, write and publish their sentiments on all subjects, being responsible for the abuse of such right."

In spite of this the State of Minnesota has a law which

[1] Editorial. *Outlook*. 150:1283. December 5, 1928.

permits a judge to decide what is defamatory or malicious and to enjoin as a nuisance the publication of it. This is not an extension of the law of libel. The law holds the publisher of a libel responsible to a jury of his peers for what he has published. This law on the contrary provides for the prevention of the utterance of the libel or anything which a judge may consider a libel. It is worse than common censorship, because it clothes the censor with judicial power to decide, punish, and suppress.

Inconceivable as it may appear, the Supreme Court of Minnesota has decided that that law is constitutional. A paper known as the *Saturday Press* of Minneapolis published charges of police connivance with racketeering vice and gambling. A judge decided that the charges were defamatory. He therefore enjoined the paper against further publication of them and suppressed the paper. He alone heard the evidence and he alone issued the order. Whether the charges were true or not is aside from the point. Those aggrieved have the right to sue and if injured to recover damages and even, if the libel is criminal, to insist on criminal prosecution. The menace in the Minnesota law is the use of the judicial power not to hold men accountable for their freedom but to suppress their freedom altogether.

This is in no sense, it should be emphasized again, a question of the character of the articles published by the *Saturday Press.* Whether they were true or false, whether they were libelous or published with malicious intent is no part of the discussion. The very essence of a free press lies in its right to be the sole judge of what it prints. The law of libel holds ample relief for the citizen attacked by unscrupulous editors. Against those who libel or slander him he may always turn to the courts, but only when the libel or slander has become a fact through publication.

The injunction is a legal instrument for which there is a legitimate use to prevent irreparable damage, but its legitimate use does not include the suppression or abridgement of what is guaranteed by any constitutional bill of rights.

This is a matter that concerns every citizen. It is not a class question, it is a public peril. Imagine a situation in which a corrupt officialdom in partnership with the underworld attempts to suppress public knowledge of crime and a corrupt or dull-minded judge is found to do the bidding of the partners in evil. What protection would the public have against such a tyranny? Such a law is the best that organized criminals could desire for their own security.

The American Newspaper Publishers' Association has in a resolution very properly appealed to all "free and loyal Americans" to take cognizance of this state of affairs and to "demand the restoration of the right of free speech."[2] The members of the Association make this appeal not alone in their capacity as publishers, but as citizens. They have raised an issue that cannot be settled until it is settled on behalf of liberty and public rights.

A VICIOUS LAW[3]

Members of the American Newspaper Publishers' Association were within their rights in adopting Colonel Robert R. McCormick's resolution pledging a united front to repeal the Minnesota newspaper suppression law. But, waiving their rights and their property interest in the subject, the publishers of the country are conserving its best traditions of liberty when they set out to cancel this incredibly pernicious law. The publisher of the *Chicago Tribune* through his newspaper has been conducting an effective struggle against the

[2] Obviously the Association meant free press and not free speech.
[3] Editorial. *New York Times*. April 26, 1929.

statute, and his presentation of the case to his associates in journalism was equally effective. These annual conventions offer a valuable forum for discussion of such evils as the Minnesota law, and the passage of the resolution suggested by Colonel McCormick again demonstrates the important opportunity for public service afforded by the American Newspaper Publishers' Association.

Publishers who heard the report were amazed that any State legislature in the Union could have passed such a law. It gives any judge the power, without jury trial or hearing, permanently to suppress any publication which, in his individual opinion, prints scandalous, malicious, or defamatory matter. On such an individual opinion the Minneapolis *Saturday Press* was suspended in 1927. A Soviet Commissar, one of the police bureaucrats who ruled Russia before the revolution, or an Oriental despot could have no greater power than this. For not only are property rights destroyed, but the source of public information is blocked or cut off. Crooked judges, and crooked politicians operating through them, are given authority which the spirit of the American governmental tradition essentially opposes. For in Minnesota articles may be suppressed even before publication. A great journalistic function of exposing wrongdoing in office and a journalistic right of criticism of public officials are both extinguished by a law of this kind.

It is difficult to believe that higher courts could hold valid such a law. As Colonel McCormick says, however, if it is constitutional in Minnesota, it is constitutional in any other state or as a Federal statute. The results of such an unthinkable condition would be the end of a free and honest press, the flourishing of controlled newspapers, and the perpetuation in office of grafters and tyrants. Minnesota, with a long record of progressive legislation, should wipe out this blot on its statutes without the necessity of pressure from outside.

MINNESOTA JOINS THE MONKEY STATES[4]

The house of representatives in Minnesota has voted to keep the press nuisance law on the statute books of the state. A bill to repeal the law had been introduced by Representative R. R. Davis. The bill was defeated in committee; the house by a vote of 86 to 30 sustained the committee.

The law permits a judge without jury trial to enjoin the publication of a newspaper which regularly prints malicious, scandalous, or defamatory matter. The law is an ideal weapon in the hands of a corrupt administration which could use it effectually to prevent criticism of itself.

Representative C. A. Peterson of Duluth said those desiring to repeal the law were suffering from hallucinations. The law does not threaten the liberty of the press, he insisted. The repeal, he thought, would be welcomed by "the army of persons waiting to begin publication of scandal sheets."

The defeat of the repeal bill is a disgrace to the state of Minnesota. When the law was enacted in 1925 it had attracted relatively little attention, and its passage could be interpreted charitably as an oversight. Today the significance of the law is plain and the refusal to repeal it indicates beyond all question that the enactment of the law was a deliberate attempt to strangle criticism in a way which enlightened men have rejected as unsound politically and morally for nearly three hundred years.

Minnesota joins hands with Tennessee, and of the two Minnesota may justly claim to be the more ridiculous. After all, it is less than a hundred years since intelligent men discarded the traditional biological notions found in the Bible. It is nearly three hundred years since John Milton stated the argument for free speech and a free press, and Milton was by no means the first champion of enlightenment in the field.

[4] Editorial. *Chicago Tribune.* March 28, 1929.

The nuisance law is an evidence that reflects upon the schools and the newspapers of Minnesota which have failed to educate this generation in American institutions. What is needed in Minnesota, apparently, is a primer devoted to the story of human liberty with special emphasis upon the rights of the citizen as established after centuries of struggle in England and America. One chapter might take as its text the remarks of the Hon. Mr. Peterson. It could show that his fear of a free press is only the echo of many similar expressions which have made the tyrants and friends of tyranny who uttered them ridiculous.

Mr. Peterson fears that the repeal of the law would set loose an army of scandalmongers. Other states are not similarly alarmed. In other states the law of libel, the consciences of editors, and the good sense of the public which supports the press are all that are required to prevent its misuse. Through centuries these safeguards have proved adequate. Mr. Peterson forces the conclusion that Minnesota is unique for the irresponsibility of its editors, for the appetite of the citizens for scandal, or for the amount of truth which ought to be made public but is now suppressed by fear of the gag law. Possibly, we may conclude, Minnesota is unique for all these reasons together.

The action of the Minnesota house has given added point to the appeal taken by the *Tribune* on behalf of the press of the nation against an injunction issued under the nuisance law. Now it is more than ever important to test the constitutionality of this statute.

THE MINNESOTA NUISANCE LAW[5]

The American Newspaper association has asked its membership whether or not it favors appeal from the decision of the Supreme court of Minnesota in the

[5] Editorial. *Chicago Tribune.* March 11, 1930.

Minnesota nuisance law case to the Supreme court of the United States. A ballot has been sent out to editors to obtain an explicit opinion. For the information of editors and other readers who have not had the Minnesota statute and the proceedings in the case of the *Saturday Press* brought to their attention the following summary may be helpful:

The Minnesota statute declares any newspaper or publication which regularly publishes malicious, scandalous, and defamatory matter a nuisance which may be suppressed by application of the injunction process. Under this law the *Saturday Press,* a small weekly of Minneapolis, was restrained from publication as a nuisance. From this order the *Press* appealed, but the state Supreme court affirmed the decision of the District court, which found against the *Press* and suppressed it as a public nuisance. At this stage the *Tribune* was informed of the statute and the proceedings against the *Press,* and as there was likelihood that an appeal would not be perfected and the time being short within which the necessary procedure must be taken, the *Tribune* acted upon its own initiative. Its regular counsel took charge of the case for the defendant and an appeal was carried at the *Tribune's* expense to the Minnesota Supreme court. There it was argued by the *Tribune's* counsel and the court again sustained the statute.

The next step is an appeal to the United States Supreme court, and it is for the approval or disapproval of this step by the American newspaper profession that the referendum is resorted to. The *Tribune* has no disposition to play Sir Galahad or Don Quixote in this matter. It has the material for testing the case and will press it if the American newspaper world agrees with the opinion which induced The *Tribune* to take up the cause in Minnesota. The *Tribune* has said editorially, and its counsel have argued in the highest court of Minnesota, that the Minnesota law is not compatible with freedom of the press and is the most flagrant device for the suppression of criticism of government that has been devised for a century. Under cover of suppressing malicious and irresponsible comment, it puts in the hands of corruptionists and malefactors in office a means of preventing exposure and robs the public of its right to know whatever is charged against their representatives in office. The ostensible restriction to "malicious, scandalous and defamatory" publication is no protection of the public, for a corrupt official, with the compliance of an allied judiciary, is free to call any exposure "malicious, scandalous and defamatory" and promptly suppress it. No better shield for venality or malfeasance in office could be devised than this summary proceeding before a judge without recourse to even a jury. The existing laws of libel are applicable to malicious, scandalous and defamatory publications, but the Minnesota nuisance law is directed to prevent publicity.

That such a device should be accepted and enacted by an American legislative body is a sorry commentary on the political conscience and intelligence of the community it represents. That it should be approved by a high court is even worse. But both the legislators and judges are elected products of a political condition in Minnesota which explains a good deal. Political power in Minnesota has been divided between a rather unusually remorseless and shortsighted moneyed interest and the excessive and not too scrupulous radical opposition it is likely to create. Moneyed power has been greedy, oppressive, and unintelligent, even as to its own legitimate interest. Rebellion against it has been given to quackery, and not careful of its weapons. What the state has needed and needs is not a bludgeon to be seized by either force but the development of an intelligent public opinion and a citizenship of character, now ineffective for its own defense in the duel between the plutocrats and the cranks. A free press is essential to the decent government of Minnesota, or any other free community, and "no abuse of a free press can be so great as the evil of its suppression."

A DANGEROUS REPRISAL[6]

The United States Supreme Court is to be asked to decide whether the Minnesota law permitting a judge permanently to suppress a newspaper is constitutional. Twice the highest court of Minnesota has held that it is. The law is directed against sheets regularly printing "malicious, scandalous, or defamatory matter," and it was aimed particularly at one published in Minneapolis. Under the process the judge sits as a court of equity and may abolish a newspaper without hearing, if, in his opinion, it comes within the purview of the law. The target, in the present instance, was small, and there is no contention that the language of the law did not cover its activities. But there is considerable anxiety—more outside Minnesota than in it—over the opportunity thus given for wrong decisions by judges against reputable newspapers. A body of opinion, expressed most vigorously by the *Chicago Tribune,* holds that the Minnesota law subverts the guaranteed freedom of the press.

For the passage of such a law, and its sympathetic reception by any court, the blame must be left on the doorsteps of the sensational press. Latterly this type has been growing in numbers and recklessness. Most of them know how generally to steer within the bounds of the libel law. When they overstep these, they count upon the unwillingness of people to take their private troubles into a court, even to secure redress against outrageous attack. To such jackals of journalism, no morsel is inedible. Decent newspapers everywhere sympathize with the public resentment which takes form in such laws as that passed in Minnesota. Yet they believe that the ordinary penal laws are sufficient, if they are invoked, to protect private citizens from libel or defamation of

[6] Editorial. *New York Times.* December 24, 1929.

character. They believe that the importance to the public of maintaining the freedom of the press is far greater than delegation of power to an individual, even a judge, to stop publication. If the Minnesota law were commonly enacted, newspapers would be at the mercy of courts, sometimes with personal spite to gratify or political purpose to achieve. The cure is worse than the malady.

FREE SPEECH; FREE PRESS[7]

In 1925 the Legislature of Minnesota enacted a law giving to county judges the right to suppress permanently, by means of injunction and without trial by jury, any "malicious, scandalous or defamatory newspaper." Under this statute a judge in Hennepin County in 1927 suppressed by injunction the Minneapolis *Saturday Press,* an unimportant weekly publication which had been devoted largely to an exposure of crime conditions in Minneapolis and criticisms of public officials. The action was instituted by the county prosecutor.

The Constitution of Minnesota provides that "the liberty of the press shall forever remain inviolate and all persons may freely speak, write and publish their sentiments on all subjects, being responsible for the abuse of such rights."

There was clearly no "abuse of such rights" in baring crime conditions in Minneapolis and in criticizing public officials. Yet the injunction of the county judge and the iniquitous statute under which it was given have been upheld by the Minnesota Supreme Court. Americans who still believe that free speech and a free press are fundamentals of liberty have interested themselves to the extent of carrying the case to the Supreme Court of the United States. The *Chicago Tribune,* through its counsel, interested itself in the litigation, and merits commendation for its efforts in behalf of a basic principle of the American bill of rights.

[7] Editorial. *Cleveland Plain Dealer.* December 8, 1928.

A law which gives to a county judge the right to suppress by injunction the publication of any newspaper is worth testing for its constitutionality. A lewd or obscene publication may be suppressed by police authority, but no such allegation was made against the Minneapolis publication. Libel may be dealt with by either the civil or the criminal courts, but no charge of libel was advanced against the *Saturday Post.* A public prosecutor merely charged that the journal was "malicious, scandalous or defamatory," and a compliant judge on this vague ground arbitrarily forbade its publication.

The case is one of vast importance. It far overshadows the specific wrong committed against an obscure and unimportant weekly publication in Minnesota. It concerns the fundamental rights of free speech [8] and free press.

PUBLISHERS TO FIGHT MINNESOTA LAW [9]

The members of the American Newspaper Publishers' Association yesterday adopted a resolution pledging a united fight to repeal the Minnesota newspaper suppression law. They also accepted a report on the law, made by a committee headed by Colonel Robert R. McCormick of the *Chicago Tribune,* which called the statute despotic.

Colonel McCormick in his report set forth the scope of the Minnesota law. It was passed in 1925, but was not invoked against a newspaper until 1927, when the Minneapolis *Saturday Press* was suspended. The law provides that any judge, without trial or hearing, can enjoin any journal which, in his opinion, publishes malicious, scandalous, or defamatory articles. The Minneapolis newspaper was subsequently permanently suppressed as a nuisance. The Colonel's report said:

[8] Of course this is not true. Neither this case nor the Minnesota Nuisance Law has anything at all to do with free speech. The full text of the law is given on an earlier page.

[9] *New York Times.* April 25, 1929.

The statute is tyrannical, despotic, unAmerican, and oppressive. It is objectionable for the following reasons: Under this statute whenever a grafting minority desires to remain in power or to prevent exposures of wrong doing, it has a ready weapon at hand with which to cover up its iniquity and suppress attempts to expose it.

This statute resuscitates the obsolete law of libels on the government, and permits the suppression of publications opposing corruption in the government. It furnishes the fetters whereby corruption in office may completely enslave and debase our free institutions without fear of public exposure.

This statute establishes courts of equity as censors and licensers of the press and permits the courts to suppress writings in advance of publication, contrary to the time-honored theory of Anglo Saxon jurisprudence (at least since the fall of the Star Chamber) that courts may not restrict or censor writings prior to publication, but may only punish for having published.

After reporting that the Minnesota law made it obligatory for a publisher to prove the truth of every inch of news in every issue—which could be done successfully with 99½ per cent of printed matter, the Colonel said, the report pointed out that time and much money would be needed to authenticate journals "en masse." The report continued:

The freedom of the press is but a shadow if the publisher is not allowed to criticize the government and its employes adversely, but must compliment and flatter them; if he prints anything derogatory to either and does so regularly and customarily, he may without hearing be enjoined from publishing his paper.

Freedom of the press means security against measures resorted to by any department of the government for the purpose of muzzling public opinion, and the phrase "responsibility for the abuse of the right" means responsibility before a jury which is the only body which has a right to determine it, and not before a court. This statute is the first attempt of a legislature since the foundation of the Union to gag the press in so drastic a manner.

The theory of the republican form of government is that the people are the rulers. When the public servants tell their masters, the people, that the latter may not find fault with them, they are overstepping the bounds of their powers and must immediately be called to account.

Needless to say, if this statute is held valid the value of newspaper properties throughout the country will be greatly diminished. If the law is valid in Minnesota, it is valid in other states. There is always the possibility of similar legislation being adopted elsewhere. Newspapers can be suppressed at the will of the legislature and a single judge sitting without a jury and, if a preliminary injunction is granted, before notice to the newspaper, or hearing.

No legitimate business can stand up under such a load. No legitimate business has ever been subjected to such a burden.

Of what value is an established business which may be suppressed overnight without notice or hearing? This is especially dangerous in view of the fact that under this law a newspaper may be so suppressed when it has printed nothing but the truth and was actuated solely by good motives and justifiable ends.

The resolution adopted set forth the main points covered in the committee report and concluded:

Now, therefore, be it resolved by the American Newspaper Publishers' Association that said statute is one of the gravest assaults upon the liberties of the people that has been attempted since the adoption of the Constitution and is inherently dangerous to the republican form of government; and be it further resolved that the members of this association cooperate in all respects to secure a repeal of said statute and of any statute similarly directed against the right of free utterance.

NECESSITY OF THE FREEDOM OF THE PRESS [10]

The printing-press is, without doubt, the most powerful weapon with which man has ever armed himself for the fight against ignorance and oppression. But it was not free-born. It was invented at a period when all the functions were most widely separated from the people; when secrecy, diplomacy, and intrigue were the chief elements of statesmanship. To such a system publicity was fatal, and from its birth Gutenberg's great invention was taken charge of in all countries by the authorities. It was assumed from the first that nothing should be printed without permission of the Church or State. The censorship of the press was not regarded by governments with the rights of individuals. It was an act of gracious beneficence to allow any man to print his opinions. In

[10] Address of James A. Garfield, delivered before the Ohio Editorial Association at Cleveland July 11, 1878. *Works of James A. Garfield.* vol. 2. p. 575-85.

France, and indeed in nearly all the states of the continent, during the first two centuries after the invention of printing, a private printing-press would have been as unlawful and anomalous as a private mint would be now. At a very early date the censorship of the press became a part of the law of England and of her colonies. For a long time it was controlled by the Church; but after the conflict of Henry VIII with the Pope, the law was administered by the civil authorities.

The English newspaper was born in London in 1622, a few months after the Pilgrims had landed at Plymouth. At that date there was no place on the earth where a printed book or paper could be lawfully published until it had received the *imprimatur* of the Church or of the sovereign; and, of course, nothing was allowed to be published but what was entirely agreeable to the authorities. In the long, fierce struggle for freedom of opinion, the press, like the Church, counted its martyrs by thousands. The prison, the pillory, the rack, the gibbet, all find their places in the bloody chapter that records the history of its emancipation.

The Anglo-Saxon race have become so accustomed to enjoy liberty of opinion, that they have almost forgotten what it cost to achieve it. They indorse the declaration of Erskine, that "Other liberties are under government; but the liberty of opinion keeps governments themselves under subjection to their duties." But they do not always remember that "this has produced the martyrdom of truth in every age, and that the world has only been purged from ignorance with the blood of those that have enlightened it." During many centuries mankind did not seem to believe that truth was more powerful than falsehood. They did not dare to let her enter the lists in equal combat. Cromwell had a glimpse of the better view when he ordered the release of Harrington's *Oceana,* which had been seized as libellous. He said, "Let him take his book. If my government is made to stand, it has nothing to fear from paper shot."

Milton saw it in its full glory, when, in his noble but unsuccessful defence of the press, he said: "Though all the winds of doctrine were let loose to play upon the earth, so Truth be in the field, we do injuriously by licensing and prohibiting to misdoubt her strength. Let her and Falsehood grapple; who ever knew Truth put to the worse in a free and open encounter? Her confuting is the best and surest suppressing." The Commonwealth did something for liberty of opinion, but that little was lost at the Restoration.

The opinion was almost universal, that to publish any of the proceedings of the government was an act of treason. In 1641 Sir Edward Dering was expelled from the House of Commons and imprisoned in the Tower, for publishing a speech which he had delivered in Parliament, and all the copies were seized and burned by the common hangman. Before the Revolution of 1688, it was unlawful to publish any reflection upon the government, or upon the character of any one employed by it.

In 1729 the Commons resolved that "It is an indignity and a breach of privilege of the House of Commons for any person to presume to give in written or printed newspapers any account or minutes of the debates or other proceedings of this House, or any committee thereof." In 1764 Mores, the editor of the *Evening Post*, was fined £100 by the House of Lords for mentioning the name of Lord Hereford in his paper. In 1771 after a long and fierce struggle, which brought England almost to a bloody revolution, custom tolerated, though the law did not authorize, the publication of the debates in Parliament. But criticism of the government was still forbidden. As late as 1792 Sampson Perry, the editor of the *Argus*, was tried and convicted of libel for saying in his paper that "the House of Commons were not the real representatives of the people."

We are accustomed to say that liberty was brought to America on board the Mayflower. But it was only after a long struggle that the germ was planted. In view of the European examples, it is remarkable that the persecution of free opinion in New England was not fiercer, and of longer duration. It required a century for the doctrines of the illustrious exile of Rhode Island to take firm root in our soil. It was two hundred years after the discovery of the continent, and seventy years after the landing of the Pilgrims, that the first newspaper was published in America, and that paper, entitled *Publick Occurrences,* published in Boston in 1690, lived but one day. It was suppressed by the Colonial authorities.

I have referred to Roger Williams as the founder of liberty of opinion in America. It has long been a matter of surprise to me that journalists have not taken more notice of him as our earliest apostle of the freedom of the press. Until his time *toleration* was the strongest expression that liberty had found. But Williams denounced toleration as a baleful word, for it implied the right of a government to refuse to tolerate dissenting opinions. Exiled into the wilderness of Rhode Island by the religious zealots of Massachusetts, in 1636 he announced the doctrine of *soul liberty,*—the right to utter his own convictions—as the inalienable right of every free man. But Williams had lain a century in his grave before his great thought was crystalized into the enduring form of constitutional law.

But little attention has been directed to a feature of our national Constitution which seems to me by far its most important provision. Our fathers sought so to distribute the functions of government that absolute power should be lodged nowhere. They divided all authority into three great groups. Certain definitely prescribed powers were delegated to the national government, certain others to the state governments; but the most important, the most sacred rights, were strictly forbidden to be exercised either by the national government or by the states. They were reserved to the people themselves. In every government that then existed, religion was the chief object of the state. Indeed, the Old World theory was that the state was organized for the defense and maintenance of religion. But our fathers considered the rights of conscience, the freedom of thought, too sacred to be delegated; hence, they provided that the care of religion, the freedom of speech, and the freedom of the press should never depend upon legislation, but should be left to the voluntary action of the people themselves. With a sublime faith in the omnipotence of truth, they left her free-handed, to fight her own way against all comers. Under the inspiration of this perfect liberty, the American press has been working out its destiny, developing its strength, its virtues, and its evils. If we were now to establish a new constitution, no thoughtful citizen would wish the press less free. If it has sometimes been weak, venal, and vicious under the reign of liberty, it would be more so under the trammels of authority.

Just now republican France is seeking to enfranchise her press. A committee of her legislature has recently made a report which ought to be published by every Anglo-Saxon journal. The report shows that there were six thousand prosecutions of publishers during the reign of the second Napoleon. It exhibits a long list of proscribed books, at the head of which stands a noble volume by a distinguished American. Then follow the works of Macaulay, Lamartine, Guizot, Cousin, Victor Hugo, George Sand, and indeed of all the foremost writers of the world. I give a single specimen of the official record of the Commission of Censure, out of hundreds equally striking: "*Essay upon the Reform of Legal Formalities regarding Mortgages.* The examiner pronounces a favorable opinion of this work, but it contains new theories not in accordance with the established order of things. Its circulation is not permitted."

Without a free press "the established order of things" can nowhere be improved. Government control has always made the press servile. I know of no better illustration than a few brief extracts from the French *Moniteur.* When Napoleon I escaped from Elba in 1815, the *Moniteur,* then the organ of Louis XVIII, thus chronicled the progress of the returning exile from day to day:

"The Anthropophagist has escaped." "The Corsican ogre has landed." "The Tiger is coming." "The Monster has slept at Grenoble." "The Tyrant has arrived at Lyons." "The Usurper has been seen in the environs of Paris." "Bonaparte advances toward, but will never reach the capital." "Napoleon will be under our ramparts tomorrow." "His Imperial Majesty entered the Tuileries on the 21st of March, in the midst of his faithful subjects."

Not for its own sake alone, but for the sake of society and good government, the press should be free. Publicity is the strong bond which unites the people and their government. Authority should do no act that will not bear the light. But freedom brings with it increased responsibility.

The chief danger which threatens the influence and honor of the press is the tendency of its liberty to degenerate into license. How far into private life it may justly carry its criticism, what influence it ought to prescribe to personal controversy, may be questions for an honest difference of opinion. I have said that the purity of government and the safety of society depend upon the publicity of all the official acts and opinions of those in authority.

Believing, as I do, in parties and in a party press, I hold it equally necessary to liberty and good government that the press shall comment with the utmost freedom upon the public acts and opinions of all men who hold positions of public trust. Here again, as in the department of news, the only just limitation is that it shall adhere to the truth. No worthy man fears the truth. Unjust criticism and false accusations are, in the long run, more injurious to the press than to its victims. Still, wrongs are sometimes committed in a month that years cannot wholly set right. Let me illustrate this by a conspicuous example.

During our late war, General McDowell, one of the noblest and most accomplished soldiers of the Union, was most unjustly assaulted by a group of war correspondents, who represented him to the country as incompetent, drunken, and perhaps disloyal. It was circumstantially stated that on one occasion he was so drunk that he nearly fell from his horse. As a consequence, he rested for a long time under this cloud of cruel and unjust suspicion. He is almost the only adult man I ever knew, of whom it can be said with truth that he never tasted spirituous liquors, tea, coffee, or tobacco; and yet several millions of his countrymen were made to believe, and perhaps many of them still believe, that he lost the Battle of Bull Run in consequence of intoxication. The fame of a worthy public man ought to be cherished as a part of the nation's possessions; yet the noblest and best citizens who have served the country in the highest capacities have won their honors and performed their duties amidst showers of obloquy.

Though there is still much room for improvement, I believe the character of the press has greatly improved during the last half-century. Possibly we now have newspapers which are worse than any in former times; certainly we have many which are far superior to any of their predecessors.

ARE NEWSPAPERS DECLINING IN INFLUENCE? [11]

One of the leading magazines of the country, the *Atlantic Monthly*, is advertising a series of articles entitled *Decline of Public Confidence in the Newspaper Press*. That the public has lost confidence in some news-

[11] By Frank I. Cobb. *New York World*. December 30, 1909.

papers and in some kinds of newspapers may be accepted as a matter of course, like the loss of public confidence in certain politicians and statesmen and theories of government. But if there is a marked decline of public confidence in newspapers as a whole, that fact is of such far-reaching public importance that it deserves the closest study and investigation.

More newspapers are printed than ever before. More newspapers are read than ever before. If the public has lost confidence in newspapers, why does it read them in such vast numbers? Merely to amuse itself? Merely to pass away the time? Merely to acquire information which it distrusts and upon which it can place no reliance? The American people have never impressed us as a nation of idiots and lunatics. They must have some definite motive in reading the newspapers, and the average American is not the sort of person who wastes his time on things in which he has no confidence.

We have observed too that the shrewd, practical gentlemen who manage the great corporations have detected no marked decline of public confidence in newspapers. Their desire to own newspapers, to influence newspapers, to shape the policy of newspapers was never so keen as it is now. They must believe that the public has confidence in what it reads in newspapers or they would not be so eager to control newspapers.

What is commonly spoken of as a decline of newspaper influence is in reality only a change for the better. Newspapers are cheaper than they were, and few men are obliged to rely upon a single newspaper. They draw information and opinions not from one source but from two or three or four sources, and their own opinion is the resultant of these various forces. This is having the excellent effect of teaching people to think for themselves. They are the surer in consequence to detect bad advice and the quicker to follow good advice. Their own opinions are clearer and saner and less prejudiced.

This does not mean a decline of newspaper influence.

On the contrary, it is a manifestation of the best kind of influence that newspapers can exert.

THE CANONS OF JOURNALISM[12]

I. Responsibility: The right of a newspaper to attract and hold its readers is restricted by nothing but considerations of public welfare. The use a newspaper makes of the share of public attention it gains serves to determine its sense of responsibility, which it shares with every member of its staff. A journalist who uses his power for any selfish or otherwise unworthy purpose is faithless to a high trust.

II. Freedom of the Press: Freedom of the press is to be guarded as a vital right of mankind. It is the unquestionable right to discuss whatever is not explicitly forbidden by law, including the wisdom of any restrictive statute.

III. Independence: Freedom from all obligations except that of fidelity to the public interest is vital.
1. Promotion of any private interest contrary to the general welfare, for whatever reason, is not compatible with honest journalism. So-called news communications from private sources should not be published without public notice of their source or else substantiation of their claims to value as news, both in form and substance.
2. Partisanship, in editorial comment, which knowingly departs from the truth does violence to the best spirit of American journalism; in the news columns it is subversive of a fundamental principle of the profession.

IV. Sincerity, Truthfulness, Accuracy: Good faith with the reader is the foundation of all journalism worthy of the name.

[12] Adopted by the American Society of Newspaper Editors, April 1923.

1. By every consideration of good faith a newspaper is constrained to be truthful. It is not to be excused for lack of thoroughness or accuracy within its control or failure to obtain command of these essential qualities.

2. Headlines should be fully warranted by the contents of the articles which they surmount.

V. Impartiality: Sound practice makes clear distinction between news reports and expressions of opinion. News reports should be free from opinion or bias of any kind.

This rule does not apply to so-called special articles unmistakably devoted to advocacy or characterized by a signature authorizing the writer's own conclusion and interpretations.

VI. Fair Play: A newspaper should not publish unofficial charges affecting reputation or moral character without opportunity given to the accused to be heard; right practice demands the giving of such opportunity in all cases of serious accusation outside judicial proceedings.

1. A newspaper should not invade private rights or feelings without sure warrant of public right as distinguished from public curiosity.

2. It is the privilege, as it is the duty, of a newspaper to make prompt and complete correction of its own serious mistakes of fact or opinion, whatever their origin.

VII. Decency: A newspaper cannot escape conviction of insincerity if, while professing high moral purpose, it supplies incentives to base conduct, such as are to be found in details of crime and vice, publication of which is not demonstrably for the general good. Lacking authority to enforce its canons, the journalism here represented can but express the hope that deliberate pandering to vicious instincts will encounter effective public disapproval or yield to the influence of a preponderant professional condemnation.

EXPURGATING THE NEWS[18]

From time to time excellent persons undertake to tell the newspapers what they should print and not print. The standard complaint is that they publish too much "crime news." Well, one apparently standard fact about the United States is that a vast amount of crime is committed. Are the newspapers to be blind to this, disguise the truth and give their readers a false, rose-colored picture of an orderly community? Writing with all her wonted logic, spirit and wit in *Commonweal,* Miss Agnes Repplier states the cardinal objection to expurgated news: "The life so indicated is not the life about us, the world so described is not the world we live in." Blinking at evil will not blot it out of existence:

> Just as the existence of a moral law lifts our soul above doubt, so the transgression of a moral law is the acid test by which judgment and justice are made clear to us. A great deal has been said about the atrocious "crime news" published in the American papers: but the atrocity lies in the crime rather than in the news. The little catechism we learned as children told us there are nine ways of being accessory to sin, and one of these is silence. It may be, and sometimes is, an evasion of duty.

Take the Leopold-Loeb murder trial last year. It was fully reported, as it should have been. As Miss Repplier happily says, "It could no more have been ignored than an outbreak of bubonic plague." That such a crime should be committed by such criminals was a cause of national humiliation. The public conscience was deeply touched. The public horror was intense. Miss Repplier infers from this general distress that vir-

[18] Editorial. *New York Times.* November 10, 1925.

tue is naturally precious to the hearts of men. Publication of evil didn't beget evil. Indeed, one might almost say that it worked an unconscious purification in many and stirred almost universally the moral sense.

Does "crime news" excite to crime? Miss Repplier contents herself with calling this "disputable"; but she dwells on the familiar habit of looking for accidental instead of real causes. In her youth the "dime novel" was a supposed fosterer of youthful crime. Yet Mr. Beadle's series, as we remember it, was always strong for virtue; and some of his books were written by an Episcopal clergyman. Now the "movies" are among the scapegoats, though so carefully censored that they show "nothing more demoralizing than imbecility." Once alcohol was the chief crime maker. The saloon is gone, but crime is more vigorous than ever.

Miss Repplier's text is the *Christian Science Monitor's* program of not reporting, with certain exceptions, "crimes, disasters, epidemics, deaths." Thus it told its readers of the Mid-Western tornado, but not of the Palm Beach fire on the same day. Seldom is Miss Repplier more refreshingly Repplierian than here:

> Just as a crime is a crime, so a disaster is a disaster. To report it is a concession to calamity, to ignore it is a concesion to pretense. Take for example the Palm Beach fire, which the *Christian Science Monitor* blithely refuses to notice. Even the idle rich are in some sort our brothers and our sisters. Any one of us might have had a widowed aunt at The Breakers when it was burned; a gay and dressy aunt, it is to be feared, perhaps even a would-be-fashionable aunt (else why The Breakers?) yet none the less a human relative, worthy of some regard. If our newspaper chanced to the the *Christian Science Monitor,* we should have liked to be told what became of her and her companions in misfortune.

Finally, the easy-going, nonchalant, bound-to-be-cheerful, quick-forgetting American needs all the knowledge that can be jabbed into him of "crime, disaster and disease." Give it to him and "let him worry all he will"—and that'll be mighty little.

THE OTHER SIDE OF YELLOW JOURNALISM [14]

We grant that the yellow journals are sensational, exaggerated, trivial, vapid, scandalous, class-appealing, unbalanced, boastful, coarse, etc. What then? Hear what John Swinton said a few weeks ago:

> The proletary, the mudsill, the clodhopper, the horny-handed upstart, the chap known in the Brooklyn churches as "offal," has learned to read, and takes the daily paper, which must be made for him as well as for the Pharisees. I say now again that this is the greatest wonder of the age. It means more for the world than aught else and all else. He is reading and so is thinking. He hasn't got to the *Critique of Pure Reason* yet—but don't be in a hurry. Sometimes you can't tell how far a man may go when he sets out.

This is the absolute truth. The yellow journals have their place as well as the London *Times*. Mother Goose and Captain Kidd lead to Milton and Scott. 'Tis better to have read and thought than never to have thought at all. Besides the yellow press takes the people's part. It represents them. What high class papers are quicker than they to help the masses, show them their rights and, if need be, fight for them? What papers side so surely with labor, whose only advocate up to this time has been itself? What papers get out injunctions to prevent Ramapo jobbers from pilfering the people's treasury, bring safely home kidnapped babies in special trains to agonized parents, or offer trips to the Paris Exposition to the most popular rag picker? We know that this transcends the ethics and province of journalism. Granted, but it is more good than bad.

In their best features the yellow journals have come to stay. They have the largest suffrage already in this country, and their circulation seems to be increasing. If we condemn them as pernicious, by implication we condemn the mass of the people. But the remarkable fact is that those very journals which have hitherto

[14] *Independent.* 52:785-6. March 29, 1900.

most bitterly attacked them are now (1900) quietly adopting many of the most successful yellow methods. Indeed the effect of their enterprise is apparent on the whole press of the country, and even the magazines are waking up.

If the yellow journals have affected the rest of the press the latter have equally influenced them. Of late their yellowness is not quite so yellow, and their gravest fault, scandal mongering, is being remedied. The crusade against two of the most flagrant offenders some time ago bore fruit, and showed them that indecency would not pay. What is printed now is often unsound, sensational, and vulgar, but it is seldom vicious.

Let us accept the good features of yellow journalism. With improvements here and there, and nobody doubts there is room for many, competition and public sentiment will doubtless do the rest. Meanwhile, the fastidious reader of the Springfield *Republican,* the Chicago *Tribune,* and the Philadelphia *Ledger* need have no fear for the future of the masses. Indeed, it might be somewhat of a moral and mental tonic if the aforesaid reader would occasionally buy a copy of a yellow journal and find out what his inferiors are thinking about. Then he might come to see that on the whole the yellow journals are doing their fair share of good in the land, as well as their esteemed contemporaries. And this we say, advising every one to read the *Critique of Pure Reason.*

A DEFENSE OF THE PRESS [15]

Any open-minded inquirer into the relations between the press and public opinion in this country will be met at the threshold by a series of paradoxes. The evidence offered him is sharply conflicting, even radically contradictory. Newspapers are all-powerful. They are also completely impotent. The press is at once dreaded and

[15] Rollo Ogden. An address before the American Political Science Association, December, 1912. *Proceedings.* 9:194.

despised, dismissed as negligible at the same time that it is fawned upon. Men in public life will at one moment make every effort to get, in the French phrase, a "bonne presse," for themselves and their measures but at the next will rail at newspaper opposition as a thing at which they may snap their fingers. Their opinion of the futility of the press, it may be noted, is usually intensified, if not originally provoked, by their ceasing to stand high in its good graces.

Newspapermen, I pause here to remark, are willing to bear testimony showing the decline of their influence. But they may be excused for objecting when the only witnesses summoned are politicians with a grievance. Some editors have memories. Those who have not have records. And by either it would be easy to prove that some of the most vehement decriers of the newspaper press have been converted to their present view with suspicious suddenness. There is, for example, that public man who for many years was the most skilful user of the press that has ever been seen. It was not simply that he had an eye for effect keener than that of any advertiser in the world; but that he flattered and cultivated pressmen with the most unblushing assiduity. His attention he showered upon all alike. Even the most indecent journalist of the age, who was for years like Donne's Anchorite, "Bedded and bathed in all his ordures," this man had no scruple in receiving on personal and confidential terms. Latterly he has begun to cry out upon dishonest and decadent newspapers. Well and good. Let him lay on. But why did he wait to go against the press until the press went against him? The same question might be put to that city executive who now fills the air with complaints of a degenerated press, though no man more earnestly than he sought the support, and sung the praises, of the very newspapers he today denounces. The men of the press, I say, may well ask for witnesses with the taint of inconsistency not so gross and palpable upon them. Those in and out of journalism who have long sought to make head against its worst types, may be forgiven if they resent this late born zeal of recent converts.

Yet the unchallenged facts arrest attention. At times, it is true, newspapers appear to have a power both vast and dangerous. At others, they seem to have none at all. Now able to do anything, they presently are capable of nothing. There are classic instances. In the city of Toledo all the newspapers of all parties were hostile to a certain candidate for the mayoralty. They had fought him before, but he had beaten them. In the campaign referred to, they decided upon the policy of ignoring him. They did not mention his name. They did not report his meetings or his speeches. They even refused to print political advertisements offered by him. But he was easily elected over this form of united opposition by suppression. There are other cases not unlike this. It has frequently happened in New York City that the press has been almost a unit against Tammany; yet Tammany has apparently shown that it could afford to despise the newspapers.

What have newspapermen to say to all this? First of all, they are not disposed to blink the facts. The influence of the press, whether good or bad, whether increasing or declining, is a theme of general discussion. Those in the business cannot be blind to this. They are aware of what is said. If outsiders are inclined to believe that the press has become "fortune's champion," merely "strong upon the stronger side," but powerless either to create or to direct public sentiment—much less to stem it—be sure that those on the inside do not shut these things from their thoughts. They can assume no airs of mystery. Their work is done in the general eye. It is fair game for the critics. Certainly the great clamorers for publicity cannot escape. Nor do they seek to. As little as men in other callings are they fond of "talking shop" in public, but on fit occasion, like the present, they are ready to submit the whole question to impartial debate.

And in their private and professional gatherings, let me add, they are as far as possible from swelling up in each other's presence with a pretense of inflated importance. . . .

In most discussions of the whole question, the test of the present-day rôle of the press in our public life is made the political test. The thing asserted or denied, that is to say, is the power of newspapers to make or break candidates for office, to carry elections. This is the region where facts are most confused and the conclusions most dubious. There are no means of absolutely correct analysis. A given anti-Tammany campaign may seem to prove, by the rough logic of votes, that the press has no influence with the electorate. But who can say that, but for the persistent attitude of the newspapers, the Tammany victory at the polls might not have been much more sweeping? The press may have influenced many votes, only not enough. There is no way of telling accurately. The inquiry, however, is always pertinent at a time when the political effect of the press appears to be near the vanishing point. Moderate or negative achievement is not the same thing as impotence. But, whatever the just inference about all this, it is a mistaken narrowing of the subject to restrict it to the political sphere. By politics alone neither man nor the daily press shall live. Campaigns are, after all, infrequent. . . . Even where the political animal is most highly developed, he has a wide range of intellectual and social interest having little or nothing to do with primaries or ballots or elections. Mr. Balfour, himself a politician, has said that nothing attempted or achieved by politicians or by political parties during the past hundred years is worthy to be named in significance for the human race alongside the mighty revolution quietly accomplished by modern science. There are, in fact, endless manifestations of the spirit of man and social movements of infinite complexity and importance, with which politics has nothing to do directly. Yet they enter more and more into the work of the press. It may be potent here even if it be conceded to have fallen away from its high estate in the matter of political influence, pure and simple.

I have just used a phrase implying that newspapers have lost power which they once had. But that is by no means certain. Great changes in the press there have undoubtedly been; its methods are not what they were; its influence, whatever it be, is excited by means and modes of expression once undreamed of. But to affirm that the press in this country had a Golden Age from which there has since been a sad decline is, in my opinion, unwarranted. It is an assertion that will not bear the weight of a good history. People can always find decadence when they look for it. The Golden Age is invariably one generation back. And if we turn to one of the earliest intelligent discussions of the American press, and of its relation to public opinion, we shall find that seventy and eighty years ago the present complaints about the decline of newspapers were anticipated. I refer to De Tocqueville. His two chapters, with scattered incidental discussions, devoted to the place of journalism in the United States, have a queerly modern sound. He, too, discovered in that far-off happy time—happy because it is far off—that "the most intelligent Americans" were much concerned about "the little influence of the press." Doubtless they would have sadly shaken their heads and told the French visitor that they could remember when American journalism was much more dignified—in the days of Frenau, for example!

De Tocqueville, however, made some philosophic observations of his own respecting our press, which are as sound now, in substance, as when he wrote them. Indeed, one in want of a guide to the understanding of the power and the limitations of our newspapers today, could not do better than take him. He declared, for example, that "the press cannot create human passions, however skilfully it may kindle them when they exist." There is a world of meaning in this. It is as true in 1912 as it was in 1831. And it applies not alone to the attempts of the press to play a great part in politics and to bring about changes in government, but as well to the whole range of intellectual interest and social concerns and the development of the humane spirit of our age, about which the press is more and more busying itself. Newspapers cannot create human passions. No, but the press can powerfully further them. Take the passion for human betterment. I have been told of a piece of advice which President Eliot is said to have given to a youth just graduating from college. He was an ardent young fellow, of good family and ample means, but filled with that sense of "social compunction" which Mrs. Ward has said to be the characteristic note of our day. He was anxious, that is, to do something for the improvement of social conditions, as he considered them, which had been impressed upon him in his own city. How to go about the work on which he had his heart? Mr. Eliot advised him to connect himself as a reporter with one of the local papers. In that capacity, he would be able, in a vivid and concrete way, to get before his public an account of the wrongs to be righted with suggestions of the way to right them. Without vouching for the truth of the story, I think that the moral of it is entirely sound, in so far as it points out the fact that social reformers find in the press today a powerful instrument ready for their hand. Through it, they may, first, disseminate the facts, often in a moving fashion; then bring about a common sentiment respecting some surviving form of human oppression, some persistent industrial or social wrong; and finally transmute that feeling into systematic agitation and an organized movement for reform by law.

All this, to go back to De Tocqueville, was clearly perceived by him. What I have been saying is but an illustration of his remark: "When many organs of the press adopt the same line of conduct, their influence in the long run becomes irresistible; and public opinion powerfully assailed from the same side eventually yields to the attack." That was true in the middle of the nineteenth century and it is true today. The press may not greatly initiate, but it wonderfully reverberates. In its franker moments, it has humbly to confess itself, with Lowell, "child of an age that lectures, not creates," but given the origination of an idea or an agitation, it can contribute mightily to its acceptance by the reading public. Here comes in its power of iteration—"damnable," if you please, in many instances, but none the less effective. The organization of news in this country yields a result nowhere else known. By means of the Associated Press, and other news-gathering agencies, it often comes about that all our millions of population are reading the same thing on the same day. This implies both an audience and a unified power of expressing it without a parallel in other lands. And no one denies that the opportunity is availed of. For good or bad, the newspaper-reading habit of Americans, combined with this ability to present virtually identical matter in every section of the republic, is a vital element in the formation of public opinion. Instance after instance could be given of the continual dropping which wears away the stone. It is, no doubt, true that newspapers "cannot form great currents of opinion which sweep away the strongest dikes, but they do offer themselves as ready channels for the flowing of such currents, once they get started in the thought and feeling of the people."

This may be a humbler function than is customarily attributed to the press, or claimed by it, but few will dispute that it is a useful one, or may be made so. The methods or devices employed to exert even this kind of influence are much in controversy, both in and out of the profession—if profession it may be called. It is frequently said that newspaper editorials are no longer of account. An editorial writer could hardly be expected to maintain the contrary. The chief emphasis is laid upon the news columns, more or less colored by the policy or the bias of the particular paper, upon the cartoons, above all upon the headlines. About the last, especially, there is much complaint. Not all of it is without justification. The headline often covereth a multitude of sins. Politicians and others attacked by the papers are heard bitterly to say that if they could write the headlines, they would not care what appeared in the rest of the paper. That an abuse lies in this, sometimes grievous abuse, no honest newspaper man would deny. . . .

If readers suffer themselves to be fooled by captions, without waiting to see whether they are borne out by the contents, what is this but one proof more that the faculty of sustained attention is disappearing? If we nowadays peruse serious books only by titles and chapter headings, and take our art merely by glances at facile reproductions, what wonder if we read newspapers on the run, and let the eye dwell upon little that is not at the top of the page?

Here is suggested the important consideration that there is something reciprocal in the relations of the press to the public. Newspapers, like party leaders, get from their constituents, as well as give to them. In either case it is a nice question whether they do not get more than they give. The press cannot be studied or fairly judged apart from its environment. It is, with all our institutions, caught in the complex of our actual state of civilization. And the whole question of bringing about reforms in newspaper methods—Heaven knows they are needed—must be discussed from both sides. Editors have their responsibility, and in some cases the responsibility for what they do is fearful; but the public is also responsible. The community always holds the power of life or death over newspapers. No form of property is more precarious. The most offensive and hurtful types of newspaper could not live a year if the public issued a really determined decree that they should die. I cannot here discuss the duty of newspaper proprietors and editors, in regard to the admitted evils of the press in our day. But the chief duty of the public is to discriminate among newspapers. Towards the vulgar and vicious it should manifest not only disgust but an active and unflagging hostility. The location of the Garden of Eden is still in dispute; but if it ever is determined and the tree of knowledge of good and evil discovered, a cutting from it should be taken and planted near every news-stand in America.

BRIEF EXCERPTS

Every community has the press that it deserves.—*Criminal Justice in Cleveland. p.* 526.

Many of the hard-won rights of man are utterly insecure.—*Walter Lippmann. Liberty and the News. p.* 20.

The press is the greatest educator and molder of opinion and ideals in the republic.—*B. O. Flower. Arena.* 38:170. *August* 1907.

A great news-gathering organization and an efficient press censorship are natural enemies.—*Edward T. Cook. Bellman.* 25:325. *September* 21, 1918.

The modern newspaper is almost forced by its readers to become a mere institutionalization of gossip.—*John Storck. Man and Civilization. p.* 270.

The press is modern democracy's weak and vital spot. In the technique of minority rule, the censor ranks ahead of the executioner.—*William Bolitho. Survey.* 57:731. *March* 1, 1927.

We believe in freedom of the press although we know that newspapers are sometimes vulgar and contribute to crime by the publication of its details.—*Independent.* 77: 433. *March* 30, 1914.

Whether sensational news in general is to any considerable extent promotive of crime or vice is a debatable question, with the direct evidence largely negative.—*Nelson A. Crawford. Ethics of Journalism. p.* 116.

If sensational trials were not reported as to be read almost universally, a great opportunity to vindicate American justice to our citizens would be lost.—*Law Notes.* 30:162. *December* 1926.

The press is justly considered among the great powers, exerting an immense influence upon the political and social destinies of mankind.—*Boris Brasol. Elements of Crime. p.* 166.

Most criminal careers are begun before there is extensive reading of the newspapers. Young offenders as a rule care for little but the comic portions.—*William Healy. Individual Delinquents. p.* 302.

The high character of most newspapers today admits them without question to the position of textbooks in the schools.—*E. Ruth Pyrtle. New Mexico School Review. March* 1930.

The Minnesota nuisance law is an ideal weapon in the hands of a corrupt administration which could use it efficiently to prevent criticism of itself.—*Lawyer and Banker.* 22:131. *May* 1929.

The Minnesota nuisance law is worse than common censorship, because it clothes the censor with judicial power to decide, punish, and suppress.—*Lawyer and Banker.* 22:1. *January* 1929.

The very essence of a free press lies in its right to be the sole judge of what it prints. The law of libel holds ample relief for the citizen attacked by unscrupulous editors.—*Lawyer and Banker.* 22:2. *January* 1929.

There are many things which ought not to be printed in the newspapers, but we don't submit our papers in advance either to a board of censors or to one man.—*Clarence Darrow. City Club Bulletin. Chicago.* 11:187. *June* 3, 1918.

Without a free press the established order of things can nowhere be improved. Government control has always made the press servile.—*James A. Garfield. Address before Ohio Editorial Association, June* 11, 1878. *Works of James A. Garfield. vol.* 2. *p.* 579.

Investigators and thinkers working in the sphere of opinion may safely be left free to speak and print because their errors will spread slowly and will probably be overtaken by the truth before they get very far.—*Edward A. Ross. Social Psychology. p.* 133.

The American yellow newspaper, which, by means of scareheads, color pictures, and gong effects, gets itself read by the foreign-born, has been a potent agent of Americanization.—*Edward A. Ross. Principles of Sociology. p.* 233.

Censorship is impracticable. The name of newspapers is legion, and their issues are prepared in hot haste during the night. Preliminary inspection is absurdly impossible.—*Thomas Templeton. Encyclopedia of Religion and Ethics. vol.* 3. *p.* 305.

The real menace to the freedom of the periodical press is not from lawmakers or courts, but from its progressive subjection to the profits motive.—*Edward A. Ross. Papers and Proceedings of the American Sociological Society.* 9:131. *December* 1914.

Were it left to me to decide whether we should have a government without newspapers or newspapers without a government, I should not hesitate a moment to prefer the latter.—*Thomas Jefferson. Writings. vol.* 4. *p.* 360.

We are governed by public opinion, as ascertained and expressed in the newspapers, to such an extent that our civilization is justly to be called a newspaper civilization. —*William T. Harris in Edwin G. Dexter's History of Education in the United States. p.* 503.

Taking the American press all in all, it seems to serve the expression, and subserve the formation, of public opinion more fully than does the press of any part of the European continent, and not less fully than that of England.—*James Bryce. American Commonwealth.* 3d *ed. vol.* 2. *p.* 275.

In summing up America's services to the human race the future historian will have to mention American journalism and American cinema films. Through its journalism and its films the United States has sent two waves of Americanism all over the globe.—*Francis McCullagh. Studies.* 18:395. *September* 1929.

As the railroad binds together portions of a continent, so the press links the minds of human beings. The newspaper is a moving picture of the world. The whole system of modern life would be impossible without the press.—*Henry K. Rowe. Society: its Origin and Development. p.* 281-2.

No one seriously expects if censorship is finally adopted to meet the conditions which we have described [newspaper reporting of crime and trials] that it can work with any degree of satisfaction even to its advocates.—*Report of the New York State Crime Commission.* 1927. *p.* 326.

No one single cause ever produces either a crime or any other social phenomenon. Therefore, in ninety-nine cases out of one hundred, we will fail to discern a causative connection between an individual crime and some specific newspaper article.—*Boris Brasol. Elements of Crime. p.* 167.

We need a much better and more trustworthy press than we possess. We cannot get on to a newer and better world without it. The remedy is to be found not, I believe, in any sort of government control, but in a legal campaign against the one thing harmful—the lie.—*H. G. Wells. Salvaging of Civilization. p.* 189-90.

Only rarely have we met the slightest indication that a newspaper story of a criminal has developed hero worship. We should be inclined to believe that there are good psychological reasons why newspapers do not have anything like the same bad effect as literature of the dime novel order or as pernicious moving and other pictures.—*William Healy. Individual Delinquent. p.* 302.

What is the liberty of the press? Who can give it any definition which would not leave the utmost latitude for evasion? I hold it to be impracticable; and from this I infer that its security, whatever fine declarations may be inserted in the Constitution respecting it, must altogether depend on public opinion, and on the general spirit of the people and the government.—*Alexander Hamilton. Federalist. No.* 84.

Imagine a situation in which a corrupt officialdom in partnership with the underworld attempts to suppress public knowledge of crime and a corrupt or dull-minded judge is found to do the bidding of the partners in evil. What protection would the public have against such a tyranny? Such a law is the best that organized criminals could desire for their own security.—*Lawyer and Banker.* 22:2. *January* 1929.

The laws of libel provide an adequate safeguard against a damaged name and they have a sufficiently restraining influence upon editors. For such newspapers as are not edited with regard for fairness and truth the actual working of the libel laws is an ample corrective. A weapon which automatically silences criticism destroys a large part of the usefulness of a newspaper.—*Editorial. Chicago Tribune. March* 19, 1929.

The freedom of the press is but a shadow if a publisher is not allowed to criticize the government and its employes adversely, but is compelled to compliment and flatter them. When the public servants tell their master, the people, that the latter may not find fault with them, they are overstepping the bounds of their power and must immediately be called to account.—*Robert R. McCormick. New York Times. November* 13, 1929.

It is its importance as a bulwark of liberty that exempts the daily newspaper [from censorship.] Public policy demands that it shall remain free despite its frequent salacity. Charges of that sort might too easily be made merely a pretext for stifling the cherished freedom of the press which the Anglo-Saxon has won only after so many sanguinary battles.—*Morris L. Ernst. To the Pure. p.* 36.

In no one single case can we in the least show that the reading of newspapers was a strong cause of criminality. We have inquired about mental influences in many hundreds of cases, and, while other factors stand out clearly as affecting mental processes, this one does not. Nor do our results contradict anything that other authors have actually been able to show.—*William Healy. Individual Delinquent. p.* 302.

Newspapers are influential in three ways: as narrators, as advocates, and as weathercocks. In the first of these regards the American press is the most active in the world. Nothing escapes it which can attract any class of readers. The appetite for news, and for highly spiced or sensational news, is enormous, and journalists working under keen competition and in unceasing haste take their chance of the correctness of the information they receive.—*James Bryce. Commonwealth.* 3d *ed. vol.* 2. *p.* 271.

The fundamental right of free men to strive for better conditions through new legislation and new institutions will not be preserved, if efforts to secure it by argument to fellow citizens may be constructed as criminal incitement to disobey the existing law,—namely, because the argument presented seems to those exercising judicial power to be unfair in its portrayal of existing evils, mistaken in its assumptions, unsound in reasoning or intemperate in language.—*Dissenting Opinion of Justices Brandeis and Holmes.* 252 *U. S.* 273.

The Minnesota nuisance law establishes a dangerous precedent. That it was designed for the suppression of disreputable publications does not insure that it will not be used as a political weapon to quiet legitimate criticism and it is an invitation for more drastic legislation. The laws of libel furnish adequate avenues for satisfaction of grievances. For those who have no justification for libel suit but who do have political influence, the newspaper injunction law offers the opportunity for dictatorial elimination of criticism.—*Editorial. Chicago Tribune. March* 6, 1929.

In criminological literature the view has been expressed by some writers that journalism invariably plays the part of a criminogenic agency, fostering delinquent impulses and inciting the moral weaklings to imitate the crimes depicted in the newspapers. Lombroso's words may be regarded as typical of this profoundly pessimistic theory. [*Crime: its Causes and Remedies. p.* 54-5.] More recently, however, this gloomy opinion was modified by the investigations undertaken by Hellwig and Fenton, whose conclusions are shared by Dr. William Healy.—*Boris Brasol. Elements of Crime. p.* 166.

So while censorship seems to be prohibited under our [state and national] constitutional guaranties of freedom of the press, yet indirectly we have made the Postmaster General a virtual censor by putting in his hands the power to exclude publications from the mails. To take away from a newspaper or periodical the second class mailing privilege, or the use of the mails altogether, is to take away the only effective means of publication and put the paper out of business. Such power as this should not be placed in the hands of any one official. —*Robert H. Wellach. North Carolina Law Review.* 4:38. *February* 1926.

The power to prohibit the publication of newspapers is not within the compass of legislative action in this state, and any law enacted for that purpose would clearly be in derogation of the [state] Bill of Rights. The power to suppress one concedes the power to suppress all, whether such publications are political, secular, religious, decent or indecent, obscene or otherwise. The doctrine of the [state] constitution must prevail in this state, which clothes the citizen with liberty to speak, write, or publish his opinion on any and all subjects, subject alone to responsibility for the abuse of such privilege.—*Unanimous decision of the Texas Court of Criminal Appeals.* 32 *Texas Crim. R.* 275. *June* 17, 1893.

We live in an age of pitiless publicity! We live in an age when freedom of speech and freedom of press are paramount issues! People should be allowed to say what they please and newspapers should be allowed to print what they please, always making themselves liable under the law of slander or the law of libel, and usually this is penalty enough to keep persons from transcending the bounds of decency and proper criticism. While courts must be protected in the administration of their judicial duties, yet courts are filled with men who are only human and they are subject to all the weaknesses and variable temperaments that beset the ordinary man. It is better that the press be free, that speech be free, that the right of assembly be free, and that the right to air our views be free, than it is that they be uttered in fear and trembling, even though oftentimes they transcend the bounds of decency and of the rights of the individual assaulted. A free people must have a free press and they must have the right to speak freely their thoughts.—*Ohio Court of Appeals of Cuyahoga County. Ohio Law Bulletin and Reporter.* 31:407-9. *March* 24, 1930.

There are certain cases where criticism upon public officers, their actions, character, and motives, is not only recognized as legitimate, but large latitude and great freedom of expression are permitted, so long as good faith inspires the communication. There are cases where it is clearly the duty of every one to speak freely what he may have to say concerning public officers, or those who may present themselves for public positions. The public have a right to be heard on the question of their selection; and they have the right, for such reasons as seem to their minds sufficient, to ask for their dismissal afterwards. They have also the right to complain of official conduct affecting themselves.—*Thomas M. Cooley. Treatise on Constitutional Limitations.* 8th *ed. vol.* 2. *p.* 908.

It is the constitutional freedom of the press that has made of America a democracy in fact as well as in name. It is the freedom of the press that permits the formation of public opinion. German newspapers have been timidly subservient to the autocratic interests of the imperial government. They have often been secretly subsidized by the German government. They have been, even in time of peace, directly controlled by the government. The most essential problem in the making of a durable peace is the dissolution of any partnership that may exist in any country between the government and the press. Interference with the free intercourse of nations through the press either by financial seduction of news agencies engaged in international news distribution or by the exercise of arbitrary powers over the press of any people that desires to be free must necessarily impede international harmony.—*David Lawrence. Annals of the American Academy.* 72:141. *July* 1917.

The inexpensive American newspaper provides a European news service of remarkable fullness, a lavish amount of information about local, state, and national politics, educational news of schools, colleges, and societies, religious and church news, news of women's clubs, articles and news about music, drama, new books, social service, and innumerable agencies of civic activity. Then there is considerable space devoted to such sports as baseball, football, racing, tennis, hockey, golf, skating, and aquatics. The commercial section embraces information about all markets and trades, and devotes much space to real estate. The Sunday supplements publish excellent photographic reproductions illustrating specially significant or interesting occurrences at home and abroad. The funny strip of the daily, and the comic page of the Sunday supplement, have apparently become one of the established institutions of the American press. —*F. Stuart Chapin. Cultural Change*. p. 286.

Censorship of the press is open to many fundamental objections. First, the policy of repression demands the exercise of control by one individual or group over another. This will inevitably lead to tyranny in the end. Second, since there are no assured means of determining what emotions or opinions are sound or of permanent value, there can be no effective selection of individuals or groups to do the censoring. Third, psychology has suggested and experience has demonstrated that the process of expression relieves the psychic pressure of distorted sentiments and disruptive opinions which might otherwise burst forth in dangerous action. Fourth, not infrequently censorship succeeds in advertising and thus popularizing the particular act, work of art, book, play, or bit of propaganda which the censors desire to suppress. On the whole the idea of censorship offers little by way of curing the sensationalism of the press, or of constructive help in improving either the literary or the moral quality of newspapers, periodicals, or other types of publication.—*Walter R. Smith. Principles of Educational Sociology. p.* 307.

Freedom of legitimate discussion must be maintained. If any editor or any public man feels persuaded that a President is working harm to the republic, he must have the right to say so plainly and emphatically. A year and a half ago Mr. Hoar, the veteran Republican Senator from Massachusetts, was profoundly convinced that the policy pursued by the [Republican] Administration was one so utterly bad that "perseverance in it will be the abandonment of the principles upon which our Government is founded, that it will change our republic into an empire;" and he so declared in the most impressive manner in a speech delivered before the Senate on the 17th of April, 1900. The right of any public man, and of any newspaper editor, to say such severe things as this about any President must be preserved, and it will be a sad day for the republic when there are no Senators ready to speak the truth as they see it. So, too, we must render it possible always for a Nast to expose a Tweed, or a Keppler a Blaine, in a cartoon which puts a whole argument in a single picture.—*Nation.* 73:239. *September* 26, 1901.

Despite many and serious defects in the American press, it renders us one great service—it holds the mirror up to American life, and shows us what that life is. It does not always show it in its right proportions. The mirror is not always a well formed mirror; it is sometimes like one of those convex or concave mirrors that stand in the agricultural fairs. Nevertheless the press does bring American people to a self-consciousness. If we do not like the records of vice and crime, of ignorance and poverty, which we read in our newspapers, let us change the life. The American press, though defective in leadership, though it appeals too much to the sensational, though it lacks in seriousness, sobriety, ernestness, conscience,—qualities which it ought to possess—does one great educative work: it brings the whole history of yesterday before us. I am glad that it brings the history of the bad as well as of the good. We do not want in America a press which only portrays our virtues and forgets our vices. Let us have from the press the truth, the whole truth, and—also—nothing but the truth.—*Lyman Abbott. Right of Man. p.* 329-30.

The people will be managed without their knowing it unless there are numerous founts of authoritative opinion independent of one another and of any single powerful organization. Let there be many towers from which trusty watchmen may scan the horizon and cry to the people a warning which no official or mob may hush. Perhaps it is impossible to secure society against delusions as disastrous as the Children's Crusade, the witchcraft persecutions, and the German megalomania of 1914, but our fairest hope lies in multiplying strongholds of free opinion. Although its growing dependence upon the receipts from advertising is bringing the newspaper under the yoke of commercial interests, we can insist that at least it shall be no jumping jack of officials. The government should not maintain a "reptile press" such as Bismarck used, nor should it censor the newspapers save in war time, and then only by a board on which private citizens preponderate. Public officials should give out impartially the news of their offices. Neither editors nor owners should be appointed to high posts in the public service lest newspapers fall into the habit of truckling to politicians. No periodical should be denied news service or forced off the news stands on account of its politics.—*Edward A. Ross. Principles of Sociology. p.* 436-7.

Among the inventions of modern times, by which the world has been powerfully influenced, and from which civilization has received a new and wonderful impulse, must be classed the newspaper. Through it the public proceedings of every civilized country, the debates of the leading legislative bodies, the events of war, the triumphs of peace, the storms in the physical and the agitations in the moral and mental world, are brought home to the knowledge of every reading person, and, to a very large extent, before the day is over on which the events have taken place. The newspaper is one of the chief means for the education of the people. The highest and the lowest in the scale of intelligence resort to its columns for information. It is read by those who read nothing else, and the best minds of the age make it the medium of communication with each other on the highest and most abstruse subjects. Upon politics it may be said to be the chief educator of the people. Its influence is potent in every legislative body. It gives tone and direction to public sentiment on each important subject as it arises, and no administration in any free country ventures to overlook or disregard an element so pervading in its influence, and withal so powerful.—*Thomas M. Cooley. Treatise on Constitutional Limitations.* 8th *ed. vol.* 2. *p.* 936-7.

Perhaps of all the inventions that occurred prior to the eighteenth century, printing has the most power in modern civilization. No other one has so continued to expand its achievements. Becoming a necessary adjunct of modern education, it continually extends its influence in the direct aid of every other art, industry, or other form of human achievement. The dissemination of knowledge through books, periodicals, and the newspaper press has made it possible to keep alive the spirit of learning among the people and to assure that degree of intelligence necessary for a self-governed people. The freedom of the press is one of the cardinal principles of progress, for it brings into fulness the fundamental fact of freedom of discussion advocated by the early Greeks, which was the line of demarcation between despotism and dogmatism and the freedom of the mind and will. In common with all human institutions, its power has sometimes been abused. But its defect cannot be remedied by repression or by force, but by the elevation of the thought, judgment, intelligence, and good-will of a people by an education which causes them to demand better things. The press in recent years has been too susceptible to commercial dominance, a power, by the way, which has seriously affected all of our institutions. Here, as in all other phases of progress, wealth should be a means rather than an end of civilization.—*Frank W. Blackmar. History of Human Society. p.* 484-5.

Strangely, the newspapers of Minnesota have not been sufficiently alarmed at the law which strikes at their rights. The established papers have been persuaded that in the application of the law they will not suffer; that it is only an instrument for the elimination of socially undesirable publications. Apparently because of their own feeling of security they have not examined too carefully into the constitutional features of the law. But the confidence of the Minnesota newspapers is unwarranted. The law provides that a publication regularly engaged in printing "malicious, scandalous, or defamatory" matter may be suppressed by injunction. Under an interpretation of this law the *Saturday Press* of Minneapolis was put out of business. It was conducting a crusade against vice conditions and the officials of Hennepin county, whom it charged with responsibility for the license in that county. One of the officials, the district attorney, who was a subject of attack by the *Saturday Press,* secured the injunction. He had recourse to libel action for protection, if he were entitled to it, but he selected to silence his enemy through the nuisance law. It happened that the *Saturday Press* was a lurid paper and its campaign was a lurid one. But thè same campaign might have been organized by a more responsible publication and carried on in a less sensational fashion. If it were fighting a politically dominant and corrupt faction its reputability would not save it from oblivion. That a bad law once has been applied, possibly for a good purpose, is no assurance that it will not be applied in future for bad purposes.—*Editorial. Chicago Tribune. March* 16, 1929.

PART IV

CENSORSHIP OF BOOKS

BRIEF

RESOLVED: *That the Federal Government should create a Board of Review for all books of fiction with power to deny the privilege of copyright and to exclude from the mails, from interstate commerce, and from importation into this country all such books that it considers obscene, immoral, impure, indecent, or that will tend to corrupt the morals of the people.*

INTRODUCTION

I. The meaning of the question.
   - A. This plan does not call for censorship in the ordinary meaning of that word.
     1. Censorship means the power of suppression in advance of publication.
     2. It means a condition where all manuscripts must be submitted to the authorities and where their permission is necessary for publication.
   - B. The proposed plan will create a board with limited powers in a restricted field.
     1. It will have jurisdiction over books of fiction only.
     2. It will have no power to forbid the publication of any book.
     3. It will be powerless to suppress any book that has been published.

C. This National Board of Review will have power to recommend or to condemn books of fiction that have been published and may hereafter be published.
  1. Its condemnation of a book will cut off its rights and privileges in copyright, importation, and transportation both in the mails and in interstate commerce.

II. The importance of the question.
  A. The publication, importation, and circulation of obscene and indecent books has become a national problem.
    1. The experts of the postal and revenue services have already placed their ban on 739 different books.
    2. The local authorities in many communities have taken action against them.
      a. In Philadelphia the prosecutor has raided a number of book shops and confiscated a large number of obscene and vicious books.
      b. The police in Boston have been active in this work.
      c. Twice in the year of 1930 the Supreme Judicial Court of Massachusetts has sustained a conviction for selling an obscene book. (171 N.E. 455, 472.)

Affirmative

I. There is urgent necessity for the appointment of a Board of Review to purify and elevate the books of fiction in America.
  A. Many of the recent books of popular fiction are obscene, indecent, and tend to corrupt public morals.

1. Many of them reek with sex smut.
   a. The Supreme Judicial Court of Massachusetts has said in a formal decision: "The conclusion of fact we have reached upon a full reading of this book is in accordance with that of the trial judge, which he formulates as follows, 'The book viewed as a whole, having regard to its significance as an entity, and not merely to certain particular parts of it viewed separately, is obscene, indecent, and impure, and manifestly tends to corrupt the morals of youth.' " (171 N.E. 456.)
2. Some of them are mere visualizations of vice.
   a. Speaking of one of Lawrence's books, Dr. Joseph Collins has said, "A large portion of the book is obscene, deliberately, studiously, incessantly obscene." (*The Doctor Looks at Literature.* p. 278.)
3. There are now a great many books of this kind being published.
   a. George F. Bowerman, the Librarian of the Public Library at Washington, D.C., has said, "The disquieting thing about the whole matter is that there are so many books published of such a character as to be candidates for censorship." (*Libraries.* 35:186. May 1930.)
   b. There are now 739 books that are excluded from the mails and from importation into this country under our present very moderate laws.

B. These vicious books are surely undermining the virtues on which our civilization is based.
   1. They are certainly corrupting the morals of our children and young people.
      a. They are poisoning the minds of great numbers of our boys and girls.
      b. Many leading people are now asking, What ails our youth?
      c. George F. Bowerman has said, "Everybody will agree that it is desirable to protect from injurious books the young and immature who are highly impressionable and whose self-control is still undeveloped." (*Libraries.* 35:184. May 1930.)
      d. Prof. Edward A. Ross has said, "No society can afford to let its members say or publish or exhibit what they please. The ordered sex relation is man's greatest achievement in self-domestication. Common sense forbids that the greed of purveyors of suggestive plays, pictures, or literature be suffered to disturb it. (*Social Psychology.* p. 126.)
      e. President Roosevelt has said that requests, made to him while President or Governor, for the pardon of a person who had been convicted and imprisoned for circulating indecent literature, "merely made me mad." (*Autobiography.* p. 305.)
   2. They have caused crime and depravity.
      a. A century ago America was a nation of high-minded and law-abiding people.
         (1) There was then but little crime in this country.

(2) The people had pure and lofty ideals.

(3) The literature was noble and inspiring.

b. In the past two generations there has been produced in this country a vicious fiction literature, and now we have more crime, in proportion to our population, than any other advanced and civilized nation in the world.

(1) We have twice as much murder as Italy, the second most murderous of nations, four times as much as Australia or South Africa, eight times as much as New Zealand, Ireland, or Spain, nine times as much as Norway, fifteen times as much as Ontario, seventeen times as much as Great Britain, eighteen times as much as Scotland, twenty-four times as much as Holland, and thirty-six times as much as Switzerland.

(2) Chicago has twenty-five or thirty times as high a murder rate as London; Detroit has a rate twice as high as Chicago; and Memphis has a rate six times as high as Chicago.

(3) Cleveland and Detroit have each more robberies each year than Great Britain with thirty-five or forty times their population.

3. They become a national menace in the hands of the feeble-minded and sub-normal people.

a. They picture vicious and immoral conduct as the ordinary and everyday actions of normal people.

b. Some of these books make crime appear attractive, picturing even the most desperate criminals as heroes, and making it appear that crime is an easy way to get rich.

c. Many of them are filled with descriptions and narrations that are suggestive of crime and vice.

4. They have prevented the development of good reading habits in thousands of the young people.

   a. They have usurped the place of wholesome and instructive reading.

   b. They have developed in many young people the habit of reading only drivel and imaginative nonsense.

   c. They have developed in many people the shallow, flightly, imaginative mind which insists that all of its reading must be for vulgar entertainment.

C. All present methods have failed to remedy this national evil.

1. They lack harmony, unity, and continuity.

   a. They are chiefly in the nature of local spasmodic crusades.

   b. George F. Bowerman has said, "Not less than sixty-eight books, sold freely elsewhere in the United States, have in the last two years been suppressed and are not on sale, at least openly, in Boston." (*Libraries*. 35:131. April 1930.)

2. They lack a standard by which the smaller towns and backward parts of the coun-

try may know what books should be suppressed.

- II. The proposed plan is wise and desirable.
  - A. It will completely remedy the evil.
    - 1. It can be applied promptly.
    - 2. It will furnish a standard.
      - a. Librarians, book sellers, parents and teachers, police and prosecutors, even judges and juries will then know how to rank and deal with any particular book.
    - 3. This will protect the young and safeguard the morals and ideals of the nation.
  - B. It will have great potential power and influence.
    - 1. It will encourage and give a substantial advantage to the reputable, clean-minded, and high grade people among the writers and publishers.
    - 2. It will put a feeling of responsibility in the criminal element among writers, publishers, and book sellers.
      - a. No writer, publisher, or book seller will dare openly to defy such a board of review.
      - b. Future books will be written and published with the view of meeting the approval of this board.
  - C. It will not interfere with the freedom of the press.
    - 1. The law has never construed the freedom of the press to be an absolute right.
    - 2. The guaranty of the freedom of the press protects the use, not the abuse of the press.
    - 3. This plan places no restraint upon publication.

D. It will not interfere with the progress of civilization.
   1. It will not obstruct the advance of science.
      a. No scientific book will be subject to review by this board.
   2. It will not interfere with the promulgation of new ideas.
   3. It will not prevent complete freedom of thought and expression.
      a. Modern fiction is mere drivel: there is no thought in it.
   4. No great work, no book of unusual literary or artistic merit, will ever be condemned by this board.
      a. The nature and duties of this board will insure the appointment of eminent experts to be its members.
      b. Such a board will command public confidence and respect.

III. The proposed plan is a practicable remedy.
   A. This board will condemn every vicious and obscene book of fiction and brand it as an outlaw.
      1. This board, made up of eminent experts, will realize that the whole world is watching their decisions.
      2. They will feel a tremendous responsibility in the way of safeguarding the morals of the nation, and will let no vicious or obscene book pass.
   B. This plan will remove the greatest obstacle in the long struggle against vicious and harmful books of fiction.
      1. The decisions of this board will set a uniform standard for the nation.

a. State and city authorities will then know what books are approved and what are condemned as obscene and indecent.
b. Writers will know what the standard is that they must meet to have their work approved.
c. Publishers will be guided by this and will not take the chances of loss by publishing a book that is liable to be condemned.

2. The question of whether a book is obscene will no longer have to be proved in court.
 a. It will be definitely and finally established by a national board that is a group of eminent experts.
 b. The courts will undoubtedly take judicial notice of all the findings of this board.

C. This plan will prevent the distribution and sale of obscene and indecent books.
 1. It will be a crime to send a book from one state to another.
 2. Any state or city can make it a crime for a person to have such a book in his possession, to sell or give away one, or to give information concerning one of them.

Negative

I. There is no need for such a drastic law.
 A. Very few of the books of fiction are obscene or vicious.
  1. Not 1 per cent of modern fiction is obscene or indecent.
   a. No book should be judged by any single sentence or passage, but should be judged as a whole.

2. The great majority of the thousands of books of modern fiction are good, instructive, inspiring, and wholly beneficial.
    a. They are instructive, picturing life as it is.
    b. They are entertaining and refreshing, relieving the strain and monotony of life for millions of people.
    c. Many of them are the best efforts of our greatest literary artists.
    d. They are the only books read by millions of our people.

B. The bad books exert little influence, doing little or no harm.
1. No evidence has been offered to show any great harm done by reading books of fiction.
    a. No evidence has ever yet been offered to show that the reading of books of fiction has ever corrupted the morals of youth.
        (1) This has always been merely an assumption.
    b. No evidence has been offered to show that the reading of fiction is a cause of crime or has caused any increase in crime.
    c. Indeed, there has never yet been any satisfactory evidence offered to show that there has been any increase in crime in recent years.
        (1) It is true that this has often been stated as a fact, but the best evidence seems to show that it is not true.
2. Any youth, who is so weak as to be led astray merely by reading books of fiction,

would probably go wrong even if he had never read any fiction at all.

- C. There are many adults who want to read what the purists call obscene and indecent books.
  - 1. The great sale of such books shows that they fill a real public demand.
  - 2. There has never been a nation in which all of the minds were up to the highest and purist levels.
    - a. There should be no legal standard of literature, bringing it all above the level of appreciation and enjoyment of millions of people.
  - 3. The real problem is to elevate and purify these minds by education and culture, and not to suppress the literature that they enjoy.
- D. Present methods are entirely adequate to handle the problem.
  - 1. There are national and state laws against publishing or selling obscene literature.
  - 2. These laws are fully enforced by the national postal, revenue, and other officials, and by the local police authorities.

II. The proposed plan is unwise and undesirable.

- A. It is wrong in principle.
  - 1. It seeks indirectly to prevent people from freely expressing their thoughts.
  - 2. In any free country the press should be left entirely free.
    - a. Laws should seek to encourage the best literature rather than to penalize and suppress the poorer works.
- B. It will not better the conditions.
  - 1. This plan does not prohibit the publication of obscene and vicious books.

2. If this plan were adopted there would be wholesale bootlegging of the condemned books.
   a. All attempts at suppression have always served only to drive obscene and vicious literature into the cellars and sewers.
   b. Under the proposed plan this type of literature would continue to circulate out of the reach of the authorities through these underground channels.
3. Even if the law were to work perfectly, we would still have the vicious magazines on almost every newstand within the reach of almost every school child.
   a. George F. Bowerman has said, "There are always the gutter magazines, easily accessible on payment of a few cents." (*Libraries.* 35:189. May 1930.)

C. The proposed plan is open to grave dangers.
1. It would be only the opening wedge for further and more harmful legislation.
   a. Legislation is a growth, one new law leading to another.
   b. All new legislation must be considered as a tendency, as an indication of the direction to which it is leading.
   c. The proposed law would undoubtedly lead to the enactment of more drastic and unwise legislation.
2. There have been many recent cases or threats of literary or scientific lynching.
   a. The mayor of Chicago recently talked about burning many of the history books in the Chicago Public Library.
   b. In 1928 the college libraries of the

two state universities in Florida were "ransacked by a committee of ten clergymen authorized by the State Senate to ferret out heretical books on history and psychology." (*New York Times Book Review*. December 8, 1929. p. 38.)

  c. The nation-wide efforts of the two hundred thousand Christian Scientists in America to suppress Dakin's biography of Mrs. Eddy are still going on.

3. There is serious danger that religious fanaticism will be fanned into a heat that will seek to crush the advance of liberal literature and even the teaching of science. (Maynard Shipley. *The War on Modern Science.*)
   a. A few states have already passed laws to restrict the teaching of science in all of their public schools.
4. It is always a dangerous thing to pass any law to stifle or suppress the free publication of any thought.
   a. It may lead to other and worse forms of censorship.

D. The proposed plan would be liable to serious abuses.
1. It gives too much and too arbitrary power to one group of men.
   a. There is no group of men in America wise enough to decide what the nation should be allowed to read.
   b. The members of the board are liable to be influenced by their own prejudices.
2. There have been many cases where the

boards of censors have changed their minds.

a. Even the Supreme Court of the United States has reversed itself on several occasions, as in the income tax case, and often it is not unanimous even in its most important decisions.

b. These are evidences that many great minds have made errors in their decisions.

3. In actual operation it will do more harm than good.

a. All forms of censorship used in recent times have often served chiefly to prohibit the good and to advertise the bad.

4. Political considerations would often be a determining factor in the decisions of this board of review.

a. Any book that criticised or ridiculed the administration or party in power would be condemned.

(1) Such a book as *Revelry* would be instantly condemned, tho its purpose and effect were good.

b. A writer of an obscene book might get it approved by flattering words about the party leaders or the administration in power.

III. The proposed plan is impracticable.

A. All forms of censorship of the press have always failed to benefit society.

1. They have done far more harm than good.

a. They have been a resistance to progress.

b. They have suppressed new ideas.

c. They have never been able to suppress all the obscene literature of any country.

2. Censorship of books has written the darkest pages of all human history. (Andrew D. White. *History of the Warfare of Science with Theology in Christendom.*)
   a. It is responsible for the burning of the library at Alexandria.
   b. It tortured Galileo on the rack.
   c. It made the Dark Ages.
   d. It burned at the stake thousands of gifted and superior people. (John W. Draper. *History of the Conflict between Religion and Science.*)

B. The proposed plan cannot be made to work out.
   1. It will be impossible to get good censors.
      a. If there are any men really well qualified for the work, they will refuse to serve.
      b. All appointments will be made primarily for political reasons.
   2. The states and cities will not obey or follow the rulings and decisions of the board of review.
      a. There will continue to be wide differences of opinion as to what books are obscene and vicious.

C. The proposed plan is a violation of the American doctrine of states' rights.
   1. Our Constitution leaves to the states all powers of government that are not specifically delegated to the Federal Government.
      a. The existence of our decentralized form of government is being threat-

ened by the constant increase in the powers and duties of the Federal Government.

(1) The state governments are slowly but surely shrinking into an unimportant place in our governmental system.

(2) The Federal Government is fast becoming an overgrown and unwieldy bureaucracy.

2. The proposed plan would be one more step in augmenting the powers of the Federal Government.

   a. It would take from the states powers that they are now exercising and confer them on the already overloaded Federal Government.

3. Any uniform standard for books of fiction is very undesirable in our vast country.

   a. Ideals in reading and standards of thought differ very greatly in the different parts of this country.

D. The proposed plan would be opposed by most of the best minds in the country.

1. Writers and publishers would be a unit in opposition to it.

2. All believers in the freedom of the human mind would oppose it.

BIBLIOGRAPHY

Bibliographies

Askew, John B. Pros and cons. 5th ed. Dutton. N.Y. '12.

Censorship of fiction, p. 34.

Putnam, George H. Censorship of the Church of Rome. G. P. Putnam's Sons. N.Y. '06.

Bibliography, vol. 1, p. xvii-xxv.

Sumner, John S. and Boyd, Ernest. Debate on censorship of books. League for Public Discussion. N.Y. 77p. '24.

General References

Books and Pamphlets

Brown, Horatio F. Venetian printing press. Putnam. N.Y. '91.

Brown, Horatio F. Studies in the history of Venice. E. P. Dutton. N.Y. '07.

The Index Librorum Prohibitorum and the censorship of the Venetian press, p. 39-87.

Catholic Encyclopedia. Robert Appleton Co. N.Y. '08.

Censorship of books, vol. 3, p. 519-27. Index of prohibited books, vol. 7, p. 721-2.

Ditchfield, P. H. Books fatal to their authors. Lond. '95.

Encyclopaedia Britannica. 14th ed. Lond. '29.

*Index Librorum Prohibitorum, vol. 12, p. 148-9.

Encyclopaedia of Religion and Ethics. Scribner. N.Y. '25.

Censorship, vol. 3, p. 304-6. Index, vol. 7, p. 207-9.

Farrer, James A. Books condemned to be burnt. A. C. Armstrong. N.Y. n.d.

Jewish Encyclopedia. Funk and Wagnalls. N.Y. '02.

Censorship of Hebrew books, vol. 3, p. 642-52.

†Monroe, Paul. Cyclopedia of education. Macmillan. N.Y. '14.

Literary censorship, vol. 4, p. 32-41.

New Schaff-Herzog Encyclopedia of Religious Knowledge. Funk and Wagnalls. N.Y. '08.

Censorship and prohibition of books, vol. 2, p. 493.

Popper, William. Censorship of Hebrew books. N.Y. '99.

Putnam, George H. Censorship of the Church of Rome and its influence upon the production and the distribution of literature. 2 vols. Putnam. N.Y. '07.

Putnam, George H. Books and their makers during the middle ages. Putnam. N.Y. '97.

Privileges and censorship, vol. 2, p. 343-463.

Searle, G. M. Plain facts for fair minds. N.Y. '95.

†White, Andrew D. History of the warfare of science with theology in Christendom. Appleton. N.Y. '96.

PERIODICALS

American Mercury. 6:74-8. S. '25. Keeping the Puritans pure. A. L. S. Wood.

Atlantic Monthly. 132:10-20. Jl. '23. Unprintable. S. P. Sherman.

Bookman. 34:185-90. O. '11. Index of prohibited books. Calvin Winter.

†Bookman. 51:460-5. Je. '20. Suppression of books. H. L. West.

Catholic World. 116:392-9. D. '22. Editorial comment.

*Congressional Digest. 9:33-57+. F. '30. Censorship of foreign books.

*Congressional Record. 71:4432-9, 4445-72. O. 10-11, '29. Customs censorship. Bronson Cutting and others.

*Congressional Record. 72:5654-70, 5731-60 (current file). Mr. 17-18, '30. Customs censorship. Reed Smoot and others.

Current Literature. 44:620-1. Je. '08. Coming censorship of fiction. B. Tozer.

Current Literature. 52:468-71. Ap. '12. Fight against poisonous literature.
Current Opinion. 55:353+. N. '13. Literary censorship and the novels of the winter.
Dial. 48:135-7. Mr. 1, '10. Literary censorship.
Dial. 50:296-8. Ap. 16, '11. Censorship of fiction. E. H. L. Watson.
Dial. 57:491-2. D. 16, '14. Our hostility to art.
English Review. 13:477-85. F. '13. Under the collar.
Independent. 65:724-6. S. 24, '08. The index crosses the Atlantic.
Ladies Home Journal. 41:20. Ag. '24. Filth uplifters.
†Libraries. 35:127-35, 182-6. Ap. My. '30. Censorship and the Public library. George F. Bowerman.
Literary Digest. 44:483-4. Mr. 9, '12. England's censorship mania.
Literary Digest. 44:533-4. Mr. 16, '12. Police as literary censors.
Literary Digest. 47:178. Ag. 2, '13. Impurity in the magazines.
Literary Digest. 53:1033-4. O. 21, '16. Confused standards of literary censorship.
Literary Digest. 58:31. S. 21, '18. The army's "index."
Literary Digest. 74:31-2. Ag. 26, '22. Shall there be a book censorship?
Literary Digest. 74:32-3. S. 2, '22. To fight literary censorship.
Literary Digest. 76:30. Mr. 31, '23. Crusade against unclean books.
†Literary Digest. 77:27-9+. Je. 23, '23. Censorship or not.
Literary Digest. 86:33. S. 19, '25. America first in lewd literature.
Literary Digest. 93:31-2. Ap. 2, '27. Boston book censorship.
Literary Digest. 93:29. Je. 4, '27. Censors and their enemies.

†Literary Digest. 93:31-2. Je. 4, '27. The Vatican on obscene literature.

Literary Digest. 100:23. F. 2, '29. Book censorship in Ireland.

Literary Review. 3:513. Mr. 10, '23. Sterilizing literature.

Literary Review. 3:637. Ap. 21, '23. On immoral books. G. E. Heath.

Living Age. 257:291-5. My. 2, '08. Coming censorship of fiction. Basil Tozer.

Munsey's Magazine. 50:493-7. D. '13. Books that are barred. Brander Matthews.

Nation. 94:205-6. F. 29, '12. Literature and morals in England.

Nation. 111:343. S. 25, '20. Again the literary censor.

Nation. 124:713-14. Je. 29, '27. Poor me and pure Boston. Upton Sinclair.

Nation. 128:570-1. My. 8, '29. Censorship in Ireland. R. M. Fox.

*Nation. 130:147-9, 175-8, 291-3. F. 5, 12; Mr. 12, '30. Christian Science censor. Henry R. Mussey.

Nation. 130:236. F. 26, '30. Who's obscene?

New Republic. 61:59-62. D. 11, '29. Christian Science censorship. Craig F. Thompson.

New Republic. 61:211-12. Ja. 15, '30. Christian science and free speech.

New York Times. Mr. 18, '23. sec. 8. p. 2. Judge Ford tells how to purge books.

New York Times. Ap. 19, '23. Likely to railroad clean book bill.

Nineteenth Century. 105:433-50. Ap. '29. Censorship of books. Havelock Ellis and others.

North American Review. 216:577-91. N. '22. Decency in literature. John Erskine.

Outlook. 86:520-2. Je. 6, '07. Censorship of the Church of Rome. G. H. Putnam.

Outlook. 94:11-12. Ja. 1, '10. Literary revolt.

Outlook. 99:353-4. O. 14, '11. Vice report and the mails.

Outlook. 149:6-7. My. 2, '28. Natural censorship. Harvey O'Higgins.

Outlook. 149:214-16+. Je. 6, '28. Boston's bogy-man. Helena H. Smith.

Outlook. 151:378-9. Mr. 6, '29. Free advertising.

Outlook. 151:536. Ap. 3, '29. Sense in censorship.

Outlook. 152:54. My. 8, '29. Obscenity brands.

Publishers' Weekly. 103:627-8. Mr. 3, '23. Renewed censorship agitation.

Publishers' Weekly. 103:940-1. Mr. 17, '23. Clean Book League: the views of its defenders and critics.

Publishers' Weekly. 103:1323-4. Ap. 28, '23. Censorship situation.

Publishers' Weekly. 103:1328-30. Ap. 28, '23. Opinions of the clean books bill.

Publishers' Weekly. 113:443-4. F. 4, '28. Embattled booksellers.

Publishers' Weekly. 113:444-7. F. 4, '28. Case for the Boston booksellers. Harold Williams, Jr.

Publishers' Weekly. 115:411. Ja. 26, '29. New censorship bill in Massachusetts.

Publishers' Weekly. 117:213-14. Ja. 11, '30. Censorship in Chicago. Milton Fairman.

Publishers' Weekly. 117:566-8. F. 1, '30. Bookseller victorious in Chicago reformers' campaign. Milton Fairman.

Review of Reviews. 75:404-5. Ap. '27. Censor for books. George H. Putnam.

Saturday Review. 142:605-6. N. 20, '26. Prudes in council.

*Scribners. 72:631. N. '22. Are we going to have a censorship of printed books? William L. Phelps.

Survey. 57:622. F. 15, '27. Youth tilts at smut and trash. Bruno Lasker.

Wilson Bulletin. 3:621-6. My. '29. Censorship of books by the library. Margery Bedinger.

World's Work. 50:323-8. Jl. '25. Can minds be closed by statute? George F. Milton.

Affirmative References

Books and Pamphlets

*Ford, John. Criminal obscenity. Fleming H. Revell. N. Y. '29.

Periodicals

American City. 33:553-5. N. '25. Effective action against salacious plays and magazines. J. S. Sumner.

Bookman. 53:385-8. Jl. '21. Criticising the critic. J. S. Sumner.

Bookman. 57:374-5. My. '23. Censorship from the inside.

†Case and Comment. 23:16-19. Je. '16. Obscene literature—its suppression. John S. Sumner.

Christian Century. 44:390-1. Mr. 31, '27. Roundsman of the Lord.

*Commonweal. 1:202-3. D. 31, '24. Uplift journals please copy. Hendrik W. Van Loon.

Congressional Digest. 9:50-1. F. '30. Is official censorship of books desirable? Reed Smoot.

Congressional Digest. 9:51. F. '30. Is official censorship of books desirable? Frederick H. Gillett.

Congressional Digest. 9:52. F. '30. Is official censorship of books desirable? Guy D. Goff.

Congressional Digest. 9:52-4. F. '30. Is official censorship of books desirable? George W. Ochs-Oakes.

Congressional Digest. 9:54-5. F. '30. Is official censorship of books desirable? John Ford.

Congressional Digest. 9:56. F. '30. Is official censorship of books desirable? Joseph Story.

Congressional Digest. 9:56. F. '30. Is official censorship of books desirable? Hendrick W. Van Loon.

Congressional Digest. 9:57. F. '30. Is official censorship of books desirable? J. Thomas Heflin.

Congressional Digest. 9:57. F. '30. Is official censorship of books desirable? Park Trammell.

Dial. 71:63-8. Jl. '21. Truth about literary lynching. John S. Sumner.

Hibbert Journal. 10:462-8. Ja. '12. Pernicious literature. H. D. Rawnsley.

*Independent. 114:686-9. Je. 20, '25. Filth on Main street. F. R. Kent.

Journal of Education. 82:458-9. N. 11, '15. Comstock and Sumner. John S. Sumner.

Literary Digest. 80:28. Ja. 19, '24. Literary worm turns.

†Literary Digest. 84:31-2. F. 21, '25. Muckraking the news stands.

Living Age. 285:90-8. Ap. 10, '15. Immorality of the modern burglar story and burglar play. H. R. D. May.

Nineteenth Century. 64:479-87. S. '08. Censorship of fiction. Bram Stoker.

Nineteenth Century. 77:432-44. F. '15. Immorality of the modern burglar story and burglar play. H. R. D. May.

Publishers' Weekly. 103:1262. Ap. 21, '23. New York's clean book legislation.

Negative References

Books and Pamphlets

Lawrence, D. H. Pornography and obscenity. Knopf. N. Y. '30.

National Popular Government League. Bul. no. 128. My. 30, '29. Shall the censorship be made absolute? Judson King.

National Popular Government League. Bul. no. 132. Ja. 4, '30. Freedom of thought and the censorship. Judson King.

Periodicals

American Mercury. 10:56-63. Ja. '27. Comstock the less. H. F. Pringle.

American Mercury. 18:281-92. N. '29. Fear, freedom, and Massachusetts. H. M. Kallen.

Arena. 36:617-21. D. '06. Our vanishing liberty of the press. Theodore Schroeder.

Atlantic Monthly. 145:13-16. Ja. '30. Theory of censorship. William A. Neilson.

Atlantic Monthly. 145:17-25. Ja. '30. Practice of censorship. Edward Weeks.

Bookman. 53:193-6. My. '21. Censoring the censor. Heywood Broun.

Bookman. 60:719-22. F. '25. Whitewashing. E. L. Tinker.

Bookman. 64:2. S. '26. Ways of censors.

Bookman. 70:258-62. N. '29. What is dirt? Robert Herrick.

Chicago Legal News. 56:253. F. 28, '24. History censorship.

Commonweal. 1:201-2. D. 31, '24. Make responsibility real. Thomas F. Woodlock.

Congressional Digest. 9:50-7. F. '30. Is official censorship of books desirable? Bronson Cutting and others.

Current opinion. 56:298-9. Ap. '14. Is censorship useless as a weapon against literary obscenity?

Current Opinion. 67:315-16. D. '19. Heywood Broun comes to the rescue of immoral books.

Current Opinion. 73:517-18. O. '22. Book censorship condemned as unAmerican and undesirable.

Dial. 70:381-5. Ap. '21. Adult or infantile censorship. Ernest Boyd.

*English Review. 4:616-26. Mr. '10. Censorship of books. Edmund Gosse.

English Review. 38:358-65. Mr. '24. Literature and the policeman. Austin Harrison.

Fortnightly Review. 93:257-67. F. '10. Responsibility of authors. Oliver Lodge.

Fortnightly Review. 108:539-51. O. '17. Freedom of the pen. John L. Balderston.

Independent. 110:191-3, 258. Mr. 17-Ap. 14, '23. Question of literary censorship. Theodore Dreiser and others.

Independent. 114:160. F. 7, '25. Readers and writers. Ernest Boyd.

Independent. 118:326-7. Mr. 26, '27. Salvation of mediocrity.

Independent. 118:467-8. Ap. 8, '27. When is a book pure? Frank Sibley.

Law Notes. 27:3. Ap. '23. Sample of literary censorship.

Literary Review. 3:641. Ap. 28, '23. A preposterous measure.

Literary Review. 4:385. D. 22, '23. Censorship.

Living Age. 265:131-8. Ap. 16, '10. Censorship of books. Edmund Gosse.

Nation. 93:308-9. O. 5, '11. Discussing the social evil.

Nation. 113:255-6. S. 7, '21. Novelist rebels.

Nation. 116:508. My. 2, '23. Censorship.

Nation. 120:346. Ap. 1, '25. Censored audience.

Nation. 123:117. Ag. 11, '26. Unwilling censor.

Nation. 123:682. D. 29, '26. Books and behavior.

Nation. 128:729. Je. 19, '29. Which law?

Nation. 130:64-5. Ja. 15, '30. My brother's peeper. Gardner Jackson.

New Republic. 34:34-5. Mr. 7, '23. It's a bad, bad book.

New Republic. 34:283. My. 9, '23. Back to the father of lies.

New Republic. 58:318-20. My. 8, '29. Enemies of society.

New Republic. 59:119-21. Je. 19, '29. Arbiters of obscenity. Duff Gilfond.

New Republic. 59:141. Je. 26, '29. Nice Nellie, the censor.

New Republic. 59:176-7. Jl. 3, '29. Customs men keep us pure. Duff Gilfond.

New York Times. Ap. 18, '23. Worst bill yet. Editorial.

New York Times. Ap. 24, '23. Publishers oppose clean books bill.

New York Times. My. 2, '23. Censorship gone daft. Editorial.

New York Times. My. 4, '23. Danger deferred. Editorial.

North American Review. 207:902-17. Jl. '18. Authorship and liberty. J. S. Auerbach.

Review of Reviews. 75:404-5. Ap. '27. Censor for books. G. H. Putnam.

Saturday Review. 6:227+. O. 12, '29. Clean hands.

Saturday Review of Literature. 5:993+. My. 11, '29. Censorship.

Saturday Review of Literature. 5:1180. Jl. 13, '29. Literary Volsteadism. Adam S. Gregorius.

Spectator. 108:147-8. Ja. 27, '12. Strachey's speech on demoralizing literature.

Virginia Law Register. 12:35-9. My. '26. Still more censorship.

Woman Citizen. 9:9-10. Ap. 4, '25. Sense or censorship? H. W. Van Loon.

World Today. 51:483-4. Ap. '28. Freedom in U. S. A.

GENERAL DISCUSSION

WHERE THE BLAME LIES[1]

Are we going to have a censorship of printed books? Is it necessary to regulate all our mental food as it has been found necessary to supervise physical food? Even the most ardent advocates of license in writing would not, I suppose, disapprove of the Pure Food Law—in other words, no one has a right to manufacture and sell any food he pleases. For it is unfortunately true that there are plenty of men who would sell poison if they could make a legal profit by doing so. Their zeal has to be regulated. And although authors and publishers are as a rule respectable persons, there are plenty of both who would be willing to sell corruption to adolescents if they were not prevented by law. Is the soul less important than the body, or is freedom to injure the mind more precious than freedom to injure the health? The question is not so simple as all that. I do not agree with those who say immoral books hurt no one; I think they hurt every one who reads them, provided the reader is a normal human being with any imagination. The difficulty is to find the right censor, probably an impossible task. And until he can be found, the criminal law which we already have is perhaps the best method to deal with unsuitable publications. Liberty is the very soul of art; and we want no cure that is worse than the disease.

Yet it should be remembered that if the censorship should be established, and we pass under arbitrary and irresponsible tyranny, it will not be the fault of the prudes and the reformers and the bigots. It will be the

[1] By William L. Phelps. *Scribner's Magazine.* 72:631. November 1922.

fault of those who destroy freedom by their selfish excesses. I should like to state in four words what I believe to be a natural law: *Excess leads to Prohibition.* It is not the fault of the Bolsheviks that Russia at present is such a hell; it is the excess of Tsarism lasting two hundred years and becoming intolerable. Had even the late Tsar ruled wisely and moderately, he might have died in his bed. The French Revolution was not the work of madmen; it was caused chiefly by Louis XIV, Louis XV, and their counsellors. In turn, the excesses of the revolutionists led to their abolition, as will probably be the case in Russia. Napoleon was not beaten by Wellington; no one but himself could ever have beaten Napoleon, and he did the job thoroughly. England and France are not the cause of Germany's downfall; she fell through the excess of her own pride and ambition. What is true of big matters is also true of little things. A man who smokes all the time eventually discovers that he cannot smoke at all. "The doctor told me I had to cut it out." Life is a dangerous game to play, and moderation is a rare virtue.

The absolute prohibition of beer and wine in America, which is theoretically an absurdity, came to pass not through the cranks and the teetotallers, but because so many people drank like professionals instead of amateurs. So if a Dark Age of literary intolerance should come upon us, do not blame the bigots and the narrow-minded; put the blame where it should justly fall, on those who wrote so abominably that in order to silence them the army of wise and high-minded authors had to wear fetters.

CUSTOMS AND POSTAL CENSORSHIP[a]

The first law which was ever passed by the Congress of the United States giving customs clerks the right of censorship was passed in 1842. The Republic managed to

[a] By Senator Bronson Cutting. *Congressional Record.* 71:4433-5. October 10, 1929.

survive for more than half a century without any censorship by the Customs Bureau. The law passed in 1842 was as follows:

> **Sec. 28. That the importation of all indecent and obscene prints, paintings, lithographs, engravings, and transparencies is hereby prohibited.**

That particular provision is rather mild. It prohibited so-called works of art which had been inspired by nothing except an indecent and a pornographic point of view.

It is quite obvious that the average customs clerk could, with comparative ease, decide the difference between a decent and an indecent postcard, drawing, photograph, or any other so-called work of art which would present itself at once to his sight and his mental vision and his understanding. It is entirely different when it comes to the question of literature, where a clerk, in order to make a correct decision, must necessarily read a book as a whole. Many books of highly moral tendency would be excluded if a man's attention were confined to one page, or one paragraph, or one sentence, or one word.

At any rate there seems to have been no particular objection to the censorship provision of the tariff act of 1842; and the United States continued to survive under that section for another half century, until the tariff act of 1890. The tariff act of 1890 provided practically the present law. It has gone on and is still in effect.

The only additional provision which was written into the bill after 1890 was the clause about lottery tickets and the advertisements of lotteries. That came in in the tariff act of 1894. I do not know why that particular section was added; but I suppose it had something to do with the Louisiana lottery scandals, which came up sometime in the nineties.

Those clauses were not enforced in any unreasonable way until about 1909. At that time a good many people realized that the tariff law of 1890, as amended in 1894, could be construed in ways which would bar out various pieces of art and literature which previously had not been barred.

In 1909 an attempt was made under this section to prevent the Field Museum, in Chicago, from importing Chinese pictures and manuscripts, very important to them, on the ground that those pictures and manuscripts were obscene.

In 1911 the postal authorities, which worked under a similar provision of the postal law, excluded from the mails the official vice report of the city of Chicago. A postal official who fails to exclude an obscene or indecent picture or book is liable to a fine of $5,000 and to a penitentiary sentence of 10 years. If he excludes a book which is later determined by the courts to be perfectly proper, he is subject to no penalty of any sort. It will therefore be evident that it is to the interest of the customs clerks who deal with this particular matter to exclude, so far as possible, anything which they think may by any chance be called indecent.

A copy of Ovid's *Metamorphoses,* sent to a professor of Johns Hopkins University, was stopped in the mails. Catalogues of books sold by booksellers which advertised for sale such works as the *Decameron* and *Elmer Gantry* were barred from the mails. Works of Tolstoi and Swedenborg—books which have been published and are still being published in this country, and can be purchased at any bookstore and can be read in any library —have been barred from the mails; and the same precedents, of course, apply to censorship by the Customs Bureau.

The reason why I refer to those cases is that this difference of opinion between the Customs Bureau and the postal censorship as to what books might be admitted and what might not, finally brought about a conference, a convention of the experts of the two departments, men who had been reading indecent literature all their lives, and felt that they were entitled to say what was or was not indecent. About a year ago these various experts met, and after comparing their experiences they got up a black list, which was subsequently added to.

This black list dates from October 27, 1928. On April 16, 1929, some further works were added to this terrible roll.

Upon this list there are 739 books.

Of those 739 more than half, or 379, are books written in the Spanish language. Of the remaining books more than two-thirds, 231, are written in the French language. Five are books in the Italian language. Ten are books in the German language. That leaves only 114 immoral books barred by the censor which are written in the English language.

I do not know that this list is of any importance in itself. I speak of it principally to show the depths of absurdity to which bureaucratic government may go. Is it conceivable that there are as many books written in Spanish as in all other languages put together which might corrupt the morals of any of our people, when we consider what a small proportion of the population are able to read books written in Spanish? Is it possible that only 114 English books could be ruled out as against over 600 written in other languages?

Books like the novels of Balzac, like the confessions of Rousseau, books which are on every library shelf, have been declared ineligible to enter the country under this provision of the tariff act. The classics, the Greek and Latin writers, who have managed to survive for two thousand years or more, and have been passed on from one generation of school children to another, are largely barred by the regulations laid down by the Bureau of Customs.

Take the works of Aristophanes, a puritan, an austere conservative, who wanted to have men like Euripides and Socrates exiled or executed because he thought they were corrupting the morals of youth. The works of that man are now two thousand years after his death being excluded from this country, but not because they contain coarse passages. There is only one of his works which is on the particular black list which I have here in my hand, and that is the *Lysistrata,* the first and most powerful argument on the futility and the brutality of warfare. I wonder whether the exclusion of *All Quiet on the Western Front* was perhaps induced by some similar motive as that which bars from the country the *Lysistrata* of Aristophanes.

The works of Ovid, the *Daphnis and Chloe* of Longus, that charming pastoral of the third century before Christ; the *Golden Ass* of Apuleius, which is read by everyone in school and college; the works of Boccaccio, and of countless more modern authors are excluded from the country.

BOOKS BANNED IN BOSTON[3]

The list of books below contains the majority of those that have been suppressed during the current Boston outbreak of censorship. The booksellers decline to give out the current list vouched for by them—the list containing those which have been on ban for a time and which now have returned to grace, and those which stand taboo at the moment.

The list is as follows:

Dark Laughter, by Sherwood Anderson
The Wayward Man, by St. John Ervine
High Winds, by Arthur Train
Blue Voyage, by Conrad Aiken
The Irishman, by St. John Ervine

[3] *New York Times.* January 24, 1930.

What I Believe, by Bertrand Russell
Circus Parade, by Jim Tully
The American Caravan, edited by E. Pettit
Move Over, by E. Pettit
Oil, by Upton Sinclair
From Man to Man, by Olive Schreiner
Mosquitoes, by William Faulkner
Pilgrims, by Edith Mannin
Horizon, by Robert Corse
The Sorrows of Elsie, by Andre Savignon
Nigger Heaven, by Carl Van Vechten
Power, by Count Keyserling
Twilight, by Count Keyserling
Black April, by Julia Peterkin
An American Tragedy, by Theodore Dreiser
The World of William Clissold, by H. G. Wells
Wine, Women and War, by John Dos Passos
Manhattan Transfer, by John Dos Passos
The Fruit of Eden, by Gerard
Count Bruga, by Ben Hecht
Kink, by Brock
Red Pavilion, by John Gunther
Ariane, by Claude Anet
The Captive, by Bourdet
Crazy Pavements, by Beverly Nichols
Young Men in Love, by Michael Arlen
On Such a Night, by Babette Deutsch
The Starling, by Doris Leslie
Pretty Creatures, by William Gerhardt
The Madonna of the Sleeping Car, by De Kobra
Dream's End, by Thorne Smith
Tomok the Sculptor, by Eden Phillpotts
The Plastic Age, by Percy Marks
The Hard-Boiled Virgin, by Frances Newman
The Rebel Bird, by D. Patrick
The Butcher Shop, by J. Devening
The Ancient Hunger, by E. Greenberg
Antennae, by Herbert Footner

The Marriage Bed, by E. Roscoe
The Beadle, by P. Smith
As It Was, by "H. T."
Elmer Gantry, by Sinclair Lewis
Doomsday, by Warwick Deeping
The Sun Also Rises, by Ernest Hemingway
Spread Circles, by Ward
Little Pitchers, by Isa Glenn
Master of the Microbe, by Service
Evelyn Grainger, by C. F. Hummel
Cleopatra's Diary, by Thompson
The Allinghams, by May Sinclair

PROSECUTOR RAIDS A PHILADELPHIA BOOK STORE [4]

Announcing an intention to arrest offending publishers as well as dealers in a campaign against indecent literature, the District Attorney's office today sent out raiders who seized books, illustrations and prints valued at $10,000 at the establishment of Horace F. Townsend in the Rittenhouse Square district and arrested Townsend.

More books and pictures were taken from a storehouse above a tea shop near by, also operated by Townsend. According to District Attorney Monaghan, the prisoner had catered to an ultra-fashionable clientele, selling books and other articles which have been banned from the country and which the District Attorney described as "disgusting in the extreme."

Among the books seized were several over which controversy has raged for years, both here and abroad. The raid was the first one in this city similar to those in Boston, and several of the volumes figured in the Boston campaign. The raid was the result of solicitation of a professional man as a prospective purchaser of the books, who complained to the prosecutor.

[4] *New York Times.* January 25, 1930.

One of the volumes seized was *Lady Chatterley's Lover,* by D. H. Lawrence, the sale of which led to the conviction of a Boston bookseller.

Mr. Monaghan said his next task would be to locate and arrest the publishers, some of whom he declared were here and others in New York.

"This is only the beginning of the drive," he declared. "That stuff we seized today is vile and rotten, there can be no excuse for it. The plaint that it represents a high type of literature above the minds of the masses is bunk. It is just pure filth and nothing else."

If convicted Townsend is liable to a fine of $1,000 or one year in prison, or both.

THE INDEX[5]

The *Index Librorum Prohibitorum* is the title of the official list of those books which on doctrinal or moral grounds the Roman Catholic Church authoritatively forbids the members of its communion to read or to possess, irrespective of works forbidden by the general rules on the subject. The earliest known instance of a list of proscribed books being issued with the authority of a Bishop of Rome is the *Notitia librorum apocryphorum qui non recipiuntur,* the first redaction of which, by Pope Gelasius, 494, was subsequently amplified on several occasions. The document is for the most part an enumeration of apocryphal gospels and acts. One of the functions of the Inquisition when it was established was to exercise a rigid censorship over books put into circulation. The majority of the condemnations were at that time of a specially theological character.

With the discovery of the art of printing and the wide and cheap diffusion of all sorts of books which ensued, the need for new precautions against heresy

[5] *Encyclopaedia Britannica.* 14th ed. vol. 12. p. 148-9. 1929.

and immorality in literature made itself felt. More than one Pope (Sixtus IV in 1479 and Alexander VI in 1501) gave special directions regarding the growing freedom of the printing press, and in 1515 the Lateran council attempted to forbid the printing of any book without previous examination by the ecclesiastical authority. The Council of Trent in its fourth session, April 1546, forbade the sale or possession of any anonymous religious book which had not previously been seen and approved by the ordinary. In the same year the University of Louvain, at the command of Charles V, prepared an Index of pernicious and forbidden books, a second edition of which appeared in 1550.

In 1557 and again in 1559 Pope Paul IV, through the Inquisition at Rome, published what may be regarded as the first Roman Index in the modern ecclesiastical use of that term. In this we find the three classes which are to be maintained in the Trent Index: authors condemned with all their writings; prohibited books, the authors of which are known, and pernicious books by anonymous authors.

At the eighteenth session of the Council of Trent, (February 1562) in consideration of the great increase in the number of suspect and pernicious books, and also of the inefficacy of the many previous "censures" which had proceeded from the provinces and from Rome itself, a commission was appointed to inquire into these "censures," and to consider what ought to be done in the circumstances. The result of its labors was handed over to the pope to deal with as he should think proper. In the following March accordingly was published, with papal approval, the *Index Librorum Prohibitorum,* which continued to be reprinted and brought down to date, and the *Ten Rules* which regulated the matter until the pontificate of Leo XIII (1897). The business of condemning pernicious books and of correcting the Index to date has been, since the time of Pope Sixtus V, in the hands of the "Congregation of the Index," which consists of several cardinals and more or less numerous "consultors" and "examiners of books."

With the alteration of social conditions, however, the Rules of Trent ceased to be entirely applicable. Their application to publications which had no concern with morals or religion was no longer conceivable, and the penalties called for modification. Already, at the Vatican Council, several bishops had submitted requests for a reform of the Index, but the Council was not able to deal with the question. The reform was accomplished by Leo XIII, who, on the 25th of January 1897, published the constitution *Officiorum* in 49 articles. In this constitution, although the writings of heretics in support of heresy are condemned as before, those of their books which contain nothing against Catholic doctrines or which treat other subjects are permitted. Editions of the text of the Scriptures are permitted for purposes of study. Translations of the Bible into the vulgar tongue have to be approved, while those published by non-Catholics are permitted for the use of scholars. Obscene books are forbidden; the classics, however, are authorized for educational purposes. Books and newspapers which outrage God and sacred things, which propagate magic and superstition, or which are pernicious to society, are forbidden. Permissions to read prohibited books are given by the Bishop in particular cases, and in the ordinary course by the Congregation of the Index.

The constitution then proceeds with the censorship of books. The examination of the books is entrusted to censors, who have to study them without prejudice. If their report is favorable, the bishop gives the *imprimatur*. All books concerned with the religious sciences and with ethics are submitted to preliminary censorship, and in addition to this ecclesiastics have to obtain a personal authorization for all their books and for the acceptance of the editorship of a periodical. The penalty of excommunication *ipso facto* is only maintained for reading books written by heretics or apostates in defense of heresy, or books condemned by name under penalty of excommunication by pontifical letters.

The constitution also prescribed a revision of the catalogue of the Index. The new Index, which omits works anterior to 1600 as well as a great number of others included in the old catalogue, appeared in 1900. The encyclical *Pascendi* of Pius X (September 8, 1907) made it obligatory for periodicals amenable to the ecclesiastical authority to be submitted to a censor for report.

BRIEF EXCERPTS

Neither Shakespeare nor the Bible is wholly occupied with virtue.—*Nation.* 123:682. *December* 29, 1926.

The time has come to do something to stop the flood of demoralizing literature.—*G. L. Strachey. Spectator* (*London*). 108:147. *January* 27, 1912.

Filth in the printed word is accepted by society under its false boast of art and literature.—*Judge George W. Martin. New York Times. January* 22, 1925. *p.* 8.

A Boston jury has again upheld the obscene-book law, under which many recent novels have been barred from the city.—*New York Times. April* 19, 1929.

Customs officials here [Boston] are barring Voltaire's *Candide,* written 170 years ago, as violating the law of decency.—*New York Times. May* 23, 1929.

I am convinced that clean books, clean plays, and clean scenarios can be produced without the aid or direction of censors.—*George B. McCutcheon. Literary Digest.* 77:58. *June* 23, 1923.

There should be some means by which the publication of unquestionably salacious books could be prevented.—*Samuel Merwin. Literary Digest.* 74:33. *September* 2, 1922.

Reason will prevail. Galileo was sent to the Inquisition in 1616, but his book was taken off the Roman Index in 1835. So in this case it took only 219 years for reason to prevail.—*Walter Lippmann. American Inquisitors. p.* 38.

You read two or three pages of a book and come to the conclusion that you do not like it. You shut it up and throw it into the dustbin, at least that is what I do with most modern books.—*G. K. Chesterton. Report of the Joint Select Committee on Stage Plays. p.* 344.

Magistrate Hyman Bushel in the Tombs Court ruled yesterday that the book, *The Well of Loneliness* by the English woman writer, Radclyffe Hall, is obscene and was printed and distributed in this city in violation of the penal law.—*New York Times. February* 22, 1929.

Still worse is the impudent discrimination in favor of the rich. It is a matter of everyday knowledge that books can be sold in expensive de luxe editions, although rigidly barred in cheaper form.—*James F. Morton. Case and Comment.* 23:25. *June* 1916.

At the present moment novels and plays may be said fairly to reek with sex. On both sides of the Atlantic the problem of indecent and unwholesome fiction and the accompanying problem of literary censorship are occupying space in almost all the newspapers and magazines.—*Current Opinion.* 55:353. *November* 1913.

There is now, there always has been, filthy writing for the sake of filth, and it should be suppressed. But it does not take a special committee to find it. Any District Attorney can recognize it when brought to his attention.—*Brooklyn Eagle. Literary Digest.* 76:30. *March* 31, 1923.

I have often wished that something could be done to check the publication of trash, moral or immoral. The appalling rubbish that litters the bookstalls of our railway stations at the present time helps us to realize the degradation of modern taste.—*E. H. L. Watson. Dial.* 50:298. *April* 16, 1911.

A second protest against the seizure by customs officials [at Philadelphia] of a 1750 edition of Rabelais and their failure to return it, was contained in a letter sent to Federal authorities today by A. E. Newton, collector of rare books and manuscripts.—*New York Times. May* 23, 1929.

Home Secretary Sir William Joynson-Hicks has suggested the establishment of a censorship of books in this country [England]. Ireland also is agitated over the question of the censorship of books, newspapers, etc. The Irish Free State Censorship of Publications bill is now before the Dail.—*New York Times. November* 4, 1928.

And many that believed came and confessed and showed their deeds. Many of them also which used curious arts brought their books together, and burned them before all men, and they counted the price of them, and found it fifty thousand pieces of silver. So mightily grew the word of God and prevailed.—*Acts of the Apostles.* 19:18-20.

Our exceedingly questionable novels are catering constantly to a most unhealthy mental attitude in the minds of those who are reading them with the greatest possible avidity, namely, our children from the age of thirteen or fourteen to the age of seventeen or eighteen. Our whole society is pervaded with this same unhealthy tone.—*Daniel Crosby. Transactions of the Commonwealth Club of California.* 16:217. *August* 1921.

Church and educational circles were stirred today by charges that a biography of Mrs. Mary Baker Eddy, founder of the Christian Science church, was being "suppressed" by Cleveland book stores. The disclosure was made yesterday by the Rev. Dilworth Lupton, pastor of the First Unitarian Church, in a sermon on the subject, "Dakin's *Mrs. Eddy.*"—*Cleveland Press. February* 3, 1930.

American and Russian literature makes bad reading for the youth of Italy, the Ministry of the Interior has decided, placing the works of Jack London, Tolstoi, Turgenieff, Gorky, and Dostoievsky on the proscribed list. Booksellers are instructed not to place the books of these authors on sale because they are polluting the moral climate in which Fascist youths must be nurtured. —*Cleveland Plain Dealer. August* 11, 1929.

In the field of books censors may usually be counted on to pick the wrong book to suppress. Few are wise enough to judge, especially to judge genius, and few are tactful enough to do the censoring cannily. When one thinks of the calibre of the officials in many of our towns and cities one shudders at what they might do if the censorship of pictures and publications were placed in their hands.—*Oswald G. Villard. Atlantic Monthly.* 137:398. *March* 1926.

The Boston police, acting in cooperation with the district attorney's office and the Boston booksellers' committee within the last few weeks have suppressed nine books, including some of the best sellers of the winter season. The police contend that certain passages in these books either "contain obscene, indecent, or impure language" or "manifestly tend to corrupt the morals of youth," and that their sale by any bookseller would be a violation of the laws of Massachusetts.—*Cleveland Plain Dealer. March* 12, 1927.

James A. De Lacey, manager of the Dunster House Bookshop here, [Cambridge, Mass.] was sentenced to one month in the House of Correction and fined $500 today for selling an alleged obscene book, *Lady Chatterley's Lover,* by D. H. Lawrence. The sentence was imposed by Judge Fosdick in Superior Court. The judge said that the book, viewed as a whole, was beyond any reasonable doubt "obscene, indecent, and impure."—*New York Times. December* 21, 1929.

A revised censorship law, designed to meet the approval of the public, the booksellers, and the guardians of Massachusetts morals, and indorsed by a distinguished committee of citizens, will be filed with the legislature next week by Representative Henry L. Shattuck of Boston. Under this revision no book of "manifest pornography" will escape the law, but every book, when adjudged in court, will be judged as a whole, and not, as under the present law, by isolated passages.—*Cleveland Plain Dealer. December* 14, 1929.

The Well of Loneliness, a book by Radclyffe Hall, English writer, who has been kicked about the courts of London and New York and was once barred by the customs service from entry into this country, today was assured a haven in the United States. Commissioner of Customs Eble declined to appeal from a customs court decision holding that it did not violate the law. Eble said he had read the book carefully and agreed with the decision that it was not offensive to clean-minded persons. London courts held the book obscene.—*Cleveland Plain Dealer. August* 30, 1929.

By a vote of 15 to 13, the Senate today killed a bill which would have changed the obscene literature law so that the entire context of a book would be considered in determining whether it was fit for publication and circulation. Under the present law a book or other publication may be condemned for a single passage which is considered improper and injurious to public morality. The bill was an outgrowth of the so-called "book war" which resulted in the banning in Boston of many of the best selling modern novels.—*New York Times. April 2, 1929.*

The *Index Librorum Prohibitorum* lists contain many inaccuracies. The names of the authors, frequently misspelled, are entered almost at random, sometimes in the vernacular, sometimes in the Latin forms. This method, or lack of method, necessarily resulted in duplicate entries, while the copyists succeeded not infrequently in omitting altogether in their transcripts writers and books of unquestioned heresy. It became increasingly impossible for the compilers to secure personal knowledge of the contents of more than a very small proportion of the books which were to be passed upon and classed as either safe or pernicious.—*George H. Putnam. Monroe's Cyclopedia of Education. vol.* 4. *p.* 38.

Llorente, the historian of the Inquisition, computes that Torquemada and his collaborators, in the course of eighteen years, burnt at the stake 10,220 persons, 6,860 in effigy, and otherwise punished 97,321. This frantic priest destroyed Hebrew Bibles wherever he could find them, and burnt 6,000 volumes of Oriental literature at Salamanca, under an imputation that they inculcated Judaism. With unutterable disgust and indignation we learn that the papal government realized much money by selling to the rich dispensations to secure them from the Inquisition.—*John W. Draper. History of the Conflict between Religion and Science. p.* 146.

Donald S. Friede, New York book publisher, today was sentenced to pay a fine of $300 for selling a copy of Theodore Dreiser's *American Tragedy* in this city (Boston) on the grounds that it is an obscene book. Friede, who came from New York today to be sentenced, was arrested here last April 18 after he had sold a copy of the book to a policeman. The arrest was pre-arranged with the Watch and Ward Society in order that a test might be made of the present law, which permits successful prosecution of such cases on the evidence provided by single excerpts from a given book without consideration of the entire context.—*Cleveland Plain Dealer. December* 5, 1929.

Detectives of District Attorney John Monaghan's staff made the round of Philadelphia book shops today in search for rare editions. Their search was of an official nature, however, as part of a drive to purge the city of "immoral" literature. In sending them out Monaghan pitted his literary judgment against that of the so-called members of the intelligentsia who are said to have patronized Horace F. Townsend's book shop and who regard the literature in question as "art." Townsend's establishment was raided today and 2,000 volumes adjudged obscene were placed under lock and key. Monaghan fears Philadelphia is becoming the distribution center for such books. Other cities in which allegedly immoral books and magazines have been seized by police lately are Boston, Chicago and Los Angeles.—*Cleveland Plain Dealer. January* 26, 1930.

The Fascist ban on "subversive" books has been widened considerably through a circular sent to the managers of the Public Libraries of Italy by Signor Belluzzo, the new Minister of Education. The librarians have been ordered to make a thorough search of their stocks in order to see if it is true that they still have books written by Socialists, or treating of Socialist subjects, at the disposal of the public. The circular concludes with the admonition that, "Such a scandal must cease at once and all such books and pamphlets must be removed from the sight of the public and from use by visitors of the libraries." For a long time no Italian booksellers have been allowed to handle the works of Jean Jaurés, Karl Marx, Vladimir Lenin, H. G. Wells, Prince Kropotkin, Romain Rolland, Henri Barbusse, Jean Jacques Rousseau and Upton Sinclair.—*New York Times. September 16, 1928.*

Among the Jews who were then the leading intellects of the world Averroism had been largely propagated. Their great writer Maimonides had thoroughly accepted it. His school was spreading it in all directions. A furious persecution arose on the part of the orthodox Jews. Of Maimonides it had been formerly their delight to declare that he was "the Eagle of the Doctors, the Great Sage, the Glory of the West, the Light of the East, second only to Moses." Now they proclaimed that he had abandoned the faith of Abraham, had denied the possibility of creation, believed in the eternity of the world, had given himself up to the manufacture of atheists, had deprived God of his attributes, made a vacuum of him, had declared him inaccessible to prayer, and a stranger to the government of the world. The works of Maimonides were committed to the flames by the synagogues of Montpellier, Barcelona, and Toledo.—*John W. Draper. History of the Conflict between Religion and Science. p.* 143-4.

We dislike the censorship. We would prefer to trust that good taste and a sense of decency on the part of publishers would prevent their publishing unclean books. But we are frequently disappointed. Even some of the most reputable publishing firms are not above producing objectionable works. There is no newspaper that will refuse to advertise them, and few newspapers that will refrain, not only from noticing, but from puffing, any novel that has literary quality, no matter how egregiously it may outrage decency. What is to be done? For Catholics the answer is plain. We have the Index, and the Index automatically forbids us to read indecent books, just as it automatically forbids the reading of heretical books. Then we have the Catholic doctrine of the Occasions of Sin. We have confession and spiritual direction. We have the Catholic tradition of holy purity, as well as the Catholic theology than any wilful sin, even in thought, against the angelic virtue, is a mortal sin. We have, finally, and most important of all, the Catholic conscience. We have every safeguard. A genuine Catholic needs no other censor. But what about non-Catholic America? The more brazen offenders against decency, be they authors, publishers, or critics, may finally go to such extremes that the American people will be driven to some such drastic measure as a federal censorship law.—*Editorial. Catholic World.* 116:398-9. *December* 1922.

Catholicism was thus weakening; as its leaden pressure lifted the intellect of man expanded. The Saracens had invented the method of making paper from linen rags and from cotton. The Venetians had brought from China to Europe the art of printing. The former of these inventions was essential to the latter. Henceforth without the possibility of a check, there was intellectual intercommunication among all men. The invention of printing was a severe blow to Catholicism, which had, previously, enjoyed the inappreciable advantage of a monopoly of intercommunication. From its central seat orders could be disseminated through all the ecclesiastical ranks and fulminated through the pulpits. This monopoly and the amazing power it conferred were destroyed by the press. In modern times the influence of the pulpit has become insignificant. The pulpit has been thoroughly supplanted by the newspaper. Yet, Catholicism did not yield its ancient advantage without a struggle. As soon as the inevitable tendency of the new art was detected, a restraint upon it, under the form of censorship, was attempted. It was made necessary to have a permit in order to print a book. For this it was needful that the work should have been read, examined, and approved by the clergy. There must be a certificate that it was a godly and orthodox book. A bull of excommunication was issued in 1501 by Alexander VI against printers who should publish pernicious doctrines. In 1515 the Lateran Council ordered that no books should be printed but such as had been inspected by the ecclesiastical censors, under pain of excommunication and fine; the censors being directed "to take the utmost care that nothing should be printed contrary to the orthodox faith." There was thus a dread of religious discussion; a terror lest truth should emerge. But these frantic struggles of the powers of ignorance were unavailing. Intellectual intercommunication among men was secured. It culminated in the modern newspaper, which daily gives its contemporaneous intelligence from all parts of the world. Reading became a common occupation. In ancient society that art was possessed by comparatively few persons. Modern society owes some of its most striking characteristics to this change. Such was the result of bringing into Europe the manufacture of paper and the printing press.—*John W. Draper. History of the Conflict between Religion and Science. p.* 292-4.

The best-oiled and smoothest-running publicity (and anti-publicity) machine operated in the United States during the twentieth century has been that controlled by the Board of Directors of the Mother Church, the First Church of Christ, Scientist, in Boston, Massachusetts. It consists of a head publicity man (called the Committee on Publication) in Boston, a publicity man (likewise called the Committee on Publication) in each State, with two for California, and local publicity men (each called the Assistant Committee on Publication) in all the cities and towns where there are Christian Science churches. Each committee, be it noted, is an individual. Back of these committees stands a little Gideon's band of about two hundred thousand loyal, enthusiastic, well-disciplined, and well-to-do Christian Scientists, on whom the committees never call in vain.

Acting thru these agencies, the directors have in

recent years reduced unfavorable publicity to almost nothing, at the same time that they have secured columns and pages of free space for their lectures and other means of spreading their gospel. They have excluded the advertising of rival groups of Christian Scientists from the press in some sections of the country, and have shut those rivals off from the channels of radio communication. They have prevented the publication of books and articles reflecting unfavorably on Christian Science and its Founder (to follow their own capitalization), and have caused to be withdrawn from circulation or have buried under a mountain of oblivion those whose publication they could not prevent. They have persuaded or forced educational authorities to withdraw from use in the public schools textbooks to which they objected, and by discreet representations they have even brought about changes in the books used in universities. They have driven out of public libraries or have had placed on reserve shelves inaccessible to the public books that they did not like. They have employed against publishers and bookstores that handle such books the method of persuasion, followed, if need be, by intimidation, and then local and nation-wide boycott. They have held over newspaper publishers the danger of advertising and other losses until they have reduced large sections of the press to a state of abject subjection; the Chicago *Tribune,* for example, did not get up its courage so far even as to publish a review of Dakin's recent life of Mrs. Eddy for months after its publication, and until the publishers' courageous fight had made it impolitic to neglect it longer. They have watched legislation in Congress and in all the States with the eyes of hawks, not only preventing the enactment of measures of health protection which they thought unfavorable to their cult, but pushing for laws that they desired, and in the State of Illinois, for example, securing the passage of the first law against slander by radio, with the avowed purpose of preventing the radio from being used to oppose Christian Science.—*Henry R. Mussey. Nation.* 130:147. *February* 5, 1930.

AFFIRMATIVE DISCUSSION

SAVE AMERICAN IDEALS[1]

American ideals never grow old and never fade. They are as eternal as God Himself Who set them up as a goal toward which a righteous people should ever strive.

Foremost among them is morality, public and private. By that term is not meant the moral tenets of any particular denomination, sect or cult, but that fundamental morality which is recognized by all religions and all civilized peoples as the foundation of well-ordered human society.

No country in the world has had so high a standard of personal conduct in this respect as our own. The foundation stones of the Republic's greatness were laid on the bedrock of sound morality. Nowhere in all the world has womanhood been so exalted and reverenced as in the United States, which has won for itself among the nations of the earth the proud title of "the paradise of women."

"The grandeur that was Rome" was won while her people adhered to their ancient rigid code of moral conduct. When the sterling virtues of the republic gave way to the profligacy of the empire Rome's doom was sealed as surely as that of Sodom and Gomorrah.

It requires but a cursory examination of existing conditions to realize how we, in this country, have begun to drift away from our old moral ideals within the past few years. Whether this is due to an essential drop in moral tone or comes as part of the aftermath of the

[1] By John Ford. *Criminal Obscenity.* As condensed in *Congressional Digest.* 9:53-5. February 1930.

World War is a moot question. Probably it should be regarded as one of the well-nigh countless evils which the war-demons scattered over the face of the whole earth.

Printed obscenity has countless distributing agencies and preys upon the souls and bodies of millions in secret. Once permit an immoral publication to go into print and it becomes a source of evil influences from generation to generation.

Parents are practically helpless to protect their children from the contamination of printed immorality. Under present conditions it is around them everywhere. Excluded from the home, it will be read outside if indeed it be not smuggled in, despite parental vigilance.

But what shall be said of the large families of children, particularly in large cities, whose parents cannot read English? Happily some are so circumstanced as to be able to safeguard their children. But what of the multitude of parents whose occupations and educational limitations render them powerless to do so? Such helpless folk should be the objects of the solicitude and care of the more fortunately situated. We live—or should—not unto ourselves alone, but unto others.

It is the rising and future generations which are endangered and our duty to these may not be shirked.

The baleful influence of such reading upon the plastic minds of young people is appalling; and there is an unceasing effort on the part of authors of a certain type to undermine the moral principles inculcated by church and parents. Licentiousness is apotheosized by them, self-control ridiculed and the libertine cast in heroic mould.

Is the decline of this nation to be rapid as its rise? Are we to regard the growing disregard of marriage ties, the promiscuity of sexual relations, the profligacy and licentiousness in all forms and the general disregard for the law as the harbinger of national decay?

Be it always remembered that these were the first signs of dissolution in every nation which having grown to greatness, is today, "one with Nineveh and Tyre."

The accumulated wisdom and experience of the ages have been able to devise but one effective method of dealing with obscene publications and that is to stamp them as criminal and punish distributors of them like other criminals.

The grotesque falsity of the charge against censorship cannot long gain credence in the minds of even the most gullible of our citizens. It is perfectly well understood by everyone who has given even casual attention to the question that no censorship of the press can be established . . . in the nation because . . . the constitution of the United States bars it. On the other hand the Supreme Court of the United States . . . has expressly declared that printed obscenity is not protected by the constitution. It is simply a crime and its perpetrators have been proclaimed outlaws by every constitution and the statutes of every state and every country under Anglo-Saxon institutions and in most of the other civilized nations.

In any form, the dissemination of obscenity is a crime. Every citizen is required by law to act as a censor of crime, that is, to reveal to the prosecuting officials any knowledge of crime which comes to him and to aid in the apprehension of the criminal and in his prosecution. This sort of censorship has always existed under our institutions and all others of English origin.

FILTH ON EVERY NEWS STAND[a]

About a year ago I went to the editor of a famous newspaper. It stands forth amidst the dreary marshes of contemporary journalism as the Rock of Tradition,

[a] By Hendrik Willem Van Loon. *Commonweal.* 1:202-3. December 31, 1924.

the one and only relic of a better and more enlightened day when newspapermen were newspapermen and dared to speak their mind without bothering about the private tastes and public prejudices of their owners, their wives, or poodle-dogs. And I spake—

> Behold, here is your chance to do a great thing in the land of Manhattan. Whenever there is a just cause that asks a champion, you sharpen the edge of your adamant Vernunft upon the granite stone of reason and bestow upon an agonized world the most convincing, the most penetrating, yea, the dullest editorials that ever were devoted to a good cause. Buckle on your most shining armor and follow me to the nearest newsstand. There you will find, available for common use (and at a small cost) the foulest collection of smut, dirt and plain pornography ever offered to an unsuspecting public in the name of literature. Smite these corrupters of our children's morals with the glorious wrath of your outraged decency, and be forever praised.

But just then a great contest was raging between two mighty political parties and the tri-cornered fight which followed took up all available space—and I had clamored in vain, for absolutely nothing was done.

Then I crossed the street and wearily betook myself to a magazine devoted exclusively to the interests of the under-dog. Never mind the color of the animal. Provided that he be a bona fide, one hundred per cent pure, A-1, three star under-dog, he is sure of a hearing within the editorial sanctum. And once more I spake and said—

> Ah, ye faithful Galahads, ye who love yellow and brown and green and pink and purple men all the way from Uvkusigsat Fjord to Tierra del Fuego, here is your chance. This time our own children, our own little darlings, are in danger. They cry out, even as my Lord Ghandi, and although they wear pantaloons and eat steaks (the largest steaks available) their need is great. Send one of your clever sleuths to the nearest newspaper stand. He will there discover a collection of sluttish, abominable and saprogenous literature in such quantities that it can pollute an entire continent. Denounce the greedy scoundrels who print it, and gain our everlasting gratitude.

But a real estate agent in an obscure suburb of a remote western town had refused to sell a house to a Negro. Hence Democracy was on the verge of collapse.

Societies for the propagation of everything and societies for the suppression of everything else were beginning to stir. Amidst the din of battle, my little suggestion was ignominiously dropped into the wastepaper basket.

But, to misquote the excellent Doctor Martinus—"I shall have my say if the world were as full of indifferent editors as New York is full of taxis." And for lack of a convenient church door, I shall hammer my theses to the hospitable wall of the *Commonweal* and I shall proclaim here and now, and as loudly as I can, that our country is being overrun with and by a putrid stream of the most despicable, the most iniquitous, and on the whole the most dangerous form of a degraded variety of literature; that this stuff is being publicly sold and publicly sent through the mails; and that so far no authority, public or otherwise, seems to be willing or able to stop the dissemination of this literary garbage. So that is that.

If the Postmaster General thinks I exaggerate, I cordially invite His Honor to meet me in New York and I shall then take him on a little tour of inspection and within one hour I promise to show him more printed filth than we would be able to find by a week of diligent searching along the wicked avenues of those wicked European cities which our professional moralists are forever holding up as the legitimate heirs to Sodom and Gomorrah.

Furthermore, this degraded stuff is not a monopoly of the metropolis. It is sold just as openly in Yellow Springs, Ohio, as in Homer, N. Y., or any other hamlet of our fair land. It is ubiquitous. It is printed by the ton and sold by the bale. It has millions of dollars behind it. And it is of recent origin. The men who publish it make the early productions of the Hearst press look like mild little Sunday school tracts. And worst of all, they commit their crime in the name of Health, of Morals, of the Purity of the Home, and they cover their tracks so cleverly that the ordinary moron who is a post-office inspector or a professional censor shouts—"Why, this is fine stuff. It reads like *The Sheik,* the book that had such beautiful passages about Arabian sunsets," and takes it home to his little girl who is studying shorthand and is making ready for a career on the grand opera stage.

Of course, it is an utter absurdity that I should be obliged to write this. I have all my life fought against censorship. I have frequently helped to hold the gate of the Republic of Letters when worthy reformers tried to push their unwelcome selves into that delectable realm of literature. Hence I can hardly qualify for the rôle of Public Prosecutor.

At the same time, I have two boys of my own. I want them to read most of the books which the Uplift Brotherhood has placed on their little index. But I shall speak words not fit for publication in a respectable magazine if I ever find them in the possession of one of those utterly corrupt sheets which Messieurs Sumner, Ford et al. in their holy zeal and their unholy ignorance have overlooked or which (as is becoming increasingly clear) they purposely overlook because they are afraid to attack a fortress which is defended by all the shyster lawyers of half a dozen metropolai.

If 'twere merely a little fly-by-night publisher, then indeed there would be a chance to gain an easy victory and derive much publicity and great credit as a public benefactor, at practically no risk. Besides, the poor publisher might try to give the world something new in literature. That fact in itself would assure the lynching party the sympathy of our half-literate millions. Their Republic "n'a pas besoin d'hommes de lettres!" But if they fail to appreciate nudity, they can understand nakedness. Hence while they would cheerfully impale the wretch who would dare to print a reproduction of some sublime bit of ancient statuary, they would just as eagerly rally to the defense of that well-beloved editor who presents them twice a week with a photograph of Lizzie the Cloak Model in diverse stages of semi-undressedness. When furthermore, said editor adds the intimate story of Lizzie's life with all its most objectionable and d'Annunzioesque details, he is their friend for life. Do they feel that their own daughters are degraded by the perusal of such nefarious drivel? By no means! For in the last paragraph, the editor (who knows his job) informs them that Lizzie has now turned over a new leaf and that she is conducting a class of darling little Sunday scholars and leads an exemplary life. Being intrinsically besotted by a perverse ideal of morality, the assembled boobs then give three cheers for the Sunday school ma'am and promptly forget the street-walker.

Here I pause to offer my apologies to the street-walker. Compared to the heroines in the aforementioned stories, the average prostitute is an honest and honorable woman. For she is bad in the accepted sense of the word. She knows that she is bad. She makes no bones about being bad. Whereas the leading ladies in aforementioned fables are nasty little creatures who are utterly corrupt, but who successfully demonstrate the truth of that lowest of all modern maxims which bids us not to worry as long as "we can get away with it."

I repeat that if the reader thinks that I am making a mountain out of a molehill, the true test lies around the nearest corner. Let him or her put on his or her galoshes and inspect a news-stand, or the magazine section of a department store. He will there find a collection of "revelations," "dreams," "romances" and "confessions" which in their true nature are nothing but thinly veiled pornography. If he or she has a spare quarter, I shall ask him or her to do me a favor. Let him buy a copy. Let him take it home and read it. Then after half an hour's gargling with strong disinfectants, I want him or her to light a cigarette and ponder upon the strange duality of our official world, which makes a cannibal feast of a book when it contains the word "belly," and which permits the publication and the dissemination of whole wagon loads of stories which Louis XV would have ordered burned by the public hangman and which would have made Casanova blush with shame.

REASONABLE RESTRAINT[3]

I gladly enter the lists to aid in arousing sentiment and urging that gaps in the law be closed so that creators and purveyors of unclean writings may not escape just retribution.

It is not a pleasant task to grapple this evil. Everyone who undertakes it becomes a butt for ridicule, a target for the jeers, jibes and lampoons of columnists, critics, authors—and alas! editors also. When the hearing on the Clean Books Bill recently was held at Albany the publishers who have been issuing objectionable matter, authors who have been writing it, magazines who have been circulating salacious stories, editors of newspapers which thrive by sensational fiction, united in the effort to throttle the measure. On the other hand, representatives of numerous religious bodies, distinguished welfare workers, men and women representing institutions, associations and movements for the moral health and protection of our people—not fanatics or extremists, but sane, upright men and women who had no end to subserve other than the protection of the plastic mind of youth from the influence of immoral books—strove valiantly for its enactment . . .

A law which sanctions the printing and sale of some of the prurient publications now debauching our youth traduces our vaunted civilization, and the blazing wrath of aroused public opinion from a people befouled and

[3] By George Washington Ochs-Oakes, Editor, *Current History Magazine.* From John Ford's *Criminal Obscenity* as condensed in *Congressional Digest.* 9:51-5. February 1930.

insulted will yet compel the authorities to dam up the polluted streams of abomination.

The most fallacious argument against more restrictive laws is the contention that the remedy should exist in the home; that the children should be taught so that they will shrink from unclean books; that youth should have such stern moral fibre that it will be unaffected by lascivious appeal. This is a palpable quibble, irrational and illogical. As well repeal all criminal statutes and put full responsibility for youthful transgressions up to the parents; pardon the thief, pickpocket, cadet and young bandit because of lack of moral strength to resist evil; absolve the tempters, the Fagins and teachers of crime who snare boys and girls because their home training should have taught them resistance to such lures; let the betrayer go scot free, because the girl was badly raised and was too susceptible. Even in the days of the saloon, barkeepers were punished for selling to drunkards or minors without clemency because the drunkard was urgent or the minor badly brought up. Should we be more considerate of, or more compassionate, toward the author or publisher who inflames the passions and arouses the baser qualities of boys and girls with lascivious books, than to the saloon-keeper who entices them to intemperance, or maddens them with vile whiskey or other poisonous decoctions?

If we did not have rigid laws to suppress barrooms, those sinks of iniquity would flourish at every street corner; if we had loose laws to suppress narcotics, the victims of degenerating, habit-forming drugs would multiply a thousand-fold; if we had weak laws to suppress gambling, those dens of vice would flaunt their lure in every city block.

I have small patience with the supercilious class of writers, editors, critics and columnists, especially some of the latter. With rare exceptions they are conceited, over-indulged coxcombs of literature, suffering from delusions of greatness and exaggerated ego, borne by the tide of their own verbal exuberance, ready to sacrifice a reputation for a wheeze or blast a good name for a quip. This type of cynic pitilessly stabs with mordant pen and cruel jest any one who even timorously expresses a judgment which does not square with his dogmatic views. Particularly is he sardonic if such opinion is a protest against the prevailing laxity in manners and customs; if it expresses itself in dissent against the present extreme style of girls' habiliments, or in remonstrance against immodest flapperism; if it demands observance of temperance, reverence for religion, obedience to law and courts, or if it seeks intelligent censorship of lascivious plays and obscene books.

We enact laws to suppress narcotics, to protect our youth from habit-forming drugs; we pass statutes to guard our stomachs from poisonous foods; we have legislation to protect our eyes from vulgar sights; our ears from foul noises, our bodies from insufficient heat, our noses from offensive smells. The senses of sight, taste, feeling, hearing, and smell are cared for; but more sensitive, more impressionable than the entire five physical faculties is the mysterious matrix of the soul, the subliminal consciousness which dwells in the human form and indelibly records all its physical reactions; that imperishable, impalpable essence which comes direct from God to be reabsorbed after death into immortality! Shall it be neglected, forsooth, because certain erotic writers must find markets for their foul productions? God forbid!

The proposition to censor works of the imagination, whether books, pictures, plays or movies, raises invariably a storm of dissent among the few sincere but misguided, and the many see their pocketbooks affected; they passionately protest that it implies a suppression of "Truth," the "hamstringing" of art, a restraint of "free expression."

But: What is "Art?" What is "Truth?" What is "Free Expression?"

Is "Art" a creation to arouse lustful emotions; is "Truth" the expression of thoughts to stimulate vicious impulses; is "Free Expression" a privilege to diffuse foul suggestions?

Who is to determine whether these sinister seeds are sown? Shall it be he or she whose moral reactions are so blunted as to be either contemptuous of or insensible to the evils that lurk behind their work? Or shall the decision rest with an unbiased judicial body of experts, chosen by legal authority—men and women—who have not the perverted artistic temperament, also who are free from the enticements of swollen box office receipts? It is a sad commentary on the depravity of human nature that the more salacious the book, the more risqué the play, the more suggestive the work of art, the wider the appeal, the greater the sale, the bigger the audiences. Publishers and producers are keenly aware of this! hence anything that may restrain unfettered latitude in appealing to this human frailty raises strong objections.

But does true art suffer by reasonable restraint?

Shall it be contended that art finds real expression only in libidinous utterance? Will the emotions evoked by imaginative work, whether of author, dramatist, painter or sculptor, evaporate unless they are inflamed by lustful appeal? To admit this is to confess that idealism, purity, ethics and morals have vanished and that our vaunted civilization is a delusion.

FILTH ON MAIN STREET[4]

Not long ago, I made a trip clear across the country and back again with the single idea of trying to discover what, if anything, is in the minds of the people. It seemed a fine time for the effort. Congress had just adjourned, there was no campaign on, no particular political excitement or propaganda, and the time to travel leisurely was

[4] By Frank R. Kent. *Independent.* 114:686-9. June 20, 1925.

available. It was a chance to do the thing differently from the time-worn "swing around the circle" of the Washington correspondents; to see and hear and talk without having to rush off to "cover" the next State. There was, too, the opportunity to visit a lot of little towns to which no one ever thinks of turning in the "search for sentiment," altho the great bulk of Americans live in them. It is so easy to forget that four-fifths of the population are completely outside our sixty-five cities of one hundred thousand and over.

Of course, such an investigation discloses nothing of a totally unsuspected and startling nature. It leads to no sensational "lifting of the veil," reveals no astonishing discoveries. It would be silly to expect such things. The feelings and thoughts, when they have any, of the American people are never hidden. There are no "concealed conditions" here, no dark secrets to be dug up. America is as open as the well-known goose. There is nothing subtle about our civilization. In these standardized, syndicated days, the same influences play on all the people. The same social customs and business methods absorb them, the same political currents saturate them, and they are afflicted with the same gross misconceptions and misunderstandings.

You find in one section exactly what you find in another. From coast to coast, the radio, the movies, golf, bobbed hair, business, short skirts, trashy literature, automobiles, lip sticks, bad newspapers, rotten liquor, absorption in money making, almost complete political inertia, and an unparalleled muddy-mindedness about public matters—that's the country today.

In the smaller towns, away from the clash and clatter of the more congested communities, it is possible to see with greater clarity the tendencies of the times, the speed and direction in which national habits are forming, the effect of the general prosperity upon the people.

Two significant attitudes stand out as vitally interesting: First, the completeness with which all liberal thought has vanished, the astounding degree to which the country has become conservatized, and the stronghold of the Coolidge propaganda on all classes of society, whether rich or poor.

Second is the truly extraordinary extent to which the country is drenched with smut by the steadily increasing stream of pornographic periodicals and dirty fiction magazines.

To deal with the last first, while it is not exactly a thing about which we like to boast or even face, the plain truth is that in the matter of literary lewdness we have taken the lead away from the French. It used to be that Paris held the palm for this sort of thing. Americans in the French capital were accustomed to marvel that a civilized nation should openly permit the sale of such filth, and it was taken to indicate that the French, as a whole, were essentially a dirty-minded people. Men used to smuggle home these Paris periodicals and stealthily pass them around among their friends.

But they do not have to do that now. They can get here in the "old home town" not only more such publications but dirtier, both as to art and as to reading matter. And not only have we produced a great smut crop of a coarseness peculiarly our own, but the more obscene of the French papers have now been translated into English and appear on the news stands along with the originals. In the small towns where they are seen in the greatest profusion, they make an imposing array. When you stop to analyze, scrutinize, and check up, there is here presented more reason for apprehension as to the future than any other single symptom in America today.

There isn't anything sudden about this prolific pornographic flood. It is a gradual growth covering a period of about five years. Some of the less lewd of the publications are even older than that. It is, however, in the last twenty-four months that the real spread has occurred, and, while the existence of this sort of thing has been casually noted, I am certain the multiplicity of the periodicals which frankly and with a surpassing vulgarity cater to the sexual appetite has not been generally grasped. It really is the most sensational development in the publishing business in years and is nationally significant in so many ways that it ought to be generally noted and understood. The place to appreciate fully its proportions is in the smaller cities and towns with populations ranging from 20,000 up to 100,000—towns, for instance, like Fairmont, West Virginia, where one news dealer sells 2,200 copies of every issue of a single monthly exclusively devoted to stories of sex experiences and the nude in art; or like Steubenville, Ohio, where out of 110 periodicals on sale in a single store, sixty were either out and out of a prurient type or bordered on the libidinous line. For reasons not possible to go into here, people in the smaller towns are more avid readers of magazines, good and bad, than in the large cities. It ought not, however, to be thought that these pornographic periodicals are not devoured with almost as much eagerness in the larger cities. They are, but they are not as conspicuously grouped or so prolifically displayed as in the smaller places.

It is not the cheap and sexually suggestive fiction magazines, although these are many and rotten, that constitute the real shock troops of these paper battalions of literary indecency so much as the smaller and more compact nonfiction affairs frankly and exclusively given over to obscenities. Some of these are published in Chicago, some in Philadelphia, but most of them in Newark, New Jersey, and are issued by the same individuals under different corporate names. They mainly contain a rehash of the dirty stories and jokes of the kind told by traveling salesmen in the smoking rooms of Pullman cars or when exchanging erotic experiences in hotel lobbies. They carry no advertisements and go to the dealers by express, not by mail. If you want to know whether these things are widely read, all you have to do is check up with any intelligent news dealer in any city, big or little, in any part of the country. The candid ones will not hesitate to tell you not only that the demand for this sexual literature is enormous, but that there is no such thing as oversatisfying it. Those who buy one of these periodicals will buy every similar one on sight. The more you feed it the keener it gets. That is why there is a constantly increasing number of these things. There have been eighteen new ones in the past three months. As fast as one lewd venture is launched and successfully established, a little twin brother, under a different name and in a dress of a different color, is sent out and is equally successful with the same clientele.

In New York and elsewhere there has been considerable commotion over some of the allegedly immoral plays of the year. From time to time, too, there is an outcry against some especially salacious novel. Except, however, in a spasmodic and entirely futile form, such as the recent gesture by the district attorney in Washington, a sermon in Canton, a councilmanic ordinance in Santa Barbara, there has been no public protest and very little comment on what is unquestionably a far more serious situation from the standpoint of the moralists than the worst plays and the most outspoken books—if only for the reason that vastly more people are touched by it. It seems incredible that more general attention should not have been centered on this great bumper American smut crop of the last two years—at least by those who professionally concern themselves about the morals of the people. Certainly, a more fruitful field for a moral crusade would be hard to conceive.

Perhaps nothing can be done about it. Perhaps, any crusade against the pornographic periodicals would result similarly to the crusades against the lewd books and the libidinous plays—namely, by greatly increasing their sale and popularity. Efforts at censorship are nearly always futile, often worse. The psychologists point out that the sexual impulse is one of the strongest of the primal instincts in human beings. Along with fear and acquisitiveness, it is inherent in the human system. This flood of sexual literature caters to a passion impossible wholly to curb or control.

Perhaps all this is true and nothing can be done about it. However, while I am a long way from being a little brother of the uplift, I still submit there is more reason to get excited about the present unchecked growth of the dirty fiction on the news-stands than about all the off-color plays and smelly novels of the past twenty-five years. There is no better index to the character and calibre of a people than what they read. The increased public demand for bad reading matter means a corresponding decrease in the demand for good. When to this disposition to make sewers out of their minds is coupled the further fact that the habit of going to the movies has become as fixed with the majority of people as eating and sleeping, it is easy to see why it is so difficult actively to interest the voters of the United States in their Government, why it is impossible to persuade a majority of them to go to the polls even to choose a President, why there is a small and ever-diminishing minority which is clear-headed and informed on public issues, why the popular mind is so muddily full of the most grotesque misconceptions, and the popular judgment so unerringly wrong.

The publication of these periodicals ought to render reflective any student of public affairs. It ought to suggest to those who think ahead and clearly that here is a greater menace to the future than any socialistic, communistic, or Bolshevistic propaganda that can be devised. Here is something real about which to see red.

It is possible you won't find these periodicals at the first news dealer's you visit, but a little hunt around will locate them. They are not in one section, they are in all sections. No corner of the country is free from them, and no step yet taken by any local government has succeeded in checking their distribution. Exactly the same reason why the Volstead Act does not prevent the sale of bootleg whiskey explains why the ordinances against obscene magazines passed here and there by the smaller cities do not stop their sale. The answer is simple—the people want both. No one with a clear mind, I think, would contend that the literature is not more poisonous than the liquor. It is like putting white lead in the coffee every morning, and the most deadly thing about it is that it is the youth of the country which is absorbing most of the literary poison. The liquor is more evenly distributed.

One of the worst things that can conceivably be said about a nation is that its people are steeped in dirty literature. If, for another year or so, this phenomenal spread in pornography is continued here unchecked, it will be possible truthfully to say so about this nation. That is a harsh assertion to make, and it will probably be resented and denied by those who have not taken the time and trouble to find out and face the facts. It is, however, true just the same, and it is further the fact that this phase of American life is the most striking and impressive to be found in any survey of the country today.

It is a subject and a situation pregnant with possibilities. Much more could be written about it as to causes, effects, remedies. Enough has been said, however, to indicate the depth and strength of the most harmful stream flowing in America today.

CUSTOMS CENSORSHIP[5]

This question is one that strikes at the morals of every young boy and girl in the United States. Mr. President, I have here books the reading of which would so disgust Senators of the United States that they would never dream of agreeing to the amendment proposed by the Senator from New Mexico [Mr. Cutting]. I did not believe there were such books printed in the world—books that the Senator from New Mexico referred to and said ought to be in the libraries of the

[5] By Senator Reed Smoot. *Congressional Record.* 72:5414-17. March 17, 1930.

people of the United States. They are lower than the beasts! I could take two of the books referred to by the Senator from New Mexico [Mr. Cutting], and if I should read them to the Senate of the United States I do not believe there is a Senator who would dare to vote for his amendment. My remarks at this time will be directed principally to the subject of so-called obscene books or literature. On the conclusion of my remarks I shall submit for the examination of Senators a number of typical importations rejected by the Customs Service. These are but a few illustrations of the filthy books that are being imported by various individuals. Thousands of these books are seized and destroyed by the customs officials every year.

Senators will notice that in most instances the names of the printers and publishers are omitted. No decent printer will allow his name to be used in connection with the distribution of this filth. This is the so-called literature which my good friend, the Senator from New Mexico, desires to have admitted to the shores of our country. I am not objecting to the admission of these books for any political reason, but I am objecting to the admission purely on my understanding of the duties of a father and an American citizen and a legislator in the interests of the great mass of our American citizenry.

I deplore the contemptuous references to the personnel of the Customs Service which ran through the debate in the Committee of the Whole. Many of the members of this personnel are veterans of the service, tried and true. I know from personal contact that many are men of education, legal training, and broad information. In enforcing the law against obscene matter they are performing an unpleasant duty in a most conscientious manner, and if I were a customs inspector, duly authorized under the present law to prevent the admission of any of this obscene literature, it would only be admitted over my dead body.

I have been saddened by the disclosure of laxity of views developed during the debate. I have been distressed that in the Senate of the United States so few voices were raised in debate against a proposal to abolish the prohibition of the importation of obscene books. I cannot refrain from expressing the opinion that some of the views expressed in that debate, while possibly only the views of the individual speakers, cannot fail to react upon the Senate as a whole and lower it in the estimation of that very large part of our citizenry whose esteem we value most, but which it would appear from the debate are included by some Senators in the "unthinking class."

It has been suggested here that the interpretation of what is moral and what is immoral should be a very liberal one, and that the people will develop moral resistance to all the improprieties the books may contain; that we should not be afraid of the distribution of literature injuring and breaking down the morals of the good, solid, substantial citizenship of America. I regard such suggestions as dangerous fallacies. I was much pleased to hear the junior Senator from Florida state that he differed with the idea that obscene literature promotes good morals and with the idea that to prohibit obscene literature conflicts with a man's liberty. I thoroughly agree with him that we would have practically no reform legislation if we listened to these arguments about liberty.

The opposition has made much of the summary seizure by customs inspectors, without opportunity for jury trial, of obscene books brought by passengers. Such seizures are made either on well-considered instructions by the department or on the judgment of the inspector himself after examination of the article and confirmation by his immediate superiors. If a customs inspector at the port of New York, with his knowledge of the world, regards on his own initiative a book as obscene it is about the nearest approach to a jury trial that can be had, and it is safe to say that his judgment would be sustained by a jury; but in either case I have heretofore pointed out how a jury trial of the question may be had. Moreover, the general accuracy of the customs judgment is confirmed by the statement of the Senator from New Mexico that he could find only one case where the courts had reversed the customs.

The senior Senator from New York has indicated objection to any classification as obscene of books for the medical profession. I can meet his objection by stating that, so far as the customs is concerned, standard textbooks of medicine and surgery for the profession have not been banned. It is only when certain extracts from such works have been made and circulated for obviously improper purposes that seizures have been made.

Unfortunately, however, there is a class of books which, with a subtle cunning almost unbelievable, seek to convey the impression that they are of a scientific or medical character. Such a book has very recently been the subject of a decision by the United States Customs Court written by the chief justice. In the opinion the chief justice uses the following language:

> In writing this book the author evidently proceeded on the theory that modesty and chastity were no longer popular conceptions of the human heart and mind, and that there has grown up, particularly among the so-called educated class a tendency that the law should be construed accordingly. . . . To assert that such a publication is impure only to the overprudish but illustrates how familiarity with obscenity tends to blunt the sensibilities, deprave good taste, and pervert the judgment.

All of which reminds me of those lines of Pope in his Essay on Man:

> Vice is a monster of so frightful mien,
> As to be hated needs but to be seen;
> Yet seen too oft, familiar with her face,
> We first endure, then pity, then embrace.

The principal point made by the opposition probably is that there is no excuse for barring the so-called classics on account of the obscene portions thereof.

I repeat what I said in the debate referred to that "it were better, to my mind, that a few classics suffer the application of the expurgating shears than that this country be flooded with the books, pamphlets, pictures, and other articles that are wholly indecent both in purpose and tendency and that we know all too well would follow the repeal of this provision," and that even if in one of these old and rare books there is any obscene matter it ought to be kept out and never permitted to go to the youth of the land.

I realize Mr. President, just as does the Senator from New Mexico, that mature, well-regulated minds may not be subverted by such matter. But such legislation is enacted to prevent such matter from coming into the hands of those whose minds are open to influence, whose morals are likely to be corrupted, and I am thinking particularly of the youth of our country, and proof that such matter would get into the hands of the young is offered by the statement made in the debate regarding the customs' rejection of such a book brought by a professor of literature in a great university to teach to his class. As the court said in United States v. Smith (45 Fed. 476):

> The most debasing topic may be presented in the choicest language. In such garb it is the more dangerous. Impure suggestion clothed in pleasing attire allures and corrupts, when bald filth would digust and repel.

Nor does the fact that such books might be imported by private collectors or for private libraries furnish any assurance that they would not reach young people for whom they were never originally intended.

It was stated in the debate that any of our citizens can go to the Congressional Library and read the obscene books that the customs bar to the public. I have caused inquiry to be made and find that such books are safeguarded in the Library and that only in proper cases is access to them permitted.

It has been suggested that there is no satisfactory definition of obscenity, and that the law should contain a definition. That supreme authority in this country, the United States Supreme Court, has given a definition or test. In Rosen v. United States (161 U. S. 29), the court said:

The test of obscenity is whether the tendency of the matter is to deprave and corrupt the morals of those whose minds are open to such influence and into whose hands a publication of this sort may fall. Would it suggest or convey lewd thoughts and lascivious thoughts to the young and inexperienced? Everyone who uses the mails of the United States for carrying papers or publications must take notice of what, in this enlightened age, is meant by decency, purtity, and chastity in social life and what must be deemed obscene, lewd, and lascivious.

Another high court, accepted throughout the Anglo-Saxon world as a great authority, has formulated a similar test. In Queen v. Hecklin (2 Q. B. 369, 1868) Chief Justice Cockburn said:

I think the test of obscenity is this, whether the tendency of the matter is to deprave and corrupt those whose minds are open to such immoral influences and into whose hands a publication of this sort may fall. Now in regard to this work (pamphlet entitled *Confessional Unmasked*) it is quite certain that it would suggest to the minds of the young of either sex, or even to persons of more advanced years, thoughts of a most impure and libidinous character.

While without authority at this moment to speak for the Committee on Finance I would be perfectly willing to have the Supreme Court's definition incorporated in the law.

But there is an exceedingly important aspect of the matter which I am inclined to believe has so far escaped the attention of the Senators.

Certain conditions in this country have become so bad that the President has appointed a National Commission of Law Observance and Enforcement. I feel sure that Senators generally are in sympathy with the purposes of the President in appointing that commission.

Before a vote was had on the amendment of the Senator from New Mexico I warned the Senate that if that amendment were agreed to all obscene books, pamphlets, papers, writings, and circulars, could come into the country freely, and that we know all too well that following the repeal of the present law this country would be flooded with books and pamphlets that are wholly indecent both in purpose and tendency. It is appalling to think of the moral and physical effects of removing the present ban. Are Senators willing to repeal this obscenity law and thereby add so greatly to the difficulties which it is the purpose of the President's commission to find ways to correct?

In the debate some of the Senators indicated that this class of books should be left for the States to deal with under their laws, one consideration being that in this way jury trials would be more practicable and likely. I have heretofore pointed out that it is not difficult under the present law to obtain a jury trial. There would, however, be no more jury trials under the State laws than there are under the present tariff law. Importers of this class of books seldom are willing to face the publicity of a jury trial. They are ashamed to be connected with the importation of books which are charged with being obscene. Besides, they think they have a better chance of convincing one man in the Treasury Department than they have of convincing a jury of 12 men, and they avoid a disagreeable publicity.

Moreover, under the Constitution, the control of interstate and foreign commerce is an exclusive Federal activity. We prevent the importation and interstate traffic in many things that poison or injure the body. Is it not equally important and desirable to cooperate with the States and protect the people in the case of what poisons the mind and the morals and so, directly or indirectly, affects the body?

The junior Senator from Washington has stated that it is not the importation but the dissemination that does the damage; that the moment a man begins to disseminate it we have the law of the land that takes care of the situation. Unfortunately, the dissemination of this class of books is often conducted in such secret, clandestine ways, like the distribution of narcotics, that detection by the State authorities is very difficult. They get into the schools and are secretly passed from one pupil to another. A sailor was recently caught on the docks smuggling in from his ship a number of books especially designed to encourage sexual vices in boys. Would Senators be willing to run the risk of the State authorities catching that sailor after he left the customs jurisdiction? I am thoroughly satisfied that the Customs Service is the only agency that can promptly and effectively detect and deal with importations of these books.

But there is a further consideration, which I think will appeal to the opposition, against leaving these books to be dealt with by the State laws. Under those laws importers would not have the advantage of the relief which the Secretary of the Treasury may now afford under the provisions of section 618 of the present tariff act. Under that section, if a book is found to be obscene, the Secretary of the Treasury will, upon a proper showing, permit the exportation of the book, whereas otherwise it would be destroyed.

I thus conclude my effort to answer all the principal arguments of the opposition. I urge the adoption of the Finance Committee's amendment in the place of the amendment adopted in the Committee of the Whole. I appeal to the Senate, as did the senior Senator from Alabama, to throw the arms of protection around the army of boys and girls who must constitute the citizenship of our country a little later on.

In submitting to the Senators for inspection the books which have been obtained from the Treasury Department, I call particular attention to the book for whose admission the Senator from New Mexico made a special appeal to Secretary Mellon, which book is pronounced by the man in the Customs Bureau who handles these books to be the vilest one that ever came into the bureau. I am told that the author of this vile book attempted to have it printed in England, but no decent printer would take the job, so it was published in another country on the Continent.

PREVENTION BETTER THAN REMEDY[6]

The amendment of the Senator from New Mexico will permit the coming in of obscene literature; it will permit the coming in of harmful books; and certainly the Congress ought to take its stand on the side of decent literature and on the side of wholesome books. I do not propose that any amendment shall pass if I can prevent it that will permit this country to become the dumping ground of all the unfit literature of the earth, to come in here to be studied by our boys and our girls, to give them wrong ideas of government, to exalt in their minds the principles of anarchism and of communism. I want to protect the young men and the young women of America from floods of literature of that kind.

We know now of instances where boys, after seeing moving pictures where murders are depicted, have gone out from those places and later committed murder themselves. The purpose to murder was traced to the harmful moving picture. Many a man and many a woman, too, have gone down to death in the United States because of a devilish book read by some boy that put the idea of murder in his mind. I want to protect this youthful crop of American citizens from contamination of that kind.

We have a law that prevents the coming in of diseased cattle; we enforce a quarantine against the foot-and-mouth disease. The Congress went on record as in

[6] By J. Thomas Heflin. *Congressional Record.* 71:4469-70. October 11, 1929.

favor of throwing the arms of protection around the cattle herds of America, around the mules and the horses. Is the Senate not willing to throw the arms of protection around the army of boys and girls who must constitute the citizenship of our country a little later on? We are doing various things to protect plant life in America. We are spending money to destroy the boll weevil that has come here. We have tried to keep it out. I went down to the State of Texas at the invitation of the legislature and made a speech at a joint session. I asked them to lay off a no-cotton zone 50 miles wide along the Rio Grande River for the purpose of keeping the pink boll worm from getting into the Cotton Belt of the United States, and they did it. The Congress appropriated several hundred thousand dollars for that purpose. We can appropriate money to keep the pink cotton worm out of the cotton fields of the South, but we cannot vote to keep out this devilish literature of the anarchists of the Old World; to prevent the impure, devilish, murderous stuff crossing the border line and coming into our country to be read and studied in dens of iniquity by men who then come out threatening to kill public men. There is no provision in the pending section that prevents the importation of such literature as that. I am for that provision heart and soul.

I do not want any literature coming in here that advocates the idea of killing public men. I note that there is in this bill, and a line has been struck through it—I wish it had been left in—a provision excluding any book suggesting the murdering of an American President. Three of them have been assassinated in the United States. Are we not willing now to go upon record on this subject when, immediately after the last election, Mr. Hoover was down in Florida and, two anarchists seeing him, one suggested to the other, "Let's blow him up; let's kill him"? Are we not ready now, with the experience we have had in the past, to put on the statute books a law saying that those things cannot be talked around in this Nation; that books containing such things cannot come here and be circulated? Who is it that is afraid to go on record as voting to keep out literature like that?

There is also a provision in the bill that immoral literature in books or otherwise shall not come in. I am in favor of that. I do not care what anybody says about my trying to prescribe situations and prevent books from circulating; I am in favor of the right kind of books being circulated, but I am no more in favor of this sort of books coming in here than I would permit the flannel-mouthed anarchist himself to come and cross the line and advocate the destruction of my Government.

I voted—and I think I have materially helped in the twenty-odd years I have served in the two Houses of Congress—to stop the unfit horde of foreigners that formerly poured in here, a million strong, every year. I helped to restrict immigration, to cut it down to a point where now it is probably less than 200,000 a year; and if I had my way about it I would shut them all out for five years and let this country take stock and see who is who in America. I have voted to keep America from becoming the dumping ground for these unfit foreigners, and I am going to vote today to keep America from becoming the dumping ground of the obscene, treasonable, and murderous literature of the anarchistic foreigner.

A great physician has said that the time to treat a cancer is in its incipient stage. The time to deal with this question is now, when a bill is up here that will put a crimp in the coming in of this character of literature. I am not going to play politics on a question like this. My party does not stand for such a proposition. The great Democratic Party does not believe in it. The Democratic Party stands for wholesome literature. The Democratic Party does not believe in permitting books to come into the United States that advocate immoral things—that is what this section means—or books that carry treasonable doctrine—there it is, right in the body of the provision—or murderous plans. There it is. We are being put in an awful situation. For Democrats to support an amendment that strikes out that provision of the bill puts us in the attitude of favoring the wholesale coming of this sort of stuff into the United States.

I believe in the fullest and freest expression of thought. I believe in it in every nook and corner of the United States, for everybody in the country and every class; but I am in favor of saying at the border line, "You shall not enter my nation with that deadly literature. Stop it! Keep it out!"

I think it is high time that this Government was taking a stand. We vote to appropriate money to kill the germs that kill the hog. We have appropriated hundreds of thousands of dollars to save the farmers' hogs of America from hog cholera; and I helped to do it. Can it be that we will not vote, when it does not cost anything, to save the boys and girls of America from this deadly, anarchistic, treasonable, murderous literature?

In the case of foot-and-mouth disease of horses and mules and cows, we come to the rescue; we grow enthusiastic; we appropriate money to treat the animals that have caught the disease here and to prevent others that have it from coming in. But when it comes to the fruits of this deadly literature that is already coming in, when murder grows out of it, when communistic doctrines are spreading over the land, when the doctrine of the black shirts of Italy is spreading over the land, when various "isms" are coming in that one day will rise up to hound us and to threaten us by their strength in this Republic, here is an opportunity; the hour has struck when we can put a stop to the coming in of literature that poisons the mind of the citizen to be and sows dragon's teeth in the path of the Republic.

I shall support the provision of the bill. It is good enough for me just as it stands. I should like to see the amendment withdrawn and the vote made unanimous to preserve the provision just as it is.

BRIEF EXCERPTS

If there is no other way to check the spirit of literary lust, I am for the censorship.—*George B. McCutcheon. Literary Digest.* 77:58. *June* 23, 1923.

The book trade is beginning to feel that some censorship is very necessary.—*H. D. Rawnsley. Hibbert Journal.* 10:466. *January* 1912.

A flood of grossly obscene publications is inundating the state. Some of the worst of them are being put into the hands of our children with special judicial commendation.—*John Ford. New York Times. March* 18, 1923.

Cannon William S. Chase declared that the book publishers were making millions every year through the debauchery of our youth.—*New York Times. March* 13, 1929.

There are many books published every year which are capable of doing an immense amount of harm to all boys between the ages of fourteen and nineteen.—*Stephen Foot. Nineteenth Century.* 105:440. *April* 1929.

There are many books which may be regarded as comparatively harmless for the adult, but which are thoroughly poisonous to the adolescent mind.—*Stephen Foot. Nineteenth Century.* 105:440. *April* 1929.

Everybody will agree that it is desirable to protect from injurious books the young and immature, who are highly impressionable and whose self-control is still undeveloped.—*George F. Bowerman. Libraries.* 35:184. *May* 1930.

The disquieting thing about this whole matter (censorship of books) is that there are so many books published of such a character as to be candidates for censorship.—*George F. Bowerman. Libraries.* 35:186. *May* 1930.

To expose boys to the unhealthy suggestion which so many modern novels contain is to undermine the whole structure, and it may easily prove fatal to the atmosphere of public schools. —*Stephen Foot. Nineteenth Century.* 105:442-3. *April* 1929.

At the moment some of our younger writers, literary infants, are now in competition to determine which can compress between the covers of a book of fiction or of an alleged scientific work the maximum amount of pornography, filth, and socially destructive instruction.—*John S. Sumner. Literary Digest.* 74:32. *September* 2, 1922.

In almost every stationery store may be found shockingly immoral books. They are conspicuously displayed in the show windows at popular prices. They find their market among the young and immature. Their influence for evil is incalculable.—*John Ford. New York Times. March* 18, 1923.

I am wondering what possible good to the people of this country could come from the distribution of circular matter, literature, advocating or urging treason, insurrection, or forcible resistance to any law of the United States?—*Arthur R. Robinson. Congressional Record.* 71:4463. *October* 11, 1929.

The defects of the old method of indictment were stated to be that the prosecution of one who had sold an obscene book did not necessarily prevent other sales of the book, and also that the legal proceedings advertised the book.—*Carrol Romer. Nineteenth Century.* 105:448. *April* 1929.

No one will seriously demand that the Watch and Ward Society be dissolved. There is a well defined field in which it may operate to safeguard children, especially from pornographic pictures and prints concerning which there is substantially no division of opinion among people of character.—*Editorial. Springfield Republican. January* 14, 1930.

The purveyor of prurient literature is in exactly the same position as the proprietor of a night club or a manufacturer of intoxicating liquor. They are all pandering to a weakness of human nature, artificially developed perhaps as the result of the war, and they are reaping a golden harvest.—*Stephen Foot. Nineteenth Century.* 105:441. *April* 1929.

I have had a long and painful experience as a Police Commissioner and a Magistrate dealing with indecent and immoral plays and books. In my opinion the law has broken down in effectively dealing with such matters. This break-down, in my judgment, is not because there is an insufficiency of statutory law, but by reason of the decisions of the reviewing courts.—*William McAdoo. New York Times. March* 13, 1923.

Some would have brought into this country any character of seditious literature, any character of obscene literature, to be carried into the home, to be absorbed and read by those of tender age in the country, and would cloak this behind the excuse that it is in the interest of freedom of the press and freedom of speech.—*Park Trammell. Congressional Record.* 72:5502. *March* 18, 1930.

The ordinary type of prurient novel which describes obscenities, or creates unpleasant situations, is generally excused nowadays on the ground that it is a work of art, though I strongly suspect that the only muse which the author considers is a golden calf. Even if it is a work of art, this does not mean that it will not do harm to a growing boy.—*Stephen Foot. Nineteenth Century.* 105:442. *April* 1929.

Judge Ford declared it impossible to curb corrupting literature under the present [New York] law, called the "censorship" charge "flubdub," and denied the contention that under the bill a book could be held obscene or indecent because of one or two passages. He said that 85 per cent of the obscene literature either originates or is sold in New York state, and for that reason other states were looking to this state to put a stop to the vile stuff.—*New York Times. March* 13, 1929.

The morals of the youth are more important than the dirty dollars of the book publishers. The publishers have found a gold mine in putting vile and degrading literature on the market, and they are working it every minute. The publishers told us once they would clean up the literature, but time has shown that they think more of the dollar than they do of the morals of the young. The gang that formerly came up here [Albany] to fight this bill [the Clean Books Bill] said they would clean up their business, but they did not keep their word.—*O. R. Miller. New York Times. March* 13, 1929.

The circulating libraries, which have a great place in England, have decided that they will not "place in circulation any book which, by reason of the personally scandalous, libelous, immoral, or otherwise disagreeable nature of its contents, is, in our opinion, likely to prove offensive to any considerable section of our subscribers." This is a move in the right direction. It is printed indecency, and not in any sense literature, with which these libraries are dealing, and it is high time that some such action as this were taken to protect innocent readers from books which are an offense to every decent person.—*Outlook.* 94:11-12. *January* 1, 1910.

Unwise newspaper publicity and the play upon crime, vice, and profligacy in literature tend to make these things attractive. Much of modern literature is filthy and vicious in the opinion of persons absolutely free from the influence of Puritan traditions. It is a reflection upon our intelligence when we permit our young people to read such matter and then punish them when they attempt to imitate the heroes and heroines. Much of modern literature is filth and few of us have the courage to call it such.

Until we have that courage it will continue to besmirch many who read it.—*Philip P. Parsons. Crime and the Criminal. p. 377.*

I differ with the idea that to prohibit obscene literature conflicts with a man's liberty. We have heard questions of liberty argued and we have heard arguments presented in this country in the name of liberty against every effort to bring about any character of reform. We would have practically no reform legislation if we listened to these arguments about liberty. I am for liberty in its true sense as vouchsafed to us in the Constitution, but do not want to adopt the definition of the anarchist of what liberty means, or what the writer of obscene and indecent literature may call liberty.—*Park Trammell. Congressional Record.* 71:4459. *October* 11, 1929.

In any case the sex appetite is more vibrant and suggestible than either of the others. [food or drink] Truly appalling is the swiftness with which sensuality and lewdness may infect a people. In a mushroom mining camp debauchery is swifter than drink in breaking down steady habits. This is why no society can afford to let its members say or publish or exhibit what they please. Lust is a monster that can be lulled to sleep only with infinite difficulty, whereas a pin prick, a single staccato note is enough to arouse. The ordered sex relation is, perhaps, man's greatest achievement in self-domestication. Common sense forbids that the greed of purveyors of suggestive plays, pictures, or literature be suffered to disturb it. —*Edward A. Ross. Social Psychology. p.* 126.

When they bring this poisonous literature in we know what it means. We have already seen it. The anarchist, Czolgolz, who murdered McKinley, had read this kind of literature. He said he had. He had read literature that defiled his mind and urged him to the dastardly deed of striking down one of the kindliest Americans that ever walked this earth, a great American President, who was murdered by the offspring of this anarchistic and communistic doctrine in the United States. Let us be true to those who sent us here and protect the boys and girls of America from the indecent, obscene, and immoral literature of foreign countries.—*J. Thomas Heflin. Congressional Record.* 72:5511. *March* 18, 1930.

The proposed amendment to the law would not strengthen the law, but would make it weaker. A jury or judges would have to decide as a matter of taste whether a given passage was decent or not and punish accordingly. The defendant would have no standard whatever to conform to, and his guilt or innocence would have to be measured by individual opinions which vary as widely as the poles. The only way that standards can be created in this matter is by censorship, and that is what these would-be regulators of literature are really aiming at. To be effective at all their proposals would have to provide for some sort of censorship.—*Jonah J. Goldstein, Attorney for the defense in the prosecution of books alleged to be immoral. New York Times. February* 26, 1923.

I hope that the Congress of the United States will not serve notice to the world that the bars are down, so far as our customs laws are concerned, to all the obscene, indecent, and salacious matter that may be published abroad. I know it is said that much of the so-called obscene matter is literature, classical literature, and that foreign classics die along with matter immoral in purpose, use, and tendency. Well, let the dead past bury its dead. It were better, to my mind, that a classic suffer the application of the expurgating shears than that this country be flooded with the books, pamphlets, pictures, and other articles that are wholly indecent both in purpose and in tendency, and that we know all too well would follow the repeal of this provision.—*Reed Smoot. Congressional Record.* 71:4458. *October* 11, 1929.

The conclusion of fact we have reached upon a full reading of this book (*Lady Chatterley's Lover*) is in accordance with that of the trial judge, which he formulates as follows: "The book viewed as a whole, having regard to its significance as an entity, and not merely to certain particular parts of it viewed separately, is obscene, indecent, and impure, and manifestly tends to corrupt the morals of youth." The several passages of this book, when read by themselves alone and out of context also warrant the trial judge in his finding that they are obscene, indecent, and impure, and manifestly tend to corrupt the morals of youth, and when so read have these baneful attributes in an even more concentrated degree than when diluted by admixture with the rest of the writing." —*Supreme Judicial Court of Massachusetts.* 171 *N.E.* 456. *May* 27, 1930.

No newspaper or magazine would dare to print their [immoral books'] abhorrent pages of filth. It is the youthful and immature who fall victims to the vicious lure of such books. And they are freely offered to your children and mine in every little book store along the avenues to be read for twenty-five cents a volume. And this in the name of liberty! These writers, publishers, and vendors claim the liberty to pollute the minds of our children, undermine the teachings of Church and parent, and desecrate the family shrine of purity and innocence. And if we presume to assert our right of self-defense against these evil influences, we are ignorant, narrow, Puritanic. I am proud to accept that characterization when acquired in doing what I may to debar these demoralizing, debasing, and degenerate publications from general circulation.—*John Ford. New York Times. February* 25, 1923.

I do not become at all disturbed on account of some extracts that may be read from some of these educators—these high-brows in the educational field. It resolves itself, in my mind, down to the practical, common-sense proposition as to whether or not we desire to ban from this country obscene and seditious literature of a foreign brand that would promote, if it could carry out its purpose, the overthrow and the destruction of our Government and its institutions; whether or not we desire to ban from our shores and from our homes obscene literature. There is no man on the face of the earth who can say that such literature will do the youth of our land any good. Shall we ban that in the interest of our land and in the interest of our homes and our future citizenship? That is the burning question of the hour.—*Park Trammell. Congressional Record.* 72:5503. *March* 18, 1930.

This improvement [censorship of the movies] is likely to spread to the censorship of books, and if it does, the publishers will have themselves to blame for it. The theory of a free press has its limits, after all. It is not safe to say youth can take care of itself. Education which comes from defilement may prove costly. I believe in censorship. Over and over again I have been asked to sign a protest against the suppression of some indecent book, but I have always refused to do so, for I am certain that, on the whole, the restraining force is salutary. Censorship is, after all, only the organized collective protest against debasing forms of art. I admit its liability to misuse and error, but the right of society to protect itself remains. The need of restraint exists, and I am willing to suffer the consequences. I am quite certain that I can say anything worth saying under such laws. Fiction, which has the power of unifying the nation by presenting sane and helpful pictures of local life, can sink to the level of pandering by presenting the baser forms of city life.—*Hamlin Garland. Literary Digest.* 80:28. *January* 19, 1924.

A crusade against the publishers and sellers of books alleged to be immoral and an agitation in favor of legislation paving the way for the successful prosecution of circulators of such literature was launched at a large meeting called by Supreme Court Justice John Ford at the Hotel Astor yesterday. The Court of Appeals, certain City Magistrates, and the "blasé literati" were roundly denounced as the defenders of bad books. The District Attorney, the Corporation Counsel, Archbishop [now Cardinal] Hayes, Bishop Manning, the National Civic Federation, the Society for the Suppression of Vice, the Lord's Day Alliance, the Boy Scouts and Girl Scouts, the Catholic Club, the Committee of Fourteen, and various churches and civic and religious organizations were represented at the meeting. The only remedy needed, according to Justice Ford and others, is an amendment to the state law to overcome the interpretation placed upon it by the Court of Appeals. "All that is required," said Justice Ford, "is to plug up the holes the Court of Appeals has made in the law."—*New York Times. February* 25, 1923.

Angered because a circulating library had placed a copy of D. H. Lawrence's *Women in Love* in the hands of his daughter, Supreme Court Justice John Ford said yesterday that he was going to seek the prosecution of those responsible for the circulation of the book and, if necessary, take a bill to the Legislature to put teeth into the present law against books likely to impair morals. When he learned that this particular volume had been under fire and that a City Magistrate had exonerated the publishers and given a good name to the book, he said, "What can ail our Magistrates? This book is a terrible thing. It is loathsome. The fact that a Magistrate may have approved of it does not alter the fact. A circulating library recommended this thing to my daughter." Justice Ford was informed that John S. Sumner, Secretary of the Society for the Suppression of vice, had pronounced the work a Sunday School book compared with some of the other volumes upheld in the Magistrate's courts. "I don't know what we are coming to if that is so," said

Justice Ford. "I have never seen anything much worse than this."—*New York Times. February* 6, 1923.

Books, particularly the fiction read by the general public, are an important force. There is no denying that much of our fiction in recent years has been a wallowing in filth, especially sex filth, under the pretense of giving us realism. The writers have regarded life and filth as synonymous terms. Now there is no objection to lifting the veil and openly acknowledging secret evils. A prudish passing by of a bad mess is both cowardly and silly. No one should be afraid to face the sinister side of life—to deal with its evil passions, ignoble emotions, its sins, big and little, with all their results, pleasant and unpleasant, with the shadows and squalors of life, and the nature and character of the people. But why abandon decency and embrace eroticism? Art and literature can so grip a person's imagination that he goes and does likewise, or at least develops moods and attitudes and reactions which the book suggests, and the bad functions as surely as the good. The novelist and any other writer or artist has a great social responsibility in connection with the suggestive material that he places before the public.—*Joyce O. Hertzler. Social Progress. p.* 256.

I select a typical example of a book which can do, and has done, an immense amount of harm to boys at public schools. I would go so far as to say that the book I have in mind has been more responsible than any other single factor for the lowering of moral tone at certain public schools. I do not mention the name of the book as I do not wish to advertise it. The book itself is not evil or obscene, but I believe its influence to be positively poisonous. The reason is simple: the author devotes a large part of the book to a discussion of immorality at public schools, and throughout the whole of this he takes the line (a) that immorality is widespread in all public schools, (b) that this has always been the case, and (c) that this must always be the case owing to the conditions under which public school boys live. In my experience the first of these statements is untrue, the second is untrue, and the third is untrue. Knowing, as I do, the harm that this book has caused, I find it difficult to write calmly about it, and feel that nothing short of a millstone can adequately meet the case.—*Stephen Foot. Nineteenth Century.* 105:441-2. *April* 1929.

We have a lot of treasonable and obscene literature circulating around the country that ought to be suppressed—communistic literature carrying doctrine that strikes at the very foundation of our Government. The home is the bedrock upon which the Republic rests. Here is communism rampant in our country, and yet some do not want to do anything to suppress it. It is true, as the Senator has said, we have grown to be a powerful and prosperous people; but it has been the history of every great nation of the earth that in their search for wealth they have neglected the search for idealism and have lost sight of right principles and spiritual values. Cults of various kinds spring up; they organize; they work quietly; and when trouble is least expected it breaks upon us. These pernicious doctrines have a hold in the country that we know nothing about because we have been too busy searching after dollars and dimes; too busy to stop and find out what is going on in the civic household of the Nation. I think it is high time that we should be laying our hands upon some of this deadly literature and suppressing its circulation. If such literature is to come in from abroad—we have already permitted immigrants who believe in that doctrine to come in—we shall have two destructive agencies hammering at the gates of constitutional government instead of one.—*J. Thomas Heflin. Congressional Record.* 71:4465. *October* 11, 1929.

I am satisfied there are but few Senators upon the floor, if any, who realize that dirty, filthy, vulgar trash is being secretively circulated around among the boys and girls of the country. If Senators could see some of the picture books which are sometimes found in homes, hidden away, if they could read some of the horrible vulgarity that is carried around in the pockets of some people in this country today, they would be horrified. I tell you, my fellow Senators, that it is a pity some of you have not seen such things; it is a pity that some of you do not realize conditions. If you will look around the jails, if you will look around some of our houses of detention, if you will look around some other kind of houses, you will find boys and girls there tonight who were put there by some scoundrel slipping dirty literature into their possession. I have practiced law, exclusively, in the criminal courts of this country for 40 years; I have defended every known kind of criminal on earth, from the murderer and the rapist down to the fellow who broke the peace; I have known them; I have seen them; I have talked with them. I have pardoned 1,555 persons in my life and I have talked with many of them; and I have found that one could trace their road to the penitentiary, their road to the chain gang, and some of the girls could be traced into bawdy houses, through the dissemination of just such vile literature.—*Coleman L. Blease. Congressional Record.* 72:5431-2. *March* 17, 1930.

NEGATIVE DISCUSSION

PROBLEMS OF CENSORSHIP[1]

That customs officials should have authority to exclude from the United States any publication which seems to them of immoral character deserves the serious consideration the senate is giving it. There is a subterranean foreign publication of clearly pornographic matter which probably would better be excluded at the customs barrier than left for local suppression. But it is the principal weakness of censorship that its limits are very difficult if not impossible to define so as to prevent abuse of power. Senator Black very truly said there is a "twilight zone" in which opinion sharply differs as to what is censorable and what not.

Virtually every rumpus over censorship occurs in this zone, although the serious evil which censorship is erected to protect society and the individual from does not lie in this zone at all. Pornographic writings surreptitiously written, printed, and distributed are the vicious stream which should be and can be prevented from reaching the immature, if we exert sufficient vigilance. Even a customs official might be trusted, with some instruction, to deal with such matters. But censorship is not content with concentrating upon this duty. The debate in the senate and every other discussion of censorship reveals why. To the champion of sweeping censorship there is no twilight zone. What he approves is for him the unquestionable norm which he proposes to establish in law and impose by the force of government upon every one else. One of the most familiar sayings attributed to

[1] Editorial. Chicago *Daily Tribune*. March 19, 1930.

Lincoln was that no man is good enough to be another man's master. That one man should dictate what another man shall read is to make the latter largely a slave to the former. But the censorship zealot has no misgivings on that score. He has no hesitation in imposing upon others, if he can, his own intellectual and moral judgments, theories, standards, or prejudices. Yet in a nation whose fundamental law guarantees freedom of speech, freedom of press, freedom of conscience, no individual or group of individuals, nor no government agency should dictate to the adult what he shall read any more than what he shall think.

Censorship is forever delivering decrees which time makes ridiculous or proves erroneous and obstructive to human progress. It has always been the servant of some sort of tyranny which a new generation or a subsequent age escapes or overthrows. The confident moral judgments of Senator Smoot are dissented from by many even of his contemporaries who under the American system are or ought to be as free to make their own judgments as he. He or they may be right or both may be wrong. The point we would have those who demand censorship in America consider more respectfully than they do is the right of the individual to his own intellectual and moral freedom.

THE CUSTOMS CENSORSHIP[2]

The standards of decency and morality vary from generation to generation. Of all the classical authors the three who might seem least likely to be barred by the customs censors under present regulations are perhaps, Homer, Dante, and Shakespeare. I should like to point out to the Senate that each one of those authors at various times has been branded as an immoral or licentious

[2] By Senator Bronson Cutting. *Congressional Record.* 71:4445-56. October 11, 1929.

author. Plato in his Republic insisted that the works of Homer, as well as those of all other poets of the classical period, should be barred as the writings of immoral and indecent authors, holding up to ridicule the religious opinions of the day.

When Savonarola came into power in Florence he burned in the public square the works of three authors, the most notorious, as he said, for licentiousness and indecency. One of the three was Dante.

The plays of Shakespeare were banned from the stage within a quarter of a century of his death as the most striking example of immorality which could be put before the people of England.

The same thing applies in many ways to works of art. It was only the premature death of one of the popes which prevented him from carrying out his plan to put draperies on all the figures of Michael Angelo's Last Judgment.

I imagine there are Senators here who remember the time when Power's Greek Slave, in the Corcoran Art Gallery, was placed in a booth, presumably with the object of insuring that none except those with a certificate of moral excellence should be allowed to see that particular work of art.

On this general subject I claim that the barring of works of literature as obscene is both unnecessary and ineffective. I believe it is unnecessary because I cannot think that the evil effect of works of literature is by any means as far-reaching as the proponents of this sort of legislation seem to believe. There has never been a nation on earth which had so widespread and far-reaching a system of universal education as has the United States, with its public schools, colleges, universities, with its libraries and night schools and correspondence courses. Is our whole educational system such a feeble thing that it cannot offset the effect of an occasional bad book from abroad? Is the foundation of the American Government so feeble that it cannot withstand subversive opinions of a few foreign theorists?

If this law is unnecessary, I claim also that it is ineffective, because the very books which are barred by the censors are protected by copyright in this country. The copyright laws themselves are very stringent against indecent or obscene or immoral literature, and yet these very books which we allow to be published, which can be had in our own Congressional Library, which can be purchased in any book store are banned from importation.

There are Senators who feel sincerely that the importation of certain books might be corruptive of the morals of youth. The question of the youth of the country, the adolescent especially, is, of course, a peculiar problem which has been extensively dealt with by psychological experts. I do not care to discuss it at this time. All I want to say is that when one thinks of the influence to which youth can be exposed, it seems rather far-fetched to believe that any particular difference can be made by any action of the Bureau of Customs.

I should like to read a quotation from Macaulay on this subject:

> We find it difficult to believe that in a world so full of temptation as this, any gentleman, whose life would have been virtuous if he had not read Aristophanes and Juvenal, will be made vicious by reading them. A man who, exposed to all the influences of such a state of society as that in which we live, is yet afraid of exposing himself to the influence of a few Greek or Latin verses, acts, we think, much like the felon who begged the sheriff to let him have an umbrella to hold over his head from the door of Newgate to the gallows because it was a drizzling morning and he was apt to take cold.

If that was the position in the time of Macaulay, what can be the position at the present time when any youth or any adolescent can take up a copy of a daily newspaper and read all the details of the Kipp Rhinelander or the Peaches Browning cases or the cases which are being reported in the daily press here at the present time, the McPherson case and the O'Donnell case? The protection of the morals of the youth of this country must be left in all common sense to their parents and to their families and to the laws of the States in which they reside.

When we deal with this matter of seditious and insurrectionary literature we are not treading on quite as firm ground as we are in connection with the question of obscenity, because the obscenity laws have been tested for a long time. We are now getting down to the base of the whole discussion, the propriety of excluding political opinion which may happen to differ from our own. I think it will be seen by anyone who studies the two statements which I have just sent to the desk for insertion in the *Record* that a customs clerk might quite plausibly exclude almost any work of advanced political thought or even of political thought which happened to disagree with his own opinion. That is the fundamental difficulty with the whole censorship matter. There is no practical appeal in an ordinary case, because it is not worth a man's time or trouble or money to prosecute an appeal in general from a decision of such clerks.

Professor Chafee makes it clear that the works of political theorists like Carl Marx, Proudhon, Bakunin, or Stirner, and even Bertrand Russell, would be excluded or might conceivably be excluded by customs clerks under the provision which we are talking of adopting. I will go further than that. If we consider the purpose for which such a provision was obviously placed in the bill I can quite conceive that any postal clerk could exclude the works of any man who would agitate a reform of any kind or any man who argued in such a way that the public spirit of unrest might be aroused. Is there any vaguer word in the English language than the word "insurrection"? It is even worse than the word "obscenity." The Declaration of Independence would certainly be excluded in English editions. If there ever was a treasonable utterance toward the government which was in power at that time it certainly was the Declaration of

Independence, and if treason means not treason against the Government of the United States but against any government, how could we admit the words of Tom Paine or Patrick Henry?

Abraham Lincoln said in his first inaugural address:

> This country with its institutions belongs to the people who inhabit it. Whenever they shall grow weary of existing government they can exercise their constitutional right of amending it or their revolutionary right to dismember or overthrow it.

If those words are not insurrectionary, I cannot conceive of any words that might be.

If the law might be interpreted to exclude the works of Thomas Jefferson and Abraham Lincoln, it would certainly exclude most of the thinkers of the present day and most of the thinkers of the past century.

It is one of the things which must clearly illustrate the danger of any such provision as has been incorporated into this bill, to think that quite possibly every statement made not only in war time but in the years after the war by Mr. Ramsay MacDonald might be excluded from this country, and may be excluded if this proposed legislation shall pass.

One of the movements which the American people should be most intent to study is the movement now going on in Russia. Those of us who disbelieve in it ought to study it even more carefully and with greater consideration than those who may happen to believe in some of its doctrines. It is one of the fundamental facts of world history. Under this provision of the pending bill, as proposed, it is quite conceivable that all books dealing with the soviet system of government would be kept out of this country. Is that really what we want? Do we really want to bury our heads in the sand like the ostrich and say that we are going ahead, without any knowledge of facts of utmost importance which are going on around us in the world?

It has been brought to the attention of the people of this country that several universities, including Harvard and Leland Stanford, are at present engaged in an extensive collection of all documents dealing with the Russian revolution. Under the terms of this bill none of them could be imported. That applies just as much to books that denounce Bolshevism as to books which uphold it, because, of course, any study of Bolshevism, whether favorable or unfavorable, must include the statement of its principles and its slogans and manifestos, which would be deemed seditious and insurrectionary under the interpretation of the average clerk in the Bureau of Customs. Those collections would be stopped.

The Congressional Library has at all times been one of the chief offenders against the obscenity statute as we have it on our books. All of those books which we bar through the Bureau of Customs we admit to the Congressional Library, and any of our citizens can go over there and read them; there is no ban on that. I imagine most of the 379 Spanish books which I spoke of yesterday can be obtained by going to the Congressional Library. If the Congressional Library keeps the proposed law, as other institutions and the citizens of the United States are supposed to keep any law, what information are we going to have as to what is going on in the world?

In line with what we have discussed as to the possible banning of certain utterances and writings by some of our great modern statesmen, here is a book which has been a classic for sixty or seventy years—John Stuart Mill on Liberty—which contains this shocking sentence, a sentence which would come under the ban of the House provision of the pending bill even before it was modified by the Senate Committee on Finance:

> There ought to exist the fullest liberty of professing and discussing, as a matter of ethical conviction, any doctrine, however immoral it may be considered. It would, therefore, be irrelevant and out of place to examine here whether the doctrine of tyrannicide deserves that title. I shall content myself with saying that the subject has been at all times one of the open questions of morals; that the act of a private citizen in striking

down a criminal, who, by raising himself above the law, has placed himself beyond the reach of legal punishment or control, has been accounted by whole nations, and by some of the best and wisest of men, not a crime, but an act of exalted virtue; and that, right or wrong, it is not of the nature of assassination, but of civil war.

How could a book which contains a sentence like that be permitted to come into the United States under the provisions proposed by the House and by the Senate Finance Committee?

The truth of the matter is that the expression of unpopular views is highly useful to the community. It is a valuable safety valve for the individual. If that sort of expression is suppressed, it leads more surely than any other method which can be adopted to discontent and in the long run to revolt. That, I think, is one of the doctrines on which our Republic was founded.

To return to Thomas Jefferson, you will remember what he said in his inaugural:

> If there be any among us who would wish to dissolve this Union or change its republican form, let them stand undisturbed as monuments of the safety with which error of opinion may be tolerated where reason is left free to combat it.

And, again quoting from John Stuart Mill:

> Popular opinions on subjects not palpable to sense are often true but seldom or never the whole truth. They are a part of the truth; sometimes a greater, sometimes a smaller part, but exaggerated, distorted, and disjointed from the truths by which they ought to be accompanied and limited. Heretical opinions, on the other hand, are generally some of these suppressed and neglected truths, bursting the bonds which kept them down, and either seeking reconciliation with the truth contained in the common opinion or fronting it as enemies and setting themselves up with similar exclusiveness as the whole truth.

The men whom we now revere as the great men of the past have usually been men who, in their own time, have been regarded as agitators, as heretics, as corruptors of the morals of youth, like Socrates, or as blasphemers, like the Founder of the Christian religion.

In the consideration of public policy it would be a very self-sufficient man who could stand up and say, "This train of thought is right and the other is wrong." It cannot be done by the Treasury Department. It cannot be done by the Bureau of Customs. In my opinion, the only policy we can accept in this matter is the belief that the American people in the long run can be trusted to take care of their own moral and spiritual welfare; that no bureaucratic guardian is competent to decide for them what they shall or shall not read.

I admit that there may be those among us who will occasionally abuse those privileges; but I insist that the same men who would abuse those privileges would abuse the privilege of the franchise. If a man is not capable of deciding what he may or may not read without injury to himself, then that man is not fit to be intrusted with the right to select his own representatives in the Government. All democracy is based on the theory that popular judgment on the average, in the long run, is more apt to bring about good than harm; that the men who are unfit to handle their own destinies form a small and negligible proportion of the population of this country. If that contention is unsound, then our whole Government goes down; but, if it is sound, we have no right to censor public thought or public opinion. The doctrine of censorship is a doctrine characteristic of the Facist government of Italy, and equally characteristic of the Bolshevist government of Russia. It has nothing to do with a democracy. A democracy, if it means anything, must be founded on the fundamental proposition that its citizens have a right to hear both sides.

You remember the old classical statement by Milton:

> Though all the winds of doctrine were let loose to play upon the earth, so Truth be in the field, we do ingloriously, by licensing and prohibiting, to misdoubt her strength. Let her and Falsehood grapple: Whoever knew Truth put to the worse in a free and open encounter?

And Jefferson said, practically echoing those words:

> Truth is great, and will prevail if left to herself. She is the proper and sufficient antagonist of error, and has nothing to

fear from the conflict unless, by human interposition, disarmed of her natural weapons, free argument and debate; errors ceasing to be dangerous when it is permitted freely to contradict them.

Whether the pretext by which we exclude a book is obscenity, or sedition, or any other reason, the fact remains that we are leaving it to the judgment of individual clerks, untrained in this particular matter, and from whose decisions, for practical reasons, there is hardly ever any appeal.

The main difficulty with the proposed legislation is that it further extends the power of bureaucracy in our Government to make decisions which may be vital to the American people. We all know in our daily experience here that this Government in its practical working is being run not by the Congress of the United States, not by the Cabinet, nor even by the President, but by a vast system of petty clerks, each one creating a precedent, each one making a ruling which in the future will influence the action of the other persons in the same department. These rulings finally become promoted to departmental policies, which thereafter balk the consideration and passage of bills which the two Houses of Congress may propose. When such bills are sent to the departments we get an adverse report, signed by the Secretary of the department which may be involved, but actually written by some subordinate who has made a specialty of the particular matter involved. The recommendation comes to us with the name of the Secretary of the department on it, and in the average case his prohibition, if it be a prohibition, is final. It prevents that particular bill from even getting out of the committee to which it has been referred.

The attempt to bar literature from the country on the ground of the opinions expressed seems to me, as Professor Chafee says in his statement, to be—

A kindergarten measure which assumes that the American people are so stupid and so untrustworthy that it is unsafe to let them read anything about revolution because they would immediately become converted.

There are many people who have that frame of mind, who believe that our people need protection, and that they are not capable of looking after themselves. It is from people of that sort, in perfect sincerity, that legislation of this character originates.

I can understand their point of view, in a way. Life is becoming increasingly complex, and if there are sincere and intelligent persons among us capable of charting out our destinies in advance, capable of laying out a high road, throwing out the radical literature to the right and the reactionary literature to the left, and fencing the road in advance so that no man can miss the way, why should they not save our people the trouble of finding the way for themselves?

The difficulty is that the road to enlightenment is not a Federal highway. It cannot be surveyed in advance. It cannot be graded or surfaced. It is not properly policed or guarded. It leads sometimes through trackless deserts and at other times over the roughest mountain trails. There are no signposts on it. Each man who travels on that road has got to find the way for himself. At each turning and at each cross-road he may have to resume that age-long grapple which Milton speaks of between truth and error or between two opinions, each one of which believes itself to be the truth.

In blazing out the trail, there is room for all of us, the conservatives and the radicals, the religious fanatics and the skeptics, the advanced dreamers and the practical men of action. But before we set out on that road let us be sure that we have our weapons with us; that we are properly equipped to take that journey, and to take note of the dangers which may meet us on that high errand. In that way alone, I believe, will we aid the general cause of public advancement in this country and elsewhere.

I believe the present situation is intolerable. I do not see that the law as it stands on the statute books today can be defended in any intelligent way, and I think the amendments which have been suggested by the House committee and agreed to by the Senate Committee on Finance will make matters worse than they are at present.

Before Senators vote on the amendment, however, I should like to read two passages. The first one is from a dissenting opinion of Mr. Justice Holmes, delivered a few weeks ago:

> If there is any principle of the Constitution that more imperatively calls for attachment than any other, it is the principle of free thought—not free thought for those who agree with us, but freedom for the thought that we hate.

The other passage is from an even more classic source —the pamphlet of John Stuart Mill on Liberty:

> If all mankind minus one were of one opinion, and only one person were of the contrary opinion, mankind would be no more justified in silencing that one person than he, if he had the power, would be justified in silencing mankind. Were an opinion a personal possession of no value except to the owner; if to be obstructed in the enjoyment of it were simply a private injury, it would make some difference whether the injury was inflicted only on a few persons or on many. But the peculiar evil of silencing the expression of an opinion is that it is robbing the human race—posterity as well as the existing generation; those who dissent from the opinion still more than those who hold it. If the opinion is right, they are deprived of the opportunity of exchanging error for truth; if wrong, they lose what is almost as great a benefit, the clearer perception and livelier impression of truth, produced by its collision with error.

THE FUTILITY OF CENSORSHIP[8]

Behind the efforts to tighten the laws affecting the publication and sale of "unclean" and otherwise dangerous books are two motives, more or less blurred. One is the honest impulse to protect society, especially the young and the weak, from sinful ideas. The other is a perversion or exaggeration of the tendency, which we all have in some degree, to impose our ideas on the other fellow. The problem is to preserve freedom of thought, the right

[8] *Nation.* 116:508. May 2, 1923.

to express daring, original, even subversive beliefs, and at the same time to prevent the circulation of words and pictures that are merely nasty and are intended to appeal to the basest instincts.

Of the various proposed measures which have recently been vexing legislatures, authors, publishers, college professors, not one seems to us to be likely to promote sound morals or sound literature. And some are positively dangerous. There are already, and there ought to be, broad flexible laws under which the vendors of deliberately lascivious, lecherous, debauching stuff can be prosecuted and their dirty trade discouraged. Each case should be judged on its merits as a whole, by magistrate or jury, according to the general principle which Mr. Justice John Ford is accustomed to lay down in his court, "a reasonable preponderance of the credible testimony." The so-called Clean-Books Bill which he has been sponsoring before the New York Assembly is not reasonable; if it passes it will be a pernicious law. It violates fundamental common sense, because it provides that any publication under question may be judged not for its dominant purpose but for any single objectionable phrase it may contain. There is even the possible danger that admitted classics, ancient and modern, may be proscribed and the publishers punished. If the protagonists of the law were as logical as they are earnest they would certainly have to begin by suppressing the Bible because parts of it are not nice reading for children.

Mr. Justice Ford has already proved himself unfit to sit in a case in which a book or a publisher may be on trial. And even more liberal judges, under a cramping law, too narrow in its definitions, might be constrained to an unfair interpretation. This is ultimately and practically a legal question, to be solved, after the legislatures have made the law, in court. And judges of law cannot be trusted as judges of literature. Who can be trusted? Perhaps not even professional men of letters. Professor

Bliss Perry, of Harvard, recently delivered before the Watch and Ward Society of Boston some strangely stupid opinions, mixed with much that was sensible and humorous. "No one," he said, "whose professional work brings him into contact with the book-making, book-selling, and book-reading classes of the community can possibly be ignorant of the very general conviction that the American public is now facing a clear and present danger through unclean books." Well, we are at least as closely in touch with those classes as is Professor Perry, and we have seen no sign of any such general conviction; indeed it is the literary classes who do not feel the danger and who resent interference; it is the non-literary who are riding the moral high horse. Professor Perry's remarks on George Moore as "a satyr in his seventieth year," and on Walt Whitman, whom he has never understood, are inept.

He is perfectly sound—and here is the real point—when he says that there are "dirty corners" in the minds of the greatest poets and thinkers. But the dashes of poison in minds that are overwhelmingly healthy and inspiring do no harm; the system takes care of them, not only the system of the sophisticated adult, but the naturally sane eliminating processes of the adolescent. People who are so afraid of the damaging effect of smutty fiction take a low view of human nature and seem to forget that they, like the rest of us, heard in youth more vile things than have ever got into print, and live through it all without very seriously blemished souls. The real danger is not from filth but from ill-advised meddling with filth, which calls attention to it and serves only to disseminate it.

The epidemic of censorship which seems to have broken out in all parts of the country is not confined to attacks on impure literature. It is aimed at ideas which are not immoral, except in an over-stretched sense of the word, ideas which certainly have nothing to do with sex or personal cleanliness. Among the most absurd of these attacks are the attempts to revise history, according to some nationalistic or economic bias, to supplant one alleged prejudice with another. The New York Assembly has been wrestling not only with Ford Clean-Books Bill, but with a preposterous Patriotic Text-Books Bill, the purpose of which is to defend the Declaration of Independence and twist the tail of the British lion by insisting that school teachers dwell upon the British injustices that led to the American Revolution. In Sacramento a patriotic society is trying to amend the early history of America in such a way as to prove that the initiative, referendum, recall, and direct primary are un-American. *The Nation* has already noted that San José, California, has banned from its libraries histories that seemed to some of its citizens too favorable to England, and Los Angeles bars *The Nation* and the *New Republic* from its schools. And the radicals are just as bad as the conservatives—Wisconsin, State of light and learning, bars from its school-rooms histories which "defame the nation's founders or contain propaganda favorable to any foreign government" (that is, of course, Great Britain). The comedy of this is that it reverses the movement that set in during the war when all history was to be made as favorable as possible to our great English-speaking ally, and the only nation which had no bright pages in its chronicle was Germany.

The difficulties of some college trustees with sinners like Darwin and Huxley, Spencer, Karl Marx, H. G. Wells, Hendrik van Loon, and James Harvey Robinson recur in the news columns almost every day. It is almost too silly to argue about. Perhaps the best comment is that which Mark Twain puts into the mouth of Pudd'nhead Wilson: "The very ink with which history is written is fluid prejudice." Every historian knows that all the great classic historians are warped and biased, and that the thing for him to do is to show his students what the biases and misinterpretations are—and then substitute his biases! It is only by the mutual correction of opposed authorities that we shall ever get a fair notion of what happened to the human race and of what is happening. And no censorship can ever save us from the intellectual and ethical errors of others or from our own.

ABSURDITY OF CENSORSHIP[4]

The absurdity of censorship lies mainly in its application. Only the highest quality of intellect and understanding is capable of acting as a censor, and it is obvious that no man or woman of fine intelligence will act in any way as a censor of the arts; therefore such activity is left in the power of those individuals who have little, if any, sense of value in literature, drama, and art generally. Certainly if there has ever been any doubt of the truth of this contention it has been recently dispelled by the printed statements of certain men who are trying to organize a board of censorship over literature and drama. Some of their opinions on books would put a school boy to shame. "The difficulty with censorship," states an editorial in the New York *Sun*, "is that it can accomplish nothing which cannot be just as well accomplished without its help." This is a truth which can be understood by anybody. No man or committee of men is qualified either by nature or education to decide whether a book is indecent or not. The social judgment is necessary and this can only be had from a widespread public opinion.

Unlike many of the men whose absurd opinions are now breaking out publicly, every publisher knows the exact difference between frankness and obscenity, and he functions according to his understanding of this. The editorial minds in any publishing house are severe and competent censors, but they judge only by intelligent standards. In a book they demand, as H. L. Mencken puts it, that it be dignified in conception, artistically honest, faithful to life and fine in workmanship. "There

[4] By Horace B. Liveright. *Independent.* 110:192-3. March 17, 1923.

is nothing pornographic in any work of literature, or even such books as can hardly be classified as literature. Pornographic books have been issued, but they are manufactured by obscure printers, in Europe and America, and are sold by peddlers; they are not issued by publishers or by reliable printers. Like a thief, they usually work in the dark and can seldom be reached by censors or anti-vice societies, and then only by accident. Their discovery is difficult, though they existed for hundreds of years and I am reliably informed that they exist today.

Certain facts of life exist, and their relation to other facts and to human behavior can only be expressed through the medium of words. These words and their meanings being part of our common tongue are printed in the dictionary. Let us then begin by confiscating all such dictionaries which have illicit words and definitions printed in them, for it is the use of these ideas by authors which make a book obscene. They create situations which offend these morality mongers, who possess an incurable inferiority complex.

Certain fiction, which seems to be the principal object of attack today, expresses itself according to the contemporary interpretation of science, abnormal psychology, psycho-analysis, and other methods of study of human behavior. Art and mind are always in process of change; a new age has a new literary and philosophic expression. But this affects only the intelligent minded; never the ignorant. Good art lives and bad art dies, that is all we know; and intelligent Americans are as capable of appreciating this fact as any other people. There is only one test and that is the test of intelligence, though a work may not be good art and yet have a useful or entertaining place in the world. "Obscenity—the word already vague enough after such repeated use—would come to mean little or nothing if the people who most fear this have their way, it is a word that will be so quickly diluted and enlarged as to drown all literature." (*New Republic*. March 7)

Frankness in literature relating to sexual matters never corrupted or depraved anyone, adult or child. It is difficult for some people to realize this, but any judge of a criminal court should know what every student of life and society knows, viz.: that the so-called depraved or vicious classes or types have no contact whatever with literature beyond the daily newspaper. This is so well known that it has become a platitude. We may become depraved by, or vicious by, economic or physical conditions, but certainly not by literature.

That very wise man, Lord Macaulay, stated the matter for all time in his famous essay on the Restoration Dramatists:

> We cannot wish that any works or class of works which have exercised a great influence on the human mind, and which illustrate the character of an important epoch in letters, politics, and morals, should disappear from the world. If we err in this matter, we err with the gravest men and bodies of men in the empire, and especially with the church of England, and with the great schools of learning which are connected with her. The whole liberal education of our countrymen is conducted on the principle that no book which is valuable, either by reason of its excellence of style, or by reason of light it throws on history, polity, and manners of nations, should be withheld from the student on account of its impurity. The Athenian comedies in which there are scarcely a hundred lines without some passage of which Rochester would have been ashamed, have been reprinted by the Pitt Press and the Clarendon Press, under the direction of Syndics and delegates appointed by the Universities, and have been illustrated with notes by reverend, very reverend, commentators. Every year the most distinguished young men in the kingdom are examined by bishops and professors of divinity in such works as the Lysistrata of Aristophanes and the sixth satire of Juvenal. There is certainly something a little ludicrous in the idea of a conclave of the venerable fathers of the church praising and rewarding a lad on account of his intimate acquaintance with writings compared with which the loosest tale in Prior is modest. But, for our own part, we have no doubt that the greatest societies which have directed the education of the gentry have herein judged wisely. It is unquestionable that a man whose mind has been thus enlarged and enriched is likely to be far more useful to the state and to the church than one who is unskilled, or little skilled, in classical learning. On the other hand we find it difficult to believe that, in a world so full of temptation as this, any gentleman whose life would have been virtuous if he had not read Aristophanes and Juvenal will be made vicious by reading them.

The virtue which the world wants is a healthful virtue, not a valetudinarian virtue; a virtue which can expose to the risks inseparable from all spirited exertion, not a virtue which keeps out of the common air for fear of infection, and eschews common food as too stimulating. It would indeed be absurd to attempt to keep men from acquiring those qualifications which fit them to play their part in life with honor to themselves and advantage to their country, for the sake of preserving a delicacy which cannot be preserved, a delicacy which a walk from Westminster to the Temple is sufficient to destroy.

A censorship over literature and the other arts is stupid, ignorant, and impudent, and is against the fundamental social principles of all intelligent Americans. There is no place for such crudity in our present civilization, and even the most conservative press and individual opinion have expressed themselves against it most emphatically. Who is really in favor of it?

CENSORSHIP A BAD PRINCIPLE[5]

Once more the so-called clean books bill is before the New York legislature. Three times it has been introduced in different sessions and three times defeated. It ought to be defeated again, if, as news dispatches indicate, it contains the same provisions that were in the former bills.

The theory of a censorship of books exercised by the state is repugnant to our institutions and to literature itself. It is not a function of government to say what books people shall read, and should such power once be conferred on it there would be no telling to what lengths of oppression and intolerance bigots in office might go.

Under the proposed New York law any book, magazine or newspaper may be condemned on a single item which certain designated public officials may declare to be in violation of the law. The possibility, nay the probability, of abuse under such legislation is apparent. No body of political administrators ought to be intrusted with the power to suppress a publication and fine and imprison its publishers, upon its own determination that a para-

[5] *Kansas City Star.* February 11, 1926.

graph or word is detrimental to public morals. Are political officials certain always to make such determination upon a sole consideration of public morals? We think not. We think they are quite as likely to make it upon political considerations.

There are now upon state and federal statute books sufficient laws to protect the public against indecent and obscene publications. Those laws are specific enough to operate with proper discrimination; they do not expose to prosecution any publisher who may happen to publish a truth unpleasant to the ears of officialdom. Therein lies the danger of literary censorship—it gives a political weapon into hands that are too likely to be unfit to wield it. Some legislators are terribly afraid the people won't be governed enough. What they seem to need is the political wisdom to recognize that the best and most effective protection to public morals is public opinion. That will very easily and very quickly terminate the life of any publication that persistently offends it.

THE CENSORSHIP OF HISTORY[*]

For two thousand years and more Herodotus was honored with the title of Father of History. Then came the nineteenth century with its passion for truth. Herodotus was weighed line by line and found light. It was proved that he had falsified events, in passages without number. His old title gave way to a new one, Father of Lies.

But the nineteenth century historians were not, after all, such white robed acolytes of the truth as their condemnation of Herodotus implied. They wrote, too often, with a political purpose, more or less subtly concealed, and political purposes seldom square with the truth. One wrote the history of Greece with a view to bolstering

[*] *New Republic.* 34:283. May 9, 1923.

parliamentary institutions. Another wrote the history of imperial Rome in justification of Bismarckian imperialism. And when nationalism went mad, toward the end of the century, every country developed its corps of historians, along with its guns and ships, as a weapon of national defence or aggression. Every political party, every social class, came to have its official manipulator of history. The historians who remained steadfast in their loyalty to the truth were helpless to check the flood of spurious historical ideas. The public preferred the debased coinage in its daily trafficking and came to regard it as standard. History had become present politics.

It is this cheapening of the standard of history that explains the tendency on the part of public and quasi public authorities to censor history books. If we are to be flooded with propaganda, let it be our propaganda. As English Americans, shall we permit our school texts and library books to denounce the British colonial policy of the eighteenth century? As Irish Americans, shall we stand for histories that imply that England had part of the law and the moralities on her side? As New Englanders with Abolitionist antecedents, shall we tolerate a too respectful treatment of the States Rights views of the Old South? As Southerners, shall we permit the historians to read Union in the very origin of the Constitution and thus convict our fathers of the crime of rebellion?

The New York Senate, by a heavy majority, has passed a bill specifying the manner in which the Declaration of Independence, the events leading up to the Revolutionary War, the military history of that war and the personal character of the Revolutionary patriots must be treated in textbooks to be used in the state. That is a beginning. Next we shall have laws fixing the characters of the early Presidents and justifying the Mexican War. Then our legislatures will give us the literally inspired history of the World War, in which, single handed almost, we overthrew the might of the Central Empires. We shall have Roosevelt or Wilson a demigod, according to the complexion of the legislature. Each political overturn will be celebrated by a state wide bonfire of the history textbooks of the defeated party. The teachers who had laboriously printed a Republican version of history on the minds of the children will have to print a Democratic version on top of it, only to put the same tables of the mind through a third printing when the Republicans come back.

Herodotus lied, but for the sake of the Muse. History, as he conceived it, was an art, as exacting as tragedy or sculpture. If the facts did not observe the proper proportions, fall into the desired rhythms, he mended them, in good faith. He never lied to advance any selfish personal or political purpose. The best thing we can do is to return to his methods. The Fathers were gallant men, often great men, but they were human. Let our historians give us purely mythical figures instead of them. Let them give us mythical wars in which all our soldiers were heroes, none of our civilians profiteers. Myth could be made infinitely edifying to the children provided they could be made to accept it. And we see no reason why they should not accept pure myth as readily as the counterfeit history prepared according to political specifications.

THE HISTORY OF CENSORSHIP OF BOOKS[1]

A brief examination of the historical aspect of the matter may here be of value to us.

We must first remind ourselves, then, that the idea of a censorship of books was a Papal invention, not by any temporal authority, but by the Church of Rome. In the beginning of the fourth century, the Council of Carthage issued a decree forbidding Christians to circulate

[1] By Edmund Gosse. *English Review.* 4:621-5. March 1910.

or to possess the writings of the authors of pagan antiquity. It would be difficult to exaggerate the loss which this act of fanaticism has entailed upon the modern world, and the spirit which inspired it is one which must always be regarded with suspicion. In times when books circulated only in manuscript, and within very limited areas, the actual destruction of a work of genius was not only possible, it was often easy. After the invention of printing, the work became more difficult, and was prosecuted with a fiercer zeal. The opening years of the sixteenth century are prominent in the annals of repression, but it took a different course. The Renaissance had done its work, and Roman prelates expended their enthusiasm and their money in the preservation of ancient literature, even though its tendency might be unfavourable to morals and religion. A new enemy was in the field, the reform inside the Church, and this was now pursued in all its literary emanations.

The earliest list of censored books is said to be that drawn up under clerical advice, by Charles V in Belgium in 1524. The theological faculty of the University of Louvain made itself dreaded throughout Europe by the fierce and reiterated attacks which it made on the freedom of the Press. In 1543 an elaborate list of prohibited books now catalogued for the first time, was issued at Venice, and in the following year the faculty of theology in Paris produced a fuller Index, and contrived heavier penalties on the sale of improper works. Pope Paul IV took advantage of the labours of the Inquisition in Venice, Milan, and Spain, to draw up the famous *Index Librorum Prohibitorum* of which so much has since been vaguely heard. He delivered the list in 1559 to the Inquisition in Rome, and this most formidable engine of literary tyranny was circulated throughout the Catholic world. In this document there were three alphabetical sections; the first comprising a list of authors whose entire writings were prohibited;

the second specified works by authors held innocuous; the third, anonymous writings. It is noticeable that an appendix contained almost all existing editions of the Holy Scriptures. This Index, after a delay during which the theological faculties in all parts of Europe were consulted, was at length published, in 1564, at the close of the Council of Trent.

It would be tedious to continue the history of these Roman Indices, which those who are curious in the matter may follow in the learned compilations of such historians as Reusch and Mendham. A recent work by Hilgers (1904) may be indicated as a useful source of information. But it is interesting in examining the early censorship of books, to notice that "immorality," except in a violent form, rarely attracted the censure of the inquisitors, which was directed mainly against theological and philosophical speculation. Heresy was the game which the censors went forth to hunt, and their principal prey were "apostates, schismatics, and every species of sectary." In 1586, the business was taken out of the hands of the Inquisition, and placed in those of the Index Congregation, a sort of committee whose duty was to keep the list of prohibited books up to date, and to grant learned and pious men special permission to read, for a holy purpose, this or that condemned work. This Congregation has never ceased its labours, and although the spread of liberal opinion has made its zeal more and more nugatory, and though that zeal has itself abated, yet its action remains of a kind which no citizen of a free community, unless biased by prejudice, can regard with satisfaction.

The desire to restrict speculative thought, although it has by no means died out, has in late years given place to a zeal for decency. It is important to notice that the tendency of a censorship nowadays is to begin with the suppression of books scandalous to morals, and then to proceed to that of books which contravene the ethical and religious ideas accepted by society at the particular moment. This latter tendency is the one which particularly justifies a resistance to any form of extra-legal repression. It is necessary to insist that to place the existence of books at the mercy of a small group of men of whose fitness for so important a charge the public can know nothing is to endanger the advance of thought. A tribunal formed today to suppress a morbid novel may go on tomorrow to boycott a Darwin or a Renan. As this has been denied, it is worth while to draw attention to what was attempted so lately as 1859. My friend, Dr. P. Chalmers Mitchell, points out to me that Whewell, Murchison, and Sedgwick appealed to Owen to stamp out Chambers's *Vestiges of Creation,* which Sedgwick called "that beastly book." A little later, the same dignified authorities used similar phrases about Darwin's *Origin of Species.* The public language of such men as Bishop Wilberforce was a direct and passionate incentive to such suppression as was possible. It is perfectly certain that if the recently self-elected tribunal had existed in 1860, when the *Quarterly Review* issued its famous blast against the theory of natural selection, as a publication "absolutely incompatible with the Word of God," an appeal to it by Sedgwick, Whewell, Murchison, and Wilberforce, supported by the scientific opinion of Owen, would have been instantly and completely successful, and the *Origin of Species* must have been withdrawn from circulation.

It is useless to pretend that such errors of judgment could not occur again. Men of light and leading in 1910 are not made of a different clay from those who represented science and society in 1860. It is always the unexampled that is unwelcome, and it is not because a Darwin is now celebrated at public banquets after half a century of fame that some one as original and as revolutionary as he will not be banned and boycotted when he takes us all by surprise. The whole history of criticism shows us that the most brilliantly equipped and most highly trained experts cannot be implicitly trusted when they censure a new theory of art or morals which runs counter to accepted tradition.

Nor is it enough that offences should be shown to exist, and that honest men should be impelled by a genuine wish to reform them. A sincere desire to check literary abuses and to maintain a high standard of decency never degenerated into more grotesque absurdity than during the reign of Charles X in France. The incidents are too near our time to possess much literary interest, and it may be that they are generally forgotten. But it is worth our while, when we are told that acts of intellectual tyranny "could never occur again," to recollect that the *censure* of the Restoration began in a very moderate and reasonable determination to put down the general public circulation of papers inimical to the restored dynasty. But it grew with what it fed upon, and when, early in 1827, the National Guards were broken up for demanding a Free Press, the suppression of literature took forms that are almost incredible when we reflect that they were imposed upon the most cultivated capital of the world in the nineteenth century.

A capable and zealous priest, apparently a man of excellent intentions, the Abbé Mutin, offered himself and was accepted as the cat's-paw of the Government, and his "reports" became more and more sweeping. The cleverest writers of the day being the most revolutionary, literary merit itself became offensive to the Abbé Mutin. He discovered, "outrages and attacks on the king, on morality, and on religion," in the most unlikely, and, one would have thought, the most innocent quarters. No less a person than Chateaubriand, having published a harmless brochure, *Les amis de la liberté de la presse,* immediately found his own writings condemned *en masse.* The classics did not escape. Voltaire, whom the Abbé Mutin called "the Great Corruptor," was not unnaturally condemned, but Le Sage and Beaumarchais soon followed. The Abbé Mutin pursued his studies, and the *Télémaque* of Fénelon fell before him. La Rochefoucauld was banned and even the mild and virtuous Vauvenargues prohibited. Pascal had long been on the Index of the Roman Congregation. If the king had not died, it seems probable that pious Frenchmen would have found the whole of their classical literature by degrees denied to them. So, with ourselves, it would be easy for a censorship, slowly developing in a fanatical direction, to discover indecency in Shakespeare, attacks on the monarchy in Milton, irreligion in Shelley, and a dangerous tendency to dwell on the details of sedition in Walter Scott.

RESISTANCE TO TRUTH[8]

More serious probably for mankind at large than any other one of the consequences of error, or perhaps than all of them combined, is the opposition that error always offers to the advance of truth. In the earliest stages there was no possibility for the truth to emerge at all from the mass of error. The error was accepted by all without any single one even so much as thinking of questioning it. All the steps toward truth were taken at later stages, chiefly in peoples that ethnologists class as civilized. Every heresy, however slightly the belief may differ from the dominant or orthodox belief, is a step toward the truth, a greater or less reduction in the amount of error in the belief. Persecution for heresy, therefore, was the first form that resistance to truth assumed.

Opposition To Science

The whole mass of primitive error was the result of a false interpretation of natural phenomena. The true interpretation of the same phenomena was the work of thousands of patient investigators continued through centuries, and was usually practically the reverse of the prevailing false interpretation. Thus shadows and reflec-

[8] By Lester F. Ward. *Applied Sociology.* p. 74-8.

tions were found to be due to the nature of light and the laws of radiation after the science of optics had been founded; echoes were explained on the now familiar principles of acoustics; dreams, delirium, insanity, epilepsy, trance, and even death are explainable on natural principles contained in the sciences of psychology, physiology, pathology, and psychiatry; and although many things are still obscure in relation to them, no specialist in any of these sciences ever thinks of calling in the aid of indwelling spirits to account for any of the facts.

All the anthropomorphic ideas upon which primitive error rests are dispelled by science. Astronomy has taught the nature of the heavenly bodies and the laws of their motions. Air is understood, and is nothing like the primitive idea of spirit, but is a mixture of gases in nearly uniform proportions. Lightning is as well understood as are any of the manifestations of electricity. And so with the whole series of physical phenomena upon which primitive man built his superstructure of life, will, and intelligence in inorganic nature.

All this truth that science revealed had to struggle against the dense mass of primitive error which it was destined to overthrow, and the resistance was enormous. The discoverers of truth have been the victims of all forms of persecution, and the truth revealed has been formally condemned and anathematized. Truth has never been welcome, and its utterance was for ages fraught with personal danger. Fontenelle advised those who possessed new truths to hold on to them, because the world would only punish them for their utterance. Nearly everybody acted upon this principle, and either refrained from investigating or from promulgating new ideas. Descartes wrote his *Traite du Monde,* but suppressed it for these reasons.[9] The chief effect was that of deterring talented men from trying to discover truth, and the greater part of all intellectual energy has been diverted into safer but comparatively useless channels.

[9] *Oeuvres de Descartes.* Paris. 1844. p. 38, 47.

The history of the later phases of this opposition to the progress of science has been so ably presented by numerous writers that it would be superfluous to enter into it here, even if space would permit. I scarcely need draw special attention to the contributions of two Americans to this subject, so familiar are their works.[10]

This opposition to science may be supposed to have some value in rendering it necessary that the discoverers of truth assure themselves beyond a peradventure of the correctness of their position before venturing to promulgate their ideas. Some have partially excused it on this ground. But for this to be true it would be necessary to suppose that anything that was absolutely demonstrated would be accepted. This has never been the case. There has never been any attempt to verify discovery. The opposition has always been dogmatic. It cannot be true because opposed to the current world view. No amount of demonstration would avail. Those who believe things because they are impossible are not going to believe anything because it is proved.

But there is no need of this kind of illegitimate opposition to truth. There is always an abundance of legitimate opposition to it.[11] There is no danger of any error in science gaining a permanent foothold. Every proposition is immediately doubted and attacked, but it is attacked with the legitimate weapons of scientific experimentation and not with the rack and thumb-screw. In other words, it is reinvestigated by others and either confirmed or rejected. Usually a part is confirmed and a part rejected, but at any rate the opposition is always compelled to admit all that is true and the original discoverer is compelled to abandon all that is not true. The difference is the amount of established truth contained in the discovery.

[10] *See* (1) Draper, John W. *History of the Conflict between Religion and Science.* 5th edition. Appleton. New York. 1875; (2) White, Andrew D. *History of the Warfare of Science with Theology in Christendom.* 2 vols. Appleton. New York. 1896; and (3) Shipley, Maynard. *War on Modern Science.* Knopf. New York. 1927.

[11] Ward, Lester F. *Pure Sociology.* p. 8-10. *How Science Advances.*

In the kind of opposition to science that we have been considering it is all loss and no gain.

Obscurantism

This is another form of persecution, only a little more subtle than the form last considered. Indeed, it is only a case of this latter, and might have been treated under the general head of resistance to truth. But by it is meant certain refined phases of this resistance practised by nations claiming to be civilized. Its principal method consists in the prohibiting or suppression of books and writings and the general censorship of the press. This has been chiefly practised by the Christian church, both the Catholic Church and the Greek Church. It is still practised by both these churches, but so far as the former is concerned it is now chiefly a matter *pour rire*. Still, within the church itself it is somewhat effective. With the Greek Church it is more serious because sanctioned by the government of the nation of which that is the state church. But for several centuries it was effective in the Catholic Church, and most of the progressive literature of that period was rendered inaccessible to the general public. For it is with books as with men; those that dissent from the current world views are the ones that contain truth. As Helvetius said in a book that he refused to publish during his lifetime: "It is only in the prohibited books that the truth is found." [12]

It is interesting to glance over the papal Index Librorum Prohibitorum. There are to be found the majority of the works that the world recognizes as great or epoch-making. This Index continues to be issued periodically, and I have recently amused myself in scanning the pages of the latest volume. The Russian government publishes a similar Index. One of its numbers has lately appeared containing the books condemned between 1872 and 1891. It contains works by Herbert Spencer, Ernst Haeckel, Lecky, Zola, Ribot, etc. The prohibition

[12] *De l'Homme*, etc. London. 1773. vol. 1. p. iv, 6, and 62.

is made effective by not allowing Russian translations to appear at all. The great mass of the people are thus effectually prevented from ever reading a book. I have never doubted that many of the books condemned by the Russian censors were so treated on account of other than religious sentiments contained in them. If it is feared that they may tend to render the people discontented with their lot or dissatisfied with the government, it is easy to find passages that can be objected to on religious grounds, and to allege these as the reasons for prohibiting a work. In the light of prevailing political opinion the ministers would scarcely dare to assign political reasons. This was attempted in Germany at the time of the publication of Frederick's diary with rather unsatisfactory results. The numbers of the Deutsche Rundschau containing the article came to America with the pages cut out. I went to a bookstore and bought for ten cents a small duodecimo pamphlet containing the English translation. Probably thousands read it that never would have done so if it had not been prohibited, at least in other countries than Germany. In a free country any such attempt at obscurantism is in the nature of an advertisement, and it is to be hoped that the time will soon come when it will be no longer possible to dam up the stream of truth. Nevertheless, in the darker ages of the world, and still at present, in the darker lands, where political liberty has not yet been achieved, it cannot be doubted that human progress has been and is being greatly retarded by cutting off the light and not allowing it to penetrate into places where it would be seen and welcomed if it could be admitted.[13]

BEYOND CENSORSHIP[14]

Literature today, in novel, magazine and pamplet form, is as bad, if not worse, than at any period in his-

[13] In reading the above article, it should be born in mind that it is from a book published in 1906, while Russia was still ruled by the Czars.—L. T. B.

[14] Rabbi Solomon B. Freehof. *Cleveland Plain Dealer.* April 4, 1927.

tory. Literature is as vulgar today as it was at its worst during the Restoration period.

The faults in modern literature are too big to be censored out of existence. Modern literature is largely exaggerated and stupid. Censorship of any kind is futile. Any attempt on the part of politically elected supervisors to say what should be written or distributed is ridiculous. It is an impossible task.

This type of literature will pass away as it always has in the past. The present era in literature will be followed by one of more austerity bordering on puritanism. The fashion in literature passes as do all other fashions. The remedy lies not in censorship of others but in censorship of self. Each individual must use his own power of resistance to such a literary appeal.

The best remedy for the present situation is to develop the character of the young people of today to the point where they can read without injury as it is virtually impossible to keep from them all of the worthless literature, so great is its volume.

The right kind of home environment with the proper kind of idealism instilled in the minds of the young will counteract the damage that might be done. It may tide them over this period. It is not so much the fact that modern novels are untruthful as that the truth comes too soon into the lives of the youngsters who read them.

BRIEF EXCERPTS

Obscenity in literature and art is an elusive and evasive quantity.—*Current Opinion.* 56:298. *April* 1914.

Censorship is impracticable. Books are too many. —*Thomas Templeton. Encyclopedia of Religion and Ethics. vol.* 3. *p.* 305.

All great literature contains the element we absurdly call "obscene."—*Havelock Ellis. Nineteenth Century.* 105:439. *April* 1929.

Adults are not considered in an attempt to make literature safe for the child mind.—*Adam S. Gregorius. Saturday Review of Literature.* 5:1180. *July* 13, 1929.

The attempt to suppress individual books simply promotes their circulation and reputation.—*Bronson Cutting. Congressional Record.* 72:5489. *March* 18, 1930.

Responsibility, not censorship, is what is needed, and it is all that is needed, but let us make responsibility real.—*Thomas F. Woodlock. Commonweal.* 1:202. *December* 31, 1924.

It is just because a censor does not bind himself to decide according to explicit rules that censorship has such a paralyzing effect upon literary production. —*Edward A. Ross. Principles of Sociology. p.* 644.

In the presence of an objectionable book there is surely one sovereign remedy always before the subscriber, namely, not to read it.—*Edmund Gosse. English Review.* 4:620. *March* 1910.

There is no doubt that some offensive books now current are by authors who are sincere. They would write for the sake of self-expression, if they knew that the sale wouldn't amount to a hundred copies.—*Editorial. New York Times. April* 24, 1923.

Justice Ford's theory that all of us must be forbidden to read books that he finds objectionable is stated so baldly that it is amusing, yet it is the principle on which the Vice Society has worked for a long time.—*Editorial. New York Times. February* 27, 1923.

There are barred from mailing in the United States books intended for the instruction and the widening of knowledge of the medical profession.—*Royal S. Copeland. Congressional Record.* 71:4435. *October* 10, 1929.

No one suggests a censorship, that is, an attempt to have books submitted to a licenser before they appear.

Let them appear, but if they are found to be within the grasp of the law let those who produce them take the consequences.—*G. L. Strachey. Spectator (London). January* 27, 1912.

It must be apparent to anyone that the phrase "containing obscene, indecent, or impure language" is an exceedingly strict qualification. Under these terms the Bible, the plays of Shakespeare, and all of the great novels could be suppressed.—*Edward Weeks. Atlantic Monthly.* 145:23. *January* 1930.

The responsibility for the policy pursued during the centuries since the advent of printing for a censorship control of literature does not rest alone with the Catholic Church. In all of the Protestant States attempts were made from time to time to control and to restrict the operations of the printing press.—*George H. Putnam. Censorship of the Church of Rome. vol.* 1. *p.* 49.

Censorship is inadvisable. History has shown that it may deprive a nation of its best leading and inspiration. No man or body of men is wise enough and tolerant enough to be entrusted with the power of controlling the expression of public opinion.—*Thomas Templeton. Encyclopedia of Religion and Ethics. vol.* 3. *p.* 305.

By far the most hopeful way of dealing with the nuisance of poisonous books is a proper awakening of public opinion. If once decent people are made to understand that public opinion will not only support them, but expects them to refuse to handle poisonous or demoralizing books, the battle will be more than half won.—*G. L. Strachey. Spectator (London).* 108:148. *January* 27, 1912.

You would not believe how, from the very commencement of my activity, that horrible censor question has tormented me. I wanted to write what I felt, but at the same time it occurred to me that what I wrote would not be permitted, and involuntarily I had to abandon the work. I abandoned, and went on abandoning, and meanwhile the years passed away.—*Leo Tolstoi. Quoted in Edward A. Ross's Principles of Sociology. p.* 645.

While it is inevitable that people, especially those responsible for the propriety of home life, should feel alarm at the inroads of indelicate and vulgar literature, it is extremely desirable not to forget the broader and, if we may say so, the historic aspects of the question. These are too commonly ignored by moralists who advocate sudden and drastic remedies of an evil which will be found to frighten more than it injures them. —*Edmund Gosse. English Review.* 4:621. *March* 1910.

The extent of the influence of the system [Censorship by the Church] is not to be measured by the number of books condemned after publication or after being put into type. It is probable that the restrictions and detriments placed in the way of literary production constituted a more important influence on the intellectual life and development of the people than the cancellation or expurgation of books that had already come into existence.—*George H. Putnam. Censorship of the Church of Rome. vol.* 1. *p.* 33.

Freedom is essential to literature and the other arts, and their essential freedom must not be jeopardized because of some slatternly and opprobrious stuff which presumes to masquerade under a sacred title. Everything on earth can be misused, and the divinest gift can be prostituted. Parents and guardians may properly feel responsibility, but they must not attempt to shift it to the shoulders of others. The danger may easily be exaggerated.—*Oliver Lodge. Fortnightly Review.* 93:260. *February* 1910.

In a little over two years sixty-eight books have been suppressed in Boston. Complaints were lodged against them only in Suffolk county, where, in most cases, they were promptly withdrawn from sale; but since officials throughout the other districts of the Commonwealth did not feel called on to take any action, we have the anomalous situation of books being banned in Boston yet being sold openly in Cambridge, only three miles away. —*Edward Weeks. Atlantic Monthly.* 145:17. *January* 1930.

There was once a bishop, the wisest and wittiest of his order, who said in his haste—or was said to have said—that he would "rather see England free than England sober." Let us take our courage in both hands and admit that we would rather see English literature free than English literature decent. Dr. Magee did not indicate, in his famous *dictum,* any approval of insobriety. When we resist with indignation the proposal to censor our reading, and to suppress such books as seem to a committee to be objectionable, it is not with the slightest wish to encourage what is ugly and vile.—*Edmund Gosse. English Review.* 4:621. *March* 1910.

Senator Smoot is so imbued with the high tariff idea that he seeks to protect American filth and American obscenity. At a time when the output of salacious literature in this country is at its peak, the Utah protectionist rallies his cohorts together in an effort to prevent the importation of any objectionable volume and to restore the censorship presided over by the customs officials. The only result of the censorship is, not to protect the United States from contamination, but to further the thriving home industry that is now turning out salacious "literature."—*Editorial. Louisville Courier-Journal. March* 19, 1930.

If we assent to censorship we will find all of our freedom gone. It is the easiest and cheapest way out of an obligation to ask the state to do everything for us, and censorship is one of the stupid strategems of democracy to find a way out of responsibility. Censorship is negative action. Negation will not help you to protect your children from the immoral and indecent play and book. I hate obscene things as much as you do, but I am afraid censorship is not the way to stop them. I am an old-fashioned freedomist. I would infinitely rather have those things than any limitation on the freedom of thinking, writing, and publishing.—*Rabbi Stephen S. Wise. New York Times. April* 23, 1923.

The intellectual life and development of Europe during the centuries between 1556 and 1800 could be traced by the lists of condemned books and these books would in themselves constitute a fairly complete library for the thoughtful student. There can be no question that a very large proportion of the world's literature that stood for intellectual activity and insight, literature which expressed the conclusions of the greatest minds of their several generations, and which stood for the development and the civilization of the community itself, had been placed by the church in the Index of condemned and prohibited books.—*George H. Putnam. Censorship of the Church of Rome. vol.* 1. *p.* 32.

When it comes to the thing called morals, for instance, there are no fixed standards and exact definitions, for the change in these standards and definitions is as inevitable as continuous. Not only does every age have its own interpretations of vice and virtue, but every race, every creed, and, it might almost be said, every community. Censors, however, not only establish fixed standards and definitions, but also determine effects. Working with a cocksure certitude that appals, they assume knowledge of the mental and emotional states of a whole people, and make hair-trigger decisions as to what will excite to lust or lawlessness or loose living. —*George Creel. Literary Digest.* 74:32. *September* 2, 1922.

The list of books which came into condemnation under Protestant censorship during the centuries in question was very much more considerable than the aggregate of all the lists of the Indexes issued in Rome or issued under the authority of the Roman Church. The censorship policy of the Protestants was more spasmodic and may be admitted to have been directed on the whole by a less wholesome, dignified, and honorable purpose. It represented very much more largely the spirit of faction or of personal grievance. While in form this Protestant censorship may be considered as less defensible than that of the Church of Rome, it may be contended that in fact it has proved on the whole much less serious in its effect upon intellectual activities.—*George H. Putnam. Censorship of the Church of Rome. vol.* 1. *p.* 51.

History discloses down through the ages that tyrants and those desiring tyrannical power have ever been opposed to the dissemination of knowledge and they have ever taken the position that the dissemination of knowledge was detrimental to the common people. They have ever taken the position that the rank and file of the people were not to be trusted to study and learn from the classics, from the literature and the knowledge of the world. The reactionaries have always taken the ground that the prohibition which they desire to set up against the dissemination of knowledge was taken not in the interest of the continuation of their own power, but to protect the rank and file of the people from gaining knowledge which would be harmful to them.—*Robert M. La Follette, Jr. Congressional Record.* 71:4460. *October* 11, 1929.

Dr. John C. French librarian of Johns Hopkins University today attacked the censorship clause of the new tariff bill as more pernicious and ridiculous than the Tennessee anti-evolution law. Dr. French said: "The new bill is more far-reaching than the Tennessee law, which affected only instruction in State-supported schools. Whereas, the Tennessee law affected a single biological theory, the House provision covers not only the field of the "obscene" but political thought as well. The political phases of the House act are much more objectionable than the so-called moral features. The danger in having the Government direct thinking of citizens is vastly greater than any possible danger arising out of the free admission of revolutionary literature." One of the principal objections made by Dr. French was the lack of any right to appeal to the courts from the decision of the Customs Service officials.—*New York Evening Post. June* 1, 1929.

It is in no sense our contention that art in its various forms is above all law and exempt from the operation of social restraints and disciplines. It is our right to speak or to write as we please, without having the propriety of our writing or speaking passed upon in advance by an individual or any body, no matter how created or how formed. But having spoken or written, we do not ask immunity. We are willing to answer for our convictions, only asking that the responsibility shall be duly subpoenaed, the offense set forth in the indictment, and the trial held in accordance with constitutional procedure. It is this orderly process that censorship defies, being a denial of the rights of the individual at every point. It is, in its essence, prejudgment. It assumes guilt rather than innocence. It substitutes the prejudices or opinions of a person or persons for the law of the land.—*George Creel. Literary Digest.* 74:32. *September* 2, 1922.

I do not think that the Senate is any better able, or any customs inspector is any better able, to say what is right and what is wrong than are the great masses of the American people. This thing of taking one or two men and placing them upon God's altar, where they can decree what is and what is not righteousness, is certainly contrary to every decent instinct of a democratic government.

I have more faith in the American people than to believe for one instant that the importation of a few magazines which might be questioned is going to drag them down into hell and damnation. I do not think we are running a Sunday school here; I think we are running a government, and religion has no place in this body, directly or indirectly. It is something which each man, according to his conscience, should decide for himself. He should not be hamstrung with a lot of regulations about what he may read and what he may not read. —*Millard E. Tydings. Congressional Record.* 71:4458. *October* 11, 1929.

Recently the Boston police have demanded that nine novels be withdrawn from the booksellers' shelves under the Massachusetts indecent literature statute. Since the books are not banned from the mails, it becomes a simple matter for curious persons to order them from neighboring New York. And the publicity attending their suppression has already increased considerably the sales of these books through the mail-order houses. All the police have gained by their act is to make slightly more difficult the purchase of the books which they deem immoral; and having made them more difficult to secure, their attractiveness and desirability, according to somewhat perverse human nature, is enhanced accordingly. Most of the novels which the Boston police have ceremoniously lifted into prominence would have slid quietly into obscurity to the accompaniment of but minor sales had they been allowed to run their course. Having now been thoroughly advertised as containing racy material, they are headed for far more success than they deserve. —*Independent.* 118:326. *March* 26, 1927.

Millions of children over the world are terrified by talk of death, hell, and eternal damnation which follows sin. But most, as they grow up, by contact with literature or life, liberate themselves from the grosser form of these terrors, and come to a true moral wisdom. In Ireland people read but little. About 95 per cent of the boys under the old regime left the national schools at the age of 12, before any real education could begin. These semi-illiterates remain with the intellectual nature and the moral nature stunted in a permanent moral infantilism. We have many, many thousands of such people, seemingly grown up, but stunted and terrified, creeping on all fours in their souls, which are in a state of infancy, feeling still all the terrors of hell with which they were made familiar so early. They form associations whose activities in other countries would bring them to jail. They invade public libraries and burn books which they have heard were evil. Of course they have never read them themselves. Tolstoy, Shaw, Maeterlinck, Turgenieff, and Balzac are some of the authors whose books were banned or burned. It was members of one of these associations who drafted the Censorship Bill and forced it on the ministers [of the Irish Free State].—*Nation and Athenaeum.* 44:435-6. *December* 22, 1928.

That book *All Quiet on the Western Front,* to my mind, as a man who was in the service over in France, is one true story of the war written in all of its phases. It tells not only about the battles where men were killed but tells about all the effects and results of warfare, and it is one of the greatest documents making for peace and the development of peace psychology I have read for a long time. Over 2,000,000 copies of it have been sold. I happen to have read the European edition, which I have in my possession, if any Senator would like to read it. The difference between the two books is due to the fact that we are looked upon as in the kindergarten class. There is nothing immoral in the book at all. It simply tells what a soldier does, and it tells the truth. Because it shows war up in all its various phases and the results of war on the minds of men, it makes it a much better book for peace than the American edition is, which eliminates practically the indirect side of a soldier's life which results from his service in the trenches. In my opinion, it is a great shame that the American people cannot get this book in its real, true edition, so that they may know what war is, because it is only through such accounts as this that we can realize what a problem it is, not only of life and death but in its other ramifications.—*Millard E. Tydings. Congressional Record.* 71:4434-5. *October* 10, 1929.

INDEX

DATE DU